The Best of Times

A Personal and Occupational Odyssey

By Paul Wasserman

615 Griswold Street • Detroit, MI 48226

Omnigraphics, Inc.

* * *

Peter E. Ruffner, *Senior Vice President*
Matthew P. Barbour, *Vice President — Operations*
Laurie Lanzen Harris, *Vice President — Editorial*
Thomas J. Murphy, *Vice President — Finance*
Jane J. Steele, *Marketing Coordinator*
Kevin Hayes, *Production Coordinator*

* * *

Frederick G. Ruffner, Jr., Publisher

Copyright © 2000 Omnigraphics, Inc.

ISBN 0-7808-0433-3

Library of Congress Cataloging-in-Publication Data

Wasserman, Paul.
   The best of times : a personal and occupational odyssey / by Paul Wasserman.
     p. cm.
   Includes index.
   "Publications": p.
   ISBN 0-7808-0433-3
     1. Wasserman, Paul. 2. Librarians--United States--Biography. I. Title.

Z720.W33 A3 2000
 020'.92--dc21
 [B]

00-060672

The information in this publication was compiled from the sources cited and from other sources considered reliable. While every possible effort has been made to ensure reliability, the publisher will not assume liability for damages caused by inaccuracies in the data, and makes no warranty, express or implied, on the accuracy of the information contained herein.

This book is printed on acid-free paper meeting the ANSI Z39.48 Standard. The infinity symbol that appears above indicates that the paper in this book meets that standard.

Printed in the United States

Table of Contents

Foreword v

Introduction vii

The Best of Times

   Chapter One 1
   Chapter Two 19
   Chapter Three 37
   Chapter Four 55
   Chapter Five 69
   Chapter Six 93
   Chapter Seven 115
   Chapter Eight 137
   Chapter Nine 165
   Chapter Ten 177
   Chapter Eleven 197
   Chapter Twelve 211
   Chapter Thirteen 231
   Chapter Fourteen 245
   Chapter Fifteen 267
   Chapter Sixteen 281
   Chapter Seventeen 297
   Chapter Eighteen 309
   Chapter Nineteen 325
   Chapter Twenty 341
   Chapter Twenty-one 361

Publications and Professional Chronology

   Publications 379
   Professional Activities and Awards 388

Index 397

This book is dedicated to my daughter Jacqueline and to her children Jennie and Shaun, to my son Steven and his children Bryan, Jason, Sarah, and David, and to my wife Krystyna, whose encouragement and invaluable assistance sustained me during every stage of its preparation.

Foreword

I have known Paul Wasserman for most of my career as a publisher and have found him to be one of the most astute persons in the field of Library and Information Services. Our friendship goes back to 1959 when we first met in Detroit while he was working on his doctorate at the University of Michigan and I was president of Gale Research Company.

Over the years, he edited numerous books published by Gale (please see his bibliography on page 379). It is a pleasure, therefore, to publish this memoir of his distinguished career in a field to which, in our separate ways, we have both devoted our lives. For I share with Paul his passion for books and the collecting and dissemination of information. In addition to his professional activities and career, he has included details of his personal life, which I found fascinating, and I hope others will as well.

And I share with many an admiration for Paul's special contributions to the field of library services. He began his career at the Brooklyn Public Library and moved on to positions as librarian and professor at Cornell's Graduate School of Business and Public Administration. Foremost, perhaps, has been his role as founding dean of the School of Library and Information Services at the University of Maryland in College Park, MD. where he launched the School of Library and Information Services in the fall of 1965. There he began a new program building on traditional elements and committed also to an interdisciplinary, technological and managerial orientation for librarianship.

During his years at College Park he initiated programs to redefine the role of library education by extending public library services to the community and to advance the research agenda in new directions. He also built an annual library administrator development program which drew senior library managers from libraries of all types from the U.S. and abroad.

Additionally, he was active internationally as library educator, management training consultant, advisor to governmental organizations, and American representative to international professional societies for library projects from Paris to Beijing.

It has been a privilege to work with such an esteemed leader in the library field and to offer this record of Paul Wasserman's life and work.

— Frederick G. Ruffner, Jr.

Introduction

In early summer 1998, I had begun to reflect upon how I might pass along to the two children of my daughter and four children of my son the means to help them understand something of their grandfather's life. The original thought was simply to prepare a brief account of selected recollections of my early years and military service. As I set out on this task, I came more and more to consider how I had also enjoyed the good fortune of living through a unique occupational history. I realized that many who had known me, even some who had been closely associated with me, had only a one-dimensional view. For some I was a library scholar and researcher. Others perceived me as an editor and compiler of reference books. Some viewed me as a business librarian. For still others, I was seen as an international educator. The sum of my professional life, the different paths which I have followed, and how and why I chose to travel them would never be known unless I were to reveal them and describe what had led me in these directions. The conclusion I reached was that the best recourse might be to narrate the full story. In this way not only my grandchildren but whoever else might be interested would be able to examine the entire record. This is what I have tried to set forth here.

The story is told essentially in two parts. The early portions treat my personal history and formative years. Later it shifts to a more central focus upon my career. The treatment, therefore, veers from the earlier details of a personal life to describing the features of an occupational history. Hopefully, this dichotomy may satisfy readers seeking to learn about my earlier years as well as those whose primary interest is in the way my career progressed during a working lifetime in librarianship and library education.

One of the principal joys of having spent an academic career spanning some forty-five years has been the satisfaction of being engaged with succeeding generations of students. In this book, however, I have assiduously avoided identifying any of the many I have come to know in the classroom, in seminars, or in my role as advisor, simply because to single out and characterize only a select handful would have been unfair to countless others. Former students, therefore, are not treated in this account except for those few who were colleagues with me on research projects or publishing efforts. Still I must acknowledge here the great joy of interacting with, learning from, and being reinvigorated intellectually and personally by the continuous line of young and not-so-young people in the United States and abroad with whom I have worked during many pleasurable years.

Reconstructing the full account has required help from many for different forms of assistance, and I am very pleased to acknowledge here those to whom I am most indebted. My mother's sister, Rose Kessler, offered vivid recollections going back as far as three-quarters of a century, unfailingly filling in numerous details of my earliest years. Invaluable research assistance in authenticating many of the facts and figures of the past was offered unstintingly and cheerfully by Yu Hsio, indefatigable librarian of the University of Maryland College of Library and Information Services. Many details of places, dates, and events were recaptured from the travel diaries and letters retained faithfully by my wife, Krystyna. Thorough checking of the full chronological record of my professional history, which forms an appendix of this volume, was carried out by Christina Prendiville. The Index to the book has been prepared by Paula Berard.

Since I relied upon my tried and true method of composing the manuscript by dictating the story from loose notes, I required a collaborator to perform the painstaking and perplexing task of word processing from audiotapes and then correcting innumerable revisions through several printed reiterations. This arduous role was good-naturedly and effectively assumed by Pat Austin, who carried out this chore over many months during what should have been her leisure hours, following a normal working schedule. Because of the heavy reliance upon technology in the course of transforming computer disks to printed pages as we moved toward the final product, data processing expertise was a continuing need. It was Norman Davis, Computing Resources Coordinator for the Wasserman Library of the College of Library and Information Services, who with his student assistant Julia Walker, offered this invaluable guidance at every stage. Deborah Phillips carried out the laborious task of editing the final manuscript, eliminating redundancies, excising the excesses of my verbosity, and introducing stylistic consistency throughout the book. The idea of incorporating pictorial content as an element of the manuscript was encouraged and enhanced by the graphic design efforts of my sister-in-law, Elizabeth Kaszubski. Ann Prentice, dean of the University of Maryland College of Library and Information Services, generously offered me full access to the college's equipment and facilities and provided support for graduate student assistance during my efforts.

I have called upon the memory and help of many colleagues and friends in seeking to corroborate particular details in this account. Insofar as feasible, I have sought to ensure the accuracy of the information included. To the extent that there are errors, they are my responsibility alone.

Paul Wasserman
Bethesda, Maryland
Fall 1999

THE BEST OF TIMES

Facing the world ahead at age 3.

Chapter One

My story begins three-quarters of a century ago. It scarcely seems so long. At the start the passing of time is like the whisper of a breeze, you scarcely feel it for it moves so slowly. As the years go by the wind picks up speed, propelling you down through the years at an accelerating rate. One is invariably left to wonder: how did it all go by so fast?

Reconstructing the past is a tortuous exercise. Unless one is methodical, there are only scattered traces remaining of the paths taken: old photos; recollections of family or friends; school yearbooks of bygone eras; yellowed pages of class notes; old report cards and diplomas. Of necessity the task becomes one of searching from within the dim recesses of the mind for memories of the way it was. The story we tell is obscured by the selective means we use in distilling from our personal history the times, the events, and the experiences that shaped our lives. We tell it from our point of view, profoundly influenced as it is by our values, impressions, prejudices and private perceptions.

What follows is a highly personal view of a life and times.

The tale unfolds in Newark, New Jersey, in January 1924. In those years, the neighborhood where my parents lived was a middle-class and predominantly Jewish section of Weequahic. We were there because my father, Joe, had lost his job in New York City. He accepted an offer from a family friend of his sister, Ida, to work as a bartender in Newark. He and my mother, Sadie Ringelescu, had been married only a short while and had very little money. Aunt Ida and her husband, who was known only by his last name, Haar, generously offered to make room for the newlyweds in their home. There they took up residence with Aunt Ida, Uncle Haar, and their three children: Jesse, George, and Gladys.

The Best of Times

For my mother, this must have been an ideal time. Aunt Ida and Uncle Haar's home was large and spacious. There were rooms for everyone and the house was comfortably furnished. Haar owned a furniture factory. He also sewed, designed, and manufactured silk walls and draperies for homes and theaters. Ida was a tall, regally attractive woman with a kind and generous disposition. As the family beauty, she was always impeccably dressed and stylish. My mother's task in our new home was to take care of me and help Ida with her homemaking duties. My parents were well liked by the family, and my father was always available as another hand for the card games that Haar and his friends indulged in every weekend.

During this period, my mother's family was living in Manhattan, in Harlem, which at that time was a predominantly Jewish neighborhood. They had gravitated to Harlem from the Lower East Side. My mother was the first child to marry. Her older sister, Rebecca, married a year later. It was around this time that my mother's family left Manhattan for Brooklyn. They moved to a neighborhood close to the borough of Queens. Their apartment was in a large, recently constructed building on Pennsylvania Avenue. It was located only two or three blocks from two different subway stations on different lines — the BMT and the IRT, which offered access to Manhattan.

Our stay in Newark was idyllic but short-lived. While we were living there, my Aunt Ida permitted my mother to invite her younger sister, Rose, to come and spend the summer with us. Rose recalls that summer as a beautiful interlude and a memorable holiday in a warm, hospitable home, where everyone was generous, loving, and cheerful — quite the opposite of the strained atmosphere in her own home. Unfortunately, by 1926, Haar's business fortunes were in decline. On the verge of bankruptcy, he had to give up the big house and move the family to more confined quarters. My mother's family had by then moved to Brooklyn, so my parents moved back to New York in 1925 to live in my grandparents' five-room apartment. My father kept his job in Newark and came home only on weekends.

My father was born in 1890 in Romania in a little town near the city of Jassi, which was close to the Russian border. Today that region is called Belarus — one of the new states that came into being with the dissolution of the Soviet Union. My father was thirteen when he and his eighteen-year old brother, Sam, decided to come to the United States. Their bold decision was likely prompted by the fact that Sam was slated for military service — a highly unattractive prospect. By

1903, my father's oldest sister, Rose Goldberg, and her husband were already living in the United States. Her husband, Adolf, whom I remember as a strapping fellow when I knew him in the late 1920's, had fled Romania with his wife, Rose, after he had killed a sergeant during a fistfight. It seems that the sergeant had insulted Adolf, who was an army private. By the time Joe and Sam left Romania, Rose and Adolf had established a restaurant on the Lower East Side of Manhattan. It was a gathering place for young Romanian immigrants looking for home cooking. Sam and Joe left by train from Jassi for the Port of Bremen in Germany. From there they sailed steerage to America. These two young boys who could barely read set off on their adventure with little more than courage and determination. But in those years America beckoned with open arms, and Ellis Island was the gateway to life in a new country.

My mother, Sadie, was born in a rural Romanian village in 1900. She arrived in the United States as a little girl with her parents, her older sister, Rebecca, and a younger brother named Morris. Another sister, Goldie, was born in 1912 in Harlem. Rose, the youngest, was born in 1914. My mother's father came to the United States after his brother had come and found a job as a waiter. My grandfather was a toy maker. He worked in factories cutting out fabric that he shaped and stuffed into teddy bears, horses, dogs, and other soft, cuddly animals.

Once in the United States, my Uncle Sam found work in the millinery industry. In those years women always wore hats. In New York City, in Manhattan, there was a large and flourishing trade in women's hats. Joe and Sam went to live with their sister, Rose, and her family. My father worked in their restaurant. My maternal grandmother had known Rose from Romania. One day the two met accidentally in New York at the market. Rose told my grandmother about her single, younger brother who was living with her. Shortly after, my mother and father met in Rose's restaurant. My father became a milliner like his brother. He learned how to block hats. This entailed shaping felt hats on a steam machine that was shaped like a human head. The work was strenuous and hazardous because of the steam heat and the chemical dyes used in the making of the hats. On one occasion my father was badly burned when his machine caught fire. He was saved only by the swift action of a fellow worker, who quickly muffled the flames. Hat making was a seasonal occupation and not an ideal way to earn a living. Before the era of unionization in the late 1920's, the pay was poor. But for a man with no education or other work skills, millinery was the work my father was obliged to remain with during his working life.

The Best of Times

For my mother, school was a joy and an escape from the home where she was constantly enlisted to care for her younger siblings. Education was not seen as necessary for young women who were destined for a life of early marriage, children, and homemaking. My mother did manage to complete her elementary school education. Her eighth-grade education at least assured literacy and some sense of appreciation for scholarly pursuits. My mother had the most beautiful penmanship and was a reader with a strong sense of the importance of a good education.

The neighborhood where my father and his brother lived teemed with Jewish, Polish, and Italian immigrants, which lent the area its European, small-town character. The family restaurant was in a building constructed in the 1880's or 1890's on Essex Street. The apartment, on the third floor, was approached by way of a dark, cold stairway. Joe and Sam slept on the floor for months before finding other accommodations. Lower East Side tenement buildings had no hot water. One toilet down the hall served several families living on the same floor. The apartments had small rooms, and privacy was non-existent, but everyone made do. Accepting these conditions was part of the ritual of becoming an American. My father's sister, Rose, had three children. The eldest, named Willy, or Velvel, was lame from birth. He was a cheerful fellow with a mellow singing voice. I remember him entertaining restaurant customers by singing Romanian and Yiddish songs. Rose's other two children were Charlie and Gussie. Charlie was a studious and serious boy, who grew up to study law at Fordham University. He retired in the 1980's from a career as Counsel to the Furriers Trade Council (the principal trade association of the fur industry in the United States). Gussie was a lively and attractive girl who was mostly interested in boys and good times. She married a man who was a jack-of-all-trades. She and her husband opened and ran a repair shop in Brooklyn Heights where he fixed radios and any other type of appliance imaginable. Their store was on fashionable Montague Street close to the Promenade — a famous walkway that offered magnificent views of the Manhattan skyline across the East River.

When my parents moved to Weequahic in 1924, it was a quiet, residential neighborhood of single and two-family homes. Jewish families, who were succeeding economically in the post-World War I period, had settled in the town. Typically, small business entrepreneurs in town had moved up from peddling to retail proprietorships of various types. Clustered in the neighborhood were shops — ranging from groceries, kosher meat markets, candy stores, newsstands, and pharmacies that featured soda fountains presided over by teenage soda jerks.

There were many specialty shops that sold exotic foods such as smoked fish, halvah, and nuts of every type. Neighborhood Jewish delicatessens featured corned beef and hot pastrami. There were also dry cleaners, Chinese laundries, shoe repair shops, as well as barbershops and beauty parlors. The community was like an island within the city of Newark. The heterogeneous population of homeowners included first-generation immigrants to America, whose children were American born. The most common aspiration for the younger generation was to shake off all traces of the Old World: from its languages — whether Yiddish or the native tongues of Poland, Russia, Romania, and Germany — to dress, manners, and mannerisms.

I remember my father as a perennial optimist. He was a modest and unassuming man who had a generous nature. He was short, stocky, and very strong — no doubt as a consequence of the strenuous work he did in millinery. He was an uncomplicated and happy person. I always had the feeling that being married to my mother, Sadie, was something he looked upon as a kind of miracle or blessing. She was the foundation of his life — the able and intelligent caretaker of our home and family. I can still see my father's smiling features, warm, loving eyes, and his somewhat mashed-in nose. We spent little time together, he and I. Occasionally, we would go on family excursions to the beach or to visit relatives. One unusual recollection of him that comes to mind was his life-long enthusiasm for cigars. My mother called them *chubuks*. I always assumed this was a Romanian word, and it was only when I heard it spoken many years later in Istanbul that I realized its origin was Turkish. When he had more money, my father bought good Havana cigars for a nickel or a dime. Usually he would shop for cigars in a neighborhood store, where the cigars were handmade by local cigar makers from Cuba. My father's cigars were little tolerated at home. He withstood a great deal of ribbing from everybody, including myself. My father also liked hot, spicy red peppers. I remember tasting one when I was an adolescent. The tears ran down my cheeks uncontrollably as my tongue burned and my mouth felt like a cauldron.

I remember once, when I was about twelve years old, my father took me on a long walk outside the neighborhood. It was Yom Kippur, and he knew the family would be fasting until sundown. When we got far enough away from our house, my father lit his cigar and led me on an exploration for an Italian restaurant, where we both had spaghetti and meatballs. My father, although clearly not religious, did acquiesce to my mother's wish that he not embarrass the family by behaving like a heathen on Yom Kippur.

My father was also an inveterate card player. His games were pinochle and rummy. I suspect that in his bachelor days card playing must have been a consuming passion. He would play with his brother Sam, their friends, and other family members. I remember that during the bleak early days of the Great Depression, around 1932 or 1933, my father would spend many evening hours engaged in neighborhood card games trying to eke out some gambling winnings when there was no work at all. President Roosevelt's New Deal Program for unemployment insurance became the underpinning of our family's sustenance during those tough years. Seasonal workers, like my father, had to apply each year to receive compensation. Between piecework wages in the busy season and insurance compensation, my father managed to earn a very modest living for his family. It was my mother's task to manage the family budget so that there would be enough money to get through the lean periods. My father cheerfully turned over his salary to my mother, deferring to her homemaking frugality. He never sought much for himself. In a time when the hallmark of a good meal was meat or beef, he always avowed how much he preferred less expensive dairy products.

At the end of a hard day's work and after an early dinner my father would read the newspaper. In the early days he read *The New York World Telegram* and later *The New York Post*. He also listened to the radio, which was a popular family pastime when I was growing up. Each evening offered a regular series of mystery, drama, comedy, or music. The news was always a popular feature as well. While my father respected and admired learning and education, it was a world that was closed to him. I never did figure out how he managed to teach himself to read without the benefit of formal schooling. We didn't talk much about my schoolwork, since it was beyond the range of what he knew. Not that he didn't take a strong interest in my progress. He would always glow with satisfaction and pride when I brought home good grades. We never talked about sports because they didn't interest my father very much. I assumed that this was because he never experienced an American childhood. The only athletic activity I ever saw him engage in was swimming, but I never discovered how he had learned to swim so well. I was never really curious or interested enough to question him about it. I do remember vividly the one time my father took me to a baseball game. It was a sandlot game played on a Sunday afternoon in a park not far from our own neighborhood. I must have been about eight years old. We left my mother and little sister and walked across the park to watch a semi-pro team called the House of David. Each player on the team sported a thick beard. I don't remember who won or lost. All that remains with me is the colorful baseball players and the fact that my father had actually taken me to watch the game.

The Best of Times

My father always remained close to his brother, Sam, even though they lived far apart. When my family lived in the New Lots neighborhood of Brooklyn, Uncle Sam made his home in the Bronx, a one-hour subway ride away. The rest of my father's family lived in Newark, except for my Aunt Rose who never moved from the Lower East Side. My mother was inseparable from her parents and her siblings. With the exception of her sister, Rebecca, who married and moved away, the rest of the family stayed together in the same apartment, or apartment building, sometimes just on the same street. They never lived more than a few blocks apart from each other.

My father spoke English without any trace of a foreign accent. I suppose this was because he had arrived in the United States at such a young age. He also spoke Yiddish but only among family. My mother's parents clung to Yiddish throughout their lives, but my father chose to read English language newspapers rather than the one in Yiddish. Both my parents spoke excellent English. I remember some of my friends' parents referring to my family as the Yankees, because they were so acculturated. Many immigrant families continued to speak only Yiddish at home.

My mother remains etched in my memory as the personification of dedicated motherhood. She was a caring and compassionate person, for whom family and home represented the essence of herself and her life's efforts. She had no personal ambition except for the well-being of her husband, children, and extended family. Her dutiful nature and devotion to those she loved put her at the center of the family. It was a role she assumed naturally. Even as a young girl she had always taken care of her siblings. Her mother, Mollie, was a bitter, disgruntled woman who seemed to despise her husband. She constantly belittled him and bemoaned her fate. My grandmother regretted leaving Europe, where her father had been a man of some small means. Illiterate, she was matched with my grandfather, a man of limited prospects and no vocation; he tended only to his personal piety. When her husband decided to travel to America to join his brother, Mollie decided to remain in Romania with her parents. In the United States my grandfather, Hyman, earned money to send for his wife and three children. My grandmother refused to come to America. Her father finally convinced her to go to New York for a visit. If she chose to return, he would send money for her travel. She agreed, but wanted to leave her oldest child, Rebecca, behind. Rebecca rebelled and insisted on going with the rest of the family. In the United States, my grandmother became pregnant with Goldie. Her son, Morris, was hurt playing in the street.

The Best of Times

Some boys had thrown his hat on to the trolley tracks. As Morris ran to retrieve it, he fell and the trolley ran over his left hand. His arm had to be amputated close to his elbow. My grandmother was so ashamed by what had happened — perhaps she felt guilty for having left Morris unattended — that she decided not to return to Romania. She deeply resented her fate and expressed her displeasure through constant scolding and a shrewish personality. It was not until the late 1930's and the 1940's, when she learned that her remaining family members had suffered and perished during the war, that she finally acknowledged her good fortune.

My mother, Sadie, had a winning smile and a cheerful demeanor. As a young girl of marriageable age she had been slender. Once married she no longer felt the need to retain a shapely silhouette. She settled into the matronly shape that was traditional among wives of that era. My mother's passion was a clean, presentable home and a healthy, well-nourished family. My mother excelled in all aspects of homemaking except for cooking. Her lack of culinary expertise was the legacy of previous generations. My grandmother prepared the meals in the same style she had learned as a girl — this entailed a ritualistic overcooking of ingredients. My mother followed suit. She never learned how to prepare tasty or appetizing dishes. So we made do with a dietary regimen of healthy, bland food that consisted of chicken boiled in soup on Tuesday and Friday nights and for lunch on Saturday. We also ate an inordinate amount of overcooked vegetables, lots of potatoes, and an abundance of dairy products. My mother never baked or fried dishes. The stove in our apartment served only to stow away pots and pans. The *specialite de la maison* was pan-grilled veal cutlets, which my mother would prepare for company on special occasions.

We rarely ate in restaurants because we couldn't afford to. In my mother's view, delicatessen foods were unhealthy. In those years there were delicatessens in every neighborhood. The closest we ever got to delicatessen food was when, after much pleading and cajoling, my mother would give in and buy frankfurters, which she boiled and served with baked beans. My favorite meal growing up was mashed potatoes and spinach with sour cream. This may explain why I actually enjoyed army food and why I bring such zeal to trying and enjoying exotic, spicy dishes from other regions of the world.

My mother's routine included daily trips to different grocery stores and shops. Only milk was home-delivered. When we lived near outdoor food markets, my mother would do much of her shopping at the open-air stalls that lined both sides of the avenue for seven or eight blocks. The streets were also crowded with peddlers' wagons. And, in the buildings behind those wagons, street-level retail stores sold dry goods, sundries, clothing, meats, baked goods, appliances, and other merchandise. The daily ritual in every season except during the bitterest cold, snow, and rain was for neighborhood housewives to look for the freshest and least expensive fruits, vegetables, and other items from their favorite peddlers. The street sellers were a hardy species. They passed each day on their feet negotiating with their choosy and demanding clientele of veteran shoppers. Sometimes after having built a following of loyal customers, the most successful of the peddlers moved up to the rental of an enclosed retail store. The general sentiment of the women shoppers was that the biggest bargains were to be found on the pushcarts, not in the stores. Peddlers had no rent or utility bills to pay that would push up prices.

My father's good-natured disposition made the world a bright and hopeful place. Sometimes this proved a frustration for me — I had a more cynical, questioning view of things. But I couldn't help but love my father's naive, accepting outlook. There was only one episode in my childhood when I managed to elicit genuine anger from him. It stands out starkly in my memory because it was so exceptional. I must have been about eleven or twelve years old at the time. We lived a block or two from a busy thoroughfare with a bus route. My friends and I liked to hitch rides by sitting on the back bumper of the bus. In groups of two or three we stayed on for a mile or two before hopping off and jumping on the back of another bus for the return ride home. It was exhilarating fun, and it was very dangerous. The bus moved fast and made frequent, abrupt stops. We had to hang on tight or risk falling down into the street or under the wheels of the bus. These joy rides were a thrilling pastime. A grownup in the neighborhood must have spied us in motion. The word got out. My father lay in wait one evening and caught me getting off the back of the bus. He took me by the hand and wordlessly led me home. Once we got home he led me directly to the bathroom. He unbuckled the strap from his trousers and gave me several belts on my buttocks. He looked as if the punishment hurt him more than it did me. I don't remember crying. I remember only my shame in making this man, who was so mild and gentle, inflict pain upon me because he loved me. I never hitched a ride on the back of a bus again. No word ever passed between us about this experience.

My relationship with my father was always deferential and respectful. He was always caring and supportive toward me. We never had strong differences. Perhaps it was simply because I understood that everything my parents did was influenced by love or economics. Both my father and mother would have preferred for us to live together in our own apartment. The lack of money often made it necessary for us to double up with my grandparents and their grown children, or with my mother's sister, Rose. I didn't like this arrangement. I detested hearing my grandmother scolding her husband and constantly lamenting her fate. I abhorred the lack of privacy and personal space. I admired but could never understand the way my father cheerfully and effortlessly tolerated it all. I don't remember him ever complaining. Even my obstreperous grandmother loved him.

I never used foul language around my parents. Nor do I ever remember hearing profanity uttered in my home. It was simply a matter of the mutual respect we all felt for each other. Once when I was a high school student a friend of mine came over and we were talking about an upcoming exam. My father came into the room. I was exasperated about some aspect of the test requirements, and I blurted out, "So, I'll flunk it." My father rebuked me later with: "Paul, you never talk like that." I was ashamed and embarrassed that he had misunderstood me. "I said *flunk* it Dad. That means fail the test." He smiled at me and said, "Oh."

Soon after we had moved back to New York from Newark, the women's hat industry began to enjoy marked success. During that period of relative affluence, my father experienced a short span of years during which he was busy for a longer season than he had been in the past. It was also during this time that the industry unionized. My Uncle Sam, who was always far more politically astute than my father, had strong ties to union leadership. Once the milliners were organized, Sam arranged to get placed in a good factory that enjoyed strong sales and a long working season. He saw to it that his young brother found employment in another plant with good prospects.

From about 1926 to 1930, my father fared reasonably well. Not nearly so well as my Uncle Sam, however. Sam and his wife, Sylvia, a Canadian immigrant from Montreal, lived with their son and daughter in a handsome apartment building near Van Cortland Park in the Bronx. The factory where my uncle worked was doing extremely well. His income was substantially higher than my father's salary. As I remember it, Sam was always the savvy older brother who connected with well-placed cronies and card-playing friends. This gave him a clear edge in the business world. He never had to work too hard on the job because of his close ties to union bigwigs. My father, on the other hand, was a more open and accepting fellow. He never complained and always seemed content with his lot.

The Best of Times

Uncle Sam attempted a few entrepreneurial schemes in his time, but they didn't succeed. It was in pursuit of one of these schemes in Montreal that Sam met his wife. My Aunt Sylvia was a proud young woman of German-Jewish background. Sam must have looked like a winner when she met him. He wasn't especially good looking. He was short, well built, cocky, and fearless. He was also indomitably optimistic about his chances. Unlike my father who was essentially a family man, Sam's world revolved around meetings, card games, and an irregular home life. We saw a good deal of Uncle Sam and his family. Sam and Sylvia had two children, Sidney and Pearl. Sidney was five or six years older than I was. Pearl was about my age.

I don't remember Sam and his family coming to visit us. Perhaps it was because we never had enough extra space in our apartment. The subway ride to their home took us over an hour, so we would stay overnight. Our visits may have reflected my father's deference to his big brother. More likely, it was because Sylvia didn't care for the long subway trip and because her home offered ample room to put us up overnight. We made the trip to Uncle Sam's about once a month on a Saturday morning. We returned home on Sunday night. I remember from my early pre-school and school years how exciting it was to travel to the Bronx. To me it was an unknown borough with spacious parks and wide boulevards, of which the Grand Concourse was the grandest of them all. It was my cousin Sidney's job to entertain me, usually by sharing his hobbies. One of these was his collection of hundreds of Indian Head pennies. One time, when I was a little older, we ventured forth in fair weather to explore the beautiful parks, playgrounds, manicured lawns, and estate-sized houses of the neighborhood. The biggest treat, however, was going to the Loew's Paradise. This celebrated movie palace had a beautifully painted ceiling that was colored blue and was lit up with hundreds of stars. With its ornate balconies, staircases, and lobbies, the theater looked like a royal castle. My Uncle Sam even owned a car in the late 1920's. Sometimes he would drive us all out to Westchester County, New York, for picnics. This city suburb was like a vast forest, accessible only by quiet country roads. We would park off the road in the woods near a stream. There wasn't a soul around for miles. Sam had his car until the early 1930's, when he had a bad accident while driving somewhere with his son. Neither of them was badly hurt, but the car was demolished and Sam never drove an automobile again.

When my Uncle Haar's business failed, and we had to leave Newark to return to New York, we lived with my mother's parents for a year in their apartment on

Pennsylvania Avenue. When my father's fortunes improved, we moved to a two-family house where we occupied the lower apartment. That was on Jerome Avenue, only a few blocks away from my grandparents. It was a quiet, tree-lined street, and our house had a front porch. We were only half a block from a main shopping avenue that was lined with retail shops. There was also a neighborhood movie house, the Miller. It was located at the corner where Sutter Avenue and Miller Avenues intersected. As the first grandchild born in my mother's family, I was treated with special importance and fussed over enormously. I grew up as a confident child, sheltered and safe in a world of loving, devoted parents and greater family. My parents, however, were not physically demonstrative. There were no great kissers, huggers, or gushers in the family. Still, mine was a loving family. I enjoyed a life with few self-doubts or insecurities. I grew up feeling that I could do whatever I set out to do.

The years between the time we moved to Jerome Street and when I started going to school remains pretty much a blank. Only one event prompted by a faded photograph remains in my memory. In those years itinerant photographers set up their cameras in neighborhood parks. For a few pennies they would capture their subjects for posterity in a picture. Like today's tourists who pose alongside life-size cut outs of politicians or movie stars, these photographers offered a variety of props. I chose a real horse. There I sit, a confused three-year-old astride a horse — a tactile reminder of a long-ago time when family memorabilia tended to be more lodged only in memory.

From Jerome Street we moved several blocks away to a modern apartment building on Riverdale Avenue. I was five years old in 1929 and we were living in what I recall as an attractive building in a pleasant neighborhood, where private houses, single- and two-family homes blended with low-rise apartment buildings. One distinctive feature of the area was a small private hospital located only half a block from our building. Proximity to the hospital may have been a factor in my parents' decision to move there. My mother was expecting a second child in 1930. My sister, Marilyn, was born in June of 1930. Children were not permitted to visit new mothers and babies. For some reason I was doggedly committed to breaking the rules and used a back staircase to gain access to my mother's room. This way I managed to visit my new sister once or twice. The hospital was small and informally administered; the nurses found my mischievous behavior amusing and looked the other way. The novelty of foiling the system soon wore off, however. The sight of my tiny baby sister did not inspire me, and my mother's concern for how well I was eating dampened my enthusiasm for continued visits. I decided to wait for my mother and sister to come home after the week's hospital stay.

There was a term used during my childhood — "fixing yourself" — which meant eating enough to stay well and strong. Even though food preparation was never a high priority in our household, getting enough food to be full after a meal was a sacred value. As the prime beneficiaries of this philosophy, children in the family tended toward plumpness. My chubbiness was the direct result of "fixing myself" at every meal. No one counted calories. Bread and starches were a staple of our diet. For only twenty-five cents my mother could buy a dozen freshly baked Kaiser rolls at our neighborhood bakery. These were devoured at every meal.

By the time my sister was born, I had been attending public school for a year and a half. The school year was divided into two semesters. I didn't turn five until January, so I entered kindergarten in the spring of 1929 and spent two terms there before entering first grade in the spring term of 1930. I enjoyed books, being read to, and listening to stories from an early age. I got along well with other kids. School held no anxiety for me. I remember that I changed schools often. In New York City in those years each neighborhood had its own brick school building. Little kids would walk to school accompanied by their mothers. Second and third graders went with friends or neighbor children. The schools for the most part had been constructed in the late 19th century. Some of the older buildings had no indoor plumbing. My first school was a more modern one, but by the time I was in the second grade, in 1931, economic conditions had seriously worsened. The impact of the Depression on the millinery industry had been delayed, but by this time my father's earnings were profoundly compromised. We had to leave our spacious and airy four-room apartment on Riverdale Avenue. We returned to the apartment building we had moved to from Newark on Pennsylvania Avenue. This time, we rented a small three-room apartment. Two rooms were bedrooms; the kitchen served as a dining room and living room.

Our building was one of ten or twelve in a row on our block. In these apartment houses there was a community of families and children to rival the scale of a small city. Families were highly transient during the Depression; they kept moving to adapt to their changing economic conditions. A perpetual stream of new kids kept coming and going. Very quickly I joined up with a bunch of neighborhood kids my age. We played together on our block in what seemed to be a place full of wonder and excitement. Our street intersected with Sutter Avenue. Sutter was a business thoroughfare with a big pharmacy and an ice cream parlor on the corner. On both sides of the street there were shops of every kind, including Woolworth's Five and Dime. Three or four blocks away there was a big, old-fashioned movie house. It was one of the theaters in the national Loew's chain. At the intersection with Blake Avenue there was a daily, outdoor market that stretched for six or seven blocks. On the opposite side of Pennsylvania Avenue was a large synagogue that had been built early in the century. Part of the building served as a Talmud Torah, a privately run school that taught children Hebrew and Jewish history. Classes were held after school and on Sunday mornings. What intrigued me and my friends the most was a construction site for the annex being built onto the school. The project had begun during the boom period of the late 1920's and was later aborted when funds ran out at the start of the Depression. The big excavation with its steel beams, cellar spaces, and unfinished walls provided my friends and me a great place for climbing and hiding from each other. We made up endless games in this maze of unfinished construction. Across Blake Avenue on Pennsylvania Avenue, covering almost an entire city block, was the relatively new Thomas Jefferson High School. Its surrounding schoolyards and outdoor play areas offered space for baseball, roller skating, and other games. My new elementary school was located about three blocks from our apartment building, in the other direction. We stayed on Pennsylvania Avenue for several years, until I was in the sixth grade. The sidewalk in front of our building was wide, and there were alleyways between the buildings. The buildings were six stories high, and their rooftops were accessible by stairway. I don't remember which floor we lived on, but there was no elevator and kids were constantly running up and down the staircase. Our apartment overlooked the street, and I could be summoned with a call from our front window. We sat out on the building's metal fire escapes in the summer. As active kids in the days before air conditioning, we slept soundly after a busy day of playing no matter what the temperature.

My mother was very busy taking care of my baby sister. I was able to run free after school and during summer vacations and holidays. By the early 1930's the Depression had deepened, and money concerns were everywhere in evidence. I can remember families being evicted from the buildings on our block when their rent money ran out. Adult conversations were preoccupied with what President Roosevelt would do to improve things upon taking office in 1933. My parents had a small savings account in a bank that was shut down. They spent several anguished months wondering whether they would ever get their money back.

Another serious concern was the unfolding drama in Germany as the Nazi party came to prominence. Virtually every family we knew had relatives in Europe. Some of them were in Germany, but many were in other countries as well. It was feared that the Nazis would succeed in extending their power beyond Germany and influence events in other parts of Europe as well. The anti-Semitic fervor of Hitler had been boldly spelled out in his treatise, *Mein Kampf.* There was great apprehension among our neighbors about the implications for Jews. When Hitler became Chancellor in 1933, the foreboding became reality.

Growing up in the 1930's as a child, Europe seemed like an unimaginably distant planet and financial problems were for grownups. Children, at least in my home, were insulated from the perils of the Depression. It was not that we didn't understand that times were difficult — anyone alive in the United States couldn't help but be aware that there was widespread unemployment and poverty in the land. We knew, however, that somehow our parents would protect us. They may have had sleepless nights, but we kids remained untroubled.

Despite hard times, I can still remember childhood treats that were part of my everyday life. There were street stands where, for a penny or at most two cents, you could buy a jelly apple — a big apple on a stick that was dipped in sweet red goo that stuck to your teeth for hours afterward. In winter there were steaming hot sweet potatoes or potato knishes to enjoy that were almost a meal in themselves. In summer there were Italian ices — cups filled with scoops of ice that was flavored by the peddler with a choice of chocolate, raspberry, or some other fruity syrup. The corner candy store offered its own dazzling array of licorice, chocolate bars, Tootsie Rolls, lollipops, and other sweets.

The local candy store was typically a family-run enterprise that besides selling candy also sold newspapers, tobacco products (cigarettes by the pack or one for a penny), and soda fountain drinks. A penny bought a large glass of seltzer. Two cents would get you a flavor mixed with the seltzer; for three cents there was the incomparable egg cream — seltzer mixed with milk and chocolate syrup. Every candy store had one or two public telephone booths as well. Few families in my neighborhood could afford to have a telephone in their apartments. At the candy store phone calls could be made with the deposit of a nickel for every three minutes of conversation. These telephones also provided a way for neighborhood kids to earn a little money. If someone wanted to reach a person living on the block, they could call the telephone number at the candy store and give that person's name and address. Kids who hung around the store would go to the address and summon the person. It was common practice at the conclusion of the phone conversation to tip the child who had gone to get the person being called. Tips ranged anywhere from one penny to a dime. The most generous tippers tended to be young women receiving calls from prospective dates or suitors. The size of the tip was subtly tied to the level of joy elicited by the phone conversation.

During my pre-teen years, boys played only with other boys. The gang usually included a dozen kids close in age. The group got together every afternoon after school. We played games or sports until dinnertime, when mothers would summon children from an open window. Evenings consisted of homework and listening to radio programs. On the weekends I was free, except for family obligations. Boys had few domestic chores to do. It was assumed that they would evolve into family wage earners.

During the summer holidays, schoolyard teams were organized based on size and age. Sometimes there were special outings arranged by playground directors to take a number of kids to see a free major league baseball game. That was how I got to Ebbetts Field once or twice to see the Brooklyn Dodgers. I also went to Yankee Stadium in the Bronx to see the New York Yankees. The seats were always in the bleachers, far away from home plate. These trips were something we looked forward to for weeks and talked about for months afterward. Until I was about ten years old, I was very happy at school and happier still when school was out. School was a challenge. I wanted to be the best, but I didn't want to have to work at it. Often I was lucky enough to earn high grades without too much effort. Homework was never as appealing as listening to radio broadcasts such as "Jack Armstrong the All-American Boy," "I Love a Mystery," "Buck Rogers in the 25th Century," "The Shadow," or the "Lone Ranger." Those were the days when breakfast cereals offered mail-in coupons for cards, stories, or games about favorite entertainment and sports figures.

Those were also the days of *Big Little Books*. These were paperback forerunners of comic books. Their square pages were bound together in a thick volume that contained adventure stories, westerns, and science fiction. The stories were light on text and heavy on illustration. I also had a passion for comic strips in the daily and Sunday newspapers. One of my favorites was "Bringing Up Father," which featured Jiggs as the *nouveau riche* Irishman who craved corned beef and cabbage, while his wife, Maggie, sought social status. Another favorite was "Blondie," in which the bumbling Dagwood was constantly in trouble with his boss. "Gasoline Alley" and "Harold Teen" were two comic strips that caught the flavor of a time when cars were a vicarious dream for most people. "Terry and the Pirates" exposed us to the exotic and mysterious Orient and to daredevil pilots.

The candy store had a flourishing traffic in the trading and exchange of pulp magazines like *Dime Detective*. I consumed these voraciously. My particular favorites were the sports magazines. In those years, baseball was the one and only passion for sports-addicted boys. We lived in Brooklyn, where everyone loved the Dodgers, but out of some childhood perversity I decided to be a Yankee fan. Maybe it was because of Babe Ruth and Lou Gehrig, or possibly because the Yankees were based in the faraway borough of the Bronx. From my friends' standpoint the only thing worse for me to have done would be to root for the New York Giants. They were in the National League and a fierce rival of the Dodgers. I had never been to the Polo Grounds where the Giants played. The Yankees were in the American League, so they never played the Dodgers unless it was a World Series. In the middle of the 1930's, the Dodgers had about as much chance of making it to the World Series as did the Keystone Cops, with whom they were sometimes compared. I followed the major league baseball season very seriously. I kept up with team standings, knew major league players' averages, and often listened to the radio play-by-play announcements of games from Ebbets Field or Yankee Stadium. The favorite announcer of that period was Red Barber who broadcast the Dodgers' games with an inimitable Deep South twang. He was a genuine folk hero of the 1930's.

Chapter Two

When I was ten years old, my parents decided it was time for me to learn Hebrew in preparation for my bar mitzvah. In families where religion was not taken very seriously, boys were sent to study with a rabbi who would instruct and prepare them for the bar mitzvah ceremony. Kids who couldn't read Hebrew were given a transliterated text, which had been converted phonically and could be rehearsed regularly. At the age of thirteen these boys would be called upon to read from the Torah (the sacred text scroll). The bar mitzvah ritual, which every Jewish boy went through, was part of "becoming a man." We lived across and down the street from the big synagogue. My parents decided that I should be enrolled in classes there. By the time I turned thirteen I should be well enough prepared to read and sing the service from the Torah and to understand and pronounce the Hebrew correctly.

The decision for me to start Hebrew studies was not a democratic one. I was dead set against it. My playtime on Monday through Thursday and on Sunday morning would be usurped by these classes. I pleaded my case. My father was sympathetic. My mother, reinforced by her mother and her brother, Morris, prevailed. Even though tuition was required (perhaps two dollars a month, a considerable sum in the mid-1930's), it was deemed a necessary and appropriate expense in order to uphold the family's standing in the community.

Once I got started at the school, I grudgingly found it pretty interesting. We learned to read, write, and understand Hebrew. We also studied Old Testament history. It was not a religious school even though it was an adjunct of the synagogue. The instructors were young, unemployed men who knew the subject matter and instructed effectively and energetically. The classes were co-ed. I could not understand why the girls were there. In those years there was no bat mitzvah ceremony for girls as there is today. Women had no role in the religious life of Judaism. On Saturdays and high holy holidays, such as Rosh Hashanah and Yom Kippur, worship at the synagogue was carried out by the men. The girls in my class may have been from more affluent families who could afford instruction for cultural reasons. In truth, I enjoyed Hebrew school. Hebrew was a new language for me with its own alphabet and accent marks. It was fun to gain mastery of it. I knew a smattering of Yiddish from listening to my mother's parents or my parents talking to them, but I couldn't read my grandfather's Yiddish newspaper, which was printed in the Hebrew alphabet. I learned that Hebrew and Yiddish were distinctly separate. Yiddish was the everyday language used among European Jews. It had been adapted heavily from the German of the Middle Ages and was interspersed with words and phrases from Hebrew and from Eastern European languages. In making the transition to the United States, Yiddish absorbed many English terms and expressions.

In biblical history class we studied in English. As we grew more proficient we studied the stories from the Old Testament in Hebrew. The instruction was not preachy, but rather offered a rich tapestry of picturesque heroes, sinners, villains, battles, and romantic adventures. I came to see history in general as a colorful panorama, not simply the stuff of long-ago dates and isolated events. It was an unending drama of human beings subject to passions and ambition from the beginning of time. I never caught the fever of deep religious conviction in spite of the biblical tales of God's potency and the making of miracles. Perhaps what put me off was the constant pious imploring to sing the Lord's praises and the zealous extolling of the power of the Almighty. The idea of sacrificing animals and sometimes human beings to demonstrate fealty was also unappealing.

Perhaps the greatest source of childhood pleasure was the movies. In the depths of the Depression money was scarce, but entertainment was cheap. Movie theaters had matinee performances every day as well as evening shows. On Saturday afternoons there was a special showing for kids. Admission was a nickel. Sometimes stores distributed free passes with a purchase. The movie fare included a double feature — two full-length Hollywood films, plus one and sometimes two different serials. Often there were special prizes and games distributed to everyone who attended. The movies were made for adults, but were suitable for kids. Many of the westerns, mysteries, horror, or science fiction movies were actually better suited to the ten-year-old mind than for adults. On the weekends, the featured movies were selected with children in mind. Weekly newsreels kept audiences up to date on current events. This is where we saw graphic displays of what was happening in Europe — scenes of a uniformed man with a mustache berating enormous crowds of hysterical, shrieking followers. For children too young to grasp the significance of these events, Hitler seemed like a vaudeville comedian, especially when he was joined on screen by his grimacing straight man, Mussolini.

The main event of the afternoon was the latest serial installment. Each week's episode started from the point where last week's episode had ended — the hero dangling by his fingertips from a roof ledge ten stories high with the bad guys poised to push him off. Somehow he would foil his enemies only to find himself in another hair-raising sequence of car chases, burning buildings, and other harrowing escapades. The weekly episode would leave our hero once again at risk from the terrible forces of evil. We knew he would somehow survive, but we still cheered, moaned, and screamed as the story progressed. In the last episode he always won the girl, or the game, or the big prize, and good inevitably triumphed over evil.

The serials starred different period celebrities, including sports heroes like Red Grange or Buster Crabb, or famous Western stars like Hoot Gibson. The scripts were always predictable, but that didn't detract from the pleasure of watching them. Sometimes the acting was so bad that even ten-year-olds would laugh when the ostensibly French-Canadian bad guy would mispronounce the word *monsieur* as "muh-shoo-er." I remember one Saturday at the Miller Theater when I had spent a longer time at the theater than usual. My parents became worried about me. My father was dispatched to look for me. He came upon me during the main feature and decided to sit down beside me. Both of us watched the film and the newsreel before returning home. My mother scolded us for making her worry so much. Another fond memory of Saturday afternoon movies is of the silver-haired matron, whose job it was to patrol the dark theater aisles in a constant and losing struggle to curb the kids' unruly behavior. Children caught screaming or shouting too boisterously were shepherded swiftly to a special row where they would continue to watch the show under the eagle eye of the matron.

By about the mid-1930's, when I was eleven, our economic fortunes reached a low point. My parents decided to economize by finding an apartment that we could share with my grandparents. Uncle Morris, Aunt Goldie, and Aunt Rose would also be living with us. Morris and Goldie were adults by then, and Aunt

The Best of Times

Rose was twenty years old. Our objective was to find an apartment large enough for nine people that would be cheaper than renting two separate units. Apartment buildings in our area did not have enough rooms to accommodate us all. Our search uncovered a five-and-a-half-room apartment in a two-family house that was located on Sheffield Avenue, next door to the home and office of a medical doctor. On the other side of the doctor's house was a public school, which occupied the rest of our side of the street. The trade-off for moving to this tranquil street was that we had to manage with only one bathroom for all nine of us. My parents and my sister occupied one bedroom. My five-year-old sister continued to sleep in a crib so that my parents could fit their bed in the room. My grandparents had their own room. My Uncle Morris and I shared a bed in a narrow sunroom. Goldie and Rose were together in another room. This left the kitchen and a small dining area for communal use. Privacy under these conditions became a fantasy. Between the constant bickering among so many people living in close quarters and the unending nagging of my grandmother, daily living became trying for everyone. Nevertheless, I remember this period as a joyful stage of my childhood. I'm sure it was our living arrangements that led my Aunt Rose to escape home through an early marriage. But for me, as soon as I had reconciled myself to a new school, a new neighborhood, and new friends, I saw it as an interesting adventure. Changing schools was not especially troublesome. I was just on the threshold of the age when making personal friendships would supplant the gang of kids who just happened to turn out on the street at the same time. Best of all, since we were far enough away from where we had lived before, it was no longer feasible for me to continue attending Hebrew school. I had many more free hours to play at the schoolyard next door, where I could join in basketball and baseball games.

We still had access to the subway—the IRT and BMT were only three or four blocks away. And we had a trolley line running along New Lots Avenue, the main street nearest to us. Pennsylvania Avenue had a bus line. Both the trolley and bus lines offered transfers to connecting lines. The move to our new neighborhood posed problems for my mother and my grandmother. Far from the open-air markets on Blake Avenue in our old neighborhood, they had to develop new strategies for shopping at stores on New Lots Avenue. But the differences might not have been so severe. Prices everywhere were very competitive, and the new community had a full range of kosher butchers, chicken stores, groceries, drug stores, and dry goods stores.

The Best of Times

Some time during my first four years in elementary school, I skipped a grade. I had moved ahead of the other kids in my class; one of my teachers decided to move me forward so that I wouldn't be bored. When I arrived at my new school at age eleven I was a half of a year ahead of my classmates. The school went through eighth grade. There was a plan to transfer the best students at the end of the sixth grade to a junior high school where they could complete grades seven through nine in two years. The junior high was quite a distance from where we lived, but it was considered to be a feather in one's cap to be selected for transfer there. I had only part of one semester to prove myself. The decision for transfer would be made in several weeks. New to the school, I tended to be mischievous in class — talking when silence was in order and generally trying the patience of my teachers. As an untried student, I was placed in the third, or slowest, section. Not many kids from this section were likely to be chosen for transfer to junior high. When time came for the selection, I did not make the cut. It wasn't long into the semester before my teacher realized that I should have been transferred after all. When I was promoted to seventh grade in the fall, I was moved up into the first section. With all the brightest students having gone on to junior high, I looked pretty good academically compared to the other kids in my class. In the middle of the year, I was moved up another grade to section 7B. A classmate and close friend, Sidney "Sonny" Bernstein, who had also missed out on placement for junior high, moved up with me.

We were placed in the lowest section of 7B in order to make up class work. Sonny and I found ourselves in a class with kids who had failed to be promoted one or two times. When we were lined up by height we were among the smallest kids. Some of the older boys were half a foot taller than we were. They were not pleased to have younger boys who were better students join them midway into the semester. One of these boys was Ralph Sadacca, who would later become my brother-in-law. The survival strategy that Sonny and I devised was to make friends with the biggest and toughest boys and to try to help them when we could with their class requirements. This tactic worked well, and by the end of the term when Sonny and I were promoted to the first section of 8A, our cronies bemoaned our departure as they went on to the lowest section.

Sonny was a considerate, self-deprecating boy with a winning smile. He had a modest way of relating to everyone. His nickname should have been "Sunny." I never knew a human being as optimistic and cheerful. He lived two blocks away from me on Alabama Avenue, near New Lots Avenue. His father had a fruit and vegetable stall in Manhattan's famous produce market. Sonny's mother was a shy woman who still retained an attractive appearance, unlike so many of the mothers who had grown rotund and shapeless by the time they turned thirty. Sonny had an older sister and two brothers. Like us, they lived in the upstairs apartment of a two-family house, while the landlord and his wife lived below. Sonny and his family occupied about the same number of rooms as we did except that there were far fewer of them in their household. I remember spending far more time at his apartment than mine.

When we started in eighth grade a new boy joined the class. We both liked him and we became fast friends. His name was Davey Plaxe. He lived on Sheffield Avenue, on the other side of New Lots Avenue. He lived with his parents and his one older sister, Yetta, on the first floor of a four-apartment building. Davey's father was a plumber. His mother was a warm, hospitable woman who always greeted Davey and his friends with a smile and a homemade cookie. Yetta was three or four years older than Davey. She was a young woman with an original cast of mind who saw the humor and dark side of life. She captured events and human frailties in colorful thought and language. Davey, on the other hand, had a thoroughly pragmatic nature. A strong boy of medium build, Davey's most obvious physical attribute was his large ears. Along with Sonny, we became an inseparable trio. Davey was less of a student, but he had an abundance of common sense and worldly wisdom. He could be counted on to size things up and make sensible judgements about anything. Not surprisingly, he grew up to become a police sergeant.

I had adjusted to my new school, my new friends, and my new neighborhood, but life at home was distressful. The family was dysfunctional. Goldie was chronically ill with some undiagnosed disorder. In retrospect it seems likely that she suffered from clinical depression. Morris was introverted; he spoke little, preferring to spend his time reading. Morris was in his late twenties by then, and Goldie was a year or two younger. Morris had taken evening college courses and was trained as an accountant. He worked in the bookkeeping department of a large firm that sold embroidered sheets, pillowcases, and towels. Provoked perhaps by work-related problems, Morris was subject to great psychological distress. For months he hovered on the edge of mental breakdown. As a boy who could not understand what was going on, I was terrified. Morris and I shared the same bed. Often he would wake during the night and scream. His mental fragility may have been due to the trolley accident that left him with a lifelong physical handicap. In an era when any handicap was cause for shame and people with disabilities were viewed as lesser beings, Morris protected himself by becoming self-contained and brooding. He had been a good student and a speedy runner, but he probably never fully realized his potential as a high school sprinter because of the physical impairment. I liked Morris very much; he was always kind to me. He was the only serious reader in the family. In a bookcase in our bedroom, he stored his modest collection of *Modern Library* books. This celebrated series of hardbound classic novels, history, *belles lettres,* and poetry printed by Random House in the 1930's sold for well less than one dollar per volume. Morris always encouraged me to read. He recommended books that he thought I would enjoy and gave me free access to the books in his collection.

It was Morris who introduced me to the theater, where I saw performances of Gilbert and Sullivan, Shakespeare, and Eugene O'Neill. During this period the Roosevelt administration's Works Progress Administration, or WPA, supported the arts, including theater and music programs. The WPA sponsored repertory companies, which gave free performances in Central Park in Manhattan and Prospect Park in Brooklyn.

When Morris became ill, I was frightened and could not understand why he was no longer the friendly uncle who had been like an older friend to me. At night, I would try to fall asleep quickly and hope that I would not hear Morris getting into bed. I prayed that he would sleep quietly without awakening and screaming during the night. I was so pleased when he finally recovered and reverted to his normal behavior.

By the time I was in the eighth grade and twelve years old my parents decided that it was time for me to begin preparation for my bar mitzvah. I would turn thirteen in January of 1937. By this time I was a long-lapsed student from the Hebrew school. It was decided that I would receive instruction from one of the teachers employed by the Talmud Torah in my old neighborhood. Having enjoyed the freedom to play without any intrusion on my free time, I was not very happy about this prospect. It was determined that I would need three sessions a week with my teacher until I turned thirteen. The bar mitzvah ceremony would take place in the synagogue across the street from our former address on Pennsylvania Avenue. I would walk the five or six blocks to the Hebrew school for after-school sessions two or three days each week. I could still read Hebrew, so this study regimen was not especially onerous. I still resented having to miss out on my free time with friends.

The Best of Times

I spent the year learning the portion of the sacred text called the *Hoftorah*, which would be the basis of the synagogue service on the Saturday morning in January 1937, when I would be called to the pulpit. The recitation was to be done in the typical singsong manner in which prayers are conducted in synagogue. I mastered the material by the time my summer holiday began — I was only twelve-and-a-half years old. In the fall, before my bar mitzvah, I would require only a short weekly review until January.

Money was scarce, so arrangements for my bar mitzvah celebration after the service were kept as inexpensive as possible. The house we lived in had a large, unused basement. The landlord gave my parents permission to use the space for our party. The morning of the ceremony was cold and wintry. The regular congregation of worshipers and our invited guests were seated in the orchestra level of the synagogue: all except the women and girls. They sat in the balcony. On that Saturday, I was the only boy celebrating his bar mitzvah. I knew my part well and performed without flaw. I'm sure my pitch must have been off key, but it didn't matter. Everybody was proud of the way I confidently got through my recitation. Following the service friends and family came back to the decorated basement for a lunch of salads, cold cuts, soft drinks, alcohol, and desserts. I later learned that among my presents I had been given about seventy dollars. In 1937 a five-dollar gift was a very generous one. I felt rich when my mother opened a bank account for me with my bar mitzvah money.

In addition to learning Hebrew in preparation for the bar mitzvah, I also learned about the religious rituals performed daily by devout Jewish men. I received the prayer shawl, yarmulke, and the small, scripture-filled leather boxes that are strapped to one's arm and forehead as part of the traditional prayer rite. I had no inclination toward religious piety, however. My father had even less interest than I. I relegated the artifacts of my bar mitzvah to a drawer in one of the household cabinets, where they were swiftly forgotten. Nevertheless, this rite of passage to manhood was an important occasion in my family. As the first grandchild, and a male grandchild at that, my bar mitzvah was a family milestone.

Around the time of my thirteenth birthday, I graduated from my elementary school and prepared to go on to high school. I had several options to consider. One possibility was to attend Brooklyn Technical High School. This school offered a first-rate preparatory program leading to a college education in science or engineering. I much preferred the humanities and the social sciences, so I ruled it out. Another possibility was Townsend Harris High School in Manhattan. This was an elite, competitive public program, which drew public school applicants from all five boroughs of New York City. Selections were based on academic records and placement tests. The third option was Thomas Jefferson High School. It was located on Pennsylvania Avenue one block away from where we had lived before moving to Sheffield Avenue. The school enjoyed a strong academic reputation and had a new principal who was a well-known poet named Elias Lieberman. My eighth-grade teacher actively promoted the idea of my applying for Townsend Harris. She asked my mother to come and chat with her about it. I was reluctant. I was going to start high school at thirteen; the prospect of spending two hours a day commuting by subway to and from Manhattan held little appeal. Besides, my friends Sonny and Davey and one or two others were all headed for Thomas Jefferson. I never bothered to take the exam for Townsend Harris. Unfortunately, in the spring of 1937, Jefferson High was overcrowded. The entire entering freshman class was destined to attend an annex in an underused elementary school that was located about two miles from where I lived. It was also not conveniently located near any form of public transportation. I went from having my school virtually next door to one that required a half an hour to walk to. It was too late to reconsider applying for Townsend Harris.

I remember starting high school trudging over piles of snow on the sidewalk in mid-winter with my friends Sonny and Davey. We bitterly complained about how we felt we were still in elementary school, since our new school building looked no different. But the subjects were different. In my English class, two sessions a week were given over to public speaking. In elementary school students were not asked to make oral class presentations except perhaps to recite a poem. The very idea of a student standing before the entire class talking about some topic seemed unimaginable to me. This requirement became one of the most memorable experiences of my first term in high school.

Our engaging teacher for this new subject was a young woman who coached us during several classes. She explained to us how to choose a topic of personal interest; how to research it; how to outline the framework and sequence of our remarks; and, finally, how to prepare our notes from which to speak. We were not to memorize the speech. The thought of appearing before the entire class of twenty or so classmates and speaking coherently without eliciting snickers or outright laughter from the class was intimidating. I prepared my oral presentation well before the day on which I would be called to speak. I was not the first student to deliver my talk. I had the opportunity to study carefully the classroom dynamics while one or two of my classmates took the floor. What I observed was that despite the student's shyness and embarrassment, everyone in the audience was psychologically bound to the speaker. We felt his or her uneasiness and awkwardness. We winced when mistakes were made. We genuinely exulted in the speaker's effective remarks. In short, we were all of us on the speaker's side.

To minimize my anxiety, I wrote out my entire ten-minute presentation and memorized it. I rehearsed it over and over again. I don't even remember what the subject was, but I do recall vividly my apprehension. As I turned to face the class, my heart was pounding and my face was hot. I looked up at my classmates. Then something extraordinary happened. Surveying the upturned faces of my fellow students, I felt suddenly completely at ease. I realized that those sympathetic faces knew exactly how I felt. To a person, my classmates were rooting for the kid who was taking his turn. I started to talk. I knew my subject, for I had studied and prepared thoroughly. I delivered my speech naturally and comfortably, dispensing with my memorized words and talking extemporaneously. I wasn't embarrassed or uncomfortable because I realized that the other students wanted me to succeed. That realization remained a lifelong lesson. With preparation, offering remarks to an audience would never hold any terror for me. There is a natural human sympathy for a fellow soul who has to hold the attention and interest of a large group.

Attending high school at the annex was like going to a ninth grade of elementary school. We were not in a high school building that could offer the clubs, sports, and other extracurricular activities that were normally part of high school. I was disappointed to not have the chance to join in after-school activities. I was left with no choice but to concentrate on academics until sophomore year, when we would be transferred to the real Jefferson High. During the winter of 1937 my friends Sonny and Davey and I hung out after school with a wider circle of boys. We congregated on a street corner close to home at the intersection of Pennsylvania and Hegeman Avenues.

During the 1930's and into the early post-World War II years, the streets of New York City, especially in the Jewish neighborhoods of the outlying boroughs, gave rise to a uniquely male culture. Street corners provided the social gathering center for adolescent and post-adolescent men. Often these groups would congregate at a candy store, drug store, or barbershop. There was no tradition for working-class, Jewish men to spend time in coffeehouses or bars. In all but the most frigid winter weather, these young men would come together on their favorite street corner to talk and joke and to plan to play ball games in the streets or playgrounds. The groups were stratified by age. Men in their early twenties made up one group, while those in their late teens made up another. On the lowest rung of the hierarchy were the thirteen- to fifteen-year-olds. While these affiliations were not formalized, the sense of belonging to one's peer group was very strong. Some of this bonding translated into the formation of sports teams that joined together to play against opposing teams drawn from groups that hung out two or three blocks away. With the exception of the genuine loners, boys would gravitate to these corner gangs after school, on weekends, and holidays. Sonny, Davey, and I spent more time with our friends than with our own families. On our street corner there was a candy store next to a drug store. On the opposite side of the street there was another candy store next door to a barbershop. We preferred to hang out at the candy store next to the drug store. The barbershop owner on the opposite side also liked having us boys around.

The barber was a man in his late thirties or early forties named Nathan Miller. He was married and lived around the corner from his store with his wife and two children. A self-conscious immigrant, Nathan Miller enjoyed vicariously the freedom of the boys who congregated outside his shop. They were young and native born and hadn't yet mortgaged their lives. They seemed to have everything before them, unlike Nathan himself, who had little more to look forward to than slaving on tirelessly to sustain his family. His brutal way with the English language was always good for a laugh. He had a heavy East European accent. But beneath the joking there was a sense of defeat and brooding self-contempt about Nathan.

Sadly, the jovial Nathan Miller was destined to suffer great personal tragedy. Around 1940, his dull and awkward fourteen-year-old son was on his way home from a movie house, where he had gone to watch a gangster film. For some reason, Nathan's son decided to enter a tailor shop and demanded money from the aged proprietor. A fight ensued, during which the boy picked up a pressing iron and struck the tailor in the head. The boy fled from the shop, but not before the tailor had screamed out for help at the top of his lungs. A man passing by on the street heard the shouting. He managed to grab young Miller and held him until the police arrived. Unfortunately, by this time, the tailor was already dead. Nathan Miller's son was taken to prison and was ultimately tried for homicide. Nathan used all his resources and borrowed heavily to engage one of New York's most celebrated criminal lawyers, the retired judge, Samuel Liebowitz. Young Miller was found guilty and sentenced to a long term in Sing Sing Prison. The tabloids ran many lurid accounts of the case and the trial. Nathan Miller, his wife, and daughter lived on in the neighborhood in anguish and shame. The good-natured and spirited barber was transformed almost overnight into a dour, gray, and aged man. No amount of joshing or high-spirited repartee by neighborhood boys could change the mood of the barbershop or raise the spirits of Nathan Miller. For him, God had passed judgement on him and his family. They were doomed to ignominy and disgrace. Gradually, the boys frequented the barbershop less and less, leaving Nathan Miller to his melancholy and sorrow.

As time passed my peer group expanded. Some boys came and went, but there was a solid core of regulars that stayed together from around 1938 until well after the United States entered World War II at the end of 1941. Davey, Sonny, and I enjoyed the company of a colorful cast of characters. Bernard "Buggy" Goodman was a carefree spirit who lacked any inhibition. He was fun loving and excelled at any sport. He earned his nickname for doing almost anything on a dare without weighing the costs or consequences. School was not his strong card. Ben Golub was a slim, handsome boy with a bright smile and a generous heart. He was hopelessly naive, however. Louis "Chink" Heckelman had a round build and slanted eyes set wide apart, hence the nickname. Irving "Itskil" Habib was a humorless fellow who was accepted by our group because his family had more money than any of ours did. We depended on him to bring the bat, football, or other sports equipment needed to get a game started. Murray Finkel was a short, scrappy boy with a sarcastic sense of humor, who was also an excellent athlete. Bernard "Bookie" Feirstein was a handsome blond boy with a good imagination. His manipulative behavior made us occasionally suspect his honesty. Maxie Lipschitz was rail thin and emaciated with a perennially hungry look. He came from a very poor home. Herman "Cousin Chaim" Rubin became loosely affiliated with our group when he moved to New York from upstate New York. Murray Finkel was his cousin. A slow moving, slow thinking boy, Herman was the personification of the country bumpkin. Leo Rubin (no relation to Herman) was a debonair fellow who sported a mustache at the age of fifteen. He would generally follow anyone else's ideas since he seldom ever had any of his own. The youngest member of our gang was Irving "Ike" Broderson. A tall and handsome boy, he constantly sought to prove his courage as compensation for his being so young. Eugene Posner, whom most us regarded as a surly, ignorant lout, was tolerated only when he was needed to fill out a team in one of our street games. Martin

"Mooky" Flamm was a sickly-looking kidder who kept us all in good humor with his tales of personal hard luck. Other boys came and went; some had stronger interests elsewhere or lived too great a distance from our favorite hangout. Some kids moved away from the neighborhood.

In those years, most of our games took place on quiet side streets or on vacant lots that were located a couple of blocks away. These lots extended for several blocks toward a large incinerator, beyond which was the Atlantic Ocean half a mile away. On those lots, fields had been cleared for baseball and football. In those days no one ever paid any attention to the heavy black smoke that poured out of the incinerator chimney. Every day, refuse trucks delivered garbage for burning. I cannot remember hearing any concerns expressed about the incinerator, which was located only a quarter of a mile from where we all lived.

During the fall before I started high school, my class made a trip to the Museum of Natural History located across from Central Park on the West Side of Manhattan. We walked through parts of Central Park during that trip and discovered fascinating rock formations and caves. The park was far more memorable to us than the museum's exhibitions and dinosaur. Sonny, Davey, and I got home and told some of our friends about Central Park. The whole gang planned to make a weekend subway trip to continue our explorations on a winter Saturday. Unfortunately, I came down with what was then called the grippe, a flu-like illness that kept me home in bed for a few days.

The trip was scheduled for the following Saturday. I returned to school that Thursday or Friday still feeling a little wobbly, but determined to accompany my friends on the Saturday outing. The day of the trip was cold, raw, and windy. My parents felt it was too soon for me to venture out for a two-hour, round trip subway ride and then a busy day at a museum. They didn't even realize that our destination would be Central Park. My passionate entreaties prevailed, and I was permitted to join my friends for the day's excursion. It was a joyous day of childish frolic, spent exploring the rock formations, paths, and caves we had discovered on our first visit. That evening, I returned home tired but exultant. The next morning, I awoke with a high fever. My grippe had returned with a vengeance. It left me with painful sinuses, and I had to sleep with my head propped up high so that I could breathe.

This sinus condition plagued me all winter and spring. My mother took me every other Saturday morning to a public health clinic on the Lower East Side of

Manhattan where nose, ear, and throat specialists would treat me. My sinuses were cleared by suction machine, but the clarifying effect lasted only ten minutes or so before my nose would clog up again. The theory was that after a sufficient number of treatments over a period of weeks and months, my sinuses would eventually return to their normal state. We kept returning to the clinic, but by the end of spring term my nose was just as clogged as ever.

My many doctor's appointments caused me to miss out on my Saturday mornings with friends. Even so, I was excited about starting high school. I couldn't wait to begin my new classes. The most pleasurable was French. My teacher was a rapid-speaking native named Monsieur Morin. He conjured up romantic visions of Paris, French cuisine, and sidewalk cafes. He was a short man with a mustache who paced back and forth in front of the room spouting long passages in what at first was an unintelligible but melodious patter of words and phrases. His English was deeply accented, exotic, and foreign sounding, unlike any speech I had ever heard. He succeeded in making the French language a challenge even though much of our time was given over to grammar and verb conjugations. With my perennially stuffed nose my pronunciation came out with just the right nasal tones, so I got on fine with Monsieur Morin. I remember walking over mounds of snow and ice on the way to school reciting verb conjugations with my friend, Sonny.

As summer approached, I still struggled with my sinuses — I breathed heavily and had difficulty sleeping. Normally, our summers were spent in the city, with the occasional day trip to Brighton Beach, near Coney Island. During the 1930's, those who could afford it rented in the Catskill Mountains or at the seashore. Our financial circumstances were limited, so we had never done this. I had never spent any time away from the streets and sidewalks of the city; the countryside was terra incognita. My health troubles must have weighed heavily on my parents, because they decided to scrape together enough money to rent a room for us in the country for the entire summer. My father would remain in the city to take advantage of the millinery industry's busiest season. He would join us for the weekends. Through word of mouth we rented a room sight unseen. The accommodations were known by the Yiddish term, *kochalayn* — literally, a "cook alone." For around seventy-five to one hundred dollars, we got a room and two beds with enough space for the four of us. How my seven-year-old sister and I managed, I don't remember. The cooking arrangements were communal. Each family had use of a stove and space in a very large icebox. We dined at large tables, where several families could eat together. The mothers developed collaborative strategies for polite, and even friendly, relationships with other families, who at first had been total strangers. Along with our clothing, we brought bedding, kitchen utensils, dishes, and appliances. We engaged a man called a hacker, who contracted to move two families at a time from the city to the Catskills.

I remember a sweltering day in June and an endless drive over winding country roads in a crowded and overheated sedan. The car made only one short stop on old Route 17 for a cold drink and a bathroom visit at a roadside restaurant called the Red Apple. At the trip's end, I emerged from the car nauseous and with a fierce sinus headache. I stood before a big, rambling house that was surrounded by a spacious lawn and a meadow. The dark forest lay beyond. I was in awe of the natural beauty of this country setting. It was so dramatically different from the cement and brick buildings that rose from the pavement back in Brooklyn.

The nearest town was a village called Woodbridge. It was about a mile away down a dirt road. It had only a few stores, but it did boast an old-fashioned movie theater. Along the deeply wooded road to town there were only two or three other houses like ours that could be seen. The nearest points of interest in the other direction were two resort hotels. The first of these was the Olympic Hotel, a quarter-mile away. On a hill some distance beyond was the grander and larger Flagler Hotel. On the weekends, when my father came up from the city, the whole family would walk, or sometimes get a ride, to one of the hotels to see whatever entertainment was being offered that evening. Musicians and other entertainers performed for the hotel guests; visitors were admitted for a modest charge.

It was a glorious summer. In no time I had made friends with boys living in our house. Exploring the woods was the greatest thrill of all. One of my friends was a boy who had been there the year before. He knew all the interesting places. He knew where to pick wild blueberries and the nearest place to go for a swim. There was enough space around our house to play baseball and punchball. Usually there were enough kids around to make up two teams. After a couple of weeks, I turned brown from the sun, and my sinuses were clear. The country air had worked its wonders; the affliction that had plagued me since January was gone. Country air and sunshine had miraculously cured me.

The summer of 1937 was a time when polio, or infantile paralysis, reached epidemic proportions. There were no known preventative treatments for this terrible disease. Old wives bromides, like wearing a camphor ball in a bag around your neck, prevailed. New York City was thought to be a fertile breeding ground for the disease, so the public schools pushed back their opening date to mid-September. We extended our stay in the country for two more weeks. That summer stretched out wondrously. I remember the smell of hay and wet foliage after a thunder shower. I remember the incomparable joy of feeling well again. I wanted that summer to go on forever.

During our summer sojourn, I learned about a part-time job from one of the older kids. I sought it out with enthusiasm. A local man had established a brisk business selling the New York City newspapers to hotel guests in the area. He needed a boy to sell *The New York Daily News*, *The Daily Mirror*, and *The New York Times* from the front steps of the Olympic Hotel. I was picked up at dawn each morning. I remember waiting bleary-eyed for the truck to turn screeching off the road up to the front of my house. The other boys on the truck who were headed to their stations at other hotels pulled me up onto the back of the truck. We went speeding along the highway to our destinations. I was dropped off along with my packages of newspapers ready to set up my wares for the hotel's early risers.

There was no time for me to get breakfast before heading out to work, and I remember how the smells of the hotel dining room wafted tantalizingly through the morning air making me hungry. My morning shift lasted until the end of the breakfast service, around nine or ten o'clock. For the first couple of days, I was famished with no prospects for food until my boss picked me up on his return rounds to collect each newsboy and his remaining stock of papers. By the third day, however, I had a strategy. Instead of standing passively on the porch waiting for customers, I took the papers into the dining room. There, I approached people while they ate their breakfast and offered to sell them a newspaper. People seemed to like this direct-to-the-table service. A number of my customers, who saw the way I longingly regarded their food, would offer me something to eat from the table. This was especially true of the maternally inclined older women who saw me as some sort of starving waif. The Olympic Hotel was one of the fabled Catskill Mountains resort hotels renowned for its bountiful servings of food. The tables were crowded with breads, bagels, sweet rolls, and pastry in addition to the cold dishes that were served. I munched on bread slathered with jam or cream cheese as I wended my way around the tables. The diners seemed amused by this grinning paperboy chewing on his bread and hawking papers. The waiters were not amused. I got in their way as they raced back and forth between the kitchen and the dining room. The bulk of the Sunday papers made it too awkward for me to make my table rounds. I remained at my post on the porch to wait there for my customers. Fortunately, some of the guests who knew me by then would remember to bring along a little snack for the paperboy with the forlorn and hungry look.

I stayed with my job until Labor Day weekend. Between my salary and tips from hotel guests, I had saved some money. I don't remember what I did with my earnings, but having worked at a regular task, responsibly and independently, gave me an appreciation for the discipline of work and the pleasure of being compensated for it.

From that summer, I remember rainy summer days on the porch, playing cards with my friends, or hitchhiking a ride into town to see a dime matinee. One film that left a vivid impression on me was "Lost Horizons" with Ronald Coleman. I loved the idea of a hidden place high in the Himalayas with its secrets of eternal life. Mostly, I recollect the joy of spending the summer in a different world where I became aware for the first time of the countryside with its woods and green meadows, far from the asphalt sidewalks of New York. The sights, smells, and open spaces dazzled this city dweller and ignited the first flames of a lifelong zeal for travel.

Chapter Three

Back in the city, I returned to school for my last semester at the annex. In January 1938, when I was fourteen, I was transferred to the main building of Thomas Jefferson High School. Jefferson High was a big, multi-story building with a student population of several thousand. Its claim to fame was the educational stature of its principal, Dr. Lieberman. My only memory of him was one fleeting, long-distance sighting during a crowded school assembly. I don't recall what he spoke about, but I was repelled by one of his ideas. He felt that until human beings stopped engaging in and celebrating violence against one another in sports such as boxing and football, there would always be wars among mankind. As an adolescent sports enthusiast, I found this revolutionary and iconoclastic idea well beyond my intellectual grasp.

In January 1938, my high school career began in earnest with classes in math, science, history, language, and other preparatory courses. I also studied German as my second foreign language during my junior year. School was always fun for me. I never had to expend much effort in order to get good grades. I focused more on extracurricular activities. During my sophomore year, I got involved with the weekly high school newspaper, *The Liberty Bell*. I enrolled in a journalism class with Mr. Pearl. He was the faculty advisor to the newspaper. I wanted to impress him so that he would assign me an editorial post on the paper. Mr. Pearl was a crusty and frequently angry man. To compensate for his lack of physical stature — he was just over five feet tall — he would bellow at students and single out the tallest boys as targets for his disdain. I was a kid of average height, so he and I had a more relaxed relationship. As a journalism teacher, Mr. Pearl was truly the gem his name implied. He was a superb editor who instructed us in the substance of newspaper writing and in the technical details of newspaper production and layout. By the end of one semester with Mr. Pearl, his students were ready to contribute to all aspects of *The Liberty Bell*. Our class was a fairly large one for an elective. There were about twenty-five of us in the class; most electives comprised no more than a dozen students. We were all competing for Mr. Pearl's favor. I clearly needed to conjure up a special strategy in order to worm my way into Mr. Pearl's good graces.

There was a fortunate confluence of events that helped me to achieve my goal. My English teacher offered her students the opportunity to go to a Saturday matinee on Broadway. Mr. Pearl had asked his students to interview anyone we wished as practice for the newspaper. The play we saw featured a well-known actor of the period, Ezra Stone. He starred in both the theater production and in a radio series as a character named Henry Aldrich. Virtually every kid of that period who had a radio could mimic Ezra Stone as he called out in a squeaky, adolescent voice, "Coming, Mother!" The plan I hatched was to go backstage and interview Ezra Stone for my journalism class. It didn't occur to me that I might have difficulty getting an audience with a Broadway star. As my classmates and I were leaving our seats, I told my teacher that I was going to interview Mr. Stone and that I would make my own way home. She wished me luck and said goodbye.

I was stopped at the backstage door by a burly guard; he wanted to know where I thought I was going. Boldly, I replied that I was a reporter for *The Liberty Bell*, an award-winning high school newspaper, and that my assignment was to interview Mr. Stone. I must have sounded impressive enough. He led me to the star's dressing room and poked his head in to tell Ezra Stone what I had said. Out of curiosity or simple kindness, Ezra Stone graciously invited me in and asked me what I was up to. Up close, the actor was a short, youthful looking man in his late twenties. He spoke in a normal adult voice quite unlike the crackling sound of his adolescent character, Henry Aldrich. I told him the truth about my class assignment and about my aspirations to join the staff of the paper. He chuckled, went back to sipping his drink and smoking his pipe, and said something like, "Okay kid, interview away." He gave me about fifteen minutes of his time and answered all my prepared questions with good humor and grace. Before I left, he gave me his autograph and asked me to send him a copy of my article. I thanked him profusely and left the theater on a cloud.

I handed in my assignment to Mr. Pearl on Monday. The next day, Mr. Pearl announced that my interview would be published in the paper along with a feature story about my meeting with Ezra Stone. I can still remember the lead of my first piece: "Stripped of the garb and paint, and minus the renowned falsetto, Ezra

Stone . . . ." I was invited to join *The Liberty Bell* staff that very week. My high school journalism career had shifted into high gear.

Around this time, my father's employment had become steadier and my parents felt that we needed a family space of our own. When I was fourteen and my sister was almost eight, it was decided that we would move away from my grandparents to our own apartment. I was determined that we not move out of the neighborhood. When we began to search for an apartment, I enlisted all my friends to help learn about vacancies in nearby streets and houses. By summer, I learned about a vacancy in a three-room apartment on Hegeman Avenue near Sheffield. It was a ground-floor apartment facing the street. The neighborhood was safe and quiet. The apartment was in one of the smaller four-to-six family buildings on the block. We moved in by September 1938.

At school things were going well. I seldom studied. I crammed for exams, concentrated during classes, and took good notes. My average kept me in the upper percentiles of the class. In the courses that interested me most, I read well beyond the course requirements. My writing skills enabled me to prepare themes and reports in record time. My favorite classes were French, German, and English. History and social studies appealed to me also, especially when I was lucky enough to have gifted teachers who brought enthusiasm and colorful insights to their subjects. In those years, the New York public schools had a strong cadre of uncommonly talented teachers. At Jefferson High we had our fair share of them. These were the Depression years, and jobs were scarce. Employment as a secondary school teacher in the city school system was a highly coveted position. The competition for teaching positions attracted some of the city's finest minds. High school teachers were part of a cultural elite; some of them even earned a good enough salary to support a summer of travel abroad.

One teacher whom I remember vividly was my English teacher, Mrs. Freeman. She was an unattractive, middle-aged woman with a warm manner. She had a winning smile that lit up her face when she spoke passionately of a poem or a short story. Mrs. Freeman professed that reading was one of life's unparalleled joys. It was from her that I caught an infectious desire to devour American fiction and dramatic literature. Before the end of my first semester with her, I was reading collections of American short stories and prizewinning dramas of the 20th century. I became a habitual user of the school library; I always checked out the maximum number of books permitted. What I missed was regular access to a public library branch. There wasn't one within a reasonable walking distance of where we lived. It was not until our next move about two years later that I lived close enough to a public library to become a committed borrower.

During my sophomore year, my neighborhood bonds became stronger. After school and in the evenings, my friends would gather on the corner to form teams and to play street games. Sheffield Avenue between Hegeman Avenue and Linden Boulevard provided an open play area. It was a lightly traveled side street where few cars were parked. Sometimes, we played basketball in the schoolyard of P.S. 190, my alma mater. Other times, we played against boys who hung out around the candy store at Hegeman Avenue and Georgia Avenue. In the winter, when the streets were too cold to stay outdoors, we often went to a school that was about half a mile away; the building stayed open in the evenings for kids who played in basketball leagues. Our group formed its own basketball team, the Raleighs. We sought out neighborhood teams of our age to play against. There weren't many teams at the school where we customarily played, so we decided to challenge teams in other parts of the city. I wrote a letter to a dozen or so orphanages in different parts of New York, offering to play against any team they might field from kids in our age group. Five or six orphanages accepted our challenge. On Saturdays we traveled by subway to play against these teams. Some of the boys we played against were rough and fiercely competitive, but we made a lot of friends from different parts of the city this way. As we ventured beyond the social, political, economic, and religious boundaries of our own neighborhood, a wider world was revealed to us. Our games with the orphanage teams provided our first introduction to Catholic boys who wore crosses and to young black boys whose speech we could barely comprehend. We realized what first-rate basketball was all about when some of these spunky kids demolished us on the court.

The neighborhood where I grew up — with the exception of the occasional gentile apartment-building custodian — was made up completely of lower-class Jewish families. There were varying degrees of religious commitment among those who lived in the community — from believers to atheists. The common thread that prevailed among us was that we were American Jews. While the community was not energized by intellectual standards, many families saw the destiny of their children tied to academic achievement. Education was seen as the primary means to transcend working-class origins. The thirties were a time of strong family ties and loyalties, but the Depression era was not an age that spawned optimism about the future. Aspirations were modest; a steady, white-collar job was an ambitious enough goal. The news from Europe, where Hitler had begun to make the plight of the Jews seem so hopeless, exacerbated an already bleak picture of the times. Our parents, who had come to America for a better life, worried about what the future might hold. Aside from their common Jewish heritage, working-class families in my time and community also shared an almost religious fervor for Franklin D. Roosevelt.

Roosevelt was seen as the hero and defender of the working class and the champion of the downtrodden and poor. Undoubtedly, there must have been pockets of nonbelievers. In the 1930's, there were many New York Jews who saw Soviet-style socialism as the world's salvation. Where I grew up, if there was any alternative for salvation beyond Roosevelt and the Democratic Party, it escaped my attention or understanding. Like most young boys, my sensitivity to political events was overshadowed by my preoccupation with sports and friends. My father might pore over and ponder the national and international events of the day, avidly reading the paper and listening to the radio news reports, but my preoccupations were with the sports section and Red Barber's broadcasts of the Brooklyn Dodgers games. Many evenings my family would listen to broadcasts of variety programs featuring Jack Benny, Kate Smith, Burns and Allen, the Lux Family Theater, and Fred Allen. The pleasure derived from listening to radio came from using one's imagination to visualize the performers. To this day I prefer listening to the radio rather than watching television.

The ethnic neighborhoods of New York at this time were like small towns where everyone knew everyone. The pace of living was slower. Difficult economic conditions may have created a pent-up desire for material goods, but there was no pressure among families to express social status through possessions. Everyone scaled back and made do with what they had. We never thought to envy those with more. There was a complete absence of the constant and remorseless media representations of the "good life" that plagues society today. We understood that there were some families that were better off, but we also observed the plight of many needy families that were far less fortunate. We accepted who we were, what we had, and counted our blessings that our lot was not such a bad one. When I reflect upon my childhood and adolescence, I feel as if I won the lottery in life. I was brought up in a sheltered, loving home by parents and relatives who cared deeply for me. I took great joy in my life and all the abundance I found in it — whether in the streets, among my friends, or in school.

The Best of Times

As a cub reporter for *The Liberty Bell* in my sophomore year, I worked diligently on all aspects of its production. I wrote stories and produced mockup pages for the weekly issues. I devoted twice the time to the paper as I did to my studies. Fortunately, I was still able to maintain a grade average that kept me in the school's honor society. In my role as journalist, I wanted to cover sports for *The Liberty Bell*. The countless hours I spent working on the paper during my first semester, coupled with my unbridled enthusiasm for all my assignments, gained me the position of sports reporter by the second term of my sophomore year. In my junior year, I was promoted to sports editor of *The Liberty Bell*. This assignment gave me the opportunity to design the sports page each week, to assign stories and photographs, and to attend athletic events. In addition, I covered the school's major football and basketball games as a stringer for *The Brooklyn Daily Eagle* and *The New York Times*. I telephoned in to the sports desks of these newspapers with the final scores and key details of each game that Thomas Jefferson played as soon as it ended. Whenever an account of the game appeared in print, which was only occasionally since high school sports were seldom newsworthy enough, I received a check for two dollars. The high point of my career as sports editor came when I convinced the editorial board and the faculty advisor, Mr. Pearl, that the sports section was incomplete without a feature column. I pointed to the daily sports columns in the major newspapers. Sports editors, including my idol, Jimmy Powers of *The Daily News*, wrote on topics of interest to their readership. I was given my big chance. The weekly column, complete with its own logo created by the staff artist and cartoonist, was called *Take It from Me*. It carried my by-line. The column was my ticket to many dividends. I got to know the school's sports elite and earned their respect. The varsity athletes, the school's nobility, invited me to sit on the bench with them during games. The coaches permitted me to interview anyone I chose to, before, after, or even during the games. For a sports-crazy teenager this was heady stuff. When I reflected on my good luck, I felt giddy. I was enamored with myself and with the notion that I was a high school celebrity. I became so absorbed in my role that, when I reached my senior year and had accumulated the credits I needed for college admission, I decided to stay on for the fall term so as not to miss out on covering a potential city championship season for the football team.

By the time I graduated from high school in January 1941, what I had learned about school athletics was how corrupt they could be. Ambitious coaches would resort to virtually any tactic in order to win. They would even put injured athletes in to play if they thought this would help the team win. There were also athletes who ruthlessly undercut their teammates as they strove for personal stardom. Illicit financial rewards from box office receipts on ticket sales often padded the pockets of players and coaches. The unbridled adulation — from cheerleaders to alumni—that was reserved for the athletes also disturbed me. The more I learned, the more disillusioned I became. When I was younger, I had worshipped baseball and its heroes without restraint. By the end of my high school career, I had come to view the world of sports with deep cynicism. I have fonder memories of the years when I was a sophomore in high school in 1938 and 1939. My classes went well and I worked assiduously on *The Liberty Bell.* My stories were becoming known among the student body. My friendships were growing stronger and I lived in an apartment that was on the very street where my crowd hung out. The troubles in Europe, while threatening to the international order, were far too distant to disturb my adolescent world. The Depression still held the economy in its thrall. Yet, if things were not improving, they seemed no worse. My view into the future was very narrow. I had only a vague sense that I would like to pursue a career in journalism, which meant that I would need a college degree. Based on my academic record, I was sure that I could attend one of the city's tuition-free, municipal colleges. I knew that my parents could not afford the cost of a private college or university. Even though no one in my immediate family had attended college, it was assumed that this would be my destiny.

As I grew older, my friends and I began to enjoy more freedom away from family constraints. In summer we would roam about the city to parks and playgrounds or get tickets to sporting events from neighborhood summer school programs. We also spent many days at the seashore. My neighborhood was located about equidistant between Brooklyn's Coney Island and Rockaway Beach in Queens. A five-cent subway ride could get us to the beach, but the trip required transfers between two different lines. It took well over an hour in hot and often overcrowded trains to reach our destination. As a teenager I shunned family excursions. Like most adolescents, I preferred the company of my peers. My friends and I chose to get to the ocean by hitchhiking. We knew all the streets and roads in Brooklyn and became very skilled in mapping out our traffic routes.

We preferred Coney Island to Rockaway for two reasons. First, there was much more traffic headed in that direction, so getting a ride was easier. More importantly, Coney Island in the thirties was a gathering place for teenagers. The beach with its famed boardwalk stretched endlessly from Brighton Beach for two or three miles through all the numbered streets of Coney Island. It was a kaleidoscope of sights and sound. There were the carnival rides, fortunetellers, sideshows, and shooting galleries. The aroma of hot dogs, cotton candy, potato knishes, French fries, Italian ices, and jelly apples mixed with the sea air. Hundreds of people crowded the beaches and strolled along the boardwalk. Coney Island was a picturesque and lively place with countless attractions to dazzle any teenager. It was also cheap. Usually, we brought along a sandwich and fruit from home and enough small change to buy a cold drink or an ice cream. These would be bought from one of the many vendors who carried their inventories slung over their shoulders. These agile entrepreneurs moved swiftly about in the sand, loudly announcing their wares. They were always on the lookout for policemen who would fine them for peddling without a license. Sometimes one of us might have an extra quarter or fifty cents to spend. We often chose to spend the money on one of the games or rides, which cost only a few pennies.

The seashore was also a place for meeting girls. In the summer of 1937 and 1938, girls were an amazing new discovery. On the beach and in the ocean, clad only in our bathing suits, the physical difference between the girls and boys was clearly in evidence. The girls came to the beach from many different neighborhoods, and they were just as interested in us as we were in them. This gave rise to boasting and tomfoolery on the part of the boys. The girls meanwhile preened, giggled, and whispered among themselves. It was an innocent, fun-filled adventure that allowed us to assert our newly won freedom from parental authority.

The major objective of our beach days was to get a fashionable suntan without being broiled by the sun. I was fair skinned and sunburned easily. I understood nothing of the sun's harmful effects. I often overdid the sunbathing and wound up badly burned. The aftermath of blisters and peeling skin made for many uncomfortable nights. I was envious of my friends with darker complexions who tanned easily. I never followed a gradual tanning strategy. I would sit in the sun at midday soaking up the sun's strongest rays. This approach contributed to the many keratoses, basal cell, and squamous skin cancers that appeared on my face, neck, chest, and back. By the time I was in my thirties, these growths had to be cut or burned off. Providentially, they seldom proved hazardous. Those sunburns from ages ago turned my face into a terrain where many small skirmishes have been fought, leaving behind innumerable craters and foxholes.

My summers were a time of freedom and high jinx. Two unusual experiences in particular remain firmly in memory. My friend Louis "Chink" Heckelman was the son of a widowed mother. His father's brother was a bachelor, and it was this uncle who helped support his brother's wife and her children. A man of means, he drove a car at a time when few people in our neighborhood owned them. He lived in a six-room apartment about two miles from where we lived, and he had a telephone in his apartment. It was unclear how Louis's uncle earned his livelihood. He seemed to be a paid functionary for an association of food stores. His apartment served as his office and headquarters. In the years before telephone answering machines, Louis's uncle needed someone to answer his phone and take messages when he was out. During the busy seasons, he hired a secretary to do this job. During the summer, he asked Louis to take on this task, perhaps as a way to augment his sister-in-law's family income.

Louis had a passion for his flock of homing pigeons. He raised and trained them on the roof of the apartment house where he lived. Sitting by his uncle's phone, he passed the time thinking about his pigeons, while his friends enjoyed playing together outdoors. As Louis reflected on his boredom, he decided he should have some company during his hours on phone duty. I suspect that Louis never asked his uncle whether this would be okay. He decided independently to invite two or three of the boys to come over. We would have the run of the apartment and access to food specialties that stocked his uncle's refrigerator and kitchen cabinets. Late one morning three of us went to visit Louis. We were greatly impressed by his uncle's expensive furniture. We bounced around on the king-sized bed and sprawled across the handsome sofas in the living room. We turned the volume up on the majestic radio and raided the choice contents of the refrigerator. All the while Louis, while enjoying our company and our "ooh's" and "aah's" of pleasure, nervously admonished us to be careful not to break anything or make a mess. After a while, the novelty of the apartment wore off and we were bored. Someone suggested that we play hide-and-seek. Everyone except Louis thought this was a great idea. Louis was "it." The rest of us had five minutes to hide. We spread out while Louis covered his eyes. The other boys headed for the bedrooms. I went down the entryway hall and let myself into a very large storage closet. There were big boxes piled up on the floor and on the shelves. I turned on a light and started to look around. My curiosity impelled me to explore the contents of the boxes. In them were rolls of printed labels for cans, jars, and bottles. These labels were from expensive brands of every specialty food product imaginable—from smoked salmon to candies and caviar.

It didn't take a great leap of imagination to comprehend that the cache I had stumbled upon was a scam that Louis's uncle was running. It was probably as simple as peeling the labels off cheaper brands and replacing them with the printed labels of more expensive brands. I quickly switched off the light and remained in the closet a little while. When I opened the door and heard no one approaching, I tiptoed to the kitchen and hid myself under a table. I never told my friends about my discovery, nor did I mention it to Louis. Once when I tried to ask him about his uncle's job, Louis squirmed and mumbled something about running the business affairs of the appetizers association. I never knew if he had ever been in the closet. I imagine that his curiosity would have led him to make the same discovery that I had. I ultimately concluded that whatever nefarious fraud Louis's uncle engaged in, some good must have come of it because of his generosity and kindness to his dead brother's sister and her children. I knew from visiting Louis's home just how difficult it was for his mother to be the sole breadwinner in the family. I decided that the people who paid for those ostensibly expensive food brands were indirectly contributing to a worthy cause.

In our neighborhood of working-class families, most were of Ashkenazi heritage from northern, middle, or Eastern Europe. There was also a sprinkling of Sephardic families who had migrated from Mediterranean countries. Unlike the Ashkenazim, who spoke Yiddish as their primary language of discourse, the Sephardim spoke Ladino, a linguistic adaptation of Spanish. Sephardic Jews also observed somewhat different traditions, rituals, and culinary practices. Despite these cultural differences, the Ashkenazim and the Sephardim co-mingled harmoniously. Some Sephardic families in the neighborhood were more affluent. The men, who were entrepreneurs in the garment industry, manufactured women's wear or children's apparel. One of these successful business proprietors, Mr. Habib, was the father of my friend, Irving "Itskil."

Mr. Russo was another businessman in our neighborhood. He was a tall, stern, and regal-looking man who had two sons. The older son was Eli. He was several years older than me. The younger brother, Irving, or "Shorty" — because he was very tall like his father — was two or three years younger. As a result of his size, Shorty hung out with the older boys in my gang. We tolerated him even though he was not too bright. He was an agreeable kid who followed our lead and shared with us whatever he bought. He typically had more money to spend than the rest of us. When I was fifteen years old in 1939, I felt that I was old enough to try to get a summer job. Jobs were scarce. Many men with family responsibilities were still unemployed. Boredom, or perhaps my recollections of the summer I spent working as a paperboy, made me want to try some kind of job. My friend Davey, who had just turned sixteen, was also interested in looking. Together, we traveled to

Manhattan by subway two or three days running and made the rounds of employment agencies. We followed up on classified ads for businesses like Western Union, which employed a lot of boys as messengers. We learned that there were no jobs for inexperienced boys without marketplace skills. In addition, there were many more just like us who needed work even more.

Davey and I were lamenting the lack of job opportunities to our friends when Shorty Russo joined the group. He told us that his father's factory was inundated with orders and was operating at full blast. Did we want him to ask his father if he could use two strong boys who were ready to work right away? We did. He went home at once, talked to his father, and came back to report that we could come to work the next morning at the factory in Manhattan's garment district. We were offered positions as general floor assistants and we would be paid twenty cents an hour. Davey and I were delighted. We thanked Shorty profusely and arranged to take the subway in the morning so as to get to the city in time to begin work at 8:30 a.m.

We reported at the address we had been given. It was a huge factory loft. Inside, it was crowded with sewing and pressing machines and with bundles of fabric that were piled in tall stacks at one end of the loft. We arrived early with the seamstresses and the pressers. The factory space already felt very warm, even though it was still early in the morning, before the machines were turned on. We looked for Mr. Russo in his small corner office, but found Eli, his older son, instead. We knew him from the neighborhood, and he had been expecting us. He explained to us what our job would be. We would carry bundles of fabric and distribute them to the sewing machine operators. They would call out to us to replenish their supply of fabric so that they could work without interruption. We would carry the completed garments to another part of the loft and hang them up. From time to time we would also be expected to transport finished goods in handcarts to other businesses located nearby. The operators were paid for piecework, rather than hourly. The factory was swamped with an unusually large number of orders to be filled. Speed was of the essence. We would be expected to move quickly and efficiently.

It sounded straightforward enough. Eli took us around the loft and introduced us to the operators as they were getting ready to start their day's work. They would call us by name when we were needed. At exactly 8:30 a.m. a bell rang. The machines started up and there was a great clatter of sewing machines humming and pressing machines steaming. The loft had been transformed into a cauldron of noise, steam, and heat. Davey and I moved into action. We worked non-stop as the loft got hotter and hotter and the workers shouted to us to bring them the bundles of fabric. We were not prepared for such strenuous physical effort in temperatures of 100 degrees or more. Within an hour we were dragging ourselves through the aisles, sore and weary and sweating and hot. Then we heard a shrill scream.

Mr. Russo suddenly appeared. Observing the slow pace of our work, he raced down the row of sewing machines and physically seized us. He then proceeded to show us how we should be doing the job. This tall, elegantly dressed man began to run in a manic frenzy back and forth through the loft carrying fabric samples and bellowing at us all the while. Davey and I were stunned. When he finally stopped berating us, we went back to our duties. We picked up our pace as much as we could. Mr. Russo kept a close eye on us, shrieking at us to move even faster. Finally, he went back to his office and closed the door. Not knowing when this hulking madman might reappear, Davey and I tried desperately to keep moving as swiftly as possible. By noon we were dog-tired. By then some of the operators were breaking for lunch. With great trepidation we gathered up the courage to ask Mr. Russo when we could go out for lunch. This just set him off once again. Why were we both there? Didn't we know that we were never supposed to leave the floor together? He allowed each of us a half-hour lunch break; when one of us returned, the other could go. "Now out of here!" he shouted. Thoroughly cowed, we returned to our stations and reconciled ourselves to eating lunch alone. The workday seemed endless. Every twenty minutes or so, Mr. Russo checked on us. He snarled at us, or at the other workers, spewing invective for some perceived inefficiency or error. He could be heard from time to time berating his own son in exactly the same nasty tones.

After what seemed an eternity, the day ended. Exhausted and disconsolate, Davey and I rode the subway home. I think we both fell asleep. At home that night, I was too embarrassed to tell my parents what had transpired. I gave only a sketchy description of what my day's work had been like. The next day, Davey and I agreed that if things did not improve we would quit at the end of the week. Things did not improve. Mr. Russo continued to berate and scold us. Davey and I stayed the course, and at the end of the week we were paid. We marched into Mr. Russo's office and told him we were leaving. He tried to frighten us into changing our minds. He said he needed time to get replacements. He yelled at us about our ingratitude and how we should be grateful for the experience he had given us. He stormed and he ranted and he raved. Then we left. Our nightmare was over. We both had lost quite a few pounds and were mad at Shorty even though we knew we should feel sorry for him: he could never be free of his father.

In the postwar years of the 1950's and 1960's, one of the business success stories of the period was a company listed on the New York Stock Exchange that manufactured women's sportswear. Full page ads for Russ Togs appeared regularly in *The New York Times Sunday Magazine.* The company's chairman and president was Mr. Russo. His son, Eli, was the executive vice-president. Irving "Shorty" Russo was the treasurer. When Mr. Russo died his sons held majority control of the company for several years. In the 1960's, the company began its decline and the value of its stock diminished rapidly. Finally, Russ Togs went bankrupt and was no more.

In July of 1939, my parents decided to move our household once again. My parents, sister, and I were living in a very small apartment. My Aunt Rose, who by then had been married for a few years, needed to find an apartment near the retail store she managed. My mother was particularly fond of her baby sister; the idea of joining Rose and her husband and sharing an apartment with them appealed to her. The move would reduce our monthly rent and would give us more living space. It would also enable Rose to walk to work. My mother would look after the house. Rose's husband worked in New Jersey at that time and was only home on the weekends. I think my mother wanted to provide Rose with a home that was filled with people who cared about her. The drawback for me was that the neighborhood where we were looking for an apartment was two miles from where we were living. For me, this arrangement seemed disastrous. How could I maintain friendships living so far away? My heated objections were unavailing. The apartment that the family decided to rent was on Shepherd Avenue, two subway stops away at the very end of the New Lots Line. The apartment itself was another seven or eight blocks beyond the subway station. We moved before the end of August in time for my sister to enroll in a new grade school. I remained at Jefferson High, but I had a fifty-minute walk to school.

I needed a strategy to remain part of my existing circle of friends. The idea of making new friends in a new neighborhood was totally out of the question. There seemed nothing for it but to do my commuting by bicycle. The last thing I wanted to do was to ask my parents for the money to buy a new bicycle. They had just paid the moving expenses. I still had nearly three dollars left from my week's wages that I earned at the factory, so I alerted everyone I knew that I was in the market for a used bike. Once word got around I began to get offers, but invariably the price outstripped my limited resources. One day, someone turned up with an ancient bicycle that was dusty and rusty from neglect. I tried it out, and except for some squeaks and squeals, it rode just fine. I paid two dollars for the bike; and, except for the occasional flat tire, it served me nobly until I went into the Army at age nineteen.

Living so far from my friends, I couldn't hang out with them the way I used to. When school started in September, I was immersed in my schoolwork and *The Liberty Bell*. Even with the bike to transport me, I budgeted my time and got back to the old neighborhood only one or two evenings a week and on the weekends. The weather proved a factor. I was reluctant to ride my bike so far in rain or cold, and spending hours on the corner bantering with the other boys began to lose its appeal. I found that my new address actually offered unexpected advantages. The neighborhood public library branch was close by — only ten or fifteen minutes away by bicycle. I could also walk to a movie house that offered daily double-feature matinees of old film favorites.

The Arlington Library was housed in a classic Carnegie building on a tree-lined street of stately homes. It was two stories high and had many intriguing nooks and crannies. The collection held many books on virtually all subjects. There was ample seating and quiet reading alcoves. The staff was friendly and helpful; they seemed genuinely pleased to welcome an adolescent boy who enjoyed roaming the stacks. After reading quietly at one of the tables, I would go home with half a dozen books. My library card was a treasured passport into a world of recorded experiences, imaginative ideas, and unknown people and places. I explored this new universe in a free ranging and undisciplined way. Serendipitous discovery, rather than selections by the library staff, informed my choices. Books were a unique source of pleasure. I felt that, when I read, I was engaged in a private conversation with the writer, who spoke directly and personally to me alone.

I remember taking shelter at the movies on rainy afternoons. There was only a handful of viewers in the audience. Films afforded me an added dimension of visual delight, with their larger-than-life images and their cast of players. The experience of watching movies, however, seemed less personal than reading.

These films did not stir my mind or provoke my imagination. In a book, I felt that the author could explain, describe, rationalize, and reason with the reader. Movies depended solely on the actions and words of the actors in order to convey their meaning. The graphic representation of life in a film could invoke emotions ranging from sympathy, horror, love, or mirth, but the effect was not profound. These portrayals appealed to sentiment more than they did to the reasoning mind.

There was no one unifying theme that propelled me toward what I read or saw. I might accidentally come upon a writer or a subject and pursue it through several books before I was swept away by a new passion or interest. Given the limited intellectual stimuli in my environment, my reading tastes were eclectic. I was exploring worlds beyond my personal world in fiction, drama, history, travel books, and anything else that caught my fancy. Films were passive pleasures, but books opened countless doors beyond my personal knowledge and experience.

In the fall of 1939, my friends and I became greatly preoccupied with girls. Our modest homes had no space where young people could get together to socialize. The street corner where we congregated was a similarly unsuitable meeting place. These limitations gave rise to a unique invention of the era: the cellar club. In many streets near where we hung out, two-family houses often had finished basements, such as the one where I had my bar mitzvah party. Landlords looking for greater financial gains often rented these basement spaces. A thriving, illegal real estate market was born. The prospective tenants were groups of boys. They would round up as many potential club members as they could and charge them a small fee to join. This way it was possible to pay the twenty- or thirty-dollar rent.

Our club was called Club Raleigh. I have no idea where the name came from, but it was also the name we used when we formed our earlier basketball team. In the fall of 1939, after many street corner conferences, we looked for a suitable basement. One turned up on Vermont Street, four or five blocks away from our customary corner hangout. It had been rented earlier to a similar group that had since disbanded. The basement had its own entrance and was already furnished with a number of well-worn chairs and sofas in the main room. There was a scarred kitchen table and some beaten up chairs in the back room. In another small room there was space for the heating system and a tiny bathroom.

Club Raleigh served two purposes: the first was gambling. Some of the boys had taken up cards and shooting craps; they used the Raleigh's back room to play on Saturday and Sunday afternoons. The chief purpose of the club, however, was to provide a place for meeting and entertaining girls in the evening. We danced all night, from about eight o'clock until the early morning hours. Our music of choice was the Big Band sounds of Artie Shaw, the Dorsey Brothers, and Glenn Miller. Besides the music that we played on the record player or on the radio, blue and red lights set up behind the couches kept the room dark enough for romantic encounters with the opposite sex. The old sofas in the basement could accommodate twelve to fourteen couples easily. On the dance floor in the middle of the room, two or three couples would sway to the music of "Stardust" or jitterbug to the syncopated rhythms of "Chattanooga Choo Choo."

Sometimes, we were invited to visit other cellar clubs in the neighborhood, and we often invited non-members to visit us. Regular use, however, was restricted to members and their girlfriends. We had about twenty members. On Friday or Saturday nights the club was invariably overcrowded. The landlord asked only that we keep the noise level down after ten o'clock at night and that we not congregate on the street outside. He didn't want anyone in the neighborhood complaining to the police, possibly alerting them to his illegal rental arrangement. We were just as eager as the landlord to avoid any disturbance that might result in our eviction. We kept the decibel level low and policed boisterous behavior among ourselves. The worst thing that could be said about Club Raleigh was that it stunk perennially of cigarettes. On weekend nights the air became polluted with a black cloud of smoke.

The club's finest dancer was Maxie Lipschitz, a thin boy from a very poor home, who always cadged cigarettes from the other boys. In return he gave dance lessons on weekday nights to any of the boys who wanted to learn. Some of us, like myself, were as graceless as bears wearing snowshoes. I'm sure we sorely taxed Maxie's patience and energies. With a cigarette dangling from his lips and smoke swirling around his head, Maxie demonstrated flawlessly every step from the fox trot to the boogie-woogie. Patiently, he helped his uncoordinated friends execute the movements. A few years later, Maxie served in Italy as a tailgunner in the Air Corps. He went down in a burst of flames from which his body was never recovered.

Now that my friends and I had shifted our attention to girls, some of the boys played the field, meeting and dating as many different girls as possible. None of us had enough money to take girls on real dates, which would have entailed the price of two movie admissions and an ice cream soda after the show. So, Club Raleigh was our party headquarters. When I was around sixteen years old, I met Clara Sadacca. She was a very pretty dark-haired, dark-eyed girl who lived several blocks away. Her good friend lived near where my gang congregated. Clara was from a big Sephardic family. She had four older brothers (one of whom, Ralph, had been my sixth-grade classmate) and a sister. It wasn't customary for kids to have very much to do with their friends' parents. Meetings usually took place on the street, at the club, or even at school.

Clara's friend, Stella Cassouto, was for a short while the girlfriend of one of my friends named Ike Broderson. Ike was tall and handsome. He seldom had anything to say, and most of the boys thought he was dumb. The girls, however, found his speechlessness alluring; it added to his air of mystery. Besides that, he owned a very classy bicycle that was the envy of all. Stella was a clever girl with a sharp wit and a remarkable flair for fashion. She was the only child of a widowed mother. Stella's mother was one of the few parents of my friends with whom I ever carried on a genuine conversation. She had been a teacher, but because of a chronic illness she was no longer able to teach full time. She was quite poor but very well read. She was an articulate woman with strong ambitions for Stella's education. Stella had no natural good looks, but she did have the imagination and good taste to transform herself into a very attractive young woman. Early on Stella learned that it was her appearance and charm that would catapult her to a higher social and economic station. Stella married before she was twenty. She married a young Sephardic man whose father was a successful clothing manufacturer, known as the "corduroy king" of New York. Stella and her husband moved to Great Neck, Long Island, where they built a home, family, and life that was far more affluent than the one she had known in Brooklyn.

Clara and I saw each other on the weekends. We both dated other people at that time. After I turned sixteen, Clara's family moved to Coney Island, more than an hour away by subway. The move made our meetings even more intermittent. I was entering my senior year at Jefferson High in January of 1940. It was clear to my parents and to me that I would be going to college rather than looking for a job in a hopeless job market. The war was going on in Europe by then, and the news accounts spoke ominously of America's need for preparedness. In my life, however, there were no discordant notes. My father was working regularly and we were living in a comfortable apartment. I don't remember any financial problems. I received a modest allowance, which I supplemented with the few dollars I earned occasionally as sports correspondent for the metropolitan dailies. During those years of social independence, I stayed out until the pre-dawn hours on Friday and Saturday nights. I slept undisturbed until noon. While my parents were not pleased with my late hours, they trusted me not to do anything foolish.

Smoking an occasional cigarette was not seen as a cardinal sin. Even so, I never smoked at home. Like most sixteen-year-olds, I saw myself as a grownup and concentrated only on my personal concerns; I was oblivious to what went on around me. I liked my family and my home. I remember fondly the small sunroom in our apartment where I set up a cot and contemplated the sky and the stars through the screened windows on hot summer nights before falling blissfully asleep. I took everything in my world for granted and vaguely assumed that somehow in the future the faith and confidence my family invested in me would be justified—that I would attain honor and success and bring great joy to the family.

My last year of high school was marked by no special achievements. I concentrated more heavily on academics in the spring term so that I would have more time in my last term to focus on sports reporting for *The Liberty Bell*. With few school requirements left, I had more time to spend with friends. I had enough time to see afternoon movies and my social life was becoming more full. Clara and I continued to date, sometimes accompanied by other friends and their dates. My days and nights were carefree and pleasurable. I was oblivious to the troubles brewing around the world and in American society.

Chapter Four

The only decision before me was which college I would attend. I knew from my reading about the joys of undergraduate life at such distant and romantic schools as Princeton or Dartmouth. I also knew that my family could not afford to send me to a private university, even if I applied and was accepted. No one in the family except for my cousin Charlie Goldberg had attended college full-time. Uncle Morris had been a part-time, evening student at City College. Charlie studied at Fordham. His high school record did not make him eligible for any of the free public colleges, so his parents paid the tuition using their earnings from the family restaurant. I had a choice between Brooklyn College and City College. Queens College was inaccessible by public transportation. My preference was for a broad liberal arts education. Brooklyn College was nearer—half an hour by subway—it was co-educational and had a more inviting, modern campus. The liberal arts center of City College, in those days, admitted men only. The campus was distinguished by its Gothic architecture that was dominated by formidable stone towers and dark cavernous corridors, halls, and classrooms. I never visited either college during my high school years. Instead, I made my decision based on the rigor of each school's admissions policy. City College had the highest standards of admission based on one's high school average. I determined that since I could qualify for the most demanding college it was there that I would go. I often reflected later on the wisdom of that naive judgement.

In order for me to get to City College, I had a ten to fifteen-minute walk to the subway station. The train, which traveled through Brooklyn and up the West Side of Manhattan to 139th Street, took another hour and fifteen minutes before reaching the station nearest City College. It took me another ten or fifteen-minute walk to finally reach the campus. The round-trip commute took two hours each way. The travel did have one important compensation: with such a long commute, I developed the habit of reading the newspaper. Morning tabloids like *The Daily News* and *The Mirror* held little appeal for a college-bound intellectual; I preferred *The New York Times* or *The Tribune*. I opted for *The New York Times*. This daily addiction, which I took up in January 1941, has remained with me ever since.

At City College, a number of surprises were in store for me. Among the school's more stringent requirements were two years of Latin, in addition to three years each of two modern languages. I had already completed three years of French and two years of German in high school, so I only needed one more year of German. There was also an ROTC program available. At a time when Europe was already in the throes of war, questions about the prospects for American involvement were everywhere under discussion. Enrollment in the ROTC seemed to offer the prospect of an army commission, if military service were to become obligatory. The smart-looking khaki uniform, with its blue ROTC insignia on the collar, courtesy of the United States government, exerted its appeal on a childish seventeen-year-old. After sober discussion about the pros and cons of joining the ROTC with my parents, I decided to sign up. My family had come a long way from the time when they had objected to my becoming a Boy Scout for fear that I would somehow wind up in the military.

Another unanticipated opportunity presented itself at City College. In those years, as a source of support for impecunious undergraduates, the National Youth Administration allocated funds to colleges to employ students from families with incomes below a certain level. I was eligible to apply and was assigned to the college library to shelve books. I was paid fifteen dollars a month for ten hours of work a week. This modest sum seemed a fair exchange for two hours of work a day, especially since much of the time I spent browsing in the stacks, surreptitiously reading whatever might be found in the section where I was presumably hard at work shelving books. The fifteen dollars I earned proved ample since I was living at home and carrying my lunch with me to school every day.

College proved to be starkly different from high school. High school had been a colorful, lively, and entertaining place. The City College population looked to me like a city of drones, where everyone moved quickly and seriously. Students were so busy and studious they even studied in the bathroom stalls. The deepest insult to my ego came during class time. In high school I had achieved a reputable standing without really developing serious study skills. I simply attended classes, completed assignments on time, and skimmed through my notes before exams. I now found myself in classes with young men from high schools all over the city who were not only just as smart as I, or smarter, but who worked hard at their jobs as students. I no longer had the edge I had enjoyed in high school when most of my classmates were far duller. Furthermore, I was no longer a school celebrity. Here, there was no *Liberty Bell*. I was just one more humorless City College drone.

I was clearly much too immature for the intellectual big league. The main extracurricular preoccupation I observed at City College seemed to be politics. The drab and drafty college cafeteria was the celebrated and central rallying point for various political factions, which were primarily left of center. Marxists, Trotskyites, Socialists, and other exotic splinter sects occupied tables from which they bellowed their polemical dialectics in strident tones. For someone as untutored as I was in the issues of class struggle, these raucous debates sounded like the burlesque routines of a Marx Brothers' movie.

College life was no fun at all. Furthermore, in a couple of my classes I was barely hanging on. Math had never been my favorite, but I had always performed reasonably well. Not now. In my math class the objective seemed to be the construction of higher math from original theories and principles. Perhaps it would have made sense to me if the instructor had spent class time in explaining how we might accomplish this. Instead, he gave us a term's worth of assignments at the start and then assiduously missed every other session through the semester. Perhaps the other people in the class had friends with whom they could discuss and sort out what was going on. I had none. It is also possible that they were simply much smarter than I and that they could figure things out by themselves without a teacher's help. Things only got worse as the term progressed. The final math exam was one of life's deep mysteries for me. The fact that fifty percent of the class failed scarcely made my grade of a "D" any more appealing.

My entry-level Latin course met five days a week for an hour. Languages had been my forte, so I expected to excel. I enjoyed Latin. I worked at the course, at least within the limits of my under-developed study habits; I was still reluctant to abandon my weekend social life for the rigors of scholarly pursuit. The instructor was disappointed in me and gave me a "C." I maintained a "B" average in my other classes, including German, science, and astronomy. In ROTC, even though I never could march in step during drills, I received an "A," and in physical education, I received a "pass."

The Best of Times

My first semester of college had been a near disaster; the pleasures of higher education proved non-existent. I was bored and angry that I had chosen City College. I would have fared more successfully and certainly would have had a better time socially if I had gone to Brooklyn College instead. I had made no new friends at City College, and there was nothing to capture my interest except difficult classes where I no longer shined. My second semester held little appeal. I foresaw nothing but weeks of long commutes and joyless classes.

The long summer of 1941 stretched before me. My friends were already out in the world of work, and somehow the prospect of another languid and lazy summer hitchhiking had lost its luster. Besides, I was genuinely curious about what it would be like to join the ranks of the employed. Jobs were still exceedingly scarce for high school graduates, but I thought word of mouth among friends and family might lead me further than had my earlier assaults on the job market through classified ads and employment agencies. My Uncle Morris gave me some hope.

For a number of years, my Uncle Morris had been employed as a bookkeeper for a large distributor of linens and domestics, Tobin, Sporn and Glaser, Inc. The company occupied several floors in a loft building on West Thirtieth Street in Manhattan, just off Fifth Avenue. Its business consisted of contracting with textile mills in the South, which supplied finely woven sheets, pillowcases, and towels. The company employed seamstresses, who embroidered these luxury cloth goods for sale to dry goods stores in the United States and Canada. Salesmen for the company sold to chain stores and traveled to different regions of the country making direct sales to independent dry goods stores. The firm's offices and showroom were on one floor. Their shipping department and inventory area occupied another two floors. The factory itself was on another level. Most of the company's work force was seasonal—orders and shipping took place in the summer and early fall, in anticipation of the Christmas season and the traditional white sales in January.

I wanted to make a favorable impression on Mr. Glaser, the company's head of internal operations. Morris thought I might have a chance at a job as a stock clerk. I knew that I would have to return to school in the fall, but if I presented myself as a candidate for summer work only, I would not get the job. Discussions at home centered on the ethical problem of misrepresenting myself for the sake of getting a job. I didn't want to compromise Morris, who had labored so long and conscientiously to establish himself. I was ambivalent. I felt that the company really couldn't hold Morris responsible for a teenager's capricious behavior. I went ahead and made an appointment to meet Mr. Glaser. I was more truthful with Mr. Glaser than I had been with my parents. This modest, tired-looking man came across as friendly and warm. I felt comfortable explaining to him how I had just completed a disappointing first term in college, and while my parents were keen for me to return in the fall, I had misgivings. To my surprise, Mr. Glaser told me my parents were right, but he also said that it was my life and I was old enough to make decisions even if they were wrong. If I really wanted to work, he suggested I could continue my studies by taking evening classes at the City College School of Business on East Twenty-third Street — just eight blocks away from the firm. He also told me that he had a son who was going to begin college in the fall and that he also might be working in the office during part of the summer. Mr. Glaser concluded our meeting by shaking my hand soberly and telling me that I could start the following Monday for twenty-five cents an hour. I was to report to the head of shipping at eight o'clock in the morning.

Working that summer at "Tobin, Shmobin and Globin", as the company was known to insiders, was my first experience beyond childhood. The millinery district of Manhattan where my father worked was just a few blocks north of Thirtieth Street, so I was able to take the subway with him every morning. We carried our paper-bag lunches prepared by my mother. Both of us read the papers; my father got *The Daily News*, while I chose *The New York Times*. We clutched a pole or a strap as the train rattled and jerked its way toward Manhattan. At Fourteenth Street we parted company as I changed to a local train that took me to Twenty-eighth Street.

My new job was tiring and physically strenuous. I spent time wheeling around a hand truck loaded with cases of baled materials, which I put into piles. To fill orders, I collected large batches of different products from their bins and carried them to the shipping department. My first days were a blur of blistered hands and sore arms and legs. I dozed off on the subway ride home and fell asleep in my bed by eight o'clock, as I listened to my favorite radio programs. After a week or so, I no longer ached. I actually felt joy in using my body and exercising my muscles. I took deep satisfaction in the exhaustion I felt when I showered and then fell into a sound, dreamless sleep at the end of each day. I reflected on how I must have been derived from peasant stock, which equipped me with the compact body and the strong arms and legs that are so well suited for the rigors of manual labor.

The Best of Times

My fellow workers lacked ambition. They did only what they needed to do. They had no other job options. Indeed, they were pleased just to be at work and off the streets. No one had serious plans; perhaps it was the times. By summer of 1941, the war in Europe was going badly. America was offering lend-lease to the British; United States involvement in the war seemed inevitable. Young, single men could imagine nothing in their future beyond military conscription. The Selective Service System with a draft of recruits had already begun. Registration at the age of eighteen was compulsory. It was an unsettling time for everyone. For an immature seventeen-year-old, the prospect of returning in September to the drab regimen of a second semester at City College held no appeal whatsoever.

I liked working and I was doing well on the job, but there was no future for me at the company. It was clear that Mr. Glaser intended to promote his son, who had shown an interest in the business. I also learned that the other principals of Tobin and Sporn had close friends and relations destined for management-level positions. I could only look forward to a job in sales, which did not appeal to me. The salesmen at the company struck me as a posturing breed of overdressed peacocks, infatuated with their self-importance. They were perennially grinning to show off their perfectly capped teeth and boasting about their sales and sexual prowess. I didn't aspire to become one of them.

In an effort to placate my parents, I decided to enroll in the business school of City College where I could take two three-credit courses in the fall. I chose classes that I could apply toward my liberal arts degree at the uptown center. One of these courses was German; the other was an introductory class in government and politics. I attended classes four evenings a week from six to eight-thirty in the evening. I usually bought my dinner of knockwurst on a Kaiser roll from a street cart on my way to class. I completed most of my assignments on the subway ride home, which enabled me to enjoy my precious weekend hours. The German instructor peppered his lectures with sly innuendoes about how the best students in his class would receive his endorsement for jobs as undercover agents in Yorkville. He was referring to the German quarter on the Upper East Side in Manhattan, which was rumored to be a nesting place for Nazi spies. If we were drafted, he offered to provide letters of reference for postings to army intelligence. As it turned out, we were at war before the semester was over.

Even though I was tired and uninspired after a long day of work, I found my new classes much more to my liking. There was little competition. Students enrolled in the business school were practical working people, mostly men in their early twenties. They came to class after a full day on the job; they had chosen the college as a means to advance their professional ambitions. Absent among my classmates were the citywide academic stars, who had populated the uptown campus. I regained my high school status and enjoyed having the academic edge again. Although my weeks were busy and my weekends full of social activity, I felt rudderless. I had no idea what I really wanted to do. The notion of my going into journalism seemed remote and fanciful. To get there, I would have to complete a college degree; even then I would need to be very lucky.

During the fall semester, I learned that a federal civil service exam was being given nationwide. High scoring applicants would receive a four-year apprenticeship at the Government Printing Office in Washington, DC. After serving their apprenticeships, these appointees would receive jobs as journeymen printers. In 1941, many dreamed of a permanent civil service position. Postal employees, teachers, and others with secure jobs, paid vacations, and guaranteed retirement pensions were the envy of all. To be eligible for appointment, one had to be eighteen years old and had to achieve a high enough score on the intelligence test. The exam was given on a Saturday morning in October. It wasn't clear from the announcement how many apprentices were going to be hired. I realized that thousands of job-seeking young men would take part in the competition. My supreme self-confidence led me to think that my chances were just as good as anyone else's. I took the multiple-choice test in a crowded gymnasium in Manhattan with several hundred applicants. I completed the test and promptly forgot all about it.

The fall of 1941 hurtled by. Between my job, evening classes, and weekend social life, I was constantly in motion. Then came Pearl Harbor Sunday. I had kept up with *The New York Times*'s accounts of discord with Japan, but like most Americans, I had no notion of the depth of the crisis before the attack. My parents were worried, not so much about American involvement in war, but about what would happen to me. In hushed tones they discussed what lay ahead. The sorrow written on their faces was tied to the fate of their not quite eighteen-year-old son. I tried to console them by suggesting that the prospect of my being drafted was still months away; perhaps by then the war would be over. They were not convinced, nor truly was I. I went to see my friends. Most of my friends turned up at the club as the afternoon progressed. By evening virtually everyone was there. We huddled around the radio, which broadcast constant accounts of the damage wrought by the Japanese attack. President Roosevelt told the nation that a state of war existed and that the country would be at war with the Axis powers in Europe. Our feelings of shock and horror for the lives lost that early morning in Hawaii were mixed with the exciting possibility that America would show the Japanese what we were made of. Beneath this jingoistic bravado, we worried about our personal fate. Someone finally switched off the radio. As if someone had given the signal, we all rose to our feet, some of us on the edge of tears, and sang out the national anthem with gusto.

It was difficult to concentrate on life's mundane routines in the immediate aftermath of Pearl Harbor. At home, at work, and in school the war absorbed everyone's thoughts and conversations. I reflected on how meaningless my job and college courses seemed during this time of dramatic upheaval. That very Friday, I received my test results from the United States Civil Service Commission—I had earned ninety-two points out of one hundred. I was placed on a list of eligibles and would be offered an appointment as soon as my name moved up to the top of the list. In the meantime, I was offered a civil service job in the Government Printing Office in Washington, DC, as a skilled assistant at the rate of sixty-six cents per hour. I could begin work one week after my eighteenth birthday on January 15, 1942. The offer, coming when it did, struck me as exactly the type of adventure I was looking for. For an eighteen-year-old who had never spent a day away from home, the prospect of living on my own in Washington, DC—the headquarters of American wartime involvement—was almost unbelievably appealing. My parents were unenthusiastic, but they understood that wartime disruptions were going to be an inevitable part of any young man's life. They knew Washington would be as safe as New York, and that I would still be able to complete my fall semester by January fifteenth. My salary of sixty-six cents per hour plus overtime was more than my father earned. Grudgingly they gave in. I sent in my job acceptance right away and agreed to report for work at 8:30 a.m. at the personnel office of the Government Printing Office on North Capitol Street in the District of Columbia.

I knew no one in Washington, but I was undaunted. Somehow, I had to find a place to live in what was reputed to be the tightest housing market in the country. Thousands of workers arrived each day from all over the country looking for rentals. All my friends and family were enlisted in the task of helping me locate a place to stay in Washington. Finally, at the very end of December, Cousin Chaim wrote to a high school acquaintance from upstate who was working in Washington. He wrote to this friend, Kenny, to tell him about my arrival in mid-January and my need for a place to stay. We had not heard back from Kenny by the time of my departure. We assumed that the mail was slow and that he would receive Cousin Chaim's letter by the time I reached Washington. My Aunt Rose loaned me a big suitcase to pack my clothes in for the trip. With the fall semester over, I said goodbye to my friends, to Clara, and to my family, and took the train from Pennsylvania Station in New York to Washington's Union Station.

During the train ride I talked to several young men and women who were headed for Washington. They all bemoaned the impossibility of finding reasonable housing accommodations in the District. I had only a few dollars with me and I began to wonder how I would pay for a hotel room, or if there would be a room for me at the YMCA. Once in Washington, Visitors' Information showed me how to get to Kenny's address by public transportation. I took the Mt. Pleasant trolley to its last stop and walked a block to a large brick house with a porch on Kilbourne Place. It was early Saturday afternoon when I knocked on the front door. A young man let me in and led me to a large parlor where several young men and women were gathered around a girl who was playing a show tune on a piano. With suitcase in hand, I entered the room: the piano playing stopped and everyone looked at me. I asked for Kenny. One of the boys answered that Kenny was his roommate, but that he had gone home for a couple of weeks and wouldn't be back until the following weekend. My heart dropped into my stomach. I asked if anyone had any suggestions about where I could find a place to live. Nobody spoke; then Kenny's roommate announced that since Kenny was gone, why didn't I take his place until I found other accommodations? This struck me as a marvelous idea.

The boarding house was a spacious four-story building. The landlady and her family lived in the back of the first floor. The upper floors each consisted of four or five rooms and a bathroom. Two or three people occupied each bedroom. I was introduced to the landlady and arrangements were made for me to rent Kenny's place until his return. Room and board was thirty dollars a month. This included room, breakfast, dinner, and a bag lunch prepared by the landlady, which could be carried to work.

The boarding house was a beehive of activity. It was crammed full of young men and women who had streamed into Washington to fill the ranks of government agencies and bureaus that were straining to increase staff as wartime activities shifted into high gear. The girls, who were secretaries or office clerks, had escaped humdrum lives in small-town America for the excitement of being part of the war effort. The boys, who were a bit older, were on borrowed time awaiting a call from the draft board. One of my boarding mates was a cartographer with the Army Map Service. He worked on secret projects drafting maps for the military. He held a college degree in geography from a university in the Midwest and had high hopes that the specialized nature of his work would gain him a draft deferment. Another boarder was an apprentice at the Government Printing Office. He had scored so high on the same exam I had taken that he was one of a handful of candidates who actually received an appointment. While his salary was far less than what the rest of us earned, he was being groomed to become a journeyman printer with the promise of lifetime employment in the federal civil service. Full-fledged printers, with whom he worked, drove their own cars and owned comfortable homes in the suburbs. His future prospects were the envy of most of us.

On Monday morning, lunch bag in hand, I boarded the trolley which took me all the way from Mt. Pleasant in northwest Washington to the Government Printing Office on North Capitol Street, just two blocks from Union Station. The trolley was crowded with eager recruits from all over the United States. At the personnel office, I was assigned to the warehouse — a smaller building, where paper used for printing was received and stored. The printing plant was across the street. The warehouse backed onto the freight yards of Union Station. Freight cars could unload the rolls and crates of paper directly into the warehouse. I was one of the crewmen who unloaded the freight cars. Hand-operated lifts and gasoline-powered trucks delivered the crates and rolls to sections of the warehouse where they would be stored until needed. We also drove stacks of paper through an underground passage to the printing plant across the street. The work was similar to what I had been doing at Tobin, Sporn and Glaser, except that now I had the help of machines to do the heavy lifting. Unlike the hectic pace of work in New York, government moved at a slow and leisurely pace, with longtime workers setting a lethargic standard. I quickly grasped that this was not a job for the energetic or ambitious. It was immediately evident to me that the interesting moments of my Washington experience would be found outside of working hours.

Washington in 1942 was a quiet, sleepy town. Except for the influx of war-related civilian and military workers, the city maintained the relaxed and unhurried mood of an overgrown village. It was a southern city with segregation firmly in place. Business in Washington had a small-town flavor as well. Early on I discovered that many of the crates and rolls of paper being delivered from upstate New York for use by the Government Printing Office were marked with the name of the Giegengack Printing Company. The name of the United States public printer also happened to be August Giegengack.

Within a week I was comfortable at work and at 1614 Kilbourne Place. By the time Kenny returned someone else had moved out. I simply switched to another room with a free bed. There I met Herbie Belon. Herbie was a short, dark-haired street-smart boy from the Bronx who had arrived in Washington in the fall of 1941. He had a job as a clerk in one of the temporary government agencies that administered the lend-lease program to England. Herbie was about two or three years older than I, but what drew me to him was what struck me as his worldly, sophisticated demeanor. Most of the occupants of our boarding house were bland, pleasant people. Herbie was flamboyant. He wore trousers tightly pegged at the ankles in the style of the zoot suit. He was also up on jazz and knew where the best parties were going on weekends that we could crash. He smoked incessantly and favored beer and Scotch over the soft drinks that others in the house preferred. He seemed to know half the girls in Washington, and when he saw one he wanted to know on a trolley or a bus, he would make her acquaintance before the end of the ride. In the vernacular of the forties, Herbie was "hep." His boisterous and extroverted manner made me feel comfortable in the role of fellow traveler. We shared several things in common: we both came from the big city; were products of New York's public schools; and we both hailed from working-class families. Unlike me, Herbie had never gone on to college. He did not care for books, but never held my own love of reading against me. Almost upon my arrival in Washington, I had discovered the closest public library branch where I checked out countless books. We both needed a sidekick for weekend socializing and just naturally gravitated towards one another.

My arrival in winter precluded most outdoor activities. There were, however, movie theatres where I could catch the weekly feature. One film that remains in my memory is "Kings Row," starring Ronald Reagan as the victim of a sadistic doctor played by Claude Raines, who needlessly amputates Reagan's legs. The movie ends with Reagan's anguished question, "Where's the rest of me?" Going to the movies had always been among my favorite activities, but it was Herbie who introduced me to jazz.

The Best of Times

In Washington in the early forties there were no public performances in theaters by black entertainers for white audiences. "Coloreds" were not admitted into theaters intended for whites. Nevertheless, Washington was a rich center of jazz, where some of the most celebrated bandleaders, such as Duke Ellington and Count Basie, performed regularly in theaters for black audiences. The mecca of jazz was the Lincoln Theater. Herbie and I would go there for matinees and evening performances to hear these extraordinary concerts. We had no difficulty buying tickets and were made to feel thoroughly at home as we sat in our orchestra or balcony seats surrounded by a sea of black people. Indeed, we were sometimes embarrassed by the attention we got from people all around us who shook our hands, welcomed us, and congratulated us on our good taste. My visits to the Lincoln Theater led to a lifelong interest in jazz.

The boarding house was located just a short walk from Rock Creek Park. In those years the park provided an idyllic setting for family outings and weekend sports. Neighborhood teams were drawn from the many rooming and boarding houses in the area. Kilbourne Place was also close to Sixteenth Street, then a flourishing boulevard of grand public and private buildings. Many exclusive and resplendent high-rise apartment houses lined the street. Washington was a city made for walking. One could take long weekend strolls along the Mall downtown, around the Capitol, and along the banks of the Potomac River.

Work had settled into a routine. Once I had learned to drive the lift and fork trucks there were no further challenges. Overtime work was readily available. At time and a half, my pay was about one dollar an hour. Apart from rent, the only out-of-pocket expenses I had were for transportation and entertainment. I bought few clothes. After all, I expected Uncle Sam to be underwriting my wardrobe before too many more months went by. I sent home most of what I earned, which my mother put in savings for me. By spring, I knew the twenty or so other boarders in the house. We all ate our meals together, and I learned about the different regions of the country they came from. The culture of the house had the flavor of a coed dormitory. In March, our landlady decided to raise the rent from thirty dollars a month to forty dollars. We formed a committee to resist the rent hike. Herbie was a member; I was not. The landlady remained steadfast in her demand. Mediation proved futile. Before the increase took effect, one of the boarders, who was a non-practicing lawyer working in a regulatory agency, filed a grievance on behalf of the renters with a local housing authority. The petition was successful. The increase was denied. Our rent stayed at the thirty-dollar rate for full room and board.

The Best of Times

Spring turned into summer. What had been comfortable living arrangements in the cold days of winter became less commodious with the approach of summer's heat and humidity. With only one window and no cross-ventilation, my crowded accommodations lost their appeal. I had not been home since my arrival in January, and I had begun to miss my family and friends. There was nothing more for me to learn at work. I was well beyond eighteen, and the draft calls in New York were being stepped up. I could be receiving my induction notice at any time.

On a Saturday night, the second week in June, Herbie and I went to a party that was being given by one of his co-workers. The house was in Adams Morgan, a neighborhood that was about half an hour's walk from Kilbourne Place. It was a lively party. There must have been eighty to one hundred people jammed into the building. There was plenty to eat and drink. I started drinking beer at about eight o'clock. Much later, I vaguely remember seeing a very inebriated Herbie admiring the ample cleavage of a blond girl, who was flustered by his leering. With slurred speech, I told Herbie that I thought it was time for us to go. He growled back, "Get lost!" I left by myself. It was almost dawn when I began to negotiate my drunken way through the streets back to the boarding house.

Back at the boarding house, I fumbled with my keys, dropped them, and cursed loudly at my bad luck. I had trouble getting the door to open; suddenly it swung open. I fell down in the entry. Once on my feet again, I groped about for the light switch and banged against a cabinet. Finally I reached the staircase. By that time, I had awakened a number of people. The landlady came forward to berate me. I mumbled something and started up the steps. I stumbled and fell, making more noise. One of the men on the first floor came to the head of the stairs and drowsily inquired if I were sick and needed help. My slurred response made him turn back to his room in disgust. Somehow I managed to find my room and fell into bed. My roommates were both awake by this time, and they regarded me with distaste.

I finally awoke about midday on Sunday and found my wobbly way downstairs. My standing in the community of the boarding house had sunk into oblivion. Everyone had either seen me in my sorry state or had heard about it. The landlady had slipped a note under my door saying she wanted to see me that afternoon. I stopped by Herbie's room. His bed was made—he had never come home at all. With my head throbbing violently with a hangover, I decided that it was time for me to leave. Washington had been interesting, but the novelty was gone. My job was a dead end. I didn't have the patience or enthusiasm to make things right with the landlady or my fellow boarders. By three o'clock in the afternoon I had written a letter to my supervisor at the warehouse telling him that I had to return home unexpectedly and that I would not be returning to work. He could send my final salary check to my New York address. I was packed and ready to go. The landlady never got the chance to scold or harangue me. I simply apologized for the night's disturbance and told her that I had to return home. Prospective tenants were in abundant supply and she would be able to charge more rent. She wished me good luck and even offered to repay me the balance of my unused room and board. I left a short note on Herbie's bed telling him that I had left. I gave him my home address and suggested that he get in touch with me some time in New York. I never saw nor heard from Herbie again.

Chapter Five

In New York, I slipped back into my earlier routines. Some changes became apparent, however. The draft and voluntary enlistment had thinned the ranks of young men at the corner hangout. Many were already serving in the military. Buggy had joined the Coast Guard. Sonny was in training in the Army Air Corps. Davey had joined the Navy but was not yet on active duty. By summer of 1942, induction notices were being sent out by the local draft boards. I had little enthusiasm for enrolling in college, knowing that I could be called up before the end of the year. My parents did not pressure me; they were happy to have me back at home. I resumed my social life. I played basketball with friends, who, like me, were marking time. I knew if I just waited around to be drafted, I most likely would end up in an unappealing part of the armed services. I discovered in *The New York Times* that there was a program in the Army Signal Corps, which offered training and instruction to young men who enlisted voluntarily. The six-month-long course enabled qualified candidates to enroll in civilian classes and to be trained as radio repairmen before being called to active duty in the Signal Corps. While my mechanical aptitude was non-existent, I figured that acceptance into the program would be based on a written exam that I could certainly pass. My parents were relieved; they imagined me safely serving in a non-combat role. By mid-summer I took the multiple-choice test in English comprehension and low-level science. I received a passing grade and was given a physical examination. I was sworn into the United States Army Signal Corps Reserve with instructions to remain available to begin my civilian, pre-active service training.

The program was offered on a full-time basis in a commercial building on Park Row in lower Manhattan, close to the Brooklyn Bridge. The courses were heavily oversubscribed. I was scheduled to begin the course in early September, but classroom shortages kept me idle until the first week in October. I bided my time, grateful to enjoy another month of free time out of uniform.

The Best of Times

Classes and labs met five days a week, eight hours a day, on a rotating schedule. Class shifts ran from 8:00 a.m. to 4:00 p.m., from 4:00 p.m. to midnight, and, finally, from midnight to 8:00 in the morning. The schedule made maximum use of the facilities. Classes began with theoretical and technical lectures on physics and electronics. Then we read and studied in the classroom — no homework was ever assigned. I enjoyed the academics and helped some of my fellow students who were floundering.

A few weeks into the course, we started laboratory exercises with soldering irons and circuit wiring. Later we moved on to troubleshooting problems, working with real radio equipment. Here I was completely at a loss. I lacked the manual dexterity and the mechanical aptitude to perform competently. Amazingly, some of my fellow students who never could grasp such abstract concepts as Ohm's law proved to be adroit at fixing real radios. There was never enough equipment to go around. We were obliged to work in teams, rather than individually. My colleagues, whom I had helped earlier during the theoretical study, bailed me out. They covered up my ineptitude at diagnosing and repairing real equipment. Instructors, who administered tests, had little stake in their jobs. Communal reinforcement by the students during testing prevailed, ensuring that everyone received a passing grade.

The rotating schedule of Signal Corps classes brought about some unsettling changes in my usual routines. It was difficult to find places to eat in lower Manhattan during our irregular dinner breaks, particularly the four-thirty a.m. break on the overnight shift. My sleeping and eating patterns were disrupted, and the customary rhythms of my family and social life were in total disarray. Other changes compounded the problem. With so many of my friends already in military service, our beloved basement club, Club Raleigh, was disbanded. Occasionally, a few neighborhood regulars would turn up at the usual street corner. I began to spend more time with Clara as my days of freedom dwindled. My physically undemanding studies and my haphazard mealtimes caused me to gain a considerable amount of weight. An extra thirty pounds changed my appearance from slightly chubby into absolutely hefty. It also became clear that no matter what credentials I may have earned, I would never be able to repair radios.

By end of March 1943, my course was over and I was instructed to await orders for military induction. The logjam of new recruits was so heavy that the induction center at Fort Dix, New Jersey, could not handle the influx. My call up to active duty was delayed for some weeks. I was frustrated by the long standby period and was itching to go when my orders for May 5 arrived. Fort Dix was only one hour by train from Manhattan. It felt like another world. The regimentation, hierarchy of authority, procedural absurdities, and impersonal treatment of the troops, quickly led me to understand that I would never like military life. I was reconciled to accept my lot. After several days of uniform distribution, physical and mental tests, inoculations, orientation lectures, dawn awakenings, and interminable waiting, my unit was shipped to a nearby Signal Corps post in New Jersey at Camp Edison. This is where I began my basic training.

The objective of basic training was to transform civilians into soldiers in just one month. Besides suffering constant insults from ill-tempered and illiterate drill sergeants, I found myself elated by the experience. The endless hours of exercise, strenuous marches, rifle practice, and maintenance, in addition to eating meals on a regular schedule, made me feel good both physically and mentally. Unlike my fellow recruits who perennially bemoaned the quality of Army cooking, I found the food to be quite good. Perhaps it was because there was a far greater variety of dishes offered than what I had come to expect in my mother's cooking. My weight plummeted in one month from 185 pounds at induction to a lean 148 pounds. I had to have my uniform refitted by the end of basic training. When I received my first weekend pass I returned home proudly to show off my healthy, suntanned face and well-conditioned torso to family, friends, and Clara.

From Camp Edison I expected to move on to Fort Monmouth in New Jersey, where we would undergo further training and build upon our civilian instruction in radio repair. The Army was full of surprises. The war against the Japanese in the Pacific had led to a Signal Corps shortage of trained telephone linesmen. My entire group, which had undergone extensive training in radio repair, was earmarked to remain in Camp Edison. We would be trained for a couple of months to become linesmen. At the end of training we would be shipped off to the Pacific to replace killed or wounded linesmen. This change of plan was greeted with vociferous complaints from all those affected. The Army brooks no dissent; orders were orders. By mid-June our unit was wearing spikes, climbing poles, and stringing telephone wires. I couldn't believe that telephone poles would actually be in place in the jungles of the South Pacific.

I was a clumsy and ineffectual telephone linesman. I was a poor climber; I had trouble securing myself by my belt and spurs to the top of the pole in the time allowed. I often dropped the wire. One time I actually missed a notch with my spur, slipped down the pole, and sprained an ankle. The procedure was repeated over and over and over again, until the process was indelibly etched into my mind. Even asleep, I would dream of shinnying up a never-ending pole that climbed to the sky like Jack's beanstalk. We were resigned to our fate as replacements destined for the Pacific. Then suddenly, new orders were received. My group was reassigned to Fort Monmouth for training in radio repair. Speculation ran high that the Japanese could easily cut telephone wires, hence radios were more effective in jungle warfare. More radio repairmen were now required to replace those whom the Japanese had killed. Whatever the rationale or illogic of the Army's strategic calculation, we were pleased to get a reprieve from imminent overseas transfer.

Fort Monmouth was only a short distance from Camp Edison. It was the major Army Signal Corps installation on the East Coast. It was equipped with classrooms and laboratories where troops were prepared for every specialized role the Signal Corps soldiers would assume either in Signal Corps units or on assignment with combat units. I knew that I would never make a competent radio repairman — all I had learned how to do was to check the battery and test the vacuum tubes. The rest was a mystery.

We started radio repair instruction in June 1943. Our course was to last six months. It appeared to cover the same material we had already covered in the civilian course in Manhattan. No one thought to question the logic of this. It was standard operating procedure for the Army to create confusion. Fort Monmouth was an attractive post close to New Jersey seaside resorts. New York City was only a short train ride away. I felt lucky to be stationed so near to home. I was uneasy about preparing for an assignment for which I knew I was unsuited. I was determined, therefore, to apply for some viable military alternative.

On a weekend pass in early August, I learned about the Army Specialized Training Program, which sounded ideal for me. A friend of mine was enrolled in this program studying Japanese at the University of Colorado. Student soldiers were enrolled in formal academic study under Army auspices in subjects that met the military's need for skilled personnel. Disciplines included various branches of engineering and foreign languages ranging from Russian to Japanese, Chinese, and Burmese. Eligible candidates had to be high school graduates and needed to score above a certain level on the Army's IQ test. On acceptance, a soldier would be shipped to a STAR unit before going to an academic institution of the Army's choice, where he would take a prescribed course of study suited to his intellectual profile. The closest STAR unit to Fort Monmouth was my old stamping grounds, City College's uptown campus. With my propensity for foreign language study, I saw myself as a natural for intensive language preparation.

Monday morning I got out of going to class and made a beeline for the personnel office. I explained my plan to a sympathetic sergeant. He checked my personnel file and concurred that I was eligible for the program. He had handled ASTP applications before and provided me with the necessary forms. Before three weeks had passed, I received word at the end of August that I had been accepted by ASTP. The only requirement that remained was a comprehensive physical and dental examination. I hastened to the medical unit and scheduled my physical the next day. The dentist who checked my teeth discovered two small cavities. I begged him to give me a clean bill of health and not delay the processing of my application. I assured him that I would get the cavities filled once I was at my new post. He insisted that I not risk any damage to my teeth. It was a Friday afternoon. He could schedule me for a filling next Tuesday morning. Despite strenuous pleading, I could not get him to let me off the hook. I had no choice but to accept his judgement.

On Tuesday morning the dentist diligently and enthusiastically filled my cavities and completed the dental health form. Clutching this document, I raced over to the personnel office and handed the form over to the friendly sergeant, explaining that this was the missing piece of documentation for my shipping orders. The sergeant grimaced and shook his head sadly. He said, "Sorry, kid. Yesterday was the last day for transfers to ASTP." The Army had just suspended any transfers indefinitely.

I resigned myself to seeing the course in radio repair to its conclusion; however, the more advanced the work became, the more frustrated I became. More and more emphasis was given over to hands-on exercises with inoperative equipment. The more I struggled, the more determined I became to explore other options. In October, two months short of the end of my course, I became aware of an Army Air Corps recruitment campaign. The stepped-up pace of the air attacks in Europe and the Pacific along with a concomitant number of crew casualties resulted in the need for greater numbers of pilots, bombardiers, and navigators. Enlisted men in other branches of the Army were strongly encouraged to apply for flight training. While I scarcely envisioned myself as a pilot (I had never in my life been off the ground in any type of equipment more perilous than a Coney Island roller coaster), my sentiments were—why not? After all, they were recruiting flying personnel, not airplane mechanics. Trainees who completed the program would also receive a commission along with their wings. The classy uniforms were an added bonus. The requisites for the training program included a high school education, a rigorous physical and vision examination, and a satisfactory score on a written test, which evaluated aptitude for training as pilot, navigator, or bombardier. I could meet the first two requirements and was confident that I would be able to surmount the third.

I went ahead and submitted my application for admission to the Aviation Cadet program. I passed the physical and learned that I had excellent vision and depth perception. I was scheduled to take the written examination in Newark, New Jersey, near the end of November. My radio repair course was due to end by mid-December. The tight timing lent special urgency to my desire to fly into the wild blue yonder. On a raw and dreary fall day I took the train from Fort Monmouth to Newark. I took the test with a group of enlisted soldiers and young civilians—predominantly college students from New Jersey academic institutions. I spent four hours taking the multiple-choice test. It was a grueling exam that left me feeling far less optimistic about my performance. It seemed to me that too many of the questions dealt with mechanical and technical problems rather than theoretical and abstract issues, which were my strong suit. There was nothing I could do but wait for the results.

The second week in December 1943, I received my scores. On a scale of one to nine, I received only a two for pilot, which disqualified me. I did score a nine for navigator, however, and an eight for bombardier. Six was the qualifying grade. I was eligible for training as either navigator or bombardier. I received notification that I had been accepted for transfer from the Signal Corps to the Air Corps. General Arnold, Commanding General of the Air Corps, sent his congratulations and welcome.

By the end of the same week my course in radio repair was over. My transfer orders were cut. I would be among a large contingent of troops being shipped by train to the Air Corps base in Miami Beach. I left on December 28, 1943. The timing could not have been better. I received a pass for Christmas and was back at camp on December 28, ready for departure to warmer climes. The troop train was crowded with newly inducted and transferred troops who were delighted to be leaving bleak, wintry New Jersey during a howling snow storm for the sunny South. After a day and a half of sitting and riding in a hard, upright seat, I woke to see rows of palm trees swaying in the sunlight as we pulled into the Miami train station. We were loaded into Army trucks and transported through balmy breezes and streets lined with pastel colored buildings. We arrived at a small, pink Art Deco hotel. Like virtually all the other hotels in the beach district this one had been taken over by the Air Corps for the duration of the war. My quarters consisted of a room with two beds and private bath, which I shared with another aspiring cadet. Our accommodations were a far cry from the crammed military barracks we were accustomed to. I felt lucky, as if I held the winning sweepstakes ticket.

The hotel was on Collins Avenue one block from Lincoln Road, a street that billed itself as the Fifth Avenue of Miami Beach. As new transfers into the Air Corps, we were held under quarantine and strictly confined to the hotel for four days. The second day was New Year's Eve. By then we had discovered an unlocked back door at street level. Everyone decided to suspend the quarantine for a few hours to join in the New Year's celebrations that were taking place in the streets by eight o'clock. We were feeling giddy. Here we were only one block from the main street of the world's most coveted winter resort, ready to embark on flying careers in the most glamorous branch of the Army.

Our elation was short lived. Once our quarantine was lifted, we started our processing. It became apparent that our cherished aviation cadet status was by no means assured. The greatest shortage of personnel was not for flying cadets but for aerial gunners. Before any of us could be advanced to true cadet status, there was another battery of physical, psycho-motor, and aptitude tests to take. Lore had it that two-thirds would fail and be sent to gunnery school. The grapevine further suggested that the recruitment campaign for cadets was simply a come-on to lure those seeking the romantic role of aviator. No one would have volunteered to serve as tail gunners. Nevertheless, it was a joy to do our calisthenics in bathing shorts on white, sunny beaches and to march along the colorful boulevards surrounded by lush tropical foliage while bellowing lustily "Into the Air, Army Air Corps." The exams were spread out over a two-week period. They were exceedingly rigorous, ranging from various physical stress tests to complicated visual and auditory exams. The aptitude testing was similar to the test I had taken in Newark. This time, however, the threshold for passing was raised to a higher level.

The Best of Times

By the end of January, I had accomplished two things: I had achieved an even and enviable suntan and I had passed the tests. I still qualified for cadet training as a navigator or bombardier. About half our number had failed this second round of testing. They were swiftly shipped out to Texas, where they were slated for aerial gunnery training. The surviving contingent remained happily and comfortably ensconced in Miami Beach awaiting transfer to the next post, where we would begin our cadet instruction.

In early February, a group of cadets for navigator training was shipped to Craig Field in Alabama. We assumed that this was the base where we would begin our pre-flight training. As it turned out, Craig Field was a training center for fighter pilots. We were only being held there until we could move on to our next post, where our true training would begin. In the meanwhile, we sat through lectures and some preliminary, pre-flight instruction, which made us eligible for observation flights in fighter aircraft on a rotating basis. Finally, we were on a base where real airplanes zoomed across the sky and where our status as aviation cadets was respected. Our billets were comfortable and all of us were given rides in the latest fighter aircraft, the P40. We discovered how much more thrilling fighter pilot training might be compared to navigator training. We became enthusiastic about going on to our next base, where we would be launched into training. After about three or four weeks at Craig Field, we were granted furloughs for two weeks and instructed that we would receive our orders while we were on leave.

I returned to New York like a conquering hero. It was a happy reunion with my parents, my sister, Clara, and one or two of my friends who were luckily stationed near the city. Three or four days into my furlough, my euphoria was shattered. While listening to the radio news, I heard General Arnold, Air Corps commanding general, bluntly pronounce that: "We shall return to the branches from whence they have come all transferred enlisted men who have not advanced beyond pre-flight training." No explanation was offered. Somehow the Air Corps had outdone itself in its recruiting zeal and had more recruits than its training facilities could process. Meanwhile, other branches of the Army were scrambling desperately to build up ground units for the imminent European invasion. I was simply a faceless pawn in this new strategy of manpower deployment. The next day a telegram arrived ordering me to report early in April to Fort Rucker, located not far from Craig Field, near Dothan, Alabama.

The remainder of my furlough passed pleasurably enough, but under a cloud of uncertainty about the fate of my continuing military odyssey. Fort Rucker was a large, sprawling infantry base. Among the swarms of recruits were seasoned soldiers, who held ranks from private to top sergeant. Many were recent draftees awaiting their first military assignment. There were two disgruntled groups among them. One was made up of those who, like myself, had been excommunicated from aviation cadet status. The other, a somewhat larger contingent, consisted of ASTP enrollees who had been reassigned out of their academic havens. All of us were to be processed for the newly reconstituted 66th Infantry Division or one of its auxiliary units. I assumed that my previous training in radio repair would take me back to the Signal Corps company attached to the division. First, we were to be interviewed by personnel and assigned to a specific unit for training.

When I went for my review, the sergeant had the full dossier of my military history before him. He asked me about any specialized skills I possessed. I replied that I had had pre-induction instruction in radio repair and that I had also completed radio repair training at Fort Monmouth. My military occupational specialty was radio repairman. He said that there was no indication in my records of any military occupational specialty. I protested. Of course I had a military occupational specialty—that is what I had been trained for from my induction in May 1943, until late December, when I transferred to the Air Corps. The sergeant showed me the form. I pleaded with him that there had been some mistake—surely the records could be checked with Fort Monmouth. "Not a chance!" was his swift retort. "Anyway the Signal Corps unit has a full complement, so they have no room for any more men," he added. I wondered whether he told me this just to avoid the trouble of checking with Fort Monmouth. "Tell you what," he said. "Headquarters company of the 1st Battalion of the 264th Regiment has room for a radio repairman/technician. You are certainly qualified with all the time you spent training in the Signal Corps."

I asked him what other options I had. He shrugged. "All we have are rifleman slots in line companies, unless you have experience as a cook or truck driver." He shuffled my papers impatiently, signaling me that the interview was over. "I guess I'll take it," I grumbled. I shuffled listlessly out of his office, reflecting on why my specialty qualification never made it into my file. My guess was that some incompetent personnel clerk had simply not bothered to record the specialty, since I was on my way to another branch of the service where it would be of no importance. The die was cast; my Army fate once again had been decided by pure chance.

As part of a freshly reorganized infantry division, under the command of General Herman Kramer, I was a lowly private first class and had advanced only

The Best of Times

one pay grade. We expected to be trained for combat right away. On our first day of training we were confronted by a fiercely shrieking figure, who spewed forth in rage: "Our destiny is to kill, kill, kill, kill the enemy!" A Herculean effort would be required to shape this group of former ASTPers, flying cadets, and draftees into a top-notch fighting division. A cadre of recent officer training graduates, reserve Army officers, a few West Pointers, and some seasoned non-commissioned officers were assigned the task of turning us into a unified unit. At least the training period offered a reprieve from immediate shipment overseas to face fighting as infantry replacements for casualties in fighting units where we would not know a soul.

It took a couple of weeks to assemble a full-strength division, to be assigned to barracks, and to fully equip the men for training. I was assigned to headquarters company, 1st Battalion, 264th Regiment of the 66th Infantry Division. The company handled the logistical and technical support requirements of the battalion. The men of the company were a diverse group. They came from different parts of the country and had wide-ranging backgrounds of social class and education. They ranged in age from barely eighteen-year-old kids to thirty-nine-year-old Sergeant Frank Koznick. First Sergeant Petit was our chief non-commissioned officer. He was a foul-mouthed, two-year veteran of stateside infantry postings. A New Englander of French Canadian background, he insisted on having his name pronounced "Pett-it." Perhaps the proper French pronunciation was for him an unwelcome allusion to his diminutive physical stature. The company commander was a haughty first lieutenant who had graduated from a four-year military college in the South and who had received a reserve commission. At this time my morale was at a new low. I had bitterly concluded that I would never achieve anything in the Army. With no hope for success, I dug in for the duration, simply trying to survive the war.

By early May 1944, our training was in high gear. We were being prepared as regular infantry. This called for a full regimen of calisthenics, marksmanship practice, weapon maintenance with our M-1 rifles, and close-order drill and field experience. Field experience meant taking twenty-five mile, overnight marches equipped with a full field pack, steel helmet, and rifle, twice a week. In a couple of weeks, we had been whipped into shape. I enjoyed the same physical satisfaction from the overnight marches as I had when lifting crates at Tobin, Sporn and Glaser. Total immersion in the boring and tiresome infantry preparation, however, left me depressed and disgusted. I felt sorry for myself and pessimistic about the future. I didn't want to worry my parents, so I wrote them occasional, vague, and joking letters about my new life in the wilds of Alabama. To Clara, I unburdened my discouragement and loneliness. I asked her to take the train to Alabama and visit me for a few days. I realized that if she came, she would probably expect a proposal of marriage. By June 1944, I was six months past my twentieth birthday. Clara had turned twenty in March. I knew my parents would oppose marriage at such an early age, even moreso during wartime. In my unhappiness, and knowing Clara's feelings on the subject, I felt that being married might prove a morale booster for both of us.

Clara came to Fort Rucker in mid-June. The Army granted me a four-day pass. On June 20, we were married in a five-minute civil ceremony by a justice of the peace at the county courthouse in Selma, Alabama. We spent the rest of my leave together. Clara boarded the train for her return journey to New York. I wrote my parents about what we had done. My mother replied that although she and my father wished we had waited, they still offered their affectionate wishes for our happiness. Clara wrote me that her father felt strongly that we should be married as soon as possible in a religious ceremony. I agreed to do this when the first occasion presented itself.

By the end of June, rural Alabama had become hot, humid, and jungle-like. Many of my fellow infantrymen speculated that we were being prepared for warfare in the Pacific. The weeks passed in an endless cycle of repetitive training rituals — long marches and bivouacs in the backwaters of the Deep South. There were mock battles and skirmishes with other division units and constant stumbling about in the insect-infested marshes and thick underbrush. On the post, we upheld our routine of close-order drills, marksmanship, and barracks inspections. Except for an allergic reaction to something that grew in the Alabama woods, which caused inflamed eyelids, I felt good physically, even while I remained discouraged about my prospects. D-Day had passed and Allied armies were advancing. Everyone hoped for an early end to the war in Europe. In the Pacific troops struggled through a succession of battles over unheard of islands and atolls that seemed never ending.

By October the division was nothing but a mass of bored and surly soldiers. Rumors were rampant by early November. The division was to be shipped to a port of embarkation on the East or West Coast for overseas transport. A few days later, the official word was that we were headed to Fort Dix, New Jersey. The post was now serving both as an induction center and as a staging base for European transfers. Most of us thought this was good news; the European Theater seemed far more promising than the Pacific. News reports informed us that the invasion was moving across France and the Low Countries. Prospects for victory in the short run appeared promising. Back at Fort Dix, I would be close to home again. My prospects for getting a weekend pass before overseas shipment looked good. I wrote Clara and my parents immediately about the expected turn of events.

By mid-November, the division had been shipped to New Jersey for overseas processing. Passes were granted liberally, and I was able to wangle a long weekend pass. Clara's father eagerly made arrangements for a religious marriage ceremony. On Saturday night, a rabbi performed the marriage at Clara's parents' apartment in the presence of our closest family members. By Sunday night, I was back in my barracks at Fort Dix. Tuesday morning, the 66th Infantry Division boarded a troop ship from a Hudson River dock and set sail for England.

We crossed the Atlantic in a multi-vessel convoy made up of several large passenger ships. We were accompanied by Navy vessels, which protected us from the German submarines. Our ten-day voyage took us through stormy weather and choppy seas. The danger of a submarine attack was shrugged off. Less easily dismissed was the perennial seasickness. Our quarters consisted of hammocks that swayed in overcrowded, overheated compartments. The other challenge was keeping our mess kits steady while eating at tables that constantly shifted with the waves. Like many others, I was miserable during the crossing. I remember commiserating with Arthur Schiller, a fellow soldier in my company, whom I had become friendly with during our train transport from Alabama to Fort Dix. It was a close contest between us over who suffered the most. We both agreed that being in the Navy would be a far worse fate. When we finally pulled into port in southern England, the dry land seemed like a vision of earthly paradise, despite the drab pier and the sheets of rain that descended in torrents. We disembarked unsteady and weary in our heavy winter uniforms and steel helmets, each carrying a rifle on one shoulder and a full duffel bag on the other.

Thanksgiving had passed uneventfully on the high seas where there had been little appreciation for the turkey and trimmings intended to boost morale. It was November's end when we landed. We were speedily transported somewhere north of London to our encampment of pitched tents, which sank into the thoroughly soaked soil. Our final training in preparation for our crossing to France is only a blurred memory. There were countless forced marches along roads surrounded by very green hills and dales. The food in England was bland and tasteless. This was blamed on the poor ingredients and incompetent cooking by the British mess units. During several half-day leaves we discovered London's pubs and ate fish and chips. Neither was sufficient to endear us to this bomb-battered city, where fog and raw, wintry blasts of cold prevailed. Shortages of everything we privileged Americans expected made us only more scornful of England. According to news accounts in early December, the end of the war was in sight. We could scarcely wait to be shipped to France.

My division had been in England just under four weeks when we received orders to ship out. We were transported to Southampton, where we boarded vessels to cross the English Channel. Near the very end of our short tour in England, the war on the continent had taken a turn for the worse. We were headed into the snow and frigid cold of what became the most severe winter Europe had experienced in decades. The Battle of the Bulge had proved a turning point for Germany. The Nazis had mounted a powerful counterattack and succeeded in pushing back the Allied forces. Huddled on a cold wet pier, we began to board during a typical British downpour. We had premonitions of our regiment being inserted into front-line combat. Two thousand, five hundred men marched up the gangplank of a huge, gray cargo vessel, into its hold. The ship, the *SS Leopoldville*, was a Belgian freighter commanded by a Belgian captain, his senior officers, a small company of British Navy personnel, and a West African crew. The remaining two regiments boarded other ships for the crossing as part of a convoy of vessels sailing to France.

The Channel crossing was expected to last six or seven hours. When the ship left the harbor the sea was choppy and the waves broke ominously against the sides. Once in our large compartment below, we were free to get as comfortable as possible in the empty hold of the rolling ship. It was then that I spotted Art Schiller, my comrade in seasickness. We paired up again, anticipating another long bout before reaching land. Schiller and I shared similar backgrounds. Like me, he had grown up in the New York metropolitan area. He had lived in the New Jersey suburbs prior to joining the Army. He had gone to college before being drafted and, just as I had, he married only a few months before being shipped overseas. He had been expelled from ASTP as I had been from my cadet training as a navigator. Schiller was a couple of years older, but we had a lot of common interests. We tended to reinforce each other's view of the absurd farce of our military misadventures.

The Best of Times

We began our shipboard reunion comparing notes about what we had been reading lately. Once we were far enough out into the Channel, nausea set in. The hold was filled with prostrate bodies. It was hot and steamy below deck. The men put their heavy overcoats on top of their duffel bags and life preservers, and leaned against the pile. The rolling and swaying of the ship and the roar of the wind above deck made us even more miserable. After about five hours at sea, we heard an explosion at the other end of the ship. We came immediately to life, donning our overcoats and life jackets, and streaming up to the deck. Art Schiller and I were part of this surging crowd moving up and out into the cold wind.

On the deck there was great confusion. Men were milling about, and officers were trying to maintain some semblance of order. There was no panic, rather a mixture of curiosity and fear. Soon the word was passed along that an explosion had ripped a massive hole in the side of the ship. Water was filling one of the holds, which had been jammed with troops. The blast was thought to have been the result of a torpedo strike from a German U-boat. A number of men had been killed at once. In that part of the hold there were a number of casualties. Soldiers were trying to get them out. For the moment, the ship maintained its upright balance and didn't appear to be sinking.

Art and I wandered along the deck together trying to determine what was going on. The sea was as rough and choppy as it had been at the start of our voyage. Keeping our balance was awkward. It was very cold, and the spray from the ocean made exposure on deck uncomfortable. The emergency had completely obliterated our seasickness. We only thought of survival. From the deck we could make out the shoreline only a few miles off. One of the other ships in our convoy pulled alongside the *Leopoldville* in an effort to transport the wounded to safety. As this ship approached, some uninjured men tried to jump from our ship to the deck of the other. The swells were so powerful that the rescue ship kept banging against the side of the *Leopoldville*. The rolling of the sea made a large gulf between the two ships before they crashed together again. Schiller and I watched one man misjudge the timing of his frantic leap. He failed to jump far enough and was crushed.

As time passed, apprehension grew about whether the *Leopoldville* could remain afloat. No one knew what the crew was doing. Nor did anyone seem to know how to make use of the lifeboats tied to the deck. Our officers had had no training in how and when to abandon a ship. They were just as concerned about their personal survival as the rest of us. Word got around that our battalion commander, Lt. Colonel Chris Rumburg, was in the thick of the casualty rescue effort in the bombed-out compartment. He had fought his way through the rushing water to carry many men out to safety. Rumburg was a hulking giant of a man, a one-time college football hero. He was renowned for his strength and good humor. Time and again, on our long marches, he would run several miles back and forth, from the head to the tail of the column, and kid around with the soldiers.

The day dragged on. The vessel that had attempted to rescue troops gave up because of the turbulent sea. I joked with Schiller about what a good war story we would have to tell when we got home. His sickly grin was more mournful than amused. An hour or two after our ship had been hit the *Leopoldville* began to list to one side. By then it was turning dark. A bright moon illuminated the sky as light faded. Schiller and I stood together at the side of the ship dressed in our military coats and wearing life preservers. I decided to jump overboard, fearing that the ship would sink swiftly. I told Art Schiller I was going overboard. Hoarsely, he told me that he couldn't swim. I told him that the life preserver would keep him afloat. As I climbed over the side, he asked me if he should keep his overcoat on. I said that it would help keep him warm in the cold water. I went over the side. As I fell, the heel of my foot smashed against the side of the ship. Then I was in the water. I looked around for Schiller but could not see him among those soldiers who had also jumped overboard. I had seen Arthur Schiller alive for the last time.

The water was freezing cold in the December sea. My greatest fear at first was that the sinking ship would cause a great eddy and pull everyone down with it. I swam as rapidly and as far as I could with the weight of my overcoat and heavy Army boots. I stopped to tread water. I figured that in the time that had passed, rescue craft would be out in numbers to rescue survivors. I struggled in spite of my fear to keep my head above water. I witnessed sights that time can never erase. As the *Leopoldville* began its final descent more and more soldiers desperately jumped overboard. Amid the panic and screaming, a number of them were grasping hold of others while trying to keep their own heads above water. The frantic clutching and pulling in rough water rapidly depleted the swimmers' energies. Many drowned. I became terrified that if I came too close to anyone else I might suffer a similar fate. I swam further away trying to distance myself from others.

The sea grew dark, but the moonlight was bright. I frantically searched my mind for long forgotten prayers and began to implore God to save me. I decided to concentrate on conserving my energy and my breath. I could see the shoreline ablaze with lights. I thought that people there had been alerted to our distress and would come to our rescue. I was freezing cold; my teeth chattered and my hands grew numb. I had heard on deck that a man could remain alive for twenty minutes before freezing to death in the winter waters of the Channel. It felt as if I had been in the water far longer. I closed my eyes. Then I thought, no, that would be the end. I opened my eyes again and kept treading water. My legs grew stiffer and more tired.

Suddenly, small boats came into sight. I mustered the last of my strength to stay afloat. As boats drew near terror-struck men tried to climb aboard. Again the frantic fighting and clawing ensued. I saw a man get chopped up by a boat propeller. For the second time since immersion in the water, I decided to stay clear of the melee. By then my energy level had diminished significantly. It was only through sheer determination that I managed to keep my head above water. A boat drew near; I tried to reach up but lacked the strength. A sailor onboard saw me. The boat's spotlight lit the water all around me. A sudden swell carried me right up to the boat's side. A strong arm reached out and firmly grasped my hand. With the next swell, I was yanked out of the water and heaved over the shoulder of a Coast Guardsman. I landed flat on my face. The last thing I remember is the smiling face of a big sailor who said, "Welcome aboard, soldier, and Merry Christmas." Then I passed out.

I recall only dimly the jumble of events that followed. In the harbor at Cherbourg ambulances transported survivors to hospitals and shelters. I vaguely remember seeing a cheerfully decorated Christmas tree in front of the hospital as I was carried in on a stretcher. At some point, my cold, soggy clothes were stripped from me and I found myself in pajamas. An Army doctor came around to check me. It was only then that I realized that my foot and ankle were in pain from the blow I had received when I jumped overboard. The doctor cursorily examined it, saw the bruise and the swelling, and decided that it could wait for X-ray until the next morning.

I was expected to improve with rest. It was impossible to predict whether I would recover fully. On Christmas day, men in my ward stood at the foot of their beds as a full Colonel marched down the line. We saluted him. He saluted us. A

Purple Heart was pinned to the chest pocket of each man's pajamas. Later we were treated to a festive holiday dinner with all the trimmings. We dined regally propped up against pillows in our fresh, clean hospital beds.

Of the more than two thousand men of the 264th Infantry Regiment aboard the *SS Leopoldville*, eight hundred had died or were missing. Bodies continued to drift ashore for several days. The hero of the disaster had been my commanding officer, Lt. Colonel Chris Rumburg of the First Battalion. After bringing wounded men from the hold to the deck, he had joined the men in the sea. There he had done what he could to keep people alive, showing them how to tread water and encouraging them to hang on until help arrived. The Colonel also helped lift the weakest swimmers out of the water to safety when the rescue craft appeared. When last seen alive, the story goes that he had told someone he was going to swim to shore. Apparently, the ordeal had sapped even his remarkable store of energy. Chris Rumburg's body was found washed up on shore; he had died of exhaustion and exposure.

We learned later that during the commotion of the ship's sinking, the African crew had commandeered the lifeboats and deserted the vessel. The ship's captain and first officer went down with the ship. It was also determined that the slow arrival of rescue craft was due to a breakdown in military and naval communication. Many of the port personnel had been released early in the day for Christmas Eve. Our ship's sinking resulted in the greatest number of men lost in any troop transport incident of the Second World War. The inept handling of every phase of the disaster brought a cloak of silence surrounding the event. News accounts of the episode appeared only months later. We were informed that our mail would be censored and we were not to describe what had happened in letters home. Colonel Rumburg was awarded only a posthumous Purple Heart. In another effort to conceal the true story, higher recommended honors for Rumburg's numerous acts of bravery, which were recounted by many eyewitnesses, were never acted on.

Some time later, I received a bitter letter from Arthur Schiller's older brother who had somehow gained sketchy details of the disaster. He asked me to write and tell him the truth about what had really happened. He wanted to instigate a congressional inquiry. I was deeply saddened by his letter. Arthur was gone among the missing; no investigation was going to bring him back. I was sure that the war had brought about many similar tragedies in badly botched military misadventures. I never replied to the letter.

The Best of Times

During my stay at the hospital in Cherbourg, my ability to walk slowly improved. On New Year's Eve, a half dozen men in my ward decided to sneak out in search of a bar. Exactly one year before I had done exactly the same thing through the back door of the Miami Beach hotel. The French winter night was cold, crisp and dry. We wore overcoats and scarves. At that time, the Battle of the Bulge was at its peak. German paratroopers, disguised in American Army uniforms, had dropped deep behind Allied military lines to carry out acts of espionage and violence. Army personnel behind the front were especially worried about this threat. Cherbourg was far from any immediate threat of hostilities. Nevertheless, in our search for a drink, we were stopped by Military Police patrols. They interrogated us about what unit we were with and where our passes were. Our reply that we were hospital patients and had no passes only heightened their suspicions. After a thorough cross-examination, which required us to recite major league baseball records and describe cartoon characters like Li'l Abner and Donald Duck, they finally permitted us to go on our way. We found a bar, where we quickly downed one cognac each. We bought two bottles and made our way back to the ward, where we shared our good cheer with those who were still awake and who hadn't been able to come along.

A couple of days later I was discharged for return to my unit. The only evidence of my experience was a slight limp in my right leg. My regiment was bivouacked in the countryside in Normandy. Survivors rejoined their units. My company commander, Lt. Harris, who had an especially domineering and self-important nature, greeted me cruelly with, "Wasserman, I thought you were dead!" I said nothing. The gaps in our regiment left by the missing and dead were rapidly filled by fresh troops from infantry replacement centers. In a few days we were shipped out to rejoin the other regiments in our division. We were shipped south and west to Brittany. There we were deployed in the cold, snow-packed fields surrounding German troops that ringed the Channel ports of Lorient and St. Nazaire.

A few months earlier, as American battle forces had secured most of France following the D-Day invasion in June, two German submarine installations on the coast had been bypassed. These had been fortified against attack to safeguard the bases and to ensure continuation of fighting against Allied Channel shipping. We often wondered whether the U-boat that had torpedoed the *Leopoldville* had come from this installation. The 66th Infantry Division was ordered to engage the well-trained and well-equipped German infantry soldiers who guarded these port operations. Despite continued Allied bombing sorties, the submarine pens remained impregnable and continued to prey upon Channel traffic. We were moved into the field and began to dig foxholes, where we tried to make life bearable in the bitter cold. Nights were spent zipped inside sleeping bags. Usually, meals consisted of K rations and C rations. We were regularly assigned to patrols against the enemy and tried to withstand the continuous battering of their powerful weapons. After a while, we could predict the timing of these attacks. As the shells screamed overhead, we buried ourselves deeper into the ground. The German soldiers were also hemmed in. Even if they were to succeed in breaking through our ranks, they had no place to go. In January 1945, the front was all the way to the east of France, close to the German frontier. The 66th Division's objective was to contain the 50,000 or so enemy troops. There were no large-scale attacks by either side, only the daily artillery duels and occasional skirmishes. The greatest danger was from artillery shells and frostbite. Keeping our feet dry in the cold, wet snow was a constant problem. Most casualties were weather induced. My second short hospital stay resulted from a case of trenchfoot—a blackening and loss of sensation in the feet. Treatment involved a two or three-day stay in a well-heated hospital, where victims could thaw out. Stricken soldiers were quickly returned to the line to make room for others.

With the first signs of spring came good news from the front. The Battle of the Bulge had ended, even though it had taken a high toll of American casualties. Our unit received combat infantry badges for coming under enemy fire; we felt lucky to have missed combat at the center of the Bulge campaign. In late March I received a three-day pass for my first visit to Paris. My high-school French came in handy. The city's inhabitants were enjoying the exhilaration of their first spring since the city had been liberated the summer before. To speak French in Paris had been a long held dream of mine.

The spring of 1945 passed rapidly. The only unhappy event was the unexpected death of President Roosevelt. This provoked widespread sorrow among many of the men in my division. Then suddenly the European war was over. Amidst the sheer exuberance of victory, we nonetheless wondered where we would be shipped to next. As soon as German prisoners of war from the units we had fought were processed, our division was moved by rail to the Rhineland. We became part of the occupying forces there. In Germany, I was able to practice my other foreign language. Opportunities for private conversation were limited; the army's non-fraternization policy was strictly enforced. However, once the word went out that I knew the language, battalion officers used me as an interpreter for discussions with civilian officials. As soon as we were settled on the Rhine in the Coblenz region, new orders were received for the division to return to France.

By the end of June, we were loaded into wartime trains called "forty and eight's," which could carry forty men or eight horses. After one more long and uncomfortable journey, we arrived in the south of France, in Provence. We lived in the field not far by Army truck from Avignon, Nimes, Arles, and Marseilles. It became clear, despite the lack of official word, that the next major military thrust would take place in the Pacific. Many new units would be needed for the invasion of Japan. Marseilles was a major shipping depot; it seemed logical that the 66th Division would be boarded onto ships for transport to the Pacific.

Summer in Provence was beautiful. The war in Europe was over, and France was a friendly nation. The French people saw American GI's as saviors who had vanquished their oppressors. It was a time of drastic shortages of virtually everything, but there was a festive mood in the air. The American military was well provisioned. Cigarettes, candy bars, and chewing gum were available and could be bartered for just about anything. The restaurants had few ingredients, yet they managed to concoct extraordinary dishes. Wine somehow was plentiful. We untutored GI's thought it of excellent quality. French entertainers sang, danced, and played the accordion at every restaurant, bistro and cafe in Provence. Soldiers were given liberal daily and weekend passes. Trucks were constantly rolling, transporting cheerful GI's into all the surrounding towns. Except for occasional rowdy, drink-induced antics, the atmosphere was one of blissful serenity.

One morning in August, the Japanese war was over. The question then became how soon we would be shipped home and discharged. The Army instituted a scoring system. Each soldier received credit for every month of active military service, for each month overseas, and for each battle decoration awarded for engagement in hostilities. Not many in my division had high enough tallies to merit an early shipment back to the States. It would be months before their turn would come. By the end of August, we were back on the troop trains. This time the units were to be disbanded. Once we reached our destination, we were to be assigned as replacements to units in which a large number of men had high enough scores to make them eligible for early return to the United States. I arrived in Austria in a boxcar crammed with many other unhappy soldiers, who were rejoining the army of occupation. My new division was the 83rd Infantry. At our new barracks in the city of Linz, we were to be assigned to units based on matching our skills with the many vacancies left by those who were homeward bound. I was determined to connect with something that would interest me and be as far removed as possible from radios.

I told the personnel interviewer about my pre-Army experience as a newspaper reporter. He seemed skeptical but said he would arrange an interview for me with the division's public relations officer. The second lieutenant I met with had an air of anxiety about him. He himself had been assigned to the division only a couple of weeks earlier. He was trying to patch together a whole range of functions and had very few people with the skills and experience to do much of anything. He wanted to know what I could do. I described my extensive newspaper career in high school and told him about my work in the Government Printing Office, where I wrote press releases. I also told him about my staff duties at *The Brooklyn Daily Eagle*. His eyes lit up. He probably didn't believe most of what I claimed, but he must have been desperate for people. He quickly said that the 83rd Division published a weekly newspaper, *The Thunderbolt*. He was short two staff members; did it interest me? It sounded like an Army version of *The Liberty Bell*. I was his man. I had finally found my true Army home.

The rapid turnover of Army personnel once the war was over enabled me to move up in responsibility on the paper's staff. It was just like running the high school paper, except that there were no classes. We enjoyed the freedom to choose stories and to edit them. We used a crackerjack photographer, who called himself Weegie, after a celebrated shutterbug of the period. The public relations officers kept being replaced with new ones. No one supervised our work. It was enough that the weekly edition came out on time and was distributed efficiently to everyone in the division. We avoided material that might offend the division's commanding hierarchy. I had no regular hours and seldom used my barrack bunk. Instead, I rented a room in a civilian family apartment near the base. I paid my rent with doughnuts from the Red Cross Center's endless supply, or with some of my weekly cigarette and candy rations. A jeep was always available to the *Thunderbolt* staff from the division motor pool. We emblazoned the Jeep with an ostentatious banner announcing "PRESS."

In 1945 Linz, Austria, was a fascinating place. The hungry and defeated citizenry of Linz looked to the conquering American heroes as the source of vital supplies. We controlled resources that could profoundly affect people's lives. Refugees from the east inundated the city — ranging from concentration camp survivors to Middle European deserters who had fled from Wehrmacht units. Civilian camps held hundreds of human beings in search of a new homeland that might offer shelter and security. In Nuremberg, the Nazi war crimes trials were beginning. Vienna, which was only an hour's jeep ride away, was teeming with excitement and intrigue under its four-power military administration — American, French, British, and Russian.

In an effort to control the economy, the Army printed a currency that was the official medium of exchange. There was a rumor that the Russians had printed limitless quantities of this paper money on the same printing presses. With all this funny money in circulation, purchasing power fell drastically. Most financial transactions were based on barter. The American dollar, however, was supreme. A real American dollar could be exchanged for twenty or thirty times its value in occupation currency. Wristwatches were being sold to Russian soldiers and displaced persons for several hundred dollars of funny money. Cartons of cigarettes were worth the equivalent of fifty dollars, while bars of soap sold for about ten dollars. The entrepreneurial frenzy was so great that some soldiers were raiding depots and stealing clothing, blankets, and food to sell on the black market. Soldiers quickly figured out that they could take occupation dollars to buy money orders at the Army post office and send these home for the value of genuine United States dollars. In the fall, General Eisenhower instituted currency controls. GIs could mail home no more than the amount they had received in pay. Currency control books contained official payroll details. Before the controls took effect, there was a two-week moratorium. Hordes of soldiers waited in line to buy money orders to send home before the clamp came down. The cost to American taxpayers must have run into the millions of dollars. At the newspaper we were permitted to write only news stories. We were not allowed to editorialize on the broader significance of these stories. I concentrated on getting to places like Vienna, Munich, and Nuremberg, to report on events for *The Thunderbolt*. I was excited to be an observer of the historical spectacle being played out everywhere around me. I smoked my full week's quota of cigarettes and gave away my candy ration to kids in the city. A German P38 pistol that I had taken from a German prisoner of war in France was stolen. It had been my most precious possession. I bartered for a replacement pistol with another GI. This was the only souvenir I would bring back from overseas.

The Best of Times

I had abundant opportunities to practice my German. In my work on the newspaper there was really no need for it, but when interviewing civilians or war refugees my German was invaluable. Most American soldiers had nothing but scorn and disdain for the local population. They saw them as losers, grubbing for things they wanted that only the soldiers had. My own experience was quite different, however. Conversations with these people gave me insight into the consequences of war for ordinary civilians. I had no great sympathy for the professions of righteous innocence that I heard from the many bureaucrats I encountered. My heart did go out to the ragged and impoverished refugees. Many of them had only recently been freed from concentration camps. They were desperately seeking to start a new life any place that would have them. Large numbers of these tragic souls were Jews, who had been reduced by years of deprivation and hunger to a gaunt frailty. The fear borne from their ordeal was still visible in their eyes. Given my own Jewish heritage, and knowing that members of my family were still in Eastern Europe at the war's start, I realized how easily I could have been one of them.

During the seven or so months I served in the 83rd Division, I appreciated how lucky the United States had been to escape the ravages of war. So much around me was in ruins. So many forlorn human beings were struggling simply to survive. Many soldiers biding their time until their return to America could dismiss the desolation around them. They could get on with their lives and put the terror of war behind them like a bad dream. I tried to spend my time in fulfilling ways and avoided counting the days before repatriation came. In letters from Clara and my mother, I learned about what was happening at home in the war's aftermath. Stories of shortages in the stores and the scarcity of rental apartments struck me as whimsical compared to the conditions I saw everywhere around me. A number of my friends from home had already been discharged from the service in the winter of 1946. Others, I learned, had perished during battles in Europe and in the Pacific. Murray Finkel had returned home a badly wounded casualty of infantry fighting on the beaches of Italy. I began to grow more impatient to return to the United States — to Clara and my family. My orders for return finally came in March 1946. I boarded a passenger train with a contingent of soldiers. We were all headed for our port of embarkation at Le Havre.

The voyage home over stormy seas lasted ten days. It was virtually a replay of my November 1944 passage to England. Again, I experienced constant seasickness. At least this time there was the promise of freedom at journey's end. The

Statue of Liberty became the object of my loving regard as it first came into sight a couple of hours before our docking at a mid-Manhattan pier. Although I had written home about my estimated date of return, there was no way to know exactly when the ship would arrive. A sleepy-looking military band greeted us at the dock. They celebrated our return by playing noisy marches and patriotic tunes. We then boarded trucks, which transported us back to Fort Dix, New Jersey. What had once been my induction center had been transformed into the largest discharge center on the East Coast. During my final physical the doctor examined my right foot and the injury I had sustained when I abandoned the *SS Leopoldville*. He determined that I was ten percent disabled. In practical terms this meant that the Veterans Administration would classify me as disabled. I was awarded a pension of about ten dollars a month for as long as my disability continued.

Chapter Six

By the end of March I received my discharge and returned to New York to begin a new life. Unlike many other homecoming veterans, I was neither disillusioned nor pessimistic about the loss of time I had spent as a soldier. I felt lucky to have survived. I was only twenty-two years old and I was healthy. Reunited with my wife and family, I had the rest of my life ahead of me. A "WELCOME HOME PAUL" banner came down the side of Clara's parents' apartment building. When the homecoming celebrations were over, Clara and I temporarily occupied a very small room in her parents' flat. We were severely cramped for space. I became acutely aware of the true extent of New York's housing shortage. Even among our wide circle of friends and family, no one could help us locate a place of our own. Finally, after a couple of weeks of desperate seeking, we rented a furnished room with a bathroom attached. It was down the hall from the apartment of Clara's future sister-in-law. We were just down the street from Clara's parents' home, and we took our meals with them. With our immediate housing problem resolved, it was time for me to concentrate on what I would do for work.

As a veteran, I was eligible to receive compensation, much like unemployment insurance, for a number of months. Clara still held a clerical position in the national office of a department store chain. Between the money Clara and I had saved, we had enough to furnish an apartment whenever we were fortunate enough find one. Given my Army newspaper experience I thought about going into journalism. My limited education was a handicap. The fact was that I couldn't even type. When the 83rd Division public relations officer had seen me using my laborious hunt and peck method in *The Thunderbolt* office, he sharply questioned how I had worked for newspapers if I didn't even know how to type. I had snidely responded that no true newspaperman could type—that was a skill for typists. I now knew that it was a skill I genuinely needed. I decided to teach myself. I borrowed a typewriter, bought a self-instruction manual, and closeted myself in our furnished room. I spent a forty-hour week, eight hours a day for five days, practicing the exercises. By week's end I gave myself a test. First, I typed some material for half an hour using my newly acquired touch-typing skills. I spent another half an hour typing the same text using my customary hunt and peck technique. Hunt and peck won out. I resigned myself to failure as a typist and dismissed the skill as akin to radio repair; it was simply not for me.

I sent my resume to countless daily and weekly newspapers within a one hundred-mile radius of New York City. My cover letter extolled my journalism achievements from high school and the military. No one bothered to reply. It occurred to me that I should apply for a job as a radio news writer. I responded to several ads in trade magazines for broadcasting jobs, which I found at the public library. In my resume and letter, I embroidered my experience to include exploits in preparing scripts for the 83rd Division's broadcasting station. Stories I had written for *The Thunderbolt* were read on the air on occasion by the station's announcers. I had never actually written anything specifically for radio. I felt supremely confident that not only could I do this kind of work, but that I could do it well. I corresponded with radio stations in relatively small markets. I did get back a couple of encouraging nibbles from places like Oshkosh, Wisconsin, and Decatur, Illinois. They sent me descriptions of the job's salary and work responsibilities. It was a rude awakening. I could not genuinely envision uprooting Clara and myself to some unknown and distant location. I felt unsure about accepting work at a job that might not work out.

I determined next that perhaps I should seek work in the advertising industry as a copywriter. Surely my writing skills would equip me well for this corollary branch of editorial work. I followed the want ads for advertising copywriters in *The New York Times*. I responded in my letters that, while I had had no experience in advertising, my high school and military newspaper work had seasoned me as a general-purpose writer. All I needed was a chance to demonstrate my abilities. Finally, I was rewarded with an interview with the head of a small agency located on the Upper West Side of Manhattan. A man of forty or so owned the firm, and I talked with him in a leisurely fashion for about an hour. He was a very sympathetic listener and seemed truly interested in my military experience. He decided to give me a try. I thought that he had probably given me the work because I was an Army veteran. I suspected that he might have had some twinges of guilt about not having served himself.

The Best of Times

I reported to work eagerly the next Monday morning. I was assigned one account on a trial basis. I have forgotten the name of the company and its product for which I was to prepare text for the newspaper ads. What I can remember is pondering long and hard in search of a theme, and how I kept coming back again and again to the image of an owl saying "It's a wise bird." It was as far as I got. After two days of suffering and drawing a blank, I confronted my boss with the meager material I had. He looked out the window a moment, and then he leaned toward me. His expression was one of sympathy, but he said, "This is banal crap." Then he added gently as an afterthought, "Try again." I walked back to my desk, disgusted with myself. After an hour of feeling sorry for myself, I returned to the owner's office to concede my failure and thanked him for his indulgence. He shook my hand warmly, wished me good luck, and paid me generously for two days of useless effort.

On the subway ride home I sheepishly contemplated my future. By then it was well into summer. My efforts so far had led me nowhere. My military severance checks would continue for a few more months, but then what? In the back of my mind I harbored the idea of completing my college education. It suddenly seemed clear that continuing my studies made more sense than thrashing about uncertainly in the labor market. The next day I began in earnest to explore readmission to college.

With support from the GI Bill of Rights, I was eligible to apply at any institution that would admit me. My high school record had been good, and I would have preferred continuing at a prestigious private university. I was married, however, and well past the age of twenty-two. A sense of personal responsibility propelled me to complete my college studies as rapidly as possible and then start work. The notion of returning to my liberal arts curriculum at City College after a five-year lapse struck me as childish. The City College Business School seemed a more reasonable option. A bachelor's degree in business administration would give me mastery of finance, marketing, and accounting—subjects that would give me a leg up in the marketplace. I arranged for a meeting at the school's Twenty-third Street center with a faculty counselor. We discussed my enrollment in the fall as a full-time student. My earlier course work would be credited towards my degree. I would also receive three credits for a correspondence course in English literature that I had completed at Texas Tech in Lubbock, while I was at Fort Monmouth. My classes in radio repair taken prior to Army induction as well as my training at Ft. Monmouth would also be credited towards a bachelor's degree. I ended up possessing forty-five credit hours towards the one hundred and twenty hours it would take to earn a business degree. I was more than one-third of the way along. Elated by this news, I sought re-admittance as an advanced student for the fall term. I made a promise to Clara and myself that I would pursue as many courses as I could in order to complete my studies at the earliest possible date. I contentedly spent the remaining weeks of summer reading in subject areas I thought might prove germane to my coming classes.

Early in September I spent a frustrating morning competing with hundreds of other students seeking to register. I wound up enrolled in nineteen credit hours composed of required subjects and purely business-oriented classes. In the fall of 1946 the school population was a peculiar blend of young students out of secondary school and older veterans. The GI Bill, which paid tuition charges as well as modest financial support for returning military, enabled many veterans an opportunity for a higher education that would otherwise have been unattainable. A number of the instructors looked like the younger brothers of the students in their classes. My intentions were deadly serious. I was going to apply myself strenuously and earn my degree as rapidly as was feasible. The student culture was decidedly pragmatic. Courses that focussed on the real world of business enjoyed great popularity. The rest were seen as irrelevant barriers. The ones I enjoyed the most, however, were precisely the ones that bored most of my fellow business students. These were the core required liberal arts requisites in English literature, European history, and the social sciences.

The school's business courses generally offered common-sense prescriptions for conducting business in the real world. They were devoid of any conceptual or theoretical basis. Among the most popular faculty were adjunct instructors drawn from the workaday world who offered their expertise through part-time appointments at the school. There were also, however, rigorous and intellectually demanding courses in the business curriculum. They included corporate finance, accounting, economics, statistics, and market research. All of these classes pushed me to the limit. But business courses did not fire my imagination. European history is where I flourished. My professor was a small, gnome-like man who spoke so softly and modestly about what we would cover during the class that I initially dismissed him as a minor lecturer. By the third class Professor Brandt had me sitting on the edge of my seat. I was enthralled by his every word and was annoyed when the bell rang at the end of class. History came alive for me during his thrilling accounts of mankind's progress from the Middle Ages forward. I avidly began to read well beyond the limits of the course requirements, delving deeply and broadly into many of the suggested readings. I spent two semesters with Professor Brandt and have never since been so profoundly influenced by a teacher. My other classes were more textbook-based. Lectures reiterated material from the book. Examinations were given at periodic intervals to test one's mastery of the material. Classes that emphasized problem solving were more challenging; they required comprehension of methods, formulae, or processes. There was only one course in which I seemed doomed from the outset. My transcript revealed that I was lacking one required course in a laboratory science. I opted for biology. The young instructor was an advanced Ph.D. student in biology at Columbia University. His lectures were quite interesting. I found the theoretical questions surrounding the matter of the course fascinating and enjoyed any number of stimulating speculative discussions about genetics, heredity, and eugenics. I read carefully and easily comprehended the material contained in the descriptive accounts in the biology textbook. The final examination, however, required students to identify with microscopes the many specimens and exhibits we had observed during our classes. For the life of me I was never able to distinguish any differences between them; they all looked like the inkblots in a Rorschach test. I pleaded my case to the instructor. He volunteered to give me special tutoring sessions. It didn't help. Everything still looked the same.

Passing the laboratory portion of the final exam would earn me a passing grade in biology, which was a requirement for my degree. My instructor understood my dilemma. Over the course of the term he and I had come to know each other. I respected and admired him. We enjoyed interchanges about philosophical and theoretical issues. He had an older brother who had also served in the Army. At the close of our last class before the final exam, he detained me as the other students filed out of the room. "I have reached the conclusion," he announced, "that you suffer from a congenital optical disorder and that it would be inappropriate for you to fail the course because of it. You'll take only the written examination part of the exam." I started to express my thanks; he held up his hands to stop me and added, "Anyway, you'll do fine in life without ever having to peer through a microscope." I received an undeserved final grade of "C" in biology.

Back in school, my life had taken on a regular and demanding routine. Our social life, for the most part, consisted of get-togethers on weekends with Clara's family at her parents' apartment. We also visited my parents on Sundays for lunch. I seldom had any time to see my old friends on the street corner. Many of them had begun drifting away, getting married and constructing a new adult life beyond the ties of our adolescent years. I still went to Nathan Miller for my haircuts, but his shop was no longer the congregating point for my cronies it had been before the war. Nathan had lost touch with most of them.

Clara and I were still living in our furnished room down the street from her parents, when her father died unexpectedly after a brief illness. He had been in poor health for a few years, but his sudden death was a shock for the family. Following the funeral, the family decided that it would be convenient and practical for Clara and me to move in with her mother. I was certainly agreeable. My mother-in-law was a warm, self-effacing human being. Even though she had lived in the United States for many years she spoke little English, preferring the Ladino of her native Turkey. She had no education, but was kind and considerate. She and I liked and respected each other very much. In addition she was a superb cook. Without any fuss or fanfare she could whip up and serve a splendid meal for any large gathering on short notice. I had been enjoying her cooking every day since my return from the service. Sharing the same apartment would suit everyone concerned.

During this time, my parents and my sister had been evicted from the apartment where they had been living since I was sixteen. The owner of the building needed the space for his own family. They wound up in a much less desirable and poorly lit flat, which they had to share with an old man. He could not meet his rent without the help of other tenants. Ironically, during the worst shortage of apartments for rent in New York City in the months following World War II, there were many two- and four-family houses for sale. My parents could have found the means to pay a modest down payment and assume a mortgage, but like so many of their generation, they remained traumatized by the Depression. They were psychologically unable to accept any financial risk.

School and family consumed all my time. I saw my old friends less and less frequently. Clara's brother, Hy, who was my favorite brother-in-law, had just married his second wife after a divorce. His new wife, Ray Sarfaty, was a widow with two young daughters. They lived in the neighborhood on Hegeman Avenue, a block and a half from where Clara and I lived with my mother-in-law. Hy was a good-natured, large, and nattily dressed man with generous ways. He worked as a garment presser and had little formal schooling, but he did have a wonderful, self-deprecating sense of humor. Hy, who was about ten years older than Clara, always treated his baby sister with something whenever he had a run of good luck at gambling. His wife, Ray, was a friendly and intelligent woman. She was the daughter of a family of merchants. Her ambition for Hy and herself was to establish a small business of their own.

At school I had renewed my acquaintance with an old high school classmate, Harry Bagon. We met again in a class in business school and later jointly registered for the same courses since we enjoyed each other's company. Harry was a short, soft-spoken, and modest man. He was the only son of a widowed mother, to whom he was very attached. Although Harry was physically plain — his alert eyes peered out from behind the thick lenses of horn-rimmed glasses — he was highly intelligent. He had a keen intellect and a highly retentive memory. A far stronger and more conscientious student than I, Harry would receive high praise from instructors on his exams and class assignments. While I was simply working toward a general business degree, Harry was majoring in managerial economics and statistics — two of the most intellectually rigorous study areas in the program.

The other high school and neighborhood friend who turned up in an occasional class was Leo Cohen. Leo's mother, Esther, was a distant family member with close ties to Clara's mother. Both women came from Turkey. Leo's father owned and operated a hot dog and orange juice counter on a busy corner in the fur district in midtown Manhattan. Even though Leo was a full-time student, he still worked many hours after school in order to help his father. Unlike Harry, Leo was far less academically inclined. He selected courses that required the least application. He was cheerful, friendly, and fun to be with.

The requirements of my classes were highly variable. Some were very demanding and called for hard work. Others required little more than regular class attendance. After one semester, I decided that if I budgeted my time carefully, I could fit in some practical work experience. What I needed was a flexible part-time job. I pored over the newspaper classifieds and came upon something that sounded as if it would fit the bill. I telephoned and was invited for an interview.

The firm was the Zuckerberg Company, located on Worth Street in lower Manhattan on the same subway line that I rode from home to school. The owner, Sam Zuckerberg, interviewed me. He was a gruff, cigar-smoking man who had built his business from the ground up — a fact that he emphasized early on. He distributed supplies to large and small laundry companies across the country. His business was growing rapidly. He needed someone to help with general administration, business correspondence, and the preparation of direct mail advertising. I explained my background to him, and he seemed impressed by my military record and my ambition to pursue a college degree. He made it clear, however, that he put no stock in formal study and believed only in the school of hard knocks. The idea of having a college man in his office seemed to tickle his fancy. He offered me the job. I worked for the Zuckerberg Company from early 1947 until the time I graduated from City College. Sam allowed me to schedule fifteen to twenty hours of work a week on a flexible basis, as long as I showed up for a few hours each day. I mostly handled the firm's customer relations. I drafted all the letters that went out to companies that bought our products and to prospective clients. Sam's talents did not embrace the niceties of composition or grammar. I became the firm's business correspondent. Sam's secretary took charge of typing, duplicating, and mailing.

Sam Zuckerberg lived with his family on the south shore of Long Island, but he spent most of his time after work playing poker in the office until late in the evening. I worked at the Zuckerberg Company for the remaining one and a half years of my undergraduate education. Sam and I were very different. He was about thirty years older than I was, but we liked and admired each other. Sam always called me "professor." He had business cards prepared for me that gave me the title of advertising manager. He once had me spend a weekend with him in Boston at a trade show. I spent virtually all my time alone manning the company's exhibition booth, while Sam cavorted with industry buddies he had met as a traveling salesman earlier in his career. Boston was a treat for me. It gave me the chance to participate in a genuine business convention. Over time I actually learned to enjoy what Sam termed, "the dirty underwear business."

During this period, television was beginning to find its way into America's living rooms. Hy and I spent one evening negotiating the purchase of two television sets; one was for his apartment and the other was for mine. Most of the programming in those early days was old radio programs transferred to the new visual format. The slapstick buffoonery of *Milton Berle's Texaco Hour* and the more sophisticated antics of *The Sid Caesar Show* gave me an excuse to play hooky from my studies. The novelty of the new medium had a hypnotic attraction for many households during these early days. Viewers would stay glued to the screen almost every waking moment. One evening while visiting my parents, I found my mother enthralled with a program in which people recounted their personal problems. Viewers would call in to offer money or help for these troubled people. Instead of receiving my mother's usual rapt attention, I found her totally besotted with this strange program. Conversation was impossible. When the show was finally over, I launched into a tirade designed to destroy any pleasure my mother might have gotten from viewing the show. She either stopped watching it or made a mental note not to have it on from then on if I happened to be in the apartment.

The spring semester of 1947 had been moderately successful. Despite my hours at work, I managed to maintain a B average. Sam Zuckerberg liked having me around and because his business was doing well, he didn't begrudge paying me more than he said he thought my reading and writing talents were worth. He seemed to be living vicariously through me the college experience he said he never wanted and didn't need. He teased me and I kidded him. He was more like a much older, tough-minded big brother to me than a boss. I think he would have liked me to stay with the company after I got my degree, but I knew that the Zuckerberg Company would be too confining for my ambitions.

During the summer session in 1947, I carried the maximum course load, so that I could receive my degree the following June. Clara was still working full time. Her salary plus the income I received as a student under the GI Bill of Rights enabled us to save some money. We spent very little beyond the cost of food and shelter. I was too busy for much indulgence in entertainment. My mother-in-law prepared our meals and I was served many appetizing eastern Mediterranean specialties, which added to my girth. The 1947-1948 school year was my senior year. I still had almost forty more credits to complete, but I had saved some soft electives in public relations, economic geography, and business ethics. I expected these courses to be less taxing than earlier ones. With completion of my studies in view, my thoughts turned to my career options. In January 1948, I would be twenty-four years old. It was high time for me to get started on my path toward some lofty business achievement.

I launched my job-seeking campaign early in my final term. I pursued leads from the college placement center and responded to newspaper ads. That spring the economy was in a mild recession, the first of the postwar era. With my general business degree I felt that my best prospect would be to join an executive training program at a large corporation. I thought that my degree in addition to my military experience would give me a competitive edge. I soon learned, however, that most companies preferred management recruits from more prestigious institutions. An undergraduate business specialization was less valuable than I had expected it to be. I did succeed in gaining several interviews, but while they seemed to go well, they never went beyond the first meeting. By the time I received my degree in June, I still had no idea what my first post-college job would be. Still, it was a time for celebration. Clara took a summer leave from her job. She hoped that I would land something promising before September so that she could resign altogether. Drawing on our savings, we rented a furnished room for the summer at the seashore close to the Atlantic Ocean beach in the Far Rockaways in Queens. I pursued my job search and planned to commute into the city once I got work. I left the Zuckerberg Company at the end of term in order to concentrate on my future career plans. Sam and I parted under the best of terms. He wished me success and offered to tell flattering lies about my abilities to prospective employers.

Ten days before we were to move to the shore, I learned from the college placement service that Consolidated Laundries, which ran a large network of laundry and cleaning establishments from headquarters in New York, was seeking applicants for their executive training program. This struck me as very promising. I had the college credential, but I also had over a year of experience working in the same industry.

I wrote to the personnel department of Consolidated Laundries and described my qualifications for the position. Almost immediately came an invitation for an interview with the screening committee. Two days later I was in a Manhattan board room, where I met with four company executives. I was informed during the interview that these men represented the major areas of the company operation: finance, sales, marketing, and plant operations. Our discussion was the first step in a process of several stages. If I proved to be a successful candidate, I would undergo further interviews with five members of the corporate board. It was the first time that Consolidated Laundries had recruited trainees for senior level responsibilities. The painstaking screening process would yield only three or four of the best candidates. The company would have preferred to recruit from within, but their employee pool did not have the education or the experience for promotion to management. I was asked detailed questions about my personal history, business course work, career ambitions, and my experience at the Zuckerberg Company. I got the feeling that they had already contacted Sam and that he had extolled my virtues as promised. At the conclusion of the interview, I was informed that I would hear from the personnel department within a few days about whether I was to be invited back for the next round. I thought the discussion had gone well. The committee had described the company's short- and long-term strategies. They suggested that trainees would be moved on a rotating basis for six to eight months to become fully familiar with all of the company's activities. New recruits would then be assigned to the part of the company that best suited their abilities. The plan sounded well thought out. I felt confident that I would make it through the entire screening process.

One week later, I was summoned to corporate headquarters for the second interview. I met with the company treasurer. He was an avuncular type, yet he interrogated me thoroughly about my knowledge of corporate finance. One of my most demanding courses at college had been finance, and my instructor had insisted that before we left his class we would be able to hold our own discussing and explaining how publicly owned companies raised, managed, and used money. My interview with the corporate treasurer became a rerun of my final exam. He seemed pleased with my responses. Once more I was informed that I would hear from the personnel department in short order. It was July now, and although I was enjoying our beach vacation, I was getting bored. It would be September before the interviewing process ended. I began to wonder whether the laundry industry was really for me.

I went for the next interview at corporate headquarters. This time I met with the vice-president in charge of plant operations. He was a tough, hard-edged man in his late fifties. He assumed a belligerent manner toward me. From his speech and general demeanor, I deduced that he had probably come up in the firm the hard way. He sounded as if he was not so sure that the route to the executive suite ought to be achieved through a detour invented for college boys. He made it clear that I would have to get my nose rubbed in real operations — from loading the trucks to operating the steam presses. He squinted at me trying to observe my reactions to his tough tone. When he completed his speech, he wanted to know if I had ever done manual labor. I told him about my experience at Tobin, Sporn and Glaser and at the Government Printing Office. This didn't seem to impress him. I also described my Army experiences: how I had marched in the swamps of Alabama carrying a full field pack and how I had dug foxholes in the frozen ground of France. He listened, seemingly with deep attention. Then he asked me in a more friendly tone about my other military background. Before we finished talking he told me about his son's Navy experience in the Pacific and how happy he and his wife had been to welcome him home when hostilities were over. The interview ended with him patting me on the back and addressing me warmly as "son." I was informed once again that personnel would be in touch.

The whole process grated on my nerves. There were still three interviews remaining. I began to wonder whether I really wanted to be in the laundry industry, even if I did get past all the hurdles. It seemed that virtually every neighborhood in the city had its own self-service Laundromat. Washers and dryers for home use were priced to attract consumers. Perhaps the laundry industry would end up like the horse and carriage business. I continued to search the classifieds hoping to find other prospects to consider.

The New York Times want ads did yield something intriguing. The Brooklyn Public Library was seeking college graduates for entry-level positions. It had never occurred to me that one might actually earn a living working in an environment of books and knowledge. The next morning I telephoned and was invited for an interview. Following a brief, perfunctory meeting with the personnel director, I was ushered into the office of the director of the library system, Milton J. Ferguson. An older gentleman with a strong presence and self-assurance, he proceeded to interrogate me. His questions ranged across a wide continuum from my personal history to my tastes in literature and to my experience with libraries. Mr. Ferguson carefully reviewed my resume. When he noted that I had just received a degree in business administration he assumed that my military service must have been with the Quartermaster Corps and asked me if this had been my branch of the Army. I said it had not. He pursued this line of questioning by asking if I had been overseas. I replied that I had. "Well, tell me, young man," he asked impatiently, "Where were you and what did you do?" I told him that I had been in Europe with an infantry division. That ended the interview. On the spot, Mr. Ferguson offered me a position at one of the branches as soon as I could begin. He offered me a salary of two thousand dollars a year.

Mr. Ferguson explained that I would start training as a pre-professional librarian. The Brooklyn Public Library was adding staff and planning to hire a number of recent college graduates. I was taken aback by the swiftness with which I had been selected. I let Mr. Ferguson know that I was under serious consideration for a management trainee role in a large corporation. I told him that the interview process had not been concluded, but that I would have to carefully deliberate the library offer. I thanked him for his confidence in me. He concluded our meeting with a philosophical comparison. He asked me to consider the difference between an occupational role in business enlisted in the cause of profits and the intellectual world of books and libraries dedicated to enlarging the human spirit. He said that I should seriously reflect on his offer, and that the library required a decision by the end of the week. If I accepted the offer, I could be assigned to begin work in one of the branches on August first.

I spent the next two days in deep soul searching. I was anxious to get started at work, and I was confident enough to think that I could succeed in either setting. Consolidated Laundries would offer me a path to higher level corporate management. The Brooklyn Public Library position was more in keeping with my self-image as a person who cared seriously about books. Thursday morning I telephoned the personnel office of Consolidated Laundries and reported that I wished to withdraw my candidacy for the management trainee position. The director of personnel asked me to hold off making an immediate decision. He asked for a phone number where I could be reached and said that he would get back to me by the end of the day. Late that morning I received a call from the secretary to the company president. I was told that there would be only one more interview before a final decision was reached. I would see the executive vice-president the following Monday morning. I gulped and replied that I was sorry, but I was not available. I telephoned the Brooklyn Public Library personnel department to accept their offer. They told me that I was to report to the branch librarian at the Saratoga Branch Library on August first at nine o'clock in the morning.

The Saratoga Branch was located in a turn-of-the-century Carnegie building. My commute from the seashore took an hour each way; from the apartment on Sheffield Avenue it took only ten minutes by subway. I reported bright and early on my first day to Cecile J. Lynch, the branch librarian. Miss Lynch had had more than twenty years of library experience. She had a college degree in the humanities, specializing in literature, classics, and history. She had a quick mind, a sharp tongue, and a fiery temperament. I spent my first morning in her tiny office on the main floor of the branch. When she asked me about my courses at business school, she was aghast at the gaps in my formal education. She was especially concerned about my limitations in such subjects as literary study and art history. She wondered whether my background was even suitable for work with the general collection of the branch, which emphasized English and American literature, poetry, fine arts, history, biography, and humanities. Could a person with a business degree really be interested in public librarianship? I explained that I had started as a liberal arts student, but as a married veteran I had shifted to business as a means of completing my studies as quickly as was feasible. From there, we went on to discuss my military service. It was then that I discovered Cecile Lynch to be a rabid patriot. She was delighted to have a returned soldier on her staff. Miss Lynch then introduced me around the library. In addition to herself, the staff consisted of an assistant branch librarian, Miss Shrewsbury, and the children's librarian, Miss Spencer. There were two full-time female clerks for circulation desk duties, and a male full-time custodian. Six part-time high school students worked as pages, reshelving books and helping at the circulation counter. I was the first male ever to be appointed to the librarian staff.

The library was pleasingly arranged. The main floor contained the circulation desk, the reference department, and the children's room. There were also the stacks, which housed the main collection. On the second floor there was an additional stack and reading area. On the library's lower level there was a comfortably appointed staff lounge and a full kitchen for staff use. My fellow staffers were friendly and welcoming, but shy and reserved. We maintained fairly formal relations among ourselves. First names were used only for the pages. Miss Shrewsbury was the eldest librarian; she was a stout, sixtyish matron who sought to disguise her kind and gentle nature behind a veneer of gruffness. Miss Spencer was a younger woman, perhaps in her early forties. She was badly disabled, which made her physical movements somewhat contorted. She was very patient and had a sweet disposition. The clerical assistants and student part-timers all liked working at the branch. Miss Shrewsbury idolized Cecile Lynch. Everyone else dreaded inviting Miss Lynch's wrath by doing something she might find inappropriate or stupid. Nevertheless, we all found her to be fair and honest.

My task was to learn about the different aspects of branch operations. At first, I worked under supervision. Later, I functioned independently at the circulation desk, the reference desk, and in the children's department. I visited the central library with Miss Lynch once every two weeks, and assisted her in selecting books for the branch from a large collection of recently published books. The library was open daily until six in the evening and until nine o'clock three nights a week. Saturdays, we were open from nine to one o'clock. Our schedules were rotated so that each staff member worked two late days, from one to nine o'clock. We also worked one or two Saturdays a month. The Saratoga Branch was like a home away from home for me. I was working with interesting, thoughtful people. The library patrons were friendly and grateful for the staff's assistance in locating materials. Except for the occasional intrusion of cranky curmudgeons, who somehow find their way into every public facility, the branch was a happy place to be. With each succeeding day I felt more certain that I had made the right decision. Public librarianship fit me far better than elbowing my way up to the executive suite of Consolidated Laundries.

After my first week at the branch Miss Lynch invited me to her office for a serious and protracted discussion. I had assumed that the route to my acceptance as a full-fledged librarian was simply to complete a period of satisfactory performance. Miss Lynch described the career path for librarians more clearly. While it was true that appointment as librarian in the past had required no more than a college degree, or sometimes even less than a full four-year degree, the situation was changing. New appointees might also attain librarian status after a year or two as pre-professionals, yet more and more the job required formal academic preparation. One would need to pursue a graduate degree at one of the institutions offering a bachelor's of science in librarianship. While neither Cecile Lynch nor any of the other staff members of the Saratoga Branch had pursued such a course, some other members of the Brooklyn Public Library staff had done so. In Miss Lynch's view they were the ones most likely to move up to senior positions, such as branch librarian. I was young and at an early stage of my career. Miss Lynch urged me to look into the possibility of enrolling in a university program. She assured me that if I were to take up such study, the branch would help me by making adjustments in my work schedule.

I had learned to trust Cecile Lynch's judgement, even though I thought that my foray into higher education was over. I had used up only two years of my four-year entitlement for subsidized study under the GI Bill. If I decided to continue my studies, the GI Bill would cover my tuition expenses. I would also be entitled to some compensation while enrolled in school. Students enrolled for full-time study, if they were disabled veterans, had no ceiling on outside earnings. I still held my ten-percent veteran disability status. It seemed that I could manage to enroll as a full-time student and keep a flexible work schedule at the library. It certainly wouldn't prove any more onerous than working for the Zuckerberg Company while I was in business school. There was only a month or so before the fall term would begin.

I learned that Pratt Institute and Columbia University in New York both offered library degrees. I decided to explore possibilities at Columbia. On my first free morning, I traveled to 116th Street in Manhattan and presented myself at the admissions office for the School of Library Service in the multi-story Butler

Library building. There, I was cordially interviewed. I was informed that the entering class of fall 1948 would be the first group to receive the newly authorized master of library science degree. The program required thirty-six credit hours. A special report project was part of the degree requirement as well. Formal admission was based on a favorable evaluation of one's college transcript. Military veterans would be most welcome. Time was short, but applications would be accepted up to September first. When I left the Columbia campus I took the catalog, application forms, and fall schedule of classes with me. I decided I would enroll in its first master's degree class if the School of Library Service would have me.

Notification of my admission to Columbia arrived in time for me to sort out necessary details with the Veterans Administration and at the branch. My schedule of fall classes comprised five courses. I would have to be on campus four days a week until midday. Miss Lynch worked out a timetable for me at the library around my school hours. I continued as a full-time employee and kept my benefits and salary. My schedule was crowded, but I was strongly motivated. If I could successfully complete my thirty-six-hour degree requirements by August 1949, I would graduate as a member of Columbia's first Master of Library Science class. As a full-time student I also received income from the GI Bill. Upon graduation, I would be immediately eligible for promotion to the position of professional librarian with an increased salary. Between my library salary and my GI Bill income, Clara and I could manage reasonably well on my earnings alone. Clara could resign from her job as planned. This arrangement—of a stay-at-home wife and a breadwinner husband—was the preferred path for any couple aspiring to middle-class social status.

I plunged into my new studies with enthusiasm and maintained my commitment to the library. It was a heady time at Columbia. The faculty included some celebrated recruits, and the student body, unlike my class at City College, came from all over the country. Many students were attracted by the MLS program, which offered a true graduate degree rather than the former, less prestigious second bachelor's degree. The allure of living and studying for a year in Manhattan's Morningside Heights was another advantage. At that time the neighborhood surrounding the campus was vibrant and safe. Some of the students brought with them considerable working experience in libraries. Others, like myself, were novices. The faculty assured us that inexperience in library work would not impede our performance as students. Among my classmates, most were in their twenties; there were a few veterans like myself. The class was composed of about two-thirds women and one-third men. The course work was not like anything I had experienced before. It concentrated on the intellectual, technical, social, ethical, and organizational concerns of libraries. As in most curricular offerings, student judgements were based inevitably on the interests, values, and biases of the individual. Looking back, I have only a few recollections from the twelve classes that remain firmly entrenched in my mind.

The associate dean of the program was Lowell Martin, from the University of Chicago. He also taught a class in library administration. As a former business student, I found his lectures very interesting. Martin was an articulate and thoughtful analyst of major concepts and broad philosophical approaches to organizational understanding. In fall 1948, his lectures were well in advance of many of the significant behavioral insights that came to light in research years later. His teaching drew on psychological and sociological perceptions and linked them to library management. My career-long preoccupation with organizational and administrative concerns of librarianship was spawned during Lowell Martin's stimulating lectures.

Maurice Tauber was editor of *College and Research Libraries* in 1948. He was among the foremost American scholars and educators who focused on cataloging and classification. He was a theorist and a consultant to large academic and research libraries. He shared joint authorship with Louis Round Wilson of the most widely read and referred to treatise on academic librarianship. Tauber's door was open wide to those who sought him out. In the classroom, at least for me, Tauber was unintelligible. My befuddlement stemmed from my complete lack of interest in technical services, which was his subject. Exercises in classification schedules and catalog codes, which were practiced in the school's only laboratory, left me in a state between total confusion and boredom. It took the charitable counsel of fellow students to rescue me from ignominious failure. I especially remember Dinah Epner, later Lindauer, and Leon Crain as my personal saviors.

Ray Trautman came straight from the military to Columbia. As an Army colonel, he had superintended the wartime book and library programs in the United States and abroad. He taught a course on libraries in the culture. The class content was negligible, but Trautman was a charming man. He was a droll raconteur, who told us about the almost unbelievable political and logistical intrigues he went through during the war to obtain books and magazines for the troops wherever in the world they were stationed.

The Best of Times

Miriam Tompkins instilled in us her visionary zeal, based on a long and distinguished career in library practice. She exuded the ethos of readers' services, emphasizing and dramatizing how libraries—public libraries in particular—played a vital role in guiding and advising lay readers. Winifred Linderman brought reference work alive, not only by guiding us through standard and invaluable printed sources, but also by underscoring the intrinsic point of reference work, which for her meant effective problem solving. In her view, reference could succeed only if the librarian was adroit enough to shepherd the client through a polite, yet steadfast and precise interrogation about the question that needed to be answered. Hellmut Lehmann-Haupt taught us to appreciate the printed book as a physical object. He demonstrated the beauty of rare books, manuscripts, and incunabula, displaying priceless examples in the class.

The school's library was a particularly rich resource. It offered a sizeable collection of books and periodicals pertaining to library science. A liberal lending policy encouraged students to use these resources both at the library and at home. Most of the students in the program were liberal arts and humanities graduates. There was only a handful of science majors among the eighty or so student body. I was the lone business major. Many students, most of whom were studying full-time with no outside work commitments, took an active role in the student government. They worked closely with faculty to build the framework for the new MLS program. The student body president was Charles Goodrum. He was an engaging, well-spoken, and politically sensitive young man who would go on to a successful career at the Library of Congress. Goodrum gained wider fame as the author of non-fiction books and murder mysteries. His first whodunit, *Dewey Decimated,* was set in a large research library and featured a distinguished and suave retired librarian as its main character.

I regretted that I could spend only a minimum amount of time on campus. I missed out on most opportunities to interact with my classmates. I knew well only a handful. In later years I would keep up only with Dinah Lindauer. Following her graduation, she went on to work at Baltimore's Enoch Pratt Library. She later returned to New York to serve with the Brooklyn Public Library while I was still on the staff. Leon Crain also worked in the branch system of Brooklyn Public Library for many years after graduation. Milton Byam, who straddled the class of 1949 and 1950, was another fellow student who began at the Brooklyn Public Library. He became the assistant director of the Brooklyn Public Library, and then moved on to the directorship of the District of Columbia Public Library. He spent the last years of his career as librarian of the Queensborough Public Library.

The Best of Times

As I pursued my studies, life went on in the library branch. I spent my nights and weekends keeping up with course readings and assignments. Social life was minimal. There were occasional evening visits with Hy and Ray, and the weekly Sunday dinner at my parents' apartment. At the branch, I found myself more and more deferred to by my colleagues, who somehow attributed to me far more knowledge about librarianship than I had yet amassed. Cecile Lynch would regularly quiz me on my classes and their content. She gained a vicarious experience of library school through me. Listening to me reinforced her view that my instruction afforded little more than she already knew, based upon her own experience and personal reading. She remained supportive and encouraging in every way she could, as did all my colleagues at the Saratoga Branch.

Several days a week I reported to the branch in early or mid-afternoon to work until nine o'clock. There were generally two or three other people on duty with me. Around three or four o'clock, the building custodian was dispatched to buy the groceries for that evening's dinner. At about five o'clock, one of my colleagues would go down to the kitchen and prepare a meal for us. Strong, mouth-watering smells would waft their way upstairs to the main floor. By six o'clock, it was time for dinner. Normally, a page would be assigned to the circulation desk as the librarians on duty adjourned to the kitchen for dinner. Whoever was responsible for that evening's meal tried to outdo her competitors. These delicious meals were served on lovely dinnerware that the branch had somehow acquired. After dinner, I was strongly encouraged to get out of the way while the dishes were cleared and washed. In spite of my frequent offers of help, I never once was permitted to lift a finger in the kitchen. That was women's work, I was told. I have always thought that being the lone male staff member of the branch in those years put me in an enviable position.

It was the beginning of 1949, and important developments were taking place at Brooklyn Public Library headquarters. Mr. Ferguson was retiring. His successor was to be Francis St. John, a vigorous, younger man who had been recruited from a high-level position in the New York Public Library. Miss Lynch returned from meetings at the central library to report on the latest news and the gossip. St. John had a reputation for ambition, innovation, and impatience. It was said that he planned to transform the Brooklyn Public Library from a traditional institution into one that would take its place in the forefront of the American public library movement. Senior members of the staff viewed these changes with trepidation. More recent staff members were charged with elation. By early spring St. John was on the scene. One of his first acts was to arrange several meetings. These were to be attended by every full-time member of the library staff at every level. I do not recall precisely what he said during the meeting I attended. What I do remember is the man. He spoke animatedly and with passion, celebrating the calling of librarianship and promising to lead the Brooklyn Public Library into the vanguard of American public libraries. I left the session with my spirits lifted and congratulated myself for stumbling into such a noteworthy occupation. I was excited to launch my career under the leadership of such an inspiring leader.

The academic year of 1948-1949 was crowded for me with new insights and understanding of libraries and librarianship. For the first time I became aware of the rich history of the institution and of the milestones in its evolution. I felt that my library career might be in reference work or administration, but it was still too early for me to settle on a philosophical or conceptual sense of the field and my role in it. I did, however, see greater potential for career development in public librarianship than in academic or special libraries. Long before graduation, the school played host to innumerable recruiters from libraries of every type, but principally from large public and academic libraries. Some of these representatives were personnel people; others were directors of libraries. All were competing vigorously for our services. They extolled the opportunities offered by their institutions. The times seemed highly propitious for new entrants to the field. It was clearly a buyer's market for the new graduates. When I could spare the time, I attended lectures and discussions to learn more about the different libraries that were seeking staff. No one who came and spoke made me feel that the institution he or she represented held out more promise or potential than the Brooklyn Public Library under the innovative leadership of St. John. I remained firm in my resolution to stay with the Brooklyn system.

By summer the Brooklyn Public Library was clearly in flux. Changes had been made in the senior levels of management. A new in-service training program was announced for newly appointed librarians, which would begin in September. The program would orient new staff to the operations and strategies of all the key departments of the library. St. John himself, and senior officers of the library's major divisions would meet weekly with staff over several months. I counted myself as fortunate to be among the first group to take part in this valuable opportunity.

By June a new dimension had been added to my busy life. Clara was pregnant and we were expecting to be parents by November. The prospect of new responsibilities reinforced my career commitment. I discussed my next assignment with

The Best of Times

Cecile Lynch. She and I both felt that with my military newspaper background, the library's public relations department might be a promising route to follow. Miss Lynch confided in me the gossip that the head of the department was planning to retire in a few months, since he was uncomfortable with the pressure of St. John's heightened demands on senior staff. She suggested that I write a letter to Mr. St. John requesting an interview with him. Within a few days I was summoned for a meeting.

In person, Francis St. John was larger than life. He was a friendly and engaging bear of a man. He was assertive and resolute, yet a thoughtful and focused listener. Before the interview he had read my file and knew a good deal about me. When I broached the subject of reassignment and proposed public relations as a possibility, he listened very carefully. He then explained to me why he felt that public relations would not be the right move for me. Public relations, he pointed out, was a staff responsibility. It was only a specialized role, not an administrative position within the library's managerial chain of command. It called for skills and performance outside the mainstream of library administration. With my background and MLS degree, he felt that I had potential for a promising and well-compensated career in public library administration. He envisioned the Brooklyn Public Library as a training ground for library managers, in which some would remain within the system while others would assume leadership roles elsewhere across the country.

The in-service training, starting in the fall, would be the first step. St. John assured me that the Brooklyn Public Library would gain national recognition as a library that developed leaders. In view of my degree in business administration, St. John suggested that I transfer to the business library of the system. There I would work with Jesse Cross, a man who had just been recruited from the New York Public Library's Economics Department to serve as the library system's head business librarian. I would receive strong training and experience in an important service center of the library. I would also capitalize on my academic preparation and remain squarely in library operations. I thanked him profusely for his advice and agreed that the business library was a logical next step. In a few days I received word that I was to report for service on July first at the business library on the upper floor of the Montague Branch located off Fulton Street in the heart of Brooklyn's business, financial, legal, and judicial district. I would miss Cecile Lynch and my other Saratoga Branch colleagues who had given me friendship and had been so generous in introducing me into the world of public librarianship; but I left for my new post with enthusiasm and eagerness.

ALA DAILY REPORTER

**Published at the American Library Association Conference 1952
By the UNITED STAFF ASSOCIATION**

BROOKLYN PUBLIC LIBRARY — NEW YORK PUBLIC LIBRARY — QUEENSBOROUGH PUBLIC LIBRARY
PAUL WASSERMAN, EDITOR

ISSUE NUMBER 5   JULY 4, 1952

LPRC AWARD TO B'KLYN COLLEGE

The Library Public Relations Council's annual award went to the Brooklyn College Library at the Town Hall Club. Rose Sellers the Chief Special Services Librarian, submitted a scrapbook which highlighted a continuing program of publicizing the activities of individual staff members. Prof. Humphrey Bousfield, Librarian at the college, accepted the award for his staff from Miss Harriet Forbes, LPRC President.

REGISTRATION RUMBLINGS

Registration had passed Chicago's figures and seemed almost certain to edge over the 5200 mark set at the last N.Y. Conference in 1937, according to ALA's Chief Accountant, Leo Weins, who's been in charge of registration. Registration's been a simple, easy flowing process right from scratch, thanks to a cooperative staff and the delegates' patience.

EQUIPMENT ACKNOWLEDGEMENTS

Charles Shaw, Equipment Chairman, on behalf of ALA, extends thanks to the public libraries of N.Y. City who provided materials, trucks and manpower. A vote of gratitude, too, to the Business Equipment Co, 300 4th Avenue, for desks, typewriter stands and chairs; to Mr. H.R. Datz and Remington Rand's Library Bureau for 20 typewriters and to the N.C. Anderson Mimeograph Co., 100 6th Ave., for the use of the mimeograph machine.

DCC'S NEW BRASS

New officers of the Division of Cataloging and Classification announced at yesterday's annual business meeting include: President, David J. Haykin, Library of Congress; Vice President, Dorothy Charles, H. W. Wilson Co; Exec Secretary, Edwin Colburn, Cleveland Public Library; Director-at-large, Sarah K. Vann Carnegie Library School; Representatives, ALA Council, Esther Peterson, Univ. of Minnesota Library, Marjorie Ann Stuff, Stephens College Library.

NY STATE TRUSTEES ELECT

At a meeting in NYPL the Library Trustee Foundation of NY State elected the following new officers for 1952-1953: Frank Ryder, Cobleskill, Chairman; Justice Francis Bergen, Albany, Vice-Chairman; Dr William Crawford, Monticello, President; Mrs. Frank C. Moore, Kenmore, Vice-President; Harold Hacker, Buffalo, Sec-Treasurer; Harold Bailey, Brooklyn, Counsel.

FLOWERS FOR FRIDAY.

Brooklyn Day today with the Kings County Association of Garden Clubs, Mrs Tutino, Pres. supplying and arranging the floral display co-ordinated by Corinne Sheppard of the B.P.L.

POST CONFERENCE TOURING?

Pick up a copy of the program schedule for the Post AIA Conference Workshop Tour of larger units of service. Sponsored by ALA's Library Extension Section and the NY State Library, the program runs July 6 through 8th. Details at their desk opposite the Ticket Desk.

BOUQUETS!

Hats off to ALA officers and the Local Chairman, to Committee Chairmen, volunteer workers and to everyone else who helped make this year's Conference a stimulating, well planned, bang up affair.
It's risky naming names, cause somebody always gets unintentionally left out, but certainly all of the following people should be cited: Francis R. St. John, Local Chairman; Charles Shaw, Equipment; Evelyn Kirkland, Local Information; Paul North Rice, Meeting Rooms; Morris Gelfand, Personnel; Maurice Tauber, Summary Reports; Harold Roth, Entertainment; Theodore Waller and Peggy Dudley, Publicity. It was a big job — well done!

NEWSWEEK DRAWING

Today's your last chance to win a year's service to Newsweek in your choice of microcard, microfilm or bound volume, at their daily drawing in Booth E-21. While you're there, don't miss catching the tele-type machine bringing the A.P. wire service direct to the Conference.

MORE ELECTION RETURNS

Public Libraries Division's Business and Technology Committee elected the following slate of officers for 1952-53: Jesse Cross, Brooklyn Public Library, Director; Gladys Sandifur, Los Angeles Public, Chairman, Milton Drescher, Milwaukee Public, Secretary; Hope Packard, Springfield Public, Treasurer, at its annual business meeting.

The first page of the final issue of the ALA Daily Reporter, *published during the American Library Association Conference in New York in 1952.*

Chapter Seven

The business library was different from the Saratoga Branch in countless ways. The telephone rang constantly, as time-harried patrons called requesting reference assistance. The clientele was disproportionately male. Visitors to the business branch tended to be well dressed and well spoken. They worked with the specialized material independently, or sought assistance by clearly defining their requirements. The collections were highly specialized and incorporated numerous expensive loose-leaf services, which provided legal, accounting, or financial information. Mr. Cross, my supervisor, proved to be the polar opposite of Cecile Lynch. He was a well built, somewhat carelessly dressed, middle-aged man. He was shy and not given to small talk or lengthy conversation. He occupied a small cubicle in the stack area, and his desk overflowed with papers, books, and periodicals in great disorder. Mr. Cross had an air of preoccupation about him, as if he were constantly pondering some staggering problem. Yet he was a kind and learned man. He carefully replied to all questions with a clear and intelligent response. Some years earlier, Mr. Cross had decided that his practice of law in Canada was not suited to his temperament. He had worked for the New York Public Library Economics Division Library for ten years, before being recruited to Brooklyn by St. John. I was to serve as a reference assistant. Working with me on the reference desk were Helen Vogel and Frank Hill. Helen Vogel was a long-time Brooklyn Public Library staff member who had gravitated to the business library from general branch work because she had a personal interest in investments and finance. Frank Hill had worked his way up at the library, starting as a clerk and gradually advancing to become a reference librarian. He was working on a graduate degree in engineering. Service at the reference desk was on a rotating basis. We took turns, including Mr. Cross. I arranged my work schedule to fit in during hours when I was not at Columbia.

The Best of Times

During the first couple of weeks, I was not assigned alone to the reference desk. This gave me the opportunity to enlist a colleague's assistance when I was at a loss for how to deal with a query. I found the reference questions extraordinarily wide ranging and I spent a great deal of time familiarizing myself with the rich resources of the collection. The more I learned of the materials, the more bewildered I became. It was daunting to find the right response to reference inquiries across such a broad spectrum. At the beginning of my third week, I poked my head into Mr. Cross's office and confided that I felt confused by the staggering amount of material in the library. I feared that I would never master it. He made no response and turned back to the papers on his desk. Twenty minutes later, Mr. Cross found me in the stack. He spoke gently. "Mr. Wasserman," he said, "I have thought about what you told me, and I am very pleased and encouraged. If after a little more than two weeks here you had expressed satisfaction that you had learned all that was necessary I would have serious misgivings. But your confusion and perplexity tells me that you appreciate how much there is to learn before feeling comfortable in this library. You're doing fine. Things will fall into place soon enough." He smiled shyly, patted my shoulder and shuffled away.

Mr. Cross was right. It took a while, but finally the pieces came together and the library's rich resources formed a mosaic I could comprehend. Every reference question was a personal challenge. To find the right solution to a question was like being in a mystery, in which I was cast as the relentless sleuth. Each hour at the desk responding to patron requirements in person and by telephone required me to exploit resources and learn more and more about the library's remarkable potential for aiding clients. Never had my work life been so pleasurable or more fulfilling. In the meantime, my MLS program at Columbia was drawing to a close. I had become used to my compartmentalized life of study and work. Clara and I had also come to depend on the GI Bill stipend I had been receiving from the Veterans Administration. There would still be one year remaining in my entitlement under the GI Bill after completion of my degree. I had grown to enjoy the Columbia campus and found graduate study much to my liking. Considering all these factors, I talked with Mr. Cross to learn his reaction to my proposed plan. If he were agreeable, and if I were accepted, I thought I might continue at Columbia to pursue further study in the Graduate School of Business. I could earn a second master's degree if I could arrange my work around my class schedule. Mr. Cross was enthusiastically supportive. He felt the additional courses would add to my expertise as a business reference librarian. A schedule to accommodate my work at the library could be easily arranged.

The Best of Times

I applied for admission to the Columbia School of Business. As a student already in residence, I was able to quickly process my application. I would begin classes in September 1949. I already held a bachelor's degree in business, so I enrolled in the one-year MS program in business economics, rather than the two-year MBA program. With my Master's of Library Science diploma in hand, signed by the University's president, Dwight Eisenhower, I transferred across the campus to start my next academic year in the Graduate School of Business. Having completed my MLS, I was promoted to the higher classification of librarian at the Brooklyn Public Library. My salary went up to $2,700 a year.

I worked a full schedule at the business library in addition to taking five courses at Columbia. I was also taking part in the Brooklyn Pubic Library's new orientation program. The orientation series offered insight into St. John's ambitious agenda, which he shared with us. Enthusiastic new department heads explained how each of the major programs would be reorganized for maximum efficiency. We learned about new approaches and discussed them fully in an open climate. Ideas suggested by the new staff members received careful consideration. The library's more seasoned librarians sought to learn everything they could from the fortunate newcomers who had been selected for the in-service training sessions.

My business courses were heavily weighted toward economics. One semester was devoted to micro-economics. The second would move on to macro-economics. My classes met in large lecture halls and in smaller discussion groups. There were lectures by a few senior professors, but Ph.D. students handled most of the work. These students made rigorous demands on us, giving frequent quizzes and exams. I found the business classes intellectually more demanding than my library classes had been. I had to spend a disproportionate amount of my study time wrestling with complex ideas. A course in the history of economic thought with Eli Ginsberg was a memorable classroom experience. He offered brilliant insights into theorists, from Adam Smith to Thorstein Veblen. The industrial relations instructor was a young Yale Ph.D. student named Ernest Dale, who was an entertaining lecturer. He brought in some of the best-known figures in union and corporate industrial relations as guest speakers. Dale later became widely known and much sought after as a management consultant specializing in corporate organizational structure. Carl Shoup dazzled us with his erudition in a seminar on tax policy. He had just returned from Japan where he had been the principal architect of the post-war Japanese tax code. Philip Taft, the author of a major treatise on personnel management, was another one of my instructors. He was teaching at Columbia while on leave from Brown University. He explained that teaching the class ranked lower on his priority list than watching the New York Yankees—his real reason for being a visiting professor in New York City.

November 1949 marked a special occasion—the birth of our first child, Jacqueline. The joy of everyone's life, she was a beautiful child with large blue eyes and golden curls. Her angelic appearance was little consolation, however, for her cranky and demanding nature. For a harried father, who was juggling both job and school, the sleepless hours spent pacing the floor late into the night with a ceaselessly wailing child added yet another dimension to an already numbing set of demands. As far as Jacqueline's three proud grandparents were concerned, this was a child who could do no wrong. Her slightest whimper was an immediate call to action. She was paraded lovingly in her carriage and shown off for all to fuss over.

At the business library I brought great zest to my role as a business reference librarian. Soon after Jacqueline's birth, Mr. Cross wrote to Mr. St. John recommending my promotion to assistant business librarian. Mr. Cross understood the increased financial burden I was under with a new addition to the family. He was also pleased with my performance. St. John approved his recommendation. As of January first, 1950, I was advanced to a higher grade and became Mr. Cross's assistant. The business library provided an ideal work situation. Mr. Cross was a man I respected highly both as a scholarly bookman and an exceptionally able collection builder. His knowledge and professionalism enabled the library to receive the necessary level of financial support needed to sustain and build the costly sets of business directories, periodicals, specialized services, monographs, and circulating materials that made the library such a crucial asset to the business community. Whether they showed up in person or telephoned, the library's patrons came from well beyond the limits of Brooklyn. They sought us out from as far as Manhattan's financial and commercial districts. The Brooklyn Public Library saw its business branch as a strategic vehicle for enhancing political support for the library's full range of public services.

Mr. Cross encouraged me in any initiative I proposed. By spring 1950, we had begun issuing *Service to Business,* a four- to six-page monthly newsletter that carried the logo: "As near as your telephone." The staff prepared the text, focusing on timely business topics and offering suggested readings from the library's collection. These selections were annotated. The public relations department took care of the printing and distribution from headquarters.

Despite my growing familiarity with the library's holdings, there were invariably questions that went beyond our collection's limitations. Conventional reference practice in those days was for a librarian to exhaustively plumb the depths of the library's collection. When nothing suitable could be found within the outer limit of a half-hour search, we would suggest that the client go to a more specialized library. Alternative libraries were usually listed in one or another of the directories of the city's public, academic, and special libraries. I found it very frustrating to have to send patrons to another place, which might or might not prove useful. I knew the business library's patrons were usually working under time constraints. I decided to come up with a different strategy.

I suggested to Mr. Cross that instead of dispatching a patron after a failed search to another library, the reference librarian could call a special subject library and attempt to get an answer to the client's question. We would be performing a value-added service as an information intermediary for the client. This approach would provide a shortcut to the alternative of traveling to another library and resuming a reference search. It also occurred to me that, instead of automatically gravitating toward the library's inventory, the reference librarian could call a specialist right away for suggestions on the best source that could provide an answer to a question. The array of prospective subject experts was limitless. They might include librarians in specialized business libraries, editors of trade journals, trade association officials, and government specialists. The prospects of searching the collection could be weighed against the benefit of identifying an answer source and telephoning that source right away on the client's behalf, whether the outcome was in print or not. Information-seeking patrons cared little whether the answer was found in a published account or in the words of an expert. Librarians, however, held an almost religious conviction that information was valid only when it could be found in printed sources.

Mr. Cross was a lawyer. He had the proper respect for the authority of words on the printed page, especially when they related to legal questions such as laws, regulations, and court decisions. He conceded that with business inquiries matters might be otherwise. He agreed that it would be interesting to experiment with alternative tactics for answering reference questions. With a green light from Mr. Cross, the other reference librarians and I began to spend more time on the telephone seeking answers to patron queries. As a result we began building an informal network of subject specialists in New York City's community of special librarians. It worked our to be a mutually advantageous arrangement. For many of the specialists we consulted, our library's rich business collection proved invaluable for serving their own clientele.

Over time we adapted our performance strategy. If we had a difficult question concerning advertising, for example, we would telephone Nathalie Frank, the librarian at Geyer, Newell and Ganger, a major Manhattan advertising agency. For a query that dealt with a highly current or unique problem in an industry, we might phone a staff member of a trade association or the editor of that industry's trade journal. Questions on current statistical data, which were not yet in print, would require help from a suitable expert in one of the government directories. We soon learned how helpful these many sources could be and how flattered they were to be helping the staff of the Brooklyn Public Library's Business Reference Library. The only negative consequence was that the library's long-distance phone bills became a cause for growing alarm in the bursar's office. A memorandum from Mr. Cross, explaining matters to the finance office, was also sent to Mr. St. John. The result was an upward adjustment in the library's telephone budget. My strategy for dealing with reference queries became an important tenet of my practice of librarianship.

I became a member of both the American Library Association and the Special Libraries Association by the fall of 1949. I was affiliated with the two parts of the ALA organization — public libraries and reference services. In the SLA, I chose the Business Libraries Division, and attended several local chapter meetings where I came to know my colleagues in fields such as publishing, advertising, finance, banking, and newspapers. With my academic background in business, I found that I shared more common professional interests with the special librarians than I did with most of my public library associates. These friendships and associations were reinforced in later years when I enlisted their help on projects of common interest.

Over time, my curiosity led me to extend my interest beyond simply responding to patron questions. I sought a greater understanding of the whole phenomenon of reference publications. I wanted to know why certain books were annually revised and reissued in more current editions while others were not. I also wanted to understand the relative utility of loose-leaf services compared to the issuance of separate, stand-alone volumes. I considered the problem of time lags — in both the accuracy of information available and the state of knowledge on a given subject — between the research and its publication. These types of questions had escaped my attention during library school. It never seemed enough to accept at face value what was at hand for the clientele. Our patrons from the business world needed their reference questions answered quickly; and they needed to know that the information proffered was accurate. They often used this information to solve immediate problems. Against this backdrop of concerns, I began to analyze carefully and analytically many of the business reference tools on which we relied.

One of the reference books we frequently consulted was a work issued by the United States Commerce Department in 1933 titled, *Price Sources*. This was an alphabetized, three hundred-page dictionary that listed thousands of different commodities, minerals, and chemicals. With each listing was cited the periodical, newspaper, or government report in which one could find current market prices. An index provided names, addresses, publishers, and subscription prices for the sources identified in the main body of the book. The book had been prepared by examining thoroughly all the sources included in the index and regrouping the information in an alphabetic commodity listing. For library patrons who wanted a commodity market price, the reference assistant would check *Price Sources* and go right to the current issue of the source identified to find the price. The technique sometimes worked flawlessly, but too often the source cited no longer existed, had changed its name, or no longer carried prices for the commodity in question. The book was by then sixteen years old. The world had changed enormously during the intervening period. Content amassed in the early 1930's had never been updated.

I discussed this problem with Mr. Cross. His view was that frequently government agencies might compile and distribute useful reference materials with no plan for revision, updating, or later editions. Sometimes the reason might be a lack of financial resources, or the agency initially responsible for a reference book might have changed its area of responsibility. Sometimes the official who had initially undertaken the project would no longer be at the agency. I felt that perhaps librarians should have some responsibility for ensuring the timeliness and continued viability of these resources. Shouldn't they play a role in seeing that the information was revised and reissued? Mr. Cross disagreed. He believed that this responsibility lay outside the limits of the reference librarian's role, which was merely to locate needed information in existing forms. I was uncomfortable with this definition. I was too busy to take on any further projects, but I filed the question away in the back of my mind knowing I would return to it at a later date.

The Best of Times

In August 1950, I received my second MS degree from Columbia University; this one was in economics, and, like the first one, was signed by Dwight Eisenhower. I had completely exhausted my eligibility under the GI Bill and would no longer receive a stipend. I felt relieved to finally be able to work at my job without the need to take classes and commute regularly to Columbia. However, I also knew that our family budget would be affected by the cutoff of about fifteen hundred dollars per year in supplementary income from the Veterans Administration. I had become used to long hours of work and study. I felt somewhat guilty about reducing my workload down to a forty-hour week. Still, I had had my fill of being a student, and I recognized that my greater concern was the reduction in my immediate income.

Not long after I had completed my program at the business school I had a long conversation at the library with a Mr. January, the headmaster of a private secondary school called Brooklyn Academy. The school was located two short blocks from the library. January was an occasional user of the business library. Over time, we came to know each other casually. The school he administered had a reputation for being a high-tuition last resort for spoiled, unruly high school students who had either been expelled or had failed in their studies at other public or private schools in the city. Mr. January explained to me that in a recent accreditation review, Brooklyn Academy had been issued an ultimatum. The school had to catalog and classify the books in its library, strengthen its collection, and introduce appropriate procedures for circulating its material. The academy would lose its state accreditation otherwise. His question to me was whether I would be interested in taking on the task on a part-time basis. I learned that the work could be done on a flexible schedule. I could work independently during evening and weekend hours. Compensation would be mutually agreed upon. I suggested that I would like to visit and look over the collection.

The library was one large room, its bookshelves filled with about eight hundred books of various types. There were two encyclopedia sets, an unabridged dictionary, a desk and a chair, and four tables and chairs, all for no more than sixteen students. I knew only the rudiments of cataloging and classification from my classes at Columbia. I was familiar with the Dewey decimal classification system, which was used at the Brooklyn Public Library. I also knew that it was possible to order pre-cataloged and pre-classified cards from the Library of Congress or from library suppliers. The hourly rate I negotiated with Mr. January was three dollars an hour for up to forty hours a month. The anticipated deadline for completion was twelve months. The extra income would be equivalent to what I had been receiving from the Veterans Administration. Also, there would be no commuting time unless I chose to work on the weekends. Working on my own I would be free to make all the necessary decisions. If I had questions, I could ask for advice from my colleagues in the Brooklyn Public Library's centralized catalog department. I started the assignment early in September of 1950.

I met with the school's faculty and administration to put forth what I thought would be the best strategy for proceeding with my assignment. I quickly learned that no one cared how or why I did my work. Their only concern was to placate the accreditation officials by demonstrating that efforts were underway to set up a proper library. I was completely on my own. I planned a schedule of work and announced that I would need three or four months until the start of the spring 1951 semester to make the library fully operative. I often spent Saturday and Sunday mornings at the Brooklyn Academy, when there were no classes in session, so that I could work without interruption or distraction.

I gradually resurrected the library. With my spring deadline looming, I decided to spend longer weekend hours at the job. On those quiet Saturdays and Sundays, when no one else was about, Dr. Sullivan, the senior academic official, often would be in his office for long periods. Quite frequently he would receive visitors. I assumed that Sullivan, a gregarious middle-aged man, was probably a bachelor and found it more comfortable spending his time in his office than facing long leisure hours at home. I could not imagine who these well-dressed men and women were as they walked past the library and down the deserted school corridor to see Dr. Sullivan. They usually stayed for half an hour or longer before departing. The mystery was solved late that fall. In a long and detailed story in *The New York Times*, I read that Dr. Sullivan was to be indicted for his part in a conspiracy. He was accused of serving as intermediary in a bribery scheme for assuring admission of students at a number of select, higher education institutions. It was only then that I deduced the likely meaning of these many clandestine conferences held at Brooklyn Academy while I toiled away at my library assignment.

Dr. Sullivan did not reappear at the school during the rest of the time I spent at Brooklyn Academy. His office was reassigned. I continued working until June. By then, the library had become a functional part of the school. It was open during certain hours under the administration of two English teachers whom I trained to supervise the library and control the circulation procedures. I never heard Dr. Sullivan's name mentioned again by anyone during the rest of the time I worked at the school.

In my regular job at the business library, I became increasingly aware of the enormous breadth and value of the library's resources. There was so much more information available for our business patrons than what they normally sought — information that could enhance their operational performance. As a business administration student, I myself had remained oblivious to the scope of available and accessible business information. It was some months after my library education, when I conceived of developing some type of instruction in business information sources for business students. In the fall of 1951, I developed an outline and syllabus for a proposed course to teach undergraduate business students how to find and use business information. I sent these materials to the deans of the business schools at both City College and Long Island University. There were some follow-up conversations with faculty members at both schools, but nothing concrete resulted.

Once my work at Brooklyn Academy had been concluded, the loss of the added income was sorely felt. My annual library salary was a little more than three thousand dollars. The Veterans Administration was in the process of reviewing my ten-percent disability pension with the aim of discontinuing it. I felt there was no reasonable way to protest its loss; I was not truly disabled and I had taken full advantage of the payments when I needed them most. I began to consider other means of increasing my modest income. There seemed to be no way I could advance my position at the business library other than to accept very limited, annual in-grade increments. I was a little more than two years beyond library school and had a total of three years work experience at the Brooklyn Public Library. I thought it might be time to try to move into a role in public library administration. Mr. St. John had explicitly spoken during his orientation talks about how the Brooklyn Public Library would be an institution committed to grooming public library administrators. I decided to seek out his counsel about my career prospects.

I met with St. John late in the fall of 1951. I described to him the financial pressure I was feeling. I asked him whether it might be time for me to try for a post as librarian of a public library in a small city. "What about becoming head of the science and industry division at Central?" he replied. "We have a vacancy there and that's a higher grade than your present level." His proposal took me by surprise. I had no background in this field; moreover, I knew that at least two of the reference staff in this department had far more experience in the library than I. All I knew about science and industry was what I had learned during my military training in radio repair. St. John was undaunted. "You'll pick up what you need on the job," was his swift retort. If he was willing, I was willing. Before I left his office, we agreed that I would be transferred from the business library to Central Library as the chief of the science and industry division, effective January 1, 1952, at a salary of $4,400 a year.

My parents had by this time relocated to an apartment better suited to their needs. My sister, Marilyn, who had completed her study at Brooklyn College, married a young engineer named Ed Foodim. Family ties with my parents, and with Clara's large number of siblings and their children, occupied a great deal of my free time. My close friends Sonny, Davey, Murray, and a number of others had all married and moved out of the neighborhood. I had gradually drifted away from them as our lives had taken different paths. Davey joined the New York City Police Department as a patrolman. Sonny was selling insurance policies to poor families. Following completion of his accounting degree, Murray had joined the staff of the Internal Revenue Service. Clara and I continued to live in the same apartment with Clara's mother and our baby daughter, Jacqueline. We tried to spend one weekend afternoon each week visiting my parents. Jacqueline had become a delighted consumer of my mother's traditional Saturday luncheon fare — the same boiled chicken and chicken soup of my childhood. The sight of her granddaughter enjoying the food gave my mother great joy. Here was a lovely child to "fix."

My new salary and savings enabled us to buy our first car. I took some driving lessons, acquired a license, and in December 1951, just short of my twenty-eighth birthday, bought my first automobile. I bought the car in Yonkers under the terms of a fleet agreement that my sister, Marilyn, arranged for me. It was the least expensive Ford four-door sedan. The price of twelve hundred dollars was the largest expenditure I had ever made in my life. A car was scarcely a necessity in New York; still, it was the luxury those of my generation avidly sought. It would make family visiting easier and permit more comfortable family outings to the parks and seashore. I would be able to forego the subway and drive daily to my new job at the Brooklyn Public Library Central Library at Grand Army Plaza.

The Best of Times

I felt wistful leaving the business library. I had enjoyed my work there and I had come to respect and admire the wisdom of my supervisor, Jesse Cross. The science and industry department was one of the major reference units in the Brooklyn Public Library's central branch. The library encompassed several other subject divisions and a children's division. Administrative offices were on the upper floors, as were the cataloging and classification departments of the library system. The director of central library programs was Corrine Sheppard. She was a gentle and gracious lady from the South who had long experience at the Brooklyn Public Library. Her deputy was Marino Ruffier, a dapper New Yorker who was impeccably attired and constantly in motion. He reminded me of a department store floorwalker. Among my colleagues as division chiefs, Sylvia Mechanic, then head of the neighboring department of social sciences, was the one with whom our subject responsibilities most closely overlapped. Sylvia was an impatient, all-business person. She had a keen, active intelligence and sound experience, making her a formidable reference person. My assistant, Dorothy Goodman, was a six-year veteran of the department. She had a far stronger subject background in the sciences than I. Each member of a subject division staff was rotated through the day and evening at the department reference service desk for about half of the time they worked. Sometimes, during peak hours, two staff members covered the desk.

My arrival was not greeted with pleasure. Fellow division chiefs felt that my promotion to senior-level department head at the Central Library was premature for someone with such limited experience and subject knowledge. Dorothy Goodman resented my leapfrogging past her, especially since I had no experience with the subject field and would need to be trained in the use of the collection. Corrine Sheppard regarded me warily as an ambitious protégé of Mr. St. John's. She perceived me as a threat to her in her position as head of Central Library services. Marino Ruffier looked upon my appointment with detachment and bemusement, waiting to see how I would adjust.

I worked with nervous zeal at mastery of as much of the subject matter of the department as I could. There was great irony in the way I had to rely on my assistant, Dorothy, for so many weeks. In spite of her sharp resentment, however, she was a painstaking and patient trainer. I sympathized with her awkward position, yet reasoned that I had not conspired to cheat her out of the promotion that she felt should have been hers. I understood fully her displeasure and sought to make her realize how much I depended upon and appreciated her help and counsel. I could never compete with her in subject mastery. I assured her that I would defer to her judgement in all matters where she was better informed. I would simply do my best to carry out my administrative duties fairly and honestly on her behalf and on behalf of the other four librarians in our unit. Dorothy Goodman possessed a strong self-deprecating sense of humor and a warm heart. In a couple of months we had become more than just colleagues; we had become good and trusting friends.

It did not take very long to get through Sylvia Mechanic's brusque veneer. We both shared a strong interest in economics, which was one of the main elements of her social sciences department. I soon discovered that Sylvia was a closet business librarian who envied my experience at the business library. She lived in Brooklyn Heights close to the business library on Montague Street and had a substantial background in finance and investments. It was not until some years later that she realized her aspiration and was transferred to the business library. A good ten years my senior, Marino Ruffier became my close friend. I admired his sleek appearance and his whimsical view of life. He had a relaxed and unthreatening demeanor in his relations with the library's users. It didn't matter whether the person was a ragged vagrant, a confused adolescent, or an expensively attired dowager; he was always helpful and pleasant. Every patron received the same patient attention and thoughtful explanation of where and how the appropriate library department would be pleased to assist.

At the central building, I was called upon to participate in system-wide activities. When I joined the main branch in 1952, Mr. St. John had engaged Irving Lieberman, a doctoral student at Columbia (he would later become the director of the University of Washington Library School), to serve as a member of the library's senior management team. He was responsible for public services and I soon found myself working with him on committees.

In June of 1952, I was called upon to carry out an exciting special assignment from the library's administrative headquarters. As a member of the American Library Association since 1949, I kept up with the ALA's workings through the library literature and the association's monthly periodical. It was in this way that I learned that the annual meeting would be held in New York in June 1952 and that Francis St. John had been appointed convention chairman. In the fall of 1951, St. John had begun to make appointments to various committees that would oversee the smooth running of the conference. Librarians from many different New York

THE BEST OF TIMES

City libraries were asked to serve. The Brooklyn Public Library staff in particular was assigned heavy responsibilities in this work. I had not been invited to participate. I thought I was being spared because I was new in my job and I needed more time to get accustomed to my new position.

By mid-February, I was summoned to meet with St. John. He politely inquired how things were going. Before I could respond he chuckled and remarked how he had heard how well I was doing. Then he got right to the point. He understood that I was an ALA member, and he wanted me to consider an idea he had: a possible innovation that he thought might add to the services provided by the convention's local arrangements committee. He wanted to issue a daily newsletter during the convention that would carry late-breaking news and features. The newsletter would be distributed free in the entrance halls to everyone attending the meetings. What did I think of this? I thought it sounded like a useful and imaginative idea. He wanted to know if I could do it. In my usual brash manner, I said that I was sure I could if I had the right help. He wanted to know exactly what I thought I would need. I blurted out that I would require half a dozen people from the Brooklyn Public Library staff who would be available for planning sessions before the conference began. They would have to be relieved of work responsibilities two days before the start of the convention and for its duration. I added that I would need access to paper, supplies, and duplicating equipment in the administrative offices, where the newsletter would be prepared. We would also need a small budget for the commercial preparation of the printing plates. The Library's staff truck and driver would be needed to deliver copies to the convention center in Manhattan for each day of the conference. St. John quickly concluded the meeting by telling me that I had the job and that I could have everything that was needed. He shook my hand, slapped my back, and ushered me out. He was true to his word. Everything I had specified was made available. I left our discussion excited by the prospect of reliving, if only for a brief interlude, my high school and military newspaper days. What I did not know then was that St. John anticipated being a candidate for the ALA presidency the following year. His work to make the 1952 convention an extraordinary success would clearly enhance his prospects for election. The daily convention paper was only one of his unique contributions. Others included a galaxy of special events and renowned speakers, most notably, Eleanor Roosevelt.

I had little difficulty assembling my editorial staff. My assistant editor was Larry Allen, who worked in a branch library. He was a key contributor and the most troublesome team member. In later years he became a well-known human relations consultant and library educator. Esther Helfand, with whom I had first worked at the Saratoga Branch when she was a part-time student assistant, joined me. So did Leon Crain, my library school classmate. St. John never once inquired about our progress. Consistent with his general managerial philosophy, once he delegated a task he left its conduct fully in the hands of the individual he had selected.

I spent that spring juggling my efforts to master my new responsibilities in the science and industry department with getting ready to produce the convention paper. Well before the conference, we had prepared our logo and headers for the *ALA Daily Reporter*. We chose the size of the paper and worked out a production schedule. Editorial responsibilities were also assigned and understood. The library staff artist had even prepared some of the cartoons that would be inserted in the columns of every issue. We were ready to go once the conference began.

The days of the ALA convention, in June of 1952, run together in my mind as a blur of long days and sleep-deprived nights. None of us on the paper's staff had time to enjoy the conference presentations or social occasions. The one treat I permitted myself was to listen to the inimitable inflections of Mrs. Roosevelt through a loudspeaker that reached the overflow of the audience in a separate room outside the main convention hall. My mind was fully engaged with reworking her inspiring remarks into a pithy summary for inclusion in the next day's issue. The editorial team tried to cover as many of the most newsworthy sessions as possible. Between times, we scouted the exhibition halls for unusual sights or events. Late each evening we returned to the library in Brooklyn and labored over the layout, makeup, and physical production of the next day's issue. By late night, the copies were assembled, bundled, and made ready for delivery to convention headquarters. We would arise wearily and travel again into Manhattan to cover the next day's program and events. In a memorandum to St. John afterward, I reported that we had distributed five daily issues: 22,000 copies in all. The costs including paper, multi-lith plates, supplies, and incidental expenses came to $269. I appended a list of do's and don't's for future editors at later conventions. The *ALA Daily Reporter* would win no Pulitzer Prize, but we had made library history producing the first daily conference newspaper.

At the library and elsewhere in the profession St. John's stewardship of the convention was seen as a personal triumph. It added to his reputation as one of the foremost public library directors in the United States. After three years of his leadership, which included the popularity of his in-service training program, the Brooklyn Public Library had gained prominence among ambitious library school graduates who sought to join its ranks. Many of the best candidates across the country were recruited. St. John developed a group of energetic senior staff as part of his top-level team. Morale was high and there was a feeling of optimism for good things to come. It was a halcyon time for the Brooklyn Public Library.

With the ALA meeting over, I settled back into my regular routine. I had by then learned enough to perform credibly as a science reference librarian. Whenever I felt out of my depth because of my limited subject competence, I would call for help from Dorothy or another of my colleagues who were better prepared to cope with subjects like chemistry or biology than I would ever be. I never achieved the self-assurance in this assignment that I had enjoyed in the business library. This lacuna in subject knowledge underscored for me that my role as division head was only a career way station. At some point, I would need to move on to another assignment. The success of the convention newspaper had bolstered my standing at the library, and I felt that my long-range prospects at the Brooklyn Public Library were highly favorable. Following the ALA meeting, I was invited to become a member of an ALA committee. With St. John's encouragement, I accepted the invitation on the basis of his assurance that the library would fund my participation in the association's 1953 meeting in Los Angeles. Late in the fall of 1952, it was announced that St. John was a candidate for the ALA presidency. He would be running against Quincy Mumford, of the Cleveland Public Library. There was little doubt among any of us who knew St. John that he would win the contest. The large contingent of Brooklyn Public Library staffers expected to attend the 1953 Los Angeles Conference was most likely part of a strategy to ensure a strong staff presence when his presidential victory would be announced.

By the summer of 1952, family matters had suddenly taken a turn for the worse. My mother, who had been plagued by illness for some months, required a serious operation from which she was struggling to fully recover. My sister, Marilyn, also became ill. By autumn my daughter, Jacqueline, who was normally very robust, developed recurrent respiratory infections. Our pediatrician advised that she spend the late fall and winter in a warm climate. Clara's oldest brother, Fred, was in Miami Beach operating a business for the season. He arranged housing for Clara, her mother, and Jacqueline near where he and his wife were living. I remained in New York while they traveled south by train to spend two or three months while Jacqueline regained her health. Meanwhile, the family was beginning to lose confidence in the elderly doctor who treated my mother. He continued to offer reassurances that it was only a matter of time before she would feel perfectly fine. I remember driving my mother to a doctor's appointment and finding the atmosphere of his office dark and depressing. During this time my sister had not yet recovered, which only added to the family's general anxiety and to my mother's own worries. Finally, in early 1953, we prevailed upon my mother to see a younger doctor who had a practice nearby. Following her visit and a series of laboratory tests, this doctor informed her that she would need another operation. Arrangements were made for surgery early in March. Clara, her mother, and Jacqueline had returned from Florida late in January. By that time, Jacqueline was once again pink and chubby and looking very healthy. I was beginning to feel more optimistic.

Then came my mother's operation. We learned immediately following surgery that the procedure had been too late. The cancer had spread and was inoperable. The incision was merely stitched back together. We were informed that she probably had only a few months to live. The family decided not to reveal the truth to my mother and to give her hope for recovery. My mother was only fifty-three years old. That spring was the worst of times. My Aunt Rose, by then the mother of two small children, accepted the role of caregiver. My mother was moved to Rose's small apartment in Queens, where she was told she would spend the time needed for her convalescence. Rose and my mother had always been close. She was pleased to be in Rose's welcoming home. Even though my mother suffered post-operative discomfort, pain medication was helpful. Everyone sought to comfort her with frequent visits, and the first few weeks went relatively well.

On the job I was greatly distracted by my anguish about my mother's condition. Everyone whom I worked with was supportive and empathetic. It was during this time that we learned that Clara was pregnant with our second child, who would be born in the fall. My mother was overjoyed to learn that she would have a second grandchild. My heart was torn by the realization that she would probably not live long enough to see the child. It was precisely at this time that I received a telephone call from the Alumni Affairs Office of the Columbia University Library School. I was told that I had been recommended for a position at Cornell University, even though I had not inquired about any opportunities. The prospect of leaving New York City during that trying period was the last thing I could imagine. I dismissed it completely from my mind. A few days later I received a formal letter from Stephen McCarthy, director of the Cornell University Library. He invited me on behalf of Edward Litchfield, the dean of the newly established Graduate School of Business and Public Administration, and himself, to come to Ithaca, New York, to discuss an appointment as librarian and assistant professor. The job would start in September 1953. I was inclined to dismiss their invitation out of hand, but before doing so I had a talk with my father. To my complete surprise, he strongly encouraged me to look into this prospect. He felt that I owed it to my family to at least learn more about the job. I conceded and unenthusiastically flew to Ithaca to meet with McCarthy and Litchfield.

The Cornell campus dazzled me. It towered majestically over the valley and Lake Cayuga. The new school and its library were lodged in McGraw Hall, a handsome older building on the west side of the main quadrangle. Stephen McCarthy hosted my visit. Ed Litchfield was constantly traveling; he would be on campus for only part of one day during my visit. McCarthy was an experienced academic library administrator. He had come to Cornell several years before on a mission to centralize coordination and standardization among a loose confederation of semi-autonomous libraries spread across the campus and closely attached to their academic units. His office was in the landmark library tower building. From McCarthy I learned in sober and measured tones, that he saw the position as something of an experiment. It was to be a joint appointment, supported equally by the library and the school. As librarian, the incumbent would report administratively to him. As an assistant professor, the chosen candidate would be accountable to the Dean. McCarthy seemed to convey little enthusiasm for this arrangement. I shrugged off his skepticism as a personality trait. My impression of the position at that point was one of indifference. Then I went to see Edward Litchfield.

As I sat waiting for my interview to begin, I could not help but feel the energy and dynamism of Litchfield's office. The phone rang incessantly. People moved with purpose around and through the offices. The air crackled with electricity. Ed Litchfield was ten minutes late. He ushered me into his office and invited me to sit in a comfortable chair facing his desk. There was a large picture window behind him that looked out on Lake Cayuga. He apologized for the delay and explained that he had been in a telephone conference with General Lucius Clay in Europe. He had worked with General Clay until a few weeks earlier as director of civil affairs in Germany.

The Best of Times

Litchfield was then just short of forty and had had a meteoric rise. Simultaneous with his recent appointment as dean of the new graduate program at Cornell, he served also as executive secretary of the American Political Science Association in Washington, DC, where he commuted regularly. He instructed his secretary that he would take no calls. He asked me to fill him in on my background and experience. I spoke for about ten minutes, highlighting my personal and professional history. He then began to speak. His manner was warm and gracious, but his words conveyed passion and conviction. He was going to build a great program, he said, in which business and public administration would find their common intersection. He believed intellectually in the universality of the administrative process—that people schooled in administration could bring their skills to bear in virtually any setting whether corporate, governmental, or non-profit. As part of such a graduate educational offering, he recognized the intrinsic importance of an outstanding professional school library. He envisaged the person who would direct the library as a teaching and research member of the school faculty. This person would offer formal instruction in bibliography and research methods and occupy an important place on the faculty. The person who took on the position would be subject to the same review and evaluative process as the other professors. He told me that there were only three people in the United States who had been identified who combined librarianship with an expertise in one of the substantive fields of the school. He had already met and talked with the other two. I had been saved for last. I was the right age, he said, ideally poised to move into the type of demanding role that he needed to fill. If I came to Cornell, I could count on his full commitment to assure the needed financial resources to build a great library. I would also have the solid support of a growing faculty that would share his views of the centrality of my role to the school's future. Litchfield was the most articulate and spellbinding speaker I had ever encountered. It was clear to me that it was his conviction, not McCarthy's, that was reflected in the unique nature of the position to be filled. We had been talking together for about half an hour when his secretary interrupted to say that he had to leave at once to make his flight to Washington. Litchfield ushered me out, looked me in the eye, and spoke convincingly about how much he hoped I would join his team. I was overwhelmed.

Before I left Ithaca, I met some of the senior staff of the library and faculty members of the school. I was driven around the town and nearby environs. It was all very impressive—the campus with its gracious buildings and age-old trees; the community's small-town flavor; the celebrated lake and park. It all seemed so picturesque, yet so fundamentally different from my big-city habitat. I returned to New York deeply uncertain about whether to consider the position seriously. One week later, I received another letter from McCarthy, written on both his and Litchfield's behalf. I was offered an appointment as assistant professor and librarian of the Graduate School of Business and Public Administration. I would start work in September 1953, at a salary of $6,000 per year.

I showed the letter to Clara. She expressed reluctance to leave her familiar haunts. The new baby was expected in late September or early October. Without her mother's help managing two kids, one newborn, in strange new surroundings would be very difficult. If I considered it a very important career step however, she would reluctantly go along. My father was totally encouraging. He thought that living in Ithaca and being associated with such a great university was too good an opportunity to miss. I decided to talk to my mother about it; she said very much what my father had. My sense was that they must have already discussed it together before I broached the subject. I painstakingly weighed the pros and cons of the move. My salary would go from $4,800 to $6000. It would be necessary to move some furnishings and buy more. Ithaca seemed an ideal setting for raising a family. I had been anticipating moving in time to a post as director of a city public library; this would be a lateral move. My earlier idea for a course in business information services, which had failed to find support, would fit exactly into Litchfield's plans. The decision was a difficult call.

It was early May 1953. The results of the ALA election were not known, but the Brooklyn Public Library had a fair-sized delegation ready to travel to Los Angeles to attend the June meeting. I arranged an appointment to talk to Mr. St. John. When we met, I described to him in candid terms my personal and family situation. I also told him that I had not actively sought another position. I shared with him my feelings about the job offer and about McCarthy and Litchfield. St. John's counsel in the past had been invaluable, and I asked again for his advice. He told me that he had heard from my colleagues that my mother was dying. He deeply sympathized and was certain that she would want me to do whatever was best for my family. Then he said that if I decided to remain in the public library field, he envisioned me moving into a job like his own within a dozen years. He regretted that there was nothing he could offer me at the moment in the Brooklyn Public Library that could compete with the Cornell offer. He added that a few years in academia doing what I had described would stand me in good stead when I was ready to move back to public library work. He thought the Brooklyn Public

The Best of Times

Library would feel the loss, and he personally would miss my presence on the staff. His considered opinion was almost the same as my father's had been; the offer was too good to pass up. I told him that, although I was scheduled to attend the ALA meeting, if I accepted Cornell's offer, I would have to leave the library at the end of August. He was adamant that I come to the meeting in Los Angeles. St. John wished me good luck and thanked me for my contributions to the library over the past five years. That night, I accepted McCarthy's offer and agreed to begin in early September.

Dorothy Goodman and Sylvia Mechanic said they would miss me and were sorry that I was leaving. I promised Dorothy that my last act as chief of the science and industry division would be to recommend her for promotion as my successor. She said that she would rather have me remain. Marino Ruffier said that he would come to visit me in Ithaca since he had always wanted to see Cornell. The ALA meeting was almost upon us, and I arranged for my first transcontinental flight to the West Coast. Shortly before the delegation was to leave for California, we learned the shattering news — Quincy Mumford had defeated St. John in the election for the ALA presidency. We were incredulous and could not understand how this had happened. St. John was so charismatic and dynamic. Mumford by contrast was a colorless candidate who seemed to epitomize a male version of the archetypal librarian, without the gray bun. It was months later when we learned that in a two-person race for the ALA presidency, the candidate from the South historically always won. Mumford was from the South, and St. John was the director of a major public library in a city that many across the country loved to hate.

Not long after the Mumford election, President Eisenhower made the first appointment in many years of a Librarian of Congress who was actually a library professional. His choice was Quincy Mumford. Over the entire period of Mumford's long and prudent tenure, I could never help but feel that St. John would have brought far greater dynamism to the appointment, if he had been the one to win the election and to receive the Library of Congress appointment. At the ALA conference, the Brooklyn Public Library contingent was enormously disappointed by St. John's defeat. He accepted the loss graciously but was not much in evidence during the sessions. The meetings were lively, the conference well attended, and it was my first visit to California. Yet, I was full of misgivings and guilt the whole time; I was leaving the library and my mother had taken a turn for the worse. Matters had reached the stage where it was difficult for Rose to deal with my mother's medical needs in her cramped apartment, where she had to constantly scold her two small daughters for being too noisy.

Back in New York, I learned that my father had made arrangements for my mother to be moved to a nursing home, where she would receive around-the-clock care. I was dismayed by how my mother had deteriorated in my short absence. By the end of June, she was in a new environment with none of the homelike qualities of Rose's apartment. She was bedridden virtually all the time. The nursing home was about twenty minutes from the library, and I visited as often as I could during the week. On the weekends, I drove my father, Clara, and Jacqueline to visit. As the summer progressed, my mother slept more and more of the time. She could eat very little and suffered considerable pain. Soon, it became too disturbing for Clara and Jacqueline to continue their visits. My mother's suffering was taking its toll on my well-being and spirits as well; I slept very badly. I struggled at work, but everyone understood my circumstances. I would soon be leaving anyway. What concerned me most was my father's anguish. He was living alone in my parents' apartment and not taking care of himself. The family invited him over for meals, but he would only occasionally accept. He was a very proud and independent person, and he didn't wish to be any trouble to anyone. He did his best to weather this difficult period, but he lost weight and was less his usual optimistic self. The summer months of 1953 were the most trying of my life. My mother finally succumbed on August 31, the hottest and most humid day of that year. The attending doctor expressed surprise that she had survived so long. The family was relieved that my mother had finally come to rest and would no longer have to endure so much suffering and pain. I left New York the day after my mother's funeral.

Chapter Eight

When I reached Ithaca, I checked into the YMCA, where I planned to remain until I could rent a suitable apartment. Very early the next day, I found my way up the hill to the deserted Cornell campus. School was not scheduled to begin for two and a half more weeks. Only a few of the faculty had returned to their offices. My office was a spacious, high-ceilinged room, which afforded a breath-taking view of Lake Cayuga. Mrs. Cassavant, a middle-aged woman who had served as the library's circulation assistant for several months, cheerfully filled me in on what had gone before. She offered to help me in any way she could. Litchfield was expected in his office later that morning, and we were to meet. When I called McCarthy's office, I learned to my surprise that he was on leave for the year on a Fulbright Professorship in Egypt. G. F. Shepherd, Jr. was the acting librarian until his return. I had met and liked Shepherd from my earlier visit, and I scheduled a meeting with him that afternoon. I plunged into my work, establishing the framework for my course preparation and laying out the library's short-term staff and acquisition requirements. The library had only a small collection; it had served principally as a reserve reading room for courses. There was scarcely any reference collection, and no reference service had ever been provided. Selection of materials and collection development would be initiated in the school, but acquisition, cataloging, classification, processing, and preparation of books for use, were all centralized for the library system. These functions were administered by the technical services department in the central library, under the direction of Felix Reichmann. Building a first-rate library was going to take a long time. I would need help to accomplish it. The only staff members were Mrs. Cassavant and a half-time office assistant. There was a very modest budget for the hiring of part-time student help to cover the circulation desk, shelve books, file services, and carry out other clerical tasks. I went to my meeting with Litchfield armed with a list of my needs for staff and for funds to support the ambitious acquisition program I envisaged.

Litchfield welcomed me warmly. He listened carefully to the agenda I presented for the library's development. He concurred with everything I proposed, and assured me that I would have his enthusiastic support in my discussions with the library officials. I left his office buoyed by his encouragement. My meeting with Shepherd was cordial and pleasant. I reported to him how I had described to Litchfield the requirements for building the library, and that I had gained his unqualified endorsement. Shepherd informed me that the library administration had budgeted only a portion of the money I would require, but he agreed to see if further money could be found elsewhere in the overall library appropriation. Our discussion was relaxed and went on far longer than the time I spent with Litchfield. Shepherd was interested in details about my family; he asked where I was staying and what arrangements I had made for moving the family to Ithaca. The conversation ended with Shepherd inviting me to come to his home late that afternoon for a swim with his family at one of the neighboring parks. I would be their guest afterward for an informal dinner.

I spent an unforgettable evening with Shep, his wife, Margaret, and his amiable teenage son and daughter. By the end of that first day on the campus, I was tired, lonely, and still deeply troubled by the events of the last few days. It was a welcome respite to find myself surrounded by such charming people. They extended their friendship and hospitality to me at a time when I badly needed a boost of morale. I came to understand later that such generosity was a Shepherd family hallmark. Every moment I spent with them that first summer evening seemed alive with joy and laughter—from splashing in the foam under the waterfall at Buttermilk Falls State Park to our meal of fresh corn, salad, and cold cuts. I left the Shepherd home that night feeling the companionable glow of their memorable introduction to the world of Cornell and Ithaca.

I spent my first weeks settling in. I searched for an apartment and prepared for teaching my class. I also began the library's development. I was so caught up in work, I felt relieved that Clara and Jacqueline had remained in New York to await the birth of the baby, instead of accompanying me. I located a modest apartment at the edge of town and furnished it simply and then concentrated completely on the other tasks before me. Litchfield had telephoned Shepherd, at my urging, to reinforce my plea for needed resources. I was encouraged to learn that our requirements would be met. At the first faculty meeting before the semester got underway, I met my new colleagues and found them fully supportive of the initiatives I had spelled out for the library's development. In my new post, I found myself linked more closely to my faculty colleagues than to my library associates. There were several reasons for this. My office and the library were located within the school building, distant from the central library. I was in frequent contact with people from the school. I also identified most strongly with Litchfield's vision for the school. My teaching role and the library's place in the program were not based on McCarthy's viewpoint, nor on the opinions of others who worked in the library. With my academic background, I shared greater common intellectual interests with the faculty than with any of the library staff. Finally, my performance would be measured based on research I submitted to a peer review of my faculty colleagues. They would gauge whether or not I met criteria for tenure and promotion to associate professor. In this respect, my professorial rank and status differed from everyone else engaged in library work at Cornell. I needed to perform well in my teaching of the required course in bibliography and research methods. I was also required to conduct a rigorous program of research and writing. My success in the library would rest on the growth of the library collection, and the development of an effective reference service for students and faculty.

Faculty members were divided between those drawn from the business and economic sector and those in public administration. The most widely recognized professor was Mel de Chazeau, an economist who concentrated on the influence of governmental regulation on business activity. John G.B. Hutchins, another senior professor, taught transportation economics and interstate trade. Arthur Nilsson and Robert "Ducky" Holmes, the first a full professor and the second an associate professor, both had worked with the Securities and Exchange Commission in Washington, DC, before joining academia to teach finance and investment analysis. Bill Shannon, who had a legal and accounting background, offered the course work in accounting. John "Mac" Rathmell was a recently appointed assistant professor of marketing. On the public side, Miller Hillhouse was a national authority on municipal administration and public finance. Paul Van Riper's specialty was the federal civil service and governmental history. Litchfield's work focused on public administration. His career had earlier led him to managerial assignments with the Panama Canal Authority followed by the most senior role in the post-war civil governance of Germany. He was responsible for teaching the required course in administration for all first-year MBA and

MPA students. Two new professors joined the faculty with me. David Thomas, who was still completing his Ph.D., taught basic and cost accounting. Richard Neustadt came to the university straight from the White House where he had been among the entourage of young intellectuals surrounding President Truman. He was slated to work with Litchfield in the teaching of administration.

While Ed Litchfield articulated the substantive commonalities between business and public administration in his lectures and writings, many of the faculty were deeply skeptical. As they saw it, business was business and public administration was government. In the fall of 1953, I may have been his most loyal disciple. The idea of identifying the elements of the administrative process that were common to every enterprise struck a chord with me. With my background in libraries and business economics, I was already a man in the middle. Litchfield was an eloquent spokesman for his position on the universality of the administrative process, and he used his unifying motif to foster openness in both areas of the program. Publicly, at least, there was no debate, or discord, about his view among the faculty. In private, however, a number of the faculty, particularly on the business side, saw Litchfield's notion as patently specious. Litchfield was aware of divided opinions. In order to allay concerns, he would bolster the faculty with early appointments of scholars, who came from neither business nor public administration, but from the behavioral sciences. He viewed these appointments as the integrating element between the two camps. He understood that research and instructional offerings in business and public administration could be enriched with insights from such disciplines as sociology and anthropology.

My commute by car to the campus took only ten minutes. I spent long days and evenings in my office. I took most of my meals at the spacious and comfortable Willard Straight Hall, which was the campus student union. From my office in McGraw Hall, the Straight was a short walk. My other dining option was the Rathskeller, an informal dining club for faculty in the newly built Statler Hotel School building, located near the Willard Straight. During those early weeks, Ed Litchfield and his wife gave a couple of cocktail parties for the faculty at their spacious modern home in Cayuga Heights—a well-to-do suburb of the campus. One or two faculty wives invited me to dinner when they learned that my family was still in New York. In no time I became acclimated to the campus and to the region with its rich beauty of enormous valleys, deep gorges, and glorious fall foliage.

The Best of Times

On September 28th, my brother-in-law, Hy, called to tell me that Clara had just given birth to our second child and first boy, Steven. I flew Mohawk Airlines from Ithaca to Newark Airport, and was in the hospital that evening to see my wife and new son. Three days later, I was back in Ithaca to teach my next class. Clara planned to fly to Ithaca in two weeks with the children. Her mother would come along to help her for a week or so.

By early October, my course was well underway and I had completed the syllabus and reading list. I also prepared the topical framework for the semester's offering. I was scheduled to repeat the course during the spring term for the second half of the first-year group of students. I met with Litchfield to learn what criteria would be used to evaluate my performance after three years, when my faculty review came up. He was clear that, in order to satisfy the promotion and tenure committee, I would be expected to publish a number of articles in reputable, professional journals, or a book issued by a recognized publisher. In order to gain promotion to associate professor, I needed a strategy that would ensure the success of my scholarly efforts. For the time being, I was too caught up between managing the library's buildup and staying one step ahead of my lectures and class meetings.

My family was with me by mid-October. By the time Clara's mother returned to New York, we were settled into a small, but comfortable, bungalow apartment near the edge of the city. Shopping and parks were nearby, and the housing development was filled with other young families. Jacqueline was almost four, so the absence of a school nearby didn't cause any concern. Living in New York with Clara's mother had habituated us to using her dishes, silverware, and the like. We had never acquired any of our own. Starting from scratch, we bought very inexpensive tableware and cutlery and deferred any unessential purchases until we had more money. With two little children under foot, such domestic niceties were the last things we were concerned about. We hadn't reckoned with the cultural conventions of one of my colleagues.

John Hutchins was a scholar and gentleman of the old school. With his New England manners, he considered an early visit to welcome a new colleague a social obligation. When he learned that my family had now come to Ithaca, his wife telephoned to announce their intention of calling on us. We invited them for afternoon tea on Sunday. It happened to be an especially chaotic day in our household. Baby Steve was crankier than usual and Jacqueline was in an obstreperous mood as well. The small living room could barely accommodate four adults. I bought some cake, but our cups, saucers, and dishes looked as if they had come straight off the low-end variety store shelves, which they had. I cringed at the thought of the dreadful impression we would make on the very proper Hutchins. Then they arrived.

The smartly attired, Mrs. Hutchins accompanied her large tweedy husband into our home. She was matronly yet endearing, while Hutchins spoke in ponderous tones. They behaved as if our cramped space were a suite at the Waldorf Astoria. John balanced Jacqueline on his lap, delighted her with an endless litany of nursery rhymes. His wife had Steve cooing and smiling from the time she took him in her arms. They sipped their tea, ate their cake, and complimented us on our charming place and our beautiful children. They thanked us generously for the refreshments. They must have spent an hour with us. They seemed perfectly relaxed during all this time and sounded genuinely appreciative of the little we had to offer. As they were leaving, they invited us to what they called, "a little dinner get-together," for some of the faculty on the following weekend. We breathed a great sigh of relief at their departure, pleased to have survived what we had feared would be a social embarrassment for us all.

A maid took our coats that next weekend at the Hutchins's spacious home in Cayuga Heights. The evening started with cocktails, and was followed by a sit-down dinner for about twenty people. The Hutchinses were just as gracious as hosts to this large throng at home as they had been when visiting our tiny apartment. I often had stormy differences with John on academic questions. We were drawn from exceedingly different class and cultural backgrounds. He and his wife, however, had endeared themselves to me forever with the warmth of their humanity and the kindness of their spirit.

Once Clara and the children had come to Ithaca, my father began to miss Jacqueline and Steven. I had seen him only fleetingly when I came to New York after Steve's birth. I was very concerned about him. Many family members and friends invited him home for meals and visits, but he was living alone and fending for himself in unaccustomed ways. My mother's final weeks had taken a physical toll on him. He kept at his strenuous work, perhaps immersing himself in his job in order to keep from brooding about the loss of his wife. He promised to come to Ithaca for a long Thanksgiving weekend. I hoped he would extend his visit into a longer respite from work. He flew up for the holiday, and took great pleasure in frolicking with the kids. The Cornell campus impressed him. He took pride in visiting my office and in seeing my name, with the designation of assistant professor beside it, on the McGraw Hall faculty roster. Clara and I tried to fatten him up. I did not tell him that I thought he looked too thin, but I did implore him to remain with us in Ithaca for a few weeks. There was no one he needed to return to in New York and his job would be waiting whenever he went back. My arguments were unavailing. He insisted on flying back to New York Sunday evening in order to be at his shop Monday morning. When I saw him off at the airport, I told him we would be driving to New York in three weeks for the Christmas recess. On Monday morning my father awoke and took the train to work in Manhattan. In the subway car he fainted and fell out of his seat. Before he could be transported to a hospital, my father was dead of a heart attack. At his funeral service there were far many more people than I knew. Many spoke to me of their love and affection for him. This was little consolation. My father was buried exactly three months after my mother.

We returned to New York again at Christmas time and stayed with Clara's mother. We visited with Rose and her family. They were living in Queens, where they ran a dry goods store. We saw my grandparents, my sister, and her husband. We saw Clara's family during the school holiday as well. I was mourning my parents, and I felt disconsolate a good deal of the time. I could scarcely wait to get back to Ithaca, where I could immerse myself in my work and keep my sorrow at bay. My course was to be over early in January, but I knew there would be major modifications needed before I could teach the class again in the spring term. I had learned a good deal about how to restructure the lectures, sequence, content, and emphasis of the class. When I invited evaluations from students at the semester's end, I was not unduly disturbed to learn that they gave the class a mediocre rating. I knew I could improve it during the second semester and that I would teach better with the experience of the first semester behind me. It was customary for new offerings to receive poor student evaluations. An experimental course put forward for the first time invariably requires a few semesters before all the elements fall solidly into place. By then, the instructor is less self-conscious and uncertain about the material. Anecdotes to punctuate the discussion are comfortably slipped in at exactly the right point. Students become happier consumers and evaluators of the class by this time. The irony is that while the course has become more polished, it has also become less creative since its debut. I learned a great deal during my first classroom experience. I saw how to improve my teaching style and the course structure, but I also realized that I could turn the class content into a book, which would serve as the vehicle to influence my promotion. During the spring term I would be able to refine my ideas. There was no summer session, so I would begin writing the manuscript during the vacation period.

I had not forgotten the idea I had during my business library days. Working again in the business field, I was aware that in 1954 the Commerce Department book, *Price Sources*, was even more hopelessly out of date. An updated edition would be a useful reference contribution, but such an index would not meet the intellectual criteria for my promotion at Cornell. It was still worth doing, however, and would be of incalculable value to business librarians and their clients. I devised a strategy for completing the task by forming a committee of interested business librarians. The work could be divided equally among the members. I would propose the project to fellow members of the Business Division as a collaborative project, when I attended the June 1954, meeting of the Special Libraries Association. The tactic succeeded; a number of colleagues agreed to share the responsibilities. Upon return to Cornell, I divided up the content and prepared a procedure manual. I dispatched an equal portion of the material to each of the people who had agreed to participate. I was to receive their completed work in two years time for the 1956 Special Libraries Association meeting. I would then revise and edit the completed manuscript for publication by the Special Libraries Association late in 1956.

It was early in 1954 when Peter Nitollo, a recent library school graduate, was asked to be assistant librarian. He was expected to arrive in June from New Jersey, where he had been working in a public library. Nitollo was an outgoing and personable young man with a background of undergraduate course work in business and economics. He wanted academic library experience. We were in desperate need of a full-time librarian for our staff and he seemed promising. During the 1953-1954 academic year, we had made considerable progress. The library and its reference collection had been strengthened. A collection development policy, which outlined selection criteria consonant with the central library and with the library of the School of Industrial and Labor Relations — a strong corollary campus library program — had been prepared. A faculty library committee had participated in this process to ensure understanding and acceptance of the library's philosophy and strategy before presenting the plan to the full faculty for adoption.

My first year at Cornell passed quickly. The second semester's teaching went far more smoothly than the first. My thinking had crystallized enough that I had prepared a detailed outline for my projected book. When I described the project to Litchfield, he picked up the phone. Before I had left his office, he had made an appointment for me to discuss the prospective volume with the director of the Cornell University Press. Before summer, I had signed a contract to deliver the manuscript to the Press by the end of 1955. All that remained was for me to write it.

My early career efforts with the *Commodity Prices* manuscript and my book project for Cornell University Press, *Information for Administrators*, were the first steps leading me toward a personal philosophy of librarianship. The foundation was quite simple. I felt the defined boundaries of professional responsibility were too limiting. In my view, an effective professional contribution required performance beyond solely reacting to questions put by library users. I envisaged a more active librarianship, in which librarians anticipated client needs and prepared material to satisfy those needs, when the tools did not already exist. It would be a number of years before my idea would be transformed into a fully thought-out strategy.

The school year ended, and many of the faculty had gone. McGraw Hall was virtually empty, but the library staff was in place. Here was the ideal opportunity for me to forge ahead with my book. Before coming to Cornell, I had already written two or three articles for library periodicals. But authoring a book posed a far more daunting challenge. There was no one to orchestrate this effort but I myself. During those early days of July, I would reach my office early and quickly work through any library matters that required my attention. Then I would stop by Dave Thomas's office, where he was working on his dissertation for the University of Michigan Business School. We would head out to the Willard Straight for coffee, where I would pick up *The New York Times*. Back in the office I would plunge into its pages. By the time I was done it was lunchtime. I would then stroll to the Statler Club, enjoy a quick lunch in the Rathskeller, and then adjourn to the faculty lounge for coffee and conversation. Later in the afternoon, I would remember that I had promised to take the family to one of the parks. I would drive home without having written a single word.

It was not until around July 10th that I became aware of how I had been sidestepping my responsibility. I finally faced up to the realization that if I did not get to work there wouldn't be a book. I immediately gave up coffee at the Straight, reading the newspaper, and having lunch at the faculty club. It was only then that I began in earnest, for at least six hours each day, to research and write the material for the book. Once I had gained momentum, I frequently took my papers home and labored far into the night. By the fall semester, I had written a draft of several of the book's first chapters. I had also laid out a schedule to follow into the next school year. I imagined that I could complete a draft of the full manuscript by the end of August 1955. The timetable was crucial. Working backward in time from spring of 1956, when the peer committee for my promotion would meet to review my fate, I realized that I needed to have already published my book, or at least have a firm and imminent publication date. Cornell University Press was expecting the completed manuscript by end of 1955. It would be tough going, but I had never been afraid of hard work. Those wasted days in July frustrated and annoyed me.

Jacqueline would begin kindergarten in the fall of 1954. We needed to move near a public school. By end of August, we found something roomier and more comfortable than our first apartment. We moved to Ithaca's South Hill into an apartment in a two-family house that was on a pleasant, quiet street in a neighborhood of young families. We were within a ten-minute walk of a relatively new public school. Cornell was on Ithaca's east hill. South Hill was a community of modest homes and apartments. We lived within a half-hour to forty minutes by foot to the downtown area. The walk to Cornell headed down South Hill across a footbridge and over a gorge emerging at East Hill on the way to the campus. Our new home put me within forty-five minutes walking time of my office. I walked to and from work every day, except when a car was essential for some special purpose. Even during later moves, I always carefully arranged to live where I could continue walking to and from my office. I kept this up from 1954 until 1987, except for occasional periods when I worked temporarily elsewhere.

By the start of the 1954-1955 academic year, I was prepared to press ahead with my manuscript. Steve McCarthy had returned from his Fulbright year abroad and Shep had reverted to his role as assistant librarian. During McCarthy's absence, we had forged ahead with the library's expansion. With budgetary support from Shepherd and Litchfield's strong encouragement, in addition to faculty support, I assumed that McCarthy would be pleased with our progress. I was mistaken. He was openly annoyed with me. He said that my aggressive pursuit of funding had made it impossible for Shep not to give in to my demands. He was disturbed by what he saw as the overly rapid rate of the library's expansion.

Our differences were a classic case of conflicting priorities. McCarthy desired a balanced, even growth in resources for the entire university library system. He wanted equal attention and funding given to all aspects of the library development. In his view, the library for the Graduate School of Business and Public Administration should not move at an accelerated pace ahead of the other libraries. McCarthy's approach was measured and prudent. He thought that I had used unfair political leverage in enlisting Litchfield and the school faculty to overwhelm Shepherd, while he was in his temporary role as acting library director in McCarthy's absence. He felt we had coerced Shepherd to accede to my unreasonable demands. From my point of view, the slow, halting growth advocated by McCarthy was anathema. I was aligned with Litchfield's and the school's more ambitious designs. My commitment was not to the university's library system. Instead, I saw myself as an agent for the faculty. I was developing the library rapidly in order to bring it up to a level that would enhance Cornell's stature among its peers. I measured our progress against comparable institutions such as the University of Pennsylvania's Wharton Business School and Stanford University. McCarthy would have preferred me to identify more closely with him, and with the university libraries, but my destiny was more closely tied to the school. I zealously pursued my mission. It had been Litchfield and the promise of the school's future that had brought me to Cornell, not McCarthy and his library system. Furthermore, I saw no political advantage in being identified with the university library. I had no ambition to advance upward in the university library's administrative hierarchy. I was a specialist, responsible for a special library that was part of a larger system. My primary allegiance was to that specialty and to the faculty and students.

Our different philosophies made the relationship between McCarthy and me somewhat rancorous. He did, however, respect the way the faculty solidly supported my efforts. He knew that in any overt public expression of our differences, the school administration would stand by me. It took years before McCarthy and I developed a closer, more trusting work relationship. Later in my career, when I taught library administration, I drew upon this contentious relationship with McCarthy as a case study, illustrating the common clash of goals between administrators of university library systems and those of librarians of professional school libraries within such larger systems.

Higher education, at least at Cornell University in 1954, seemed to me to be undergoing a transformation in the ranks of its younger faculty. Older faculty members, like my colleague John Hutchins, were from a more affluent class. Before the War, the long years needed to pursue a doctorate that would lead to a teaching position required financial means that were only available to a select few. It was not until the GI Bill took hold that this changed. For the first time in American history, young men who had previously viewed working toward advanced degrees as impractical were now making their way into the teaching and research ranks. The presence of these newcomers was reflected in their differences in lifestyles. The older, more financially secure faculty would typically reside in the more exclusive suburbs. Those teachers who were new to academia gravitated toward lower middle-class communities in and around town. Differences in style of dress, though more subtle, were also in evidence. Younger faculty tended to wear less formal clothing. The cars were another badge of class. Established faculty drove big, expensive models and sports cars. The university itself was a democracy of the intellect. Sociological distinctions did not influence the more important academic or substantive issues facing the faculty community.

The fall of 1954 brought an influx of new faculty to Cornell. In keeping with Litchfield's strategy to build on the commonalities between business and public administration, he had encouraged the faculty to augment their ranks with teachers from the social sciences. Litchfield's view was that the study of administration would remain static without insights from the behavioral sciences. Here resided the logic for the addition of several new faculty: James Thompson, a sociologist; William McEwen, an anthropologist; and William Gore, a political scientist trained in the behavioral sciences. My former Columbia University instructor, Ernest Dale, served as an adjunct professor, flying into Ithaca from New York City two days a week. By then, Dale was well past his Ph.D. study; he had become a prominent management consultant and a best-selling American Management Association author. During this period, the university had received support from the Sloan Foundation to establish the Sloan Institute of Hospital Administration. This teaching and research program was designed to prepare students within the framework of the two-year MBA and MPA degree program for careers in hospital administration. The institute would have a director and several faculty members to provide a limited number of specialized courses and to advance the institute's research.

I had a strong interest in the administrative process, and I had been sitting in on some of Litchfield's and Neustadt's lectures. In the fall of 1954, Neustadt abandoned Cornell for Columbia University's political science department. With Litchfield committed to other responsibilities, Jim Thompson had to bear the brunt of teaching the required course in administration. Litchfield continued as executive secretary of the American Political Science Association in Washington, and served as a board member of several large American corporations. During this time, Litchfield's wife, Ann, was diagnosed with cancer. I found myself drawn to Thompson's lectures in administration; I wound up reading the class assignments as well. Once my curiosity was piqued, I sought to extend my understanding of the behavioral sciences through close and frequent interaction with Thompson, McEwen, and Gore. A year later, when the school decided to publish the *Administrative Science Quarterly* under Thompson's editorship, I was invited by Thompson to serve as the book review editor. I assumed this role from 1956 to 1961.

New faculty, new ideas, and Litchfield's ambitious plans made Cornell an exciting place in 1954 and 1955. The tempo of events was exhilarating. Many distinguished visitors were drawn to the campus for special colloquia. One outstanding occasion was a public lecture by Robert Moses, the celebrated power broker behind the development of New York City's highways, parks, and infrastructure. The event was enhanced when Litchfield invited the faculty to dine informally with Moses in a private room at the Statler Club. Moses regaled the group with an off-the-record, blunt, and hilarious account of his exploits. It featured vignettes of the egotism and ineptitude among the state and national political elite.

Work on my book was gradually moving forward, but at a slower pace than I would have wished. At the close of the fall semester, I learned from Nitollo that he would be leaving on February 1, 1955, to accept a post in New Jersey. The news caught me off balance. It was customary for people who had accepted a new library assignment to remain for at least a full academic year. I pointed this out to Nitollo, but he explained that the opportunity was too good to pass up. He and his wife wanted to return to New Jersey. He had already accepted the new position and made plans for moving. This meant that we had to begin our search for a successor at once. What at first seemed an unfortunate turn of events led to the fortuitous selection of Betsy Ann Olive. She was a promising young North Carolinian with a library degree and business experience in Chicago. She joined the library in the summer of 1955. The absence of Nitollo in the spring disrupted my writing timetable. Teaching class and devoting more time to library duties kept me fully occupied. I impatiently anticipated Betsy Ann's arrival, so that I could go on with my book project. Once Betsy Ann was in place, I feverishly resumed my work on the book. With two years of teaching behind me, I received the benefit of testing the ideas put forward in my book on four successive student groups.

Information for Administrators: A Guide to Publications and Services for Business and Government was intended to serve as a guide through the maze of information resources in the broad fields of business and governmental management. It synthesized the published sources with details of agencies, programs, and associations. It also explained how to identify and apply these resources. Some chapters were arranged by topic (legislation and regulation, local areas, international information, business administration, and public administration), while others were organized by source (governmental programs, trade groups, chambers of commerce, reference books, periodicals, and newspapers). Still other chapters dealt with methods of investigation, such as statistics and research. The novelty of this approach, and what seemed to appeal to Cornell University Press, was that the book was not intended as a bibliography or list of publications. It was designed to serve as an executive's manual of authoritative and up-to-date information that offered approaches useful in decision making.

Before the fall semester began, I had written all but one chapter. The concluding chapter was to be an exhaustive outline of all the data sources needed to build a full-scale profile of a city or county. It would include the key economic, sociological, cultural, and political facts, organized under twenty-eight major categories. For each topic there were to be innumerable sub-topics that identified the published sources in which the information could be found. I was following a method of analysis first advanced in *Outline for Making Surveys,* by the United States Bureau of Foreign and Domestic Commerce in 1944. I knew that the necessary research would slow me down once classes started. In an effort to meet my December deadline, I prevailed upon Dean Litchfield to allow me to use the services of the school's secretariat. They could type the final manuscript for me in a timely fashion. I also telephoned my friend Marino Ruffier at the Brooklyn Public Library and pleaded with him to review the drafts of chapters I had completed. While Ruffier read through everything, I would devote myself to completing the last unfinished chapter. I asked Betsy Ann to insulate me from any interruptions on library matters while I was in my office. At home, I explained the urgency of my submitting the work by year's end. If I did not complete the work by Christmas recess, we might have to forego our customary holiday sojourn in New York.

Everything went according to plan. Marino graciously read the chapters and mailed them to me with his editing suggestions. The school's office staff good-naturedly assigned priority to typing the material as they received it. I toiled ceaselessly to complete the detailed forty pages of the last chapter. Fortunately, the nature of this chapter's content made editing unnecessary. By December 15, the final manuscript was ready. I submitted it to the Cornell University Press before Christmas. By January 15, Dean Litchfield had prepared a preface in which he identified the book as the first in a series from the school to be known as the Cornell Studies in Policy and Administration. Betsy Ann Olive, whose interest was aroused by my dedication to this seemingly endless project, offered to prepare the index. It was then that I handed in an introduction to the volume. I acknowledged my indebtedness to all those who had made the book's completion possible. The Cornell University Press completed its final editorial review and put the book into production. In early March, I received the galley proofs for correction. One set of these galley proofs went to the faculty committee on promotion and tenure at the end of March. Soon afterward, Ed Litchfield informed me of the committee's unanimous recommendation for my promotion to associate professor. The finished product including Betsy Ann's index was 380 pages long. It appeared in print on June 1st, 1956. The dedication read: "To the memory of my parents, Sadie and Joe."

In time Clara and I had become used to life in Ithaca. We had become accustomed to the differences between small-town living and New York City. We didn't really miss the antics of impatient New Yorkers. However, the seeming indifference of Ithaca's local merchants to consumer demands was perplexing, when compared to the competitive retail strategies pursued in New York. We made do in Ithaca's small shops, and saved our more serious shopping for our visits to the city. Downtown Ithaca in the 1950's consisted of one long main street called State Street. This shopping area boasted only one small department store, Rothschilds. The store was a turn-of-the-century emporium with a sparse inventory that was located on three floors. The rest of downtown consisted of a number of smaller shops and restaurants, along with the usual range of service establishments. Ithaca had four movie theaters at that time; two of them had regular showings of foreign and art films, which appealed primarily to students and faculty from Cornell and Ithaca College. Ringing the town were manufacturing establishments, including the Morse Chain Company and the Ithaca Gun Company. These companies were major employers in the immediate area. A large agricultural cooperative also had its central office in a building close to downtown. The main business of the community, however, was Cornell. The university on East Hill boasted a school-year population of about fifteen thousand students and four thousand faculty and staff. Ithaca College was at that time located downtown, before its later move high up on South Hill. The divide between town and gown was as pronounced in Ithaca as in any other college community.

The Best of Times

Being removed from any major cities, Cornell developed its own self-sustaining culture. It provided its university family with many facilities and recreational opportunities: sporting events; musical and theatrical performances; and lecturers drawn to Ithaca as part of the circuit of American universities. All our ties and associations in Ithaca were faculty related. Our friends were usually close colleagues in the school's faculty. We also connected with a few families in other departments and in the university's library community. Gormley Miller, librarian of the School of Industrial and Labor Relations, who was actively engaged in local Democratic party politics, was a friend, as was the Shepherd family. The families with small children, who lived on our street in South Hill, also became friends. John Summerskill was a neighbor who served as a resident psychologist in the university's clinic. He was an avid ice hockey enthusiast and a Canadian. He announced Cornell's hockey games, which we attended at Lynah Rink. He became a Cornell vice president before moving to San Francisco State University, where he endured a stormy tenure as university president during the tempestuous days of student protests in the early 1970's.

Clara and I enjoyed parties and dinners at the homes of fellow faculty members. Living so far from New York, we only visited family during school breaks. We would spend time with Clara's family and with my Aunt Rose and her family. My sister, Marilyn, and her husband, Ed, had moved to Huntington, Long Island, where they were just starting their own family. The Ithaca winters were considered to be the worst in western New York State. There was heavy and frequent snowfall. We gradually learned to take the snow in stride; the kids became adept at sliding down their favorite snow-covered hill on the campus. They borrowed Willard Straight cafeteria trays as their sleds. Summer season was the ideal time to enjoy the area. The students were gone and the campus took on a sleepy aura. The town was pretty much deserted. Opportunities to swim were abundant in the nearby state parks, and in Lake Cayuga. Nearby vacation sites were never crowded. There were many farm stands that offered sweet and freshly picked corn for sale. We seldom wanted to be anywhere else but in Ithaca for the summer.

Around this time, I began to participate frequently in the annual meetings of the Special Libraries Association and occasionally went to those of the American Library Association as well. When I was still at the Brooklyn Public Library, I had taken on the chairmanship of the business division of the Special Libraries Association. I was filling in for a person who had resigned unexpectedly. I found myself immersed in the affairs of the division on a continuing basis. It was also at this time that I became a good friend of Bill Woods, executive secretary of the Special Libraries Association in New York. It was Bill who proposed that the book on commodity prices be published by the Association. He successfully steered the proposal through to acceptance by the Association's publications committee.

In the early planning stages of the *Administrative Science Quarterly,* I became even more actively interested in pursuing the study of administration. My informal tutors were two behavioral science colleagues, Thompson and McEwen. Following their suggestions, I studied the evolution of management theory—from Weber on bureaucracy to Frederick Winslow Taylor's work in scientific management. I also took on the writings of the more modern behaviorists like Chester Barnard and Herbert Simon. My reading served to inform my understanding of the research and empirical studies which would find their way into the pages of *Administrative Science Quarterly*. It also helped me to select the monographs appropriate for review in the *Quarterly*'s forthcoming issues. I was in the process of building an intellectual foundation, which would serve me when I later began to offer instruction and write on library administration.

My first three years at Cornell were a heady introduction to a world that I had never dreamed I could become part of. It was a surprise and a novelty to find myself at home in this setting. I became quite at ease with the blend of freedom and personal responsibility that my work offered. I enjoyed the feeling that I could set my own goals and shape my own scholarly agenda. Much of the allure of Cornell, and many of the satisfactions I experienced there, were due to Ed Litchfield. His dexterous and high-profile leadership brought excitement and made the school a place where innovation was not just possible, but was actively encouraged. Like Francis St. John of the Brooklyn Public Library, Litchfield profoundly influenced my career.

Not everyone at the school or at Cornell was enamored of Litchfield. The faculty was split; the traditionalists in the business school rejected the idea that public administration had anything in common with business. The public administration faculty tended to support Litchfield. Elsewhere across the campus, Litchfield was often perceived as an ambitious self-promoter. A reporter preparing a feature article on Litchfield for *Fortune Magazine* interviewed me at the end of his campus stay. He confided that only two people on the campus with whom he had spoken were firmly in Litchfield's camp. The president of the university was one and I was the other. It came as a shattering revelation, when I learned late in the spring of 1956, that Litchfield was moving in the fall to the University of Pittsburgh as its chancellor. During the year, his wife, Ann, had died, and Litchfield may have wanted to make a new start in life. Litchfield had joined the boards of several very large corporations and was becoming widely known nationally. Word had it that members of a dynastic Pittsburgh family had offered him virtually unlimited financial resources to elevate the academic stature of what was regarded as a provincial institution. Pittsburgh University was celebrated only for its football prowess. It would be Litchfield's task to turn the school into one of the nation's leading universities. Litchfield had brought the Graduate School of Business and Public Administration far along during his tenure. Doubtless, he required a wider playing field for his vision. I felt his departure keenly. Not only was Litchfield leaving, he was taking Jim Thompson, the first editor of the *Administrative Science Quarterly*, with him.

By the fall term of 1956, the school had begun to change. Mel de Chazeau was serving as acting dean. New faculty was also being added. Harold Bierman, a University of Michigan accounting Ph.D., had come to offer course work in finance and managerial accounting. Seymour Smidt, a young product of Chicago University's economics program, was added to teach managerial economics. Earl Brooks came from Cornell's School of Industrial and Labor Relations, where he had been assistant dean to instruct in personnel management and human relations. The new person with whom I would associate most closely and develop strong ties of friendship was Robert Presthus. Presthus came from the University of Southern California. His field was public administration and he had co-authored a widely used textbook on the subject. He had earned his Ph.D. from Chicago in political science, but his orientation had been shifting toward a more psychological and sociological view of administration. It was this aspect of his background that led to his appointment as Thompson's successor as editor of the *Administrative Science Quarterly*. Betsy Ann Olive was proving to be a great asset as assistant librarian. Her gracious and endearing southern manner was balanced with an organized and purposeful work style. She afforded me the luxury of concentrating on my teaching and writing commitments. I felt completely at ease knowing that Betsy had the daily management of the library in hand. During the 1956-1957 school year, however, I began to have misgivings about whether I should remain at Cornell pursuing a career in academia.

Temperamentally and intellectually university life appealed to me. Nevertheless, I had some doubts. With Litchfield gone, my relationship with Steve

McCarthy might grow more strained, particularly if the next dean were to see my teaching role and the library's significance as less integral to the school's program. I had earned a tenured position on the faculty, but even though I held two professional master's degrees, the customary rite of passage for the professoriat was the Ph.D. This limitation might constitute a formidable barrier were I to seek mobility in the university world. I had the sense that my time at Cornell had been only a way station along the route to a directorship at a large public library. I had demonstrated that I could succeed in the academic world. My book had been published, and perhaps it was time to gravitate back to the public library field. It was the sum of these factors that led me to consider possible alternatives.

In February of 1957, I came upon an announcement in the *Library Journal* describing an opening for director of personnel at the public library known as the Philadelphia Free Library. The librarian was Emerson Greenaway, a prominent figure who had first come to national attention as director of the highly regarded Enoch Pratt Library in Baltimore. The information I requested made it clear that my background qualified me for consideration. In March, a series of personal interviews would be conducted in Philadelphia for all eligible applicants. The first interviews were with senior library staff. A panel drawn from the city administration and the library's board also would interview candidates. These interviews were to focus on each applicant's understanding and views of public library administration and personnel management. The library was included in the civil service system; according to regulations, military veterans were placed above all other applicants in the order of selection. I completed the necessary forms and within ten days was invited to Philadelphia. The examination would consist of a review of my experience; a series of interviews were scheduled on the same day. The city provided no expenses for travel or lodging, but I felt my chances were good enough to make the trip worthwhile. Even though I had studied personnel administration and was well versed in management theory, I thought it was a good idea to spend some time reviewing the personnel literature before my appearance.

In Philadelphia, I learned that there were six applicants. Four of them were women with years of public library administrative experience. None of them was a veteran, however. I was one of two men applying for the job; both of us had military experience. This meant that unless we failed the examination completely, we would automatically be considered as number one and two on the list of eligible candidates. My competitor was a man in his mid-thirties who had been working in the public library field in Baltimore for several years. I felt that my interviews went exceedingly well. My discussions with Emerson Greenaway and several of his deputies were cordial and interesting. During my talk with Greenaway, he asked casually how soon I could come to Philadelphia if I were selected. I suggested that I could move soon after classes ended, around June 1st or June 15th. In the half-hour session with the panel I felt I had made a good impression. I left Philadelphia with the feeling that I had an excellent chance of being offered the position.

I received notice from the Philadelphia Civil Service Commission on April 10th. I had been placed at the top of the eligible list. I assumed that I would hear shortly that I had been offered the post, and began tentatively to plan the move before summer. After ten more days, having heard nothing further from Philadelphia, I became impatient and decided to telephone Mr. Greenaway to inquire where matters stood. When I reached his office, I was told that he would not be available until the afternoon. I reached him late in the day and asked what had happened. He told me that he regretted having to report that I had not been selected, but that the person second on the list had been offered the position. I asked him why I had not been chosen, especially since I had scored highest in the competition. Greenaway reminded me that I had said that I could not report for work before June. The Philadelphia library needed someone sooner as the position had been vacant already for six months. I asked what starting date my competitor had offered. He said he thought he would be there by May first and no later than the fifteenth. I asked why Greenaway hadn't informed me of this time consideration, and why he had not given me the opportunity to make special arrangements to arrive earlier. He was evasive. He then went on to explain that he felt I was highly qualified, and that he was certain I would have no difficulty advancing to an important position in public library administration. Furthermore, because he now knew my background and qualifications, he would be pleased to serve as a future reference. We concluded our conversation on what he may have felt was an amiable note, but I was not mollified.

I spent a day or two reflecting on what had happened. I checked into the background of the man who had been given the post. I learned that he had worked as an administrative assistant to Greenaway during Greenaway's tenure as director of the public library in Baltimore. This made me angry. It seemed I had unwittingly played the fool in a drama that Greenaway had cleverly orchestrated. His intention from the outset was to give the job to his former aide. I could not simply shrug off what had happened. I resolved to have a conversation about what had transpired with my friend and colleague, Dave Thomas. Dave was a patient and thoughtful listener, not given to rash opinions. He listened to my account and inquired about Greenaway's stature and importance. He believed that I was in a no-win situation. No matter what I did or said, the position had gone to the other man; that could not be changed. All I could do was vent my wrath. If I were to do that, Greenaway would still prevail. If I embarrassed or insulted him, I would only invite his hostility. As long as he remained nationally influential he would be an unseen enemy who might damage my career in untold ways. Dave's advice was simple — forget it. Of course he was right, but I couldn't forget it.

The next day I wrote a letter. I explained the entire sequence of events from the time of the interviews in Philadelphia to the telephone conversation with Emerson Greenaway. I added the information that the man who received the position had worked as an assistant to Greenaway in Baltimore. I made no charges or accusations. I suggested only that this matter was worthy of close scrutiny by the responsible parties. My letter went to the office of the Mayor, the Director of the Civil Service Commission, and to each member of the board of the Free Library. After two weeks, I received a brief letter from a staff member in the Office of the Director of the Civil Service Commission notifying me that regulations in Philadelphia permitted agency heads to choose the first or second person from the eligible roster. There had been no violation of the regulations. Another week passed before I heard from the chairman of the library's board. His letter was somewhat more personal. He thanked me for writing to the board members. They had talked with Mr. Greenaway about my concerns. They wished to assure me that in the future, when the first eligible candidate was to be passed over in favor of the second for a senior administrative post in the Free Library, the board would be fully apprised of the circumstances before the final selection was made. I never crossed paths with Emerson Greenaway again.

Matters seemed to be looking up at Cornell in the summer of 1957. A new dean was expected to be in place by fall. He was C. Stewart Sheppard, a British national who had been assistant dean at the business school of New York University. Presthus had by then assumed the editorship of *Administrative Science Quarterly*, and our associations on and off the job had grown stronger. McCarthy and I were getting along reasonably well. Both of us were waiting to see where the new dean stood on some of the issues that had caused us some discord in the past. My book had been well received and, for a university press imprint, was selling moderately well. The royalties might help toward the purchase of a house, if we remained in Ithaca. By that time, I had completed four years at Cornell. In two more years, I would be eligible for a sabbatical. I began to wonder whether it might be worthwhile to use that time to work toward a Ph.D.

As a result of the success of my book, The American Management Association invited me to New York to lecture on information for management decision making. I would speak at several seminars during 1957 and 1958. The executive secretary of the McKinsey Foundation for Management Research asked me to submit a proposal to support research dealing with information useful for managerial study and practice. At the same time, the Sloan Institute of Hospital Administration was conducting an empirical study of decision making. This subject was of growing concern to many scholars across a range of disciplines. It seemed to me to be a subject for a bibliographic guide. In my presentation to the McKinsey Foundation, I sought assistance to conduct a survey of the scattered writings on decision making in the various behavioral and scientific fields. I wanted to bring order to the subject by rationally arranging and classifying its literature. McKinsey quickly approved and funded the request. I enlisted the assistance of Fred Silander, a doctoral student in administration and economics. I began work in the summer of 1957 with guidance from a Sloan Institute committee and other faculty. As the project advanced, many other scholars on campus and at other institutions offered counsel and suggestions. The published volume, *Decision Making: An Annotated Bibliography*, appeared in 1958 under the imprint of the school, and was distributed as part of its publication program.

With my newly gained insights into administration, and the support of my associate, Bill McEwen, I set out to write an assessment of where matters stood in the study and teaching of library administration. What I learned corroborated for librarianship what Litchfield had observed about the field of general management in his 1956 article in *Administrative Science Quarterly*'s first issue. Management practice in libraries was far ahead of theory, empirical analysis, and research. In what I saw as my first intellectual contribution to the periodical literature of my own field, I sought to analyze why this was so. I also outlined what I thought to be promising directions for moving the discipline forward. The article appeared in *College and Research Libraries* in July 1958. It was titled, "Development of Administration in Library Service: Current Status and Future Prospects." It was the first expression of a theme that would become a fundamental element of my belief system and aspirations for librarianship—the need for change.

The Best of Times

The positive reception of the work on decision making led to the McKinsey Foundation encouraging me to undertake a follow-up effort. During the mid-1950's, American management was manifesting a heightened interest in organizational assessment. Nowhere was this concern more evident than in management consulting. McKinsey Company was a leading management consulting firm. I received their financial support by late 1957. I repeated the efforts that had resulted in *Decision Making*. An informal advisory committee of faculty members again advised me on content, arrangement, and scope. This time, the subject was measuring and evaluating performance. Earlier publications had centered primarily on technical tasks and operating systems. Little attention had yet been focused on administrative activities. These were less precise and quantifiable. The topics reviewed would include goal definition, performance standards, means of selecting performance measurement systems, applying measurement tools to performance, comparison of performance results with standards, and determination of the significance of differences between performance results and the established standards of performance, in order to modify the value-producing process or the standards. I would analyze literature ranging across business and public administration. It would also encompass other fields of administrative activity in the military, education, libraries, and health.

In early 1958, with this project well underway, Miller Hillhouse, a close colleague who was giving a seminar in municipal administration, invited me to visit his class to discuss measuring performance in public libraries. I accepted, but soon felt that the writing available on the subject did not address this subject coherently. The literature was devoid of any theoretical or substantive base. Measurement in public libraries was simply built on a value system of faith in numerical counts. Circulation statistics, numbers of reference questions asked, volumes added to collections, and similar such yardsticks were all that were taken into consideration. The underlying assumption was that the larger the numbers, the more effective the library's performance. Qualitative standards were virtually absent. There was no study that compared results with objectives or goals set by the organization. The best I could do when I met with Hillhouse's class was to describe measurement tools then in use, and to explain why and how they fell short of providing any reasoned basis for assessing the success or failure of organizational performance. This opportunity to point up the shortcomings of public library evaluation measures became the basis for my first research investigation.

The Best of Times

At the start of the 1957-1958 academic year, I had firmly decided not to seek a position in public librarianship. I would remain in the academic world. The new dean was by then in residence. It was too early to tell how the school would fare under his stewardship, but his early actions and statements seemed supportive of my role and of the library as important elements of the program. My family had been living in the apartment on South Hill for three years. We enjoyed life in the community, but felt it was time to move to larger quarters. Just a short distance from where we lived, at the city's southern edge, there was a tract of land just to the north of what had once been the site of freight railroad tracks. The city decided to divide up the land into lots zoned for private residential construction, and to sell them at public auction. I liked the location with its view of Lake Cayuga to the north. If I could buy one of the lots at a reasonable price, it would make sense to build a house there. We could move without leaving the immediate area or disrupting Jacqueline's progress at South Hill School, where she was entering the third grade. I attended the auction early in October, and bought the lot I had set my sights on for two thousand dollars.

Within a couple of weeks, we arranged for a mortgage and engaged a local contractor to construct a six-room, ranch-style house, which was a prefabricated National Home. The house sections would be delivered from the factory. Once the builder had prepared the foundation and the utilities were in place, construction could be done in a matter of days. We anticipated moving in by mid-November. The builder contracted to have the house ready for occupancy by November 15th. I expected the project to move forward flawlessly. I was mistaken. The construction schedule was delayed by more than the usual mishaps and mistakes. The house was not ready for occupancy by November 15th. Our apartment already had been rented to another family, so we were obliged to move into a motel and have our furnishings stored. The house was finally ready five days late. We quickly adjusted to our more spacious quarters and returned to a normal routine. I was now only three semesters short of eligibility for a sabbatical leave. I decided to use the leave to pursue a doctorate. The scant attention paid to measurement concerns in public librarianship seemed to offer a promising research theme, which would serve as the raw material for a doctoral dissertation.

When I was not teaching or dealing with library matters, I divided my time between the McKinsey project and working on a research proposal that would deal with the measurement of performance in public libraries. I came to appreciate how much my work in surveying the literature of decision making and measurement had provided a solid foundation for such study. I understood how public library service, like social welfare and education, was a field of activity where the legislative standard was undefined. It was characterized by a lack of clearly articulated notions of what constitutes good service. The result was that public library administration afforded great discretionary power over both the means and ends of organizational activity. In the absence of clearly stated goals, library performance could only be measured in vague terms like circulation figures. Until the values, objectives, and goals of any organization's activities were clearly articulated, any evaluation or assessment of performance would be impossible. Clear, unambiguous identification of a public organization's goals had to be the most difficult, yet the most crucial, element in an evaluative process. The specification of goals was essential, not only for public libraries, but for other types of public institutions as well. My research task might be to figure out how to design and test a method by which a public library could arrive at a set of concrete goals. The organization's performance success or failure could then be measured in a meaningful way. I was not yet clear about how I could effectively accomplish this.

Once again I turned to my colleagues as sounding boards for my thoughts and as the source of ideas on how I should proceed. Seymour Smidt was exceedingly helpful. There were in that period social science research centers on a number of college campuses, including Cornell. These were local councils funded externally with the mission of reviewing, advising, and providing modest financing for deserving research projects. Once I had crystallized my thoughts, I laid out a preliminary plan and met with members of the Cornell Social Science Research Center. Some of the best minds in the social sciences in the United States offered me counsel. The panel included distinguished scholars such as John Dean, Edward Devereux, and William Foote Whyte. With the input of these experts, I revised and adapted my proposal and submitted it for formal consideration. My proposal was accepted. I received sufficient support to engage a graduate assistant and secretarial aid. By summer of 1958, I began to conduct a comparative test of my methodology in three different public libraries in small cities of comparable size. All of them were within a radius of sixty miles of Ithaca. By the fall, my field work was complete. The secretary spent the fall term completing the transcription of the interviews I had conducted. I did not plan to complete the final analysis or to write up the research findings until the propitious time. My hope was that I would be able to build my Ph.D. dissertation based on this data.

The Best of Times

Early in the fall of 1958, I began in earnest to determine where to seek the doctorate. I was unsure whether to concentrate my work in a business or library school. I needed to identify a program where I could satisfy the residence requirement in one year, since that was all the time I would have for my sabbatical. The two business Ph.D. programs that I looked into seriously at the University of Chicago and at Columbia University did not meet my time needs. I decided to limit myself to librarianship. I considered the programs offered at three universities: Columbia, Illinois, and Michigan. I felt I should not make this important decision until I had visited each institution and had interviewed the deans and faculty.

I visited Columbia University first. The dean of the library school at that time was Robert Leigh, a renowned social scientist. He had come to library education from the directorship of the celebrated mid-century Public Library Inquiry. Leigh was highly encouraging. He offered to do whatever he could to induce me to come to Columbia. He conceded, however, that Columbia could only offer a DLS—a professional doctorate in library science, rather than a Ph.D. University politics precluded the school from awarding the Ph.D. Even though I would miss the opportunity to live in New York with my family, I decided against Columbia. The research degree I wanted was the Ph.D. I went next to the University of Illinois. Before my arrival there I had written to the dean, Harold Lancour, to tell him the date and the purpose of my visit. When I reached the library school and announced myself, I was informed that Dr. Lancour would not be in his office that day. If I liked, I could speak with other members of the faculty. I was told where their offices were. I stopped by one office and met an agreeable professor, but he didn't know who I was. When I told him the purpose of my visit, he expressed great surprise that I would go to so much trouble. I concluded that the Illinois doctoral program was not for me and immediately left the campus.

The University of Michigan was my last attempt. I had written to Rudolph Gjelness, chairman of the library science department, and received a warm letter in return inviting me to come. Gjelness was a tall, reserved man who was uncomfortable with small talk. He was welcoming and seemed pleased that I was considering Michigan. He arranged for me to meet several faculty members. After I spent some hours on the campus and in the school, Gjelness and I met again for a longer talk. I explained to him about my research and how I hoped that it might serve as the basis for my dissertation. Not only did he think that my idea was feasible, but he volunteered that my committee might include one or two members from the public administration faculty, who would have an interest in my study. He hoped that I would decide on Michigan because of my interesting background. He added that he was certain that scholarship support would be available were I to choose to come. I left Ann Arbor very encouraged. The Michigan program held additional appeal for me because the Ph.D. required not only a masters degree in librarianship, but a second masters degree in a subject field. I already satisfied this requirement. My residency could be spent solely in preparing for the comprehensive examinations. Gjelness had assured me that I could accomplish everything I needed to in one year's time. By the time I returned to Ithaca, I had made up my mind. I would be going to Michigan.

I moved ahead quickly to gain approval for my sabbatical leave and to make formal application to Michigan. With both approvals in hand by mid-November, I decided to make the most of my leave time by arranging to move with the family to Ann Arbor as soon as Jacqueline got out of school in June of 1959. I would be able to get an early start on my program before the start of the summer session. I worked at an accelerated pace to finish my measurement book before the end of the spring semester. The second McKinsey Foundation annotated bibliography, *Measurement and Evaluation of Organizational Performance*, was published by the Cornell Graduate School of Business and Public Administration in May 1959.

The Michigan Ph.D. required reading competence in two foreign languages. When I lived in New York I had subscribed intermittently to a French language newspaper published in the United States called, *France Amérique*. I also read some fiction in French. I was confident that I would do well in French. German was another matter. I had not spoken German in years, and it had been at least eighteen years since I last read it. I would need remedial study to prepare for an examination in this language. I arranged to sit in on an intermediate German class during the spring term at Cornell in order to refresh my reading competence. Among other arrangements to be made for my year of absence was to ensure that Betsy Ann Olive would have someone to assist her while she held the fort directing the library in my absence. Steve McCarthy invited Sue Perella to join the library staff as reference assistant for the year. Chester Lewis, the library director at *The New York Times* became my substitute teacher for my course in bibliography and research methods. He agreed to serve as an adjunct professor for the 1959-1960 academic year. Lewis would teach the class once a week, enabling him to minimize his commute between New York and Ithaca. The final task was to rent our house. The family of a professor from Lincoln University took a year's lease.

Chapter Nine

We moved to graduate student housing in Ann Arbor in mid-June. After two days of driving, we arrived with a U-Haul trailer hitched to our car and moved into a furnished two-bedroom apartment on Michigan's North Campus. The community was swarming with kids. Steven was entering first grade in September. Both he and Jacqueline were going to attend a public school nearby. A shuttle bus ran regularly between the housing project and the main campus. I bought a bicycle to commute to the university in fifteen minutes during temperate weather. Limited campus parking made it difficult to drive there. In a few days, we had made friends with the families in our neighborhood and felt right at home.

My first order of business was to take the language exams. Once I had officially established residence, I went to see the graduate school's foreign language examiner. He turned out to be a cordial, senior faculty member who had assumed this role for many years and was on the verge of retirement. He explained the simple regimen he followed. I was to select a book in my subject field of at least three hundred pages. The examination would consist of his selection of one page of text somewhere in the book. I would be required to translate this text within a prescribed time, using a dictionary if needed. My next step was to choose the two books, one written in French and one in German, from the school library's collection. Selecting a recently published work in French was easy. There were many possibilities available. Choosing the German volume proved more difficult. There were very few German books in the collection published later than the early 1930's. They tended either to be short monographs or lengthy historical tomes, written in a style that I found very difficult to follow. Finally, I came upon one work dealing with the evolution of books, printing, and the publishing industry. I felt that I could master this book with time. I learned from another

Ph.D. student that the benign professor who handled the language testing was retiring by the first of July. The foreign language departments were expected to implement exams using a more formal and demanding testing procedure. I stopped by the professor's office and made an appointment to take both tests on June 28th, which gave me only one week to study. I spent my time trying to work through the four hundred pages of the German book. My time ran out. I did as much as I could, but had managed to cover only half the text before the exam. As a last desperate act, I opened and reopened the heavy book many times at a place about one-third of the way into it. My idea was that, if one were to let the volume fall open, it would naturally open at this point.

The day of the test I gave the two books to the examiner. He sat me in a room next to his office, opened the French volume, and left me to write the translation. I was done in less than the time allowed and gave him the book and my exam booklet. With my heart pounding, I watched his next move. He looked at the title page of the German book for a moment and then opened the book to the page I was to translate. It was exactly where I had trained the volume to open. I completed the translation within the specified time with only minor reliance on my dictionary. The professor read both tests before I left his office. He congratulated me on having successfully passed both the French and German doctoral examinations. I had surmounted the first hurdle on the track toward my Ph.D.

I enrolled in two courses for the summer session. They were both taught by practicing academic librarians who came to Ann Arbor each year to serve as members of the summer faculty. One of them was Charles Shaw, librarian of Swarthmore College, who was best known for a selection guide he had prepared, *Books for College Libraries*. The other was Edmon Low from the University of Oklahoma. He was very active in the higher reaches of the American Library Association. Shaw's course was in academic library administration. Low offered a seminar in library technical services.

Two days into the term I had concluded that Charles Shaw did not have a clue about administration. His lectures consisted of anecdotes from his experience working as a college librarian. He made few demands on the students, other than to attend the class and read the few selections on the reading list. There were two other doctoral students in the class, and we all felt that the course was pedestrian. It actually seemed to us that Shaw was embarrassed by our presence in the class. Lowe's seminar was meatier. It dealt with issues of concern to those actively engaged in managing cataloging and classification operations. My background in this area was far more limited than in almost any other area of librarianship. I could discern little relevance in Low's lectures or assigned readings to my interests or research agenda.

After three weeks of the six-week term, I scheduled a meeting with Gjelness. I raised with him as delicately as I could the question of whether it would be necessary for me to register for formal courses, in order to meet the year's residence requirement. I asked if it might be possible, instead, for me to study independently for the written comprehensive doctoral examinations. He advised me to take the class in the history of books and printing, which would be given in the fall. An "A" or "B" grade in this class would satisfy the requirements of passing one of the four comprehensive examinations. This would leave me with only three other tests. In light of published work in the field of administration, he was also prepared to waive the examination in library administration. I was down to only two examinations—one in reference and one in cataloging and classification theory. Gjelness suggested that I meet with the reference instructor, Wallace Bonk, to learn how I might best prepare independently for the examination in his subject area. Gjelness was the examiner for cataloging and classification. He offered to provide me with an extensive bibliography, which I could use as a study guide to prepare for the test. The meeting was very helpful. I thanked Gjelness for his sympathetic hearing and told him how pleased I was to have come to Michigan. Almost as an afterthought, Gjelness asked whether I could be prevailed upon to teach a course on business information sources one evening a week in the fall. It would be given in the school's extension program in Detroit. I had not expected to teach while in Ann Arbor. I was afraid that it might interfere with my primary objective of completing the Ph.D. requirements. In the light of all that Gjelness had done to ease my passage, however, I told him I would be pleased to teach the course.

As promised, Gjelness gave me a lengthy list of books and journal articles for which I would be held accountable in the examination in cataloging and classification theory. I was familiar with only a few of the readings. The fall semester would give me ample time to work through the rest of the material, however. What I learned from Bonk was far less heartening. The comprehensive examination in reference service would include questions requiring Ph.D. students to provide details for virtually every reference work in the fields of general reference, the humanities, the social sciences, and the sciences. This requirement struck me as absurd. I appreciated that reference librarians needed a thorough grounding in the tools of their craft. Yet, having to commit to memory details about content, arrangement, and index features of hundreds and hundreds of reference sources boggled the mind. I felt strongly that the more rational approach was to use bibliographic guides to reference books to find one's way to particular works. New titles were constantly appearing in increasing number to replace or supersede existing reference books. Knowing and relying only upon existing reference books at a particular time created in librarians a dependency on a fixed collection of tools. What frustrated me at a more basic level was such a fundamentally anti-intellectual element in Michigan's Ph.D. program. When I asked another Ph.D. student what he thought would be the best way to prepare for such an examination, my question was met with a shrug. I was then told that there were sets of cards that gave details about the reference works we needed to know about. This would be akin to memorizing vocabulary cards for foreign language mastery. I had no choice but to learn the information by rote if I were to gain a passing grade.

My fall term also included the course in the history of books and libraries, which met twice a week with Professor Raymond Kilgour. I spent several hours studying in a library carrel. I divided this time between reading in cataloging and classification, and memorization of the contents of countless reference books from my reference card file. I also made the weekly commute every Tuesday evening to the university's engineering education center in Detroit to teach the business information class. Two other Ann Arbor faculty members taught in Detroit on the same evening. We carpooled together and ate dinner in the center's dining room before our classes began. One of these colleagues was an education professor whose specialty was comparative education. Frequently, he would bring along an international visitor to lecture in his class. One of his guests had been a teacher and friend of Anne Frank.

For my class, I relied on my Cornell teaching material. I adapted it from business and public administration to librarianship. This was my first experience with library education. The students were working librarians from special libraries in the Detroit area. All were enrolled as part-time master's degree students in the Ann Arbor program. Taking a cue from my colleague in education, I thought it might be worthwhile to invite an occasional guest speaker. My contacts in the business library field in Detroit were few. There was one person I wanted to meet, however. I thought it would also be interesting for the students to hear him. The man I had in mind was Frederick G. Ruffner, Jr.

The Best of Times

In the 1950's, Fred Ruffner had published the *Encyclopedia of Associations* at Gale Research Company in Detroit. At that time, I reviewed this new reference volume for the *Library Journal*. I wrote that this was a very useful reference source and that it would become even more valuable with the appearance of later expanded and updated editions. Ruffner's publishing office was in downtown Detroit. I telephoned him and explained who I was. I invited him to join me for dinner at the engineering center on a Tuesday evening in early October and to talk to my class about publishing business reference books. He accepted.

Fred Ruffner remembered my review of the *Encyclopedia of Associations* and was familiar with my book *Information for Administrators*. He seemed interested to learn that I would be in Ann Arbor for the 1959-1960 academic year. Ruffner invited me to visit the Gale Research offices in the Book Building that Friday. During my visit, Mr. Ruffner described a new Gale project. It was a directory that would provide details about research groups in American higher education. I said I thought this would make a useful reference tool for libraries. He asked me if I would edit the book. He said I could do the work from Ann Arbor communicating by phone and mail. He offered to give me a Dictaphone machine with tapes, which could be mailed back for transcription. He was prepared to turn over his working notes and let me take charge of developing the questionnaires and building the mailing list. I would be responsible for writing the entries that would form the book's content. Ruffner expected that the manuscript could be completed by the summer of 1960 for publication early in the fall. I considered my other commitments, which included the course I was taking and the one I was teaching, as well as the two comprehensive examinations in December. If I were to work at home spending no more than fifteen or so hours a week on the Gale project, I could work with Ruffner. My decision was influenced somewhat by the reduced income I was receiving while on half salary during my sabbatical. Before leaving the Gale office I accepted the editorship of what would become the first edition of the *Directory of University Research Bureaus and Institutes*. Neither Fred Ruffner nor I knew that our close association would endure through all those years to the present day.

In Ann Arbor, a fellow Ph.D. student and I forged a lasting friendship. His name was Anthony Kruzas. Tony, his wife, Florence, and daughter, Mary, made their home in Ann Arbor. Tony was an instructor in the library school faculty. The Kruzas family became our closest friends. Tony was my resident guide to people, places, and life at the university. I spent many Saturday afternoons, in the fall of 1959, in the grandstands watching the colorful spectacle of the Big Ten Michigan football team. Clara and the kids joined me. The Ann Arbor campus was bigger than Cornell's. There was also a far larger student body and faculty. The community of Ann Arbor supported many more social and shopping opportunities than Ithaca. My sabbatical year in the Midwest was a welcome change after living for six years in western New York State.

I spent October and November memorizing details about reference books, a task of sheer boredom and drudgery. The study of the theory and development of cataloging and classification principles, codes, and standards was more stimulating. My interest would flag, however, after about an hour or two spent wading through this literature. An unexpectedly pleasant surprise was the course in the history of books, printing, and publishing. When I was at Columbia studying with Lehmann-Haupt, I had barely scratched the surface of this subject. Professor Kilgour lecturing was not a stellar classroom experience. The lectures were really no more than droning recitations of events and dates. Slides illustrating the lectures were often so primitively made as to be virtually unrecognizable. Perusing the course bibliography, I discovered to my amazement that the reading selections proved fascinating. I was soon caught up in the colorful history of how texts were transformed into gloriously illuminated manuscripts. I pored over accounts of how the technology of printing made books a source of widespread public communication. What had started as a burdensome chore for fulfilling a Ph.D. requirement opened a door to the full sweep and range of all that had come before. I became caught up in this literature, avidly reading one account after another. I felt just as I had as an adolescent after discovering a favorite author. The selections from Kilgour's class enabled me to understand and fully appreciate the remarkable heritage and evolution of books, which had led to modern-day institutions of publishing and libraries.

My two comprehensive examinations were scheduled on a day early in December. Before the reference test I had been having a recurring dream: thousands of three by five cards, each covered with unintelligible marks, marched endlessly forward as in a military parade. Fortunately, I remembered enough to pass the reference examination. The test in cataloging and classification theory called for several short essays. I had absorbed enough in my independent study to write coherent compositions. I passed the exam. Only the completion of the course in the history of books and publishing was left. With all the voracious reading I had done, I was confident that I would receive a high grade. Two tasks other than my dissertation remained. One was teaching my weekly Detroit class until the end of the term, in early January. The other was continuing the work on the Gale directory. By December, I had made good progress on this assignment. Working with college and university catalogs and details included in several existing higher education directories, I had prepared the mailing list for Ruffner by the end of October. The questionnaire was written, arranged, and revised. After a final review, it was reproduced in Detroit. The questionnaire mailings to the research bureaus had started to go out in mid-November. By early December, completed questionnaires were returned to Detroit and mailed on to me for editing. We anticipated that most of the completed questionnaires would be in hand by early January. A second mailing was scheduled for February, with necessary follow-ups in mid-spring. My July deadline remained feasible.

By mid-December, I was ready to proceed vigorously with my dissertation. I met with Professor Gjelness to tell him that the only outstanding requirement still incomplete would be fulfilled by early January, when I would receive my grade for Professor Kilgour's class. I was anxious to start with my dissertation, so I requested Gjelness's help in forming my dissertation committee. He remembered what I had told him about my earlier study, and how I had requested that my committee include someone from the public administration faculty. He thought the chairperson should be from librarianship. He asked if I would find him acceptable as chairman. I assured him that I would be very pleased to have him direct my dissertation committee. He suggested Mary Duncan Carter, a senior professor with special interest in public librarianship, and assistant professor Wallace Bonk, the reference specialist, as other faculty for the committee. I had not taken any courses with Dr. Carter, but agreed that it would be helpful to have her on the committee. I did know Bonk. He had been my nemesis in the matter of reference book memorization. I liked him personally and knew that he had a quick wit and a keen intelligence. He also had a reputation for being fair. I told Gjelness that I found him acceptable as well. Gjelness asked me to identify someone from public administration who would be interested in my dissertation subject and who would serve on the committee. I had already met and talked with several of the public administration faculty. I had discussed in detail my research with Dr. Robert Pealy and suggested that he be our public administration representative. Gjelness convened the first meeting of my doctoral committee in his office in mid-December.

I thought the meeting went very well and that the group seemed comfortable with each other. I noticed that the library faculty tended to defer to Pealy, since they felt my research was really a methodological study in public administration. Pealy in turn was deferential to them, since he saw the research as being public-library focused. When I distributed my proposed outline of content for the thesis, there were no objections. Nor did anyone find it inappropriate that I had completed the design and field study before coming to Michigan, leaving only the analysis of data and the writing undone. I suggested that I could give them each chapter to review and criticize as I completed it, instead of submitting the completed work for their review. They all agreed that this would be preferable. On this happy note Gjelness concluded the meeting. All that remained was for me to do the writing.

The winter and spring were divided between my time spent completing the dissertation and the Gale directory. My residence requirement would be fulfilled when I registered for dissertation preparation in the spring term. With luck, I would be finished at Michigan by June and could return to Ithaca in July with the Ph.D. in hand. It did not happen exactly that way. Once I had cleared the process with the committee, I buckled down to the writing. The study was divided into eight chapters. The supplementary appendixes, tables, and bibliography were already prepared. The first chapter laid out the theoretical bases of library performance measurement and evaluation. The second described the empirical analysis in the three libraries. Working from notes I had prepared earlier, I wrote the first two chapters by mid-January. Ann Arbor in 1960 was home to a cottage industry of dissertation typists, who were steeped in the university's arcane style requirements. I found an agreeable graduate student wife among their number. She was experienced and ready to commit herself to work with me through the whole process. She promised to type the first two chapters and three legible carbon copies in two or three days. She kept her word.

I gave a copy at once to each of the committee members for their criticism. I assumed that the material would be read and returned with comments within a short time. I was mistaken. The most serious problem I faced in completing the dissertation was retrieving material from my committee. Gjelness, Bonk, and Pealy normally got the draft chapters back to me within a week. Mary Duncan Carter did not. After four weeks, when I finally pried Chapters I and II from her, she offered only one observation. She suggested that I revise the designation of the three public libraries from library "1," library "2," and library "3" to library "X," library "Y," and library "Z." I could not distribute any more material to the committee until I received back what I had handed in to all four readers.

The Best of Times

Two other matters arose during January 1960, both related to the Special Libraries Association. In 1956, once the Special Libraries Association Business Division voted at their meeting to sponsor the preparation and publication of an updated version of *Price Sources*, a working committee drawn from the division membership was formed and efforts on the project had begun. I expected to have the completed assignments in hand for final editing before publication by the Association in 1958. The work dragged on and on. Two of the original contributors withdrew and needed to be replaced. I could not do the final editing until all parts of the entire manuscript had been received. It wasn't until January 1960 that I finally received the last section. To keep the content from becoming any more outdated, I dropped all other work to spend two weeks finishing the manuscript. The roster of contributors to the project included some of the best known names in American business librarianship: Eleanor Allen, Winifred Baum, Lorna Daniell, Charlotte Georgi, Marie Goff, Robert Goodrich, Paul Kruse, Thelma Morris, Margaret Rocq, Idair Smookler, Paul Wiley, and Jean Wesner. *Sources of Commodity Prices: A Project of the Special Libraries Association Business and Finance Division* (the Business Division had merged with the Finance Division in 1958) was published later in the year. The effort had taken almost four years to complete. I learned an important lesson from this experience. Publishing by committee was hopelessly frustrating. I promised myself that I would never do it again.

The other development concerning the Special Libraries Association came in the form of a telephone call from Grieg Aspnes, librarian of Cargill Corporation and chairman of the Special Libraries Association's nominating committee. He had located my whereabouts from my office at Cornell and invited me to accept the nomination for the first vice-presidency of the Special Libraries Association in their upcoming spring election, for the term of 1960-1961. The first vice-president automatically succeeded to president the following year. I was astonished. The only active office I had held in the SLA was as a substitute chairperson of the Business Division. I told Aspnes that I was a complete unknown to most of the membership and that I would not be a worthy opponent against the other nominee. He pressed me, arguing that I was better known than I thought—special librarians used my business information book all the time. I wavered. He insisted. I told him I would need to think about it and to get back to me in a few days. To commit so much of my time to such a demanding national office would require support from my institution. I phoned Dean Sheppard at Cornell. He said he would talk to Steve McCarthy. He felt that both of them would be enthusiastic about my running for the office. Two hours later, McCarthy called to suggest that I accept the nomination. When Aspnes called again, I asked him if he was at liberty to tell me who would oppose me. He said that was not possible. I then accepted the nomination. The election was held in April 1960. My opponent was Eugene Jackson, librarian of the General Motors Corporation Library. Jackson was among the best known and most highly respected special librarians in the United States. He defeated me by a wide margin.

Once the manuscript for *Sources of Commodity Prices* had been sent off, I resumed work on my dissertation and the Gale directory. The directory was moving forward, but I could not move any faster on the dissertation than the pace at which my committee members would return the material with their comments. Based on my experience with the first two chapters, I decided to give them only one chapter every three or four weeks. There would still be ample time to conclude well before June.

The work on the Gale directory was a unique learning experience. I became habituated to using dictating equipment. This required that I organize my thoughts coherently before speaking. I learned the discipline of talking in grammatical sentences and paragraphs, even to the degree of punctuating as I dictated. Even more importantly, I gained understanding of all that went into the process of bringing a reference book into being—from the initial idea to its planning and execution. I had prepared material for publications before, but I had never been so thoroughly enmeshed in the entire sequence. This expertise would stand me in good stead for many years to come. My work on the directory was the catalyst for an effort I had been mulling over in my mind for a number of months.

I had been using *Information for Administrators* in the classes I taught. I had mostly envisaged the primary use of the book as a tool for students and practitioners. My business students, however, felt that, while the book was a convenient general guide, it fell short of what was needed most. They wanted a volume that could name the exact publication where particular information could be found. I had been considering how to design just such a tool for locating statistical information. There were many general guides. There was also the widely used government annual, *Statistical Abstract of the United States*. No compendium served as a comprehensive reference source that could lead a person directly to any and every type of publicly or privately issued statistical information. Sitting on a bench on campus one spring day, I tried my idea out on Tony Kruzas. What did he think of designing a reference book that gave an alphabetical listing of all the possible topics about which statistics might be sought, followed directly by details describing the exact publication in which such statistics could be found? His reaction was immediate. Based on his experience as a reference instructor, he thought such an index would be very useful. Before we got up from the bench that afternoon, I had conceived the basic outline and designed the method for constructing such a reference book. I told Tony that I would like two colleagues I knew I could count on to work with me on the project. He was one. The other would be Charlotte Georgi, librarian of the Graduate School of Business at the University of California, Los Angeles. She had been a disciplined and responsible editorial collaborator on the *Commodity Prices* project. Even though he was busy with teaching and trying to complete his Ph.D., I convinced Kruzas that his effort on the statistics project would take only a little time if we put the book on a two-year timetable, for completion in the spring of 1962. Somewhat grudgingly, but good-naturedly, he agreed to participate. I wrote at once to Charlotte to lay out the plans. I invited her to be the second associate editor. She agreed enthusiastically. Soon thereafter, at my next meeting in Detroit with Fred Ruffner, I explained the book project and offered it as a prospective publication for Gale Research Company. He offered to publish it without any hesitation. Within days contracts were drawn up and work was begun. The manuscript's delivery date was spring 1962. Two years later the first edition of *Statistics Sources* appeared in time for display at the American Library Association's June Conference.

The scheduled publication date for the first edition of the *Directory of University Research Bureaus and Institutes* was late summer 1960. In the mean time, my dissertation chapters were read by my committee and came back to me without any criticism. I was hopeful that I would have the last chapter returned in time to schedule my oral defense by mid-June. By then, I would have satisfied the last requirement for the Ph.D. I hadn't reckoned with Professor Gjelness's priorities, however. He decided to have me teach two courses in the summer session. By the time I learned this, I had already made plans to move the family back to Ithaca at the end of June. I would have to fly back to Ann Arbor for the teaching stint once we had settled back into our house. Moreover, there was a graduate school regulation that precluded holding an oral defense while a Ph.D. candidate was teaching courses. The committee accepted my completed dissertation, *Toward a Methodology for the Formulation of Objectives in Public Libraries*. My oral exam was scheduled for early August. The delay in my oral exam date was a minor annoyance measured against the myriad ways in which Gjelness and the Michigan faculty had facilitated my fulfillment of the doctoral requirements in record time.

The classes I taught that summer included the business information course that I had offered for the extension program in Detroit, and another one in library administration. I had never before taught a course in library administration. I was eager to adapt the Cornell management course for business and public administration students for a library school audience. In the article I had written for *College and Research Libraries* in 1958, "Development of Administration in Library Service," I included a critique of teaching administration in library schools, based on a survey of the syllabi, outlines, and reading lists received from schools offering administration courses. I had concluded that libraries were scarcely influenced by the insights of other disciplines and drew little from the literature of business, public administration, or administrative behavior. During a brief stay in Ithaca, before returning to Ann Arbor on the summer teaching assignment, I reworked the outline for the Cornell management course. My revision drew heavily on writings on the administrative process and organizational behavior, blending them with selections from the library literature that offered reasoned insights and germane case illustrations. My purpose was to structure a course in management focused on the processes of administration that were intrinsic to organizations of all types. I took libraries as the case in point. My lectures drew upon the insights, concepts, and theories embedded in the readings in order to illustrate their relevance to the management of libraries.

That first offering of the course in library administration must have tried the patience of my Michigan students. I overloaded the reading list and required a weighty paper, all during an abbreviated summer term when normal ground rules called for a much less taxing set of demands. Other than placing an unfair burden on the students, I became convinced of the intellectual usefulness of this orientation. This framework, adapted through continuous incorporation of newer, more relevant contributions to replace earlier writings, served as the basis for later years of instruction in library administration, when I shifted my base from business and public administration to education for librarianship.

Chapter Ten

Back on the Cornell campus in the fall of 1960, I resumed my responsibilities as before. Even though I was very grateful to the Michigan faculty for their support in expediting the completion of the doctoral requirements, as a learning experience the year had been quite limited. What I felt I had missed was any type of introduction to the new technology then beginning to bear upon the field of librarianship. Individuals like Hans Peter Luhn at IBM and organizations like the Western Reserve University Center for Documentation Research were experimenting and reporting new approaches to handling and retrieving information. None of these ideas had yet permeated the Michigan library education scene. I received the Ph.D. without any exposure to these new developments, which would have such a strong impact on the evolution of library practice. I also realized that being in a program of business and public administration, I was at best a mixed breed. In business and public administration I was seen as a librarian. In librarianship, I was viewed as an adherent of business and public administration. Perhaps I had gone as far as I could in my role as faculty member and librarian in a professional school. A year's immersion in library education and library relationships had led me to wonder if it might not be more rewarding to be fully lodged within my own discipline. If I were ever to make an impact on my field, maybe this was where I belonged. Caught up once again in life at Cornell, these thoughts were for the moment set aside.

In the fall of 1960, I was invited to serve as a director of the newly formed Library Organization and Management Section of the Library Administration Division of the American Library Association. A bit later I gained elective office as the section's vice-chairman, and then chairman, ending my term in 1964. At Indiana University's School of Business a Cornell doctoral alumnus, James Patterson, was making a reputation as a marketing professor. Referring to the

Cornell model, he put forward the idea of establishing a graduate business school library at the university that would be presided over by someone who could also teach, do research, and publish. Indiana's dean, Arthur Weimer, had the energy and imagination to understand that the Cornell model might be worth emulating. He engaged me as a consultant to help design a comparable program for the Indiana Graduate School of Business. I spent two years and several pleasurable stays in Bloomington working on this project. I finally realized that my consulting assignment was actually an attempt to lure me to Indiana. I had little interest in doing the same thing twice and concluded the association.

At a library conference in New York City later that fall of 1960, I had a chance meeting with Francis St. John. I caught up on developments at the Brooklyn Public Library, and filled him in on my career since 1953. St. John was interested in the public library focus of my doctoral research. He informed me that the directors of the three New York City library systems in Brooklyn, Queens, and New York were planning to commission a study of readership patterns of library use. St. John told me he would be pleased if I would put forward a proposal for such a study. Back in Ithaca, I discussed the idea with a marketing colleague, Hart Walters. Walters's background was in psychology and marketing research. He thought the use of motivation research techniques with a limited sample, rather than a quantitative study employing a fixed questionnaire with a great number of respondents, would be the most useful strategy. I agreed. We drafted a proposal and sent it to St. John. Soon afterward we were invited to a meeting with the library directors in New York where we elaborated our study plan. Sentiment was divided about whether to support such an unorthodox research method, but with St. John championing our effort a decision was made to go forward.

During a three-week period between mid-December 1960 and early January 1961, Walters and I conducted a total of twenty-seven in-depth interviews with male and female adults living in regions served by the three library systems. Sampling was opportunistic, but cut across all social categories, including income level, ethnic origin, educational background, and the distance respondents lived from libraries. Respondents were encouraged to discuss freely every aspect of their reading and use of libraries. Interviews ranged from fifteen minutes to one hour. In addition to direct and indirect lines of inquiry, word associations and cartoon identifications were employed. With permission from our subjects, we taped these interviews. While the conclusions of the research were highly tentative, resulting as they had from a small sampling during an exploratory analysis, they did afford some very suggestive hypotheses. These were elaborated under eighteen categories in the report submitted to the library directors. In a section on directions for further study, we suggested further explorations to verify some of our findings. We would expand the number of respondents to two hundred, eliminate certain areas of questioning in order to deepen the line of analysis, and add some new question categories.

The insights identified in the pilot study suggested the need for a more thorough analysis, potentially leading to revised approaches and strategies with the library audience. One finding, however, deeply disturbed all three of the library directors. It dealt with the potential for attracting adults who were currently non-readers and non-users. We had learned that the public library was irrelevant to the purposes and requirements of this group. Walters and I suggested that if further evidence corroborated what we had found in the pilot study, the library systems would be trying to go against a structure of behavior and supporting attitudes that were fundamental to the individuals involved. Strong evidence from advertising and public relations indicated that it was virtually impossible to effect profound change in an individual's general conditions of life by seeking to alter attitudes and behavior. If on further study this hypothesis were fully verified, it would be reasonable to write off such people as potential users. We had qualified our remarks by indicating that this was not the same as saying that *all* non-users should be ruled out as potential users. What was implicit, however, was that virtually all adult non-users might need to be written off as a lost cause for becoming an appreciable segment of the library systems' future audience.

Walters and I had inadvertently assaulted a basic tenet of library faith: that non-user and non-reading adults might be redeemed by the public library. St. John and his two colleagues were outraged. They angrily rejected the evidence of our findings. Needless to say, they were not disposed to lend further support to such heresy in full-scale, follow-on research. The report was not disseminated beyond the three directors. Moreover, they denied permission for publication of any portion of the research in any other medium. The study report and findings have never been seen or discussed anywhere outside the occasional seminar, in which Walters and I later made use of the material. Thenceforward, I was perceived as suspect for betraying the public library cause. Sadly, the rapport I had long enjoyed with St. John was over.

During my absence in Ann Arbor, the Sloan Institute had determined that there was need for a review and analysis of the information facilities serving hospital administration and related disciplines. I was engaged to synthesize, order, and assess these information sources. A committee of specialists and experts in the field advised me in this effort, which resulted in a publication by the Graduate School of Business and Public Administration. This monograph identified and characterized library facilities, government programs, statistics sources, fact-finding sources on individuals and organizations, periodicals, indexes, abstracts, specialized services, professional, research, and university programs. It also covered the literature and bibliography of the health management field. My colleague, Betsy Ann Olive, prepared a thorough index to the content. The work, *Sources for Hospital Administrators: Publications and Facilities Serving the Health Administration Field*, was issued in 1961.

My experience with the Sloan project and my work on the *Gale Directory of University Research Bureaus and Institutes* led me to compile a full-scale directory of organizations in the health field. I began work in late 1960 with student assistance provided by the Sloan Institute of Hospital Administration. I patterned my methods after the procedures I had used when compiling and editing the Gale publication. Under the auspices of Cornell University's Graduate School of Business Administration, *Health Organizations of the US, Canada and Internationally* was published in 1961.

With the positive reception accorded *Sources for Hospital Administrators*, it was clear to me that a wide audience would find value in comparable works on many business management subjects. I envisaged developing a continuing series of volumes, each covering one distinct subject. The content of each would incorporate the full range of information sources on that topic. I discussed the idea with Fred Ruffner. He was encouraging. He saw the proposed series contributing to the literature of management, research, and reference work, with Gale Research Company as the publisher.

Once the idea had been accepted and the publisher identified, the next step was to find suitable authors who could prepare the volumes. Special librarians, working in unique collections, with their understanding of and access to information on important subjects, would make suitable prospective volume editors. If they could be convinced to bring their expertise into play, they could contribute source books that would be highly valued by a wider constituency, beyond the organizations where these librarians worked. I felt strongly that the image of librarianship would be enhanced if librarians themselves brought their subject knowledge to bear on a publication that offered practical information in a particular field.

The Best of Times

The first discussions with potential contributors took place at the Special Libraries Association Conference in 1961. A number of special librarians, known for their subject competence, were invited to consider editing individual volumes. By fall, they had agreed to participate. Operating guidelines were drafted, and memoranda governing formats and citation form were issued. Gale Research Company drew up formal contracts for each of the contributors. By a fortunate coincidence, Janice Babb and Beverly Dordick, both with the National Association of Real Estate Boards, had been considering doing a book on information sources for the real estate field. Their work was soon underway. By early 1963, *Real Estate Information Sources* appeared as the first volume in the Gale Management Information Guide Series. This work proved a model and prototype for succeeding volumes in its comprehensiveness, meticulous preparation, careful editing, and thorough index. Reviews in both the library media and in the real estate journals were laudatory. The young in-house editor who worked with me and with the authors was Dedria Bryfonski. She eventually became chief executive officer at Gale Research Company. Thirty-eight volumes were published in the series. The last was published in 1983. With only two exceptions, all the authors were special librarians. They constituted a distinguished roster of the field's finest.

Like many thesis writers, I wished to broadcast the conceptual thinking and research evidence from my dissertation. I sought to publish in a periodical with wide readership. The article "Research Frontiers" appeared in the July 1961 issue of the *Library Journal*. It was there that I advanced, in more popular style, the basic thinking embodied in the thesis. I identified how and where research evidence might further the effective practice of the administration of public libraries. Another article appeared in the December 1961 issue of *Illinois Libraries*. It was written at the invitation of Mary Lee Bundy, who was then with the Library Research Center at the University of Illinois Library School. This was a special issue given over to management topics. My paper was titled, "Policy Formulation in Libraries." The piece dealt with four themes: decision-making authority, organizational planning methods, characteristics of supervisory personnel, and administrative controls and supervision. The article is less important than the fact that in the course of doing it, Mary Lee Bundy and I came to know each other. Our acquaintance formed the basis for closer professional ties in the future.

In the summer of 1961, I revisited Ann Arbor. There, I repeated the two courses I had taught the previous summer. My second offering of the library administration class brought about a drastic revision and reduction in the demands upon the students. As a result, student sentiment improved dramatically. During the academic year of 1961-1962, I made a considerable effort to complete the first edition of *Statistics Sources*. Georgi and Kruzas finished on schedule the sections of the work that they were responsible for. The final manuscript was ready and mailed to Gale Research Company for late spring publication in 1962. Back at Cornell, working with graduate students of business and public administration, I once again received comments on the limits of my 1956 book, *Information for Administrators*. They wanted something that would lead directly to material on any business management topic. By then, I had become very familiar with preparing reference books and I had grown confident in my ability to create new works. What the students were proposing was a new and different kind of reference tool. I knew this would be a daunting task if I were to undertake such a project. For several months I pondered what such a work might contain, how it could be arranged, and what strategy I would use in its compilation. These deliberations led to a plan with several distinctive characteristics. First, the work would be arranged alphabetically by specific business topics. Second, cross-references would be liberally included in the alphabetical listings, which would redirect the user of an unused term to the subject where the information could be found. Third, the subjects included would run the gamut across the widest range of business and management topics. Finally, under every topic, details would be given about current and pertinent sources for learning more about the subject — including resources ranging from handbooks, dictionaries, directories, and bibliographies to journals, newsletters, encyclopedias, trade associations, and research organizations.

The intent of the work would be to provide an array of sources on hundreds of subjects, thus anticipating questions on these topics by pre-arranging all the pertinent sources. Information seekers or librarians would have access to a ready-made tool, obviating the need to do "look-up" searches on these subjects. A subject list was the first step to putting together the book. Terms would be drawn from existing subject indexes like *Business Periodicals Index*, *Public Affairs Information Service Bulletin*, and specialized business dictionaries. For each subject included in the final list of topics, a reference search would fill in the sources germane to that topic. Trial efforts were begun to test the viability of this approach. While this process was underway, the idea for this publication was discussed with Fred Ruffner. The novelty of the content design and the uncertainty that the finished product would meet the requirements of its intended audience led Ruffner to suggest that the work be published on an experimental basis, without attribution to Gale Research or to me. The publisher would be identified only as Business Guides Company. The work would, however, be advertised and distributed by Gale Research Company. If the book was favorably received, later editions would bear the Gale imprint. The three-volume work, *Executive's Guide to Information Sources,* was more than two years in the making. It was not published until 1964. Market reception proved favorable. A widely used business reference tool, *The Executive's Guide,* became the nucleus for subsequent publication as the *Encyclopedia of Business Information Sources.*

I returned to Michigan in the summer of 1962. By then, the novelty of summer teaching was beginning to wear thin. Back in Ithaca in August, a new and unusual opportunity came my way. During Litchfield's deanship, Cornell had built relationships with overseas institutions. Litchfield's visit to the University of Indonesia in the mid-1960's resulted in a contract with the government foreign aid agency—later known as the Agency for International Development, or AID—whereby Cornell built a library in public administration for shipment to Indonesia. Our responsibility had included the selection and acquisition of books, in addition to their full cataloging and classification by the central technical services unit of the Cornell library system. Cards were made and filed in a catalog. Finally, the book collection of some two thousand volumes and the catalog were shipped to Indonesia. More recently the school had developed an interinstitutional relationship with Middle East Technical University in Ankara. This higher education institution offered classes conducted in English. Junior faculty from the university in Ankara came from Turkey to study at Cornell toward the doctorate. In return, Cornell faculty were invited to spend one or two years in Ankara as visiting professors. In addition to teaching, the visiting faculty helped develop a new curriculum in administration. Given the previous experience in setting up the Indonesian library, it was decided that an essential element of the Cornell/Middle-East Technical University association should include a strong administration library as part of the university library in Ankara. I was invited to travel to Turkey as a consultant for three weeks during September 1962. During that time, I would serve as library advisor to the Agency for International Development and its other Turkey-based projects.

I had not been outside the United States since my return from military service in Europe in 1946. I welcomed the opportunity to revisit the continent. As part of my itinerary, I built in a two-day stopover in Paris to savor once again a bit of its Gallic flavor. In 1962 the dollar was very strong everywhere in Europe. The Paris I rediscovered during this trip suffered from no shortages. My visit was all too brief, and I resolved to try to return again.

The Best of Times

Ankara was unlike any city I had experienced in the West. Everything seemed exotic and strange—from the unique language to the heavy smog from coke-burning furnaces. The furnishings of hotels and offices were in the style of 1930's America. My colleague, Seymour Smidt, and his wife had only recently arrived before me to begin a two-year visiting professorship. Once established in my centrally located hotel, my AID host arranged appointments for me with the chairman of the administration faculty and the president of the university. I knew that my time in Turkey would be very brief, so I was keen to make every hour count. I got right to work on my assignment. The AID official took me at once to the office of the university librarian. After making introductions, he excused himself.

William Bennett was the university library director. He had been serving for some months as a UNESCO appointee. The university was the recipient of support from a number of international bodies as well as from AID. Bennett, a burly outgoing black American of considerable personal humor and charm, greeted me warmly. As we sat and talked about mutual colleagues and librarianship in the United States, Turkish coffee was brought in. Our random chat continued for another forty-five minutes or so as we sipped the thick, sweet brew. When I tried to shift the conversation toward my assignment and the timetable of my work, Bennett dexterously returned the discussion to generalities about life and culture in Turkey. I grew impatient. My time in Turkey was limited and I was itching to get to work. A secretary came in to announce that the chairman of the faculty committee was waiting to see Bennett. Thus, our first meeting ended without any substantive discussion at all. We made a date to meet again the following day. As I was ushered out and reflected on my interview, my assessment was that if I were Bennett, an academic librarian from Atlanta, the Middle East Technical University assignment would be an attractive sinecure. The slow pace and the easy-going social discourse was far easier than concentration on getting things done under pressure as was customary in the United States. I did not understand that Bennett had been instructing me in the ways of Turkey. Business was never conducted in a hurry. More important by far was the establishment of relaxed interpersonal relations. I was simply too brash and insensitive to understand the lesson Bennett was trying to teach me.

Early in my stay I met Ann Davis, the United States Information Services librarian who covered Turkey and Greece as regional librarian for both countries. She was my first introduction to American overseas librarianship. She served as the model against which I would assess the USIS librarians I would later meet in other parts of the world. Ann was exemplary in every respect. She was highly astute politically and had her finger on the pulse of everything bearing upon books, libraries, education, and the cultural scene in Turkey. Her efforts transcended the normal boundaries of library practice. She was engaged actively in spearheading the translation of important American books into Turkish. She was knowledgeable about Turkish government developments, and maintained associations with key political figures. She saw to it that they had access to American publications relevant to their responsibilities. She worked energetically with local educational institutions, individual librarians, and library associations. She also got involved with library education programs in Ankara and Istanbul. While Bill Bennett became my advisor on the library and political context at Middle East Technical University, Ann Davis guided my understanding of the higher education scene in Istanbul and elsewhere in Turkey. It was she who helped me gain access to key figures in other universities, with whom our efforts at Middle East Technical University were related.

Despite my busy work schedule, I still had time to enjoy the excellent cuisine and fine Turkish wines so little known outside the country. Sy Smidt accompanied me on visits to Istanbul University and Robert College in Istanbul. There I enjoyed the sights and sounds of this crossroads between Europe and Asia. I also became hopelessly lost in the maze of stalls in the famous covered bazaar. Grueling work, professional activities, social events, and tourism were all crammed into my short three-week stay. On my return trip I scheduled a weekend stop in Athens, where I frenetically dashed about to every single tourist highlight. I wrote a draft of my report on the homeward flight. I returned home exhausted but exhilarated by the experience.

The first night home I awoke during the night and fainted in the bathroom. When I saw the doctor the next morning, I was instructed to go at once to the Tompkins County Hospital for admittance. The X-rays my doctor ordered confirmed his preliminary diagnosis; I was suffering from a bleeding ulcer. After a week in the hospital of bed rest and a light bland diet, a later X-ray revealed that the ulcer had healed. It was only after another week at home of eating carefully and limiting my exercise that the doctor permitted me to return to work. A combination of spicy Turkish cuisine and an overzealous work pace had most likely brought about the ulcer. My sudden illness taught me that I could not change the world in three weeks and that I would need to accept cultural conditions as they were. If the phones do not work, one must be patient. When a meeting does not begin on schedule, it will begin somewhat later. I had tried to measure events in a foreign land against my own compulsive yardstick. In order to survive and succeed in any overseas context, I would need to create for myself an alternate persona—one of patience, tolerance, and acceptance. My hospital stay had been a costly way to learn this lesson, but it became indelibly etched into the fiber of my personality for a lifetime.

My fall course during the 1962-1963 school year had been disrupted by my illness. I did not meet my first class until after three weeks of the term had passed. By the fall of 1962, however, Steve McCarthy and I had finally achieved a more cordial relationship. He seemed pleased with the recognition that the library of the school had gained both on and off the campus. Betsy Ann Olive had become highly regarded in the campus library community. We fit well within the framework of the Cornell library system and were no longer regarded with suspicion. A more tangible factor in my solidified association with McCarthy resided in the fact that neither one of us had much confidence in Litchfield's successor, Stewart Sheppard. In spite of his friendly, personal style and constant assurance of agreement and understanding, Sheppard would frequently be inconsistent. Sheppard's strong card was public relations and the appearance of good will. He sought to please everyone and ended up pleasing no one. This led McCarthy and me to draw closer, based on mutual trust and respect. I continued my sporadic consulting visits to the University of Indiana Graduate Business School and worked actively in both the Special Libraries Association and the American Library Association. In the Special Libraries Association, I served as chairman of the finance committee. During this time, I was also continuing my efforts with the Organization and Management Section of the Library Administration Division of the ALA. These responsibilities entailed regular attendance at the annual meetings of both organizations, as well as the mid-winter meetings of the American Library Association. More than two years had passed since I concluded my doctoral study. I had misgivings about gaps in my understanding of the ever more rapidly encroaching world of computer technology. Caught up as I was in a full schedule of teaching, library association meetings, and writing commitments, I could not conceive of any way to learn what I felt I should know.

On a return flight from the ALA meeting in January 1963, I wound up seated next to Jesse Shera, dean of the Western Reserve University library school. During our conversation I shared with him my disquiet about my lack of technology awareness. Shera's reaction was immediate and to the point. He proposed that I spend an academic year as a post-doctoral scholar at Western Reserve, where I could sit in on sessions in the Center for Documentation Research at the library school. I could also sit in on selected classes at Case Institute of Technology, located adjacent to Western Reserve University. He offered to arrange an alumni financial stipend of several thousand dollars to help finance me. If I could identify one or two other sources of support, he felt the study year should be feasible. I thanked him for his generous invitation and said that I would see what I could work out. When I discussed the prospective study plan for academic year 1963-1964 with Sheppard and McCarthy, both gave their approval. I would have to take unpaid leave, and my salary would be used to pay for someone to work in the library during my absence. A substitute in my teaching role would also need to be compensated. I needed to find the means to supplement the Western Reserve grant in order to make the study year possible.

I applied for fellowship support from the Tangley Oaks Foundation of United Educators, Inc. This was a Chicago-based grant-making organization affiliated with an encyclopedia publishing firm. It offered financial awards to librarians seeking to carry out study programs intended to enhance their ability to contribute to the field of librarianship. The application required a resume of education and experience and details of the proposed study and its prospective benefits to the recipient and to library service. I also wrote to Fred Ruffner at Gale Research Company. I explained to him what I hoped to do, and asked whether he might have a project that I might work on for him during 1963 and 1964. Seeking further support, I applied to the American Philosophical Society in Philadelphia. In the proposal, I outlined my plans for the year of post-doctoral study. The funds sought would be used for travel to selected sites at academic and research centers to observe at first hand developments in library automation and technological research bearing directly on the future of library operations.

Fred Ruffner responded first. He telephoned to say he did not know what project he might need me for, but he would use me as a consultant, and I could count on that income. I received word from Tangley Oaks in March. I was designated a Tangley Oaks fellow and was awarded a financial grant. It was not until May that favorable word came from the American Philosophical Society. They offered me the travel funds I had applied for. By then I had already phoned Dean Shera to inform him that I planned to move to Cleveland with my family and to spend the next academic year in post-doctoral study at Western Reserve. He said that he and his colleagues looked forward to greeting me in September. In mid-summer

The Best of Times

I made a stopover in Cleveland, while en route somewhere, and arranged to rent a furnished apartment in East Cleveland. The apartment was only a half-hour walk from Western Reserve University. That summer, we sublet our house in Ithaca, and planned for the transfer of Jacqueline and Steven to a public school in East Cleveland for the next school year.

Dean Shera welcomed me on my first visit to the campus. He arranged office space for me and introduced me to his colleagues. The person who facilitated most aspects of my work was Margaret Kaltenbach, the assistant dean. Shera was the imaginative and eloquent public symbol of Western Reserve. Kaltenbach made the classes run on time. I was most interested in the Center for Documentation Research, which was then under the management of Alan Goldwyn. He served as associate director under Dean Shera. Two impressive junior faculty in the center at the time, who later distinguished themselves in library education and research, were Alan Rees and Tefko Saracevic. The announced purpose of my independent study was met with a degree of skepticism and suspicion. No one had ever been a post-doctoral scholar at Western Reserve. People wondered what my real motives were. After I arranged to audit two classes at the center in data processing and information retrieval and after I had gotten to know the staff better, my presence was viewed in a more relaxed manner. Shera invited me to attend faculty meetings if I chose to (which I did not), and Margaret Kaltenbach eased my acceptance as an auditor in two classes at Case Institute of Technology. One class was on automation; the other was about operations research.

I planned to spend the year sitting in on classes and pursuing an independent course of readings about machine technology and data processing in libraries. I also wanted to prepare an account of my experiences. I would conduct a small study of Midwest academic library administrators on automation applications in their institutions, and carry out a series of site visits to institutions and centers, where I could see the installation of systems and research-in-progress on library automation. The only commitment I brought with me from Cornell was to continue work in collaboration with Fred Silander—by then an associate professor at DePauw University—on a supplement to the earlier *Decision Making* book. We wanted to include more recent selections from the burgeoning new literature that had appeared since the original bibliography was published. Ann Matthews at Cornell assisted us in abstracting and editorial activities throughout the compilation. *Decision Making: An Annotated Bibliography (Supplement 1958-1963)* was published by the Graduate School of Business and Public Administration in

June of 1964. The size of this five-year supplement was twice that of the original volume. My consulting relationship with Gale Research Company led to no specific or regular editorial assignment by the time the school year had begun. I suspected that Fred Ruffner was loathe to encumber my study with too demanding a responsibility. I resisted, but Shera prevailed upon me to teach a course. It was to be on library administration during the spring semester. I had already taught the course twice at Michigan, so I felt the assignment would not prove too onerous.

For the first time in my life I had the freedom at Western Reserve to pursue an independent course of study. I could choose what to read and which classes to attend. The fall term proved stimulating and enriching. My colleagues at the Center for Documentation Research were very helpful. They discussed with me in detail any technical issues that interested me. In the spring, I arranged for a similar class program. Between the classes I audited and the course I taught, my spring schedule included a series of field trips. Perhaps most instructive of the seven or eight visits I made were those to Washington University in St. Louis, the University of Illinois at Chicago, and Stanford Research Institute in California. At Washington University, I met with Ralph Parker, director of the library and a pioneer in computer applications in libraries. Parker demonstrated for me the library's automated systems. At the Chicago campus of the University of Illinois, Louis Schultheiss and Ed Heiliger showed me their data processing installation. During my visit to Stanford Research Institute, Charles Bourne explained his research investigations of automated retrieval systems, performance evaluation, and cost analysis. The other element of my travel program took me to Paris, where I participated in a short seminar directed by the archeologist, Jean Claude Gardin, who had created an ingenious automatic data retrieval system, SYNTOL, for every type of physical artifact.

Another pleasurable and enlightening element of my stay in Cleveland was attendance at the occasional colloquium lectures offered by visiting scholars. These visits invariably offered ample time for personal discussions. This was how I came to know Professor Wilfred Saunders, who was on an American fact-finding tour before embarking on his efforts to inaugurate a graduate program in library and information science at the University of Sheffield. Jack Mills was another itinerant Briton from Northwestern Polytechnic in London who passed through and spoke about interesting work being done by the British classification research group. The year at Western Reserve reinforced my identification with librarianship. It afforded me a new and revised perspective on the dramatic opportunities available in the field. I felt strongly that I could contribute new and untried approaches to education for librarianship, if I were given the opportunity. In the spring, Rudolph Gjelness invited me back to Michigan to teach in the summer school program once more. I had completed work on the *Decision Making* supplement. The questionnaire data from academic library administrators had been received and recorded, and the notes from my year's study program had been edited. When I moved the family back to Ithaca in June, prior to flying to Ann Arbor, my plans while teaching in Michigan in July and August were expanded to incorporate the preparation of a manuscript about my study year.

While I was in Cleveland, the promotions committee at Cornell had voted for my promotion to full professor. A new dean had been appointed in our school. He was William Carmichael from the Ford Foundation where, even though he was only in his mid-thirties, he had served as a senior official. During my study leave, a new building had been completed. It housed the Graduate School of Business and Public Administration and its library. It was named for Deane Malott, who had been president of the university during much of the 1950's and 1960's. He had been very supportive of the program in business and public administration. In Cleveland, I had decided it was time for me to divest myself of the responsibility for directing the library. During both my Ph.D. year and the Western Reserve post-doctoral year, Betsy Ann Olive had managed the library effectively. It was time for me to step aside and let her have the title and rewards of being recognized as the library administrator. In order to facilitate Betsy Ann's promotion, I decided to leave the library and devote myself entirely to teaching and research in the school. My new understanding of data processing and information retrieval would allow me to augment my repertoire in teaching research methods and business information systems. The university libraries and Steve McCarthy might still avail themselves of my services, but only as a consultant in library management and retrieval. I knew that McCarthy and Shepherd deeply respected Betsy Ann Olive's competence, and would welcome her in the post of business and public administration librarian. If I failed to gain the new dean's support for such a change, I would view it as a signal for me to move on. A professorial appointment in a library school might be a logical next step. That summer, however, I still faced the task of writing the book. I was eager to describe for the academic library field exactly where I saw the discipline in relation to the emerging new technology.

The monograph that resulted was *The Librarian and the Machine: Observations on the Applications of Machines in the Administration of College and University Libraries*. In ten brief chapters I presented my observations, not from the point of view of a systems analyst or engineer, but, rather, from the user of such systems. The volume reported on recent developments in the mechanization of library processes, based on published reports as well as site visits. The book moved on to document innovations in technical systems and structures that were having an impact on academic librarianship. The characteristics and expertise of individuals in the vanguard of these evolving practices were also examined. I outlined the various paths these leaders had chosen as they developed their new technologies. The contributions and the limitations of the three principal professional associations — the American Library Association, the Special Libraries Association, and the American Documentation Institute (later known as the American Society for Information Science) — were also presented. The computer industry and its influence on future directions were profiled in later chapters, which also included an evaluation of the status of library education in 1963-1964. The timely incorporation of curricular adaptations, reflective of emerging technological directions in the practice of librarianship, was advanced as well. The next to last chapter reported the results of the small sample survey of Midwest library directors. It identified how fully half their number could be characterized as concerned but inactive. Many librarians felt uncertain about the uses of technology and were therefore unable to move toward innovation in their organizations. Many others preferred to wait and see; they remained unconvinced that any change in procedure would represent a forward step in their libraries. Less than twenty percent of the respondents felt a deep personal need to adapt to machine procedures. They were already exploring the prospects or actively engaged in implementing change. The final chapter summarized the main findings. The implications for education in librarianship included several critical factors. There was a need to retool library personnel and to make administrative choices between choosing data processing as a comprehensive system or opting for an isolated element of the process. The utility of a central clearing house on library data processing was illustrated, as were the prospects for information retrieval in the academic library during the coming months. The chapter concluded with some thoughts about the potential for library associations to catalyze technological innovation. An annotated bibliography of books and monographs, in the order in which I had read them, was included along with a personal assessment of the relevance of each selection. Beverly Brewster prepared the index. She was a former graduate student of mine at the University of Michigan. Gale Research Company published the book early in 1965.

Once I was back at Cornell, I settled into a new office in the school's new building. My first task was to revise my course to incorporate elements from my study. I wanted to augment the content by demonstrating how technological advances bore upon managerial information. In mid-September, I received the first overture I ever received from the field of library education. Ralph Shaw, widely known for his path-breaking efforts in applying machine processes at the Department of Agriculture Library, and the founder of Scarecrow Press, had been appointed the dean of a newly established library education program at the University of Hawaii. He was also the director of the university's library. He put out a feeler to determine my possible interest in becoming associated with him. A professorial appointment in such an exotic location, paired with the opportunity to work with a pioneer in the field, seemed an ideal opportunity. This was before I learned the details of the job description. Shaw was working from a conceptual framework, in which he saw the faculty functioning in teaching and research, in addition to the practice of librarianship. The post he proposed was as joint appointee between professor of librarianship and head of the university library's reference department. This arrangement was very similar to the role I had assumed at Cornell. The only difference was the substitution of a library school for a school of business and public administration. I found myself at odds philosophically and intellectually with Shaw's construct. I understood the need to forge active links between professional education and occupational practice. If I were to move into library education, however, it would have to be a full professorial commitment. I considered what he proposed to be an overloaded and schizoid responsibility. Ralph Shaw and I had had our differences in the past. Once during a panel discussion, in which we had both participated, I made what I felt was a totally innocent observation. He was so incensed that he had not spoken to me for months thereafter. As graciously as I was able, I wrote to Shaw to say thank you, but no thank you.

Shortly after Shaw's overture I received a letter from R. Lee Hornbake, Vice President for Academic Affairs at the University of Maryland. He invited me to apply for the position of dean of a yet-to-be-established library school in College Park. I had never contemplated a move into a university administrative post. I identified myself as a teacher and scholar, rather than as an administrator. The prospect of bringing into being a wholly new academic enterprise, unencumbered with past traditions or expectations, intrigued me very much. I aspired to no more than a professorial role, but my curiosity was aroused. If the institution was seriously committed, and if the resources to build a program of distinction were forthcoming, such an assignment might well be worth investing a period of years. It was a chance to construct the type of exemplary professional school where I might take pleasure in serving as a faculty member. After only a day's reflection, I wrote to Hornbake and enclosed my resume. While I awaited further word from Maryland, I scheduled an appointment with Dean Carmichael to discuss with him my desire to change my appointment in the school. Carmichael listened carefully and told me that he would need time to consider carefully what I was proposing. A week or two later, Hornbake telephoned to invite me to the Maryland campus. I would meet with the dean selection committee, which he was chairing. When I explained and apologized for the fact that in the coming three or four weeks I was too heavily committed with teaching responsibilities to leave the Cornell campus, Hornbake inquired whether I would object to his coming to Ithaca to meet with me. I assured him that I would be pleased to welcome him at Cornell.

Hornbake's career had been spent exclusively in public institutions of higher education. Cornell, steeped as it is in tradition and history and extraordinary in its grounds and architecture, had the effect of enhancing Hornbake's assessment of the candidate he had come to interview. We met first in my handsomely appointed office located in the impressive new building that housed the school. Lunch was at the faculty club in the Statler Hotel School building. When we later strolled the quadrangle of the lower campus and looked out over the valley and Lake Cayuga, I felt that he was not only reviewing me as a prospect, but seeing me in the context of this prestigious institution. My long association with Cornell was perceived as an asset. Hornbake, then and for as long as I have known him, came across as an unassuming, modest, and friendly man. I liked and trusted him from that very first meeting. During our time spent together, he gave me the background on Maryland's decision to launch a new professional school. He laid out the steps needed to bring the program into being by September 1965. My questions related to resources, political and bureaucratic constraints, and managerial flexibility. In sum, I wanted to know the degree to which the founding dean would enjoy decision-making prerogatives and the latitude to move forward expeditiously. I also informed Hornbake that I was committed to Cornell through the end of the 1964-1965 academic year. If I were to be Maryland's choice, I felt it might be feasible to reduce my responsibility at Cornell in the spring to a half-time appointment. That way I might be able to arrange to spend half my time in College Park. I could concentrate on accomplishing all the necessary tasks to make the fall opening date possible. By the time Hornbake departed, his questions and mine had been answered to our mutual satisfaction. Hornbake told me he would report our discussion to the selection committee. If the committee were so disposed, I would then be invited to the Maryland campus early in December to meet with the committee and with Wilson Elkins, president of the University. I thought our meeting had gone well and felt I would be a serious contender for the Maryland deanship.

Lee Hornbake called me a week after his visit to ask whether I could come to College Park to meet with the committee. I scheduled the trip for the earliest possible date. During a whirlwind two-day stay, I spent most of my time in meetings with the full search committee made up of faculty members and deans of two colleges. I also met with members individually. The hospitable climate for the new school, reflected in the remarks of the search committee, encouraged me. I was more concerned about the limited quarters allocated for the new school's use on the upper two floors of the already overcrowded university library building, McKeldin Library. Hornbake offered assurance that all the space needs of the program would be met by the time of the school's startup. He also explained that should I accept the post, the university would underwrite the travel and living expenses I would incur during the period from January until June, when I would be moving to College Park. By the time I met with the president on the afternoon of the second day, Hornbake and I had even discussed the salary level for the post. The move would represent no improvement in my earnings, when the twelve-month nature of the deanship was compared to my Cornell academic year appointment.

Before I left, I saw Wilson Elkins, the president. He was very candid. A number of inquiries had been made about me, he explained, virtually all of them favorable. Hornbake had apparently learned of me from someone I had known casually as a fellow Ph.D. student at Michigan, Russell Munn. Munn was the very erudite dean of libraries at the University of West Virginia. He was the son of a distinguished public librarian, Ralph Munn, who for many years had served as director of the highly regarded Carnegie Public Library in Pittsburgh. Russell Munn told Hornbake that if Maryland were seeking someone to lead the new school in the mainstream of library education, I would be the wrong choice. If, however, Maryland was willing to go with a risk-taker inclined to chart new directions, then I might be the right selection. Elkins also reported to me a conversation he had with Stewart Sheppard, my dean at Cornell before he moved to the faculty of the University of Virginia business school. Sheppard had described me as quite competent, but made the point that I was given to aggressive behavior. What Elkins seemed to be communicating was that I might try to rein in my forceful performance style in a prospective deanship. I didn't comment on his observations. Neither did I explain how several years earlier I had been a member of the faculty at Cornell which had given Sheppard a vote of no-confidence, thus obliging him by the end of the academic year to leave and accept a professorship at Virginia. I finally realized that I had been told these things because Elkins was preparing to offer me the deanship and the rank of professor in the still unnamed professional school. When he formally extended the offer, I thanked him and told him that I would need a week's time to consider it. I returned from my trip pleased yet undecided.

Moving the family from Ithaca, our home for more than eleven years, to a new region was not a decision to be taken lightly. Moreover, if Carmichael were to accede to my proposal, my situation at Cornell would be adapted to permit me to concentrate fully on teaching, research, and writing. I had no administrative aspirations. Yet the Maryland deanship offered a once-in-a-lifetime opportunity to build an academic program from scratch. After the foundations were firmly in place, I would be able to revert to a faculty role in a professional school in my own discipline. To clarify my choice, I decided to press Carmichael for a decision. He was out of town and would not be back in the office until Saturday. By then he would have had a number of weeks to consider my proposal. I had promised Lee Hornbake I would make a decision by Monday. I resolved to confront Carmichael on Saturday morning. That day proved to be a busy one at the school. A special faculty meeting was scheduled for late morning. Carmichael was caught up in preparing for it. I told his secretary that I needed no more than ten minutes of his time. She informed me that he was too busy to see me. On the way to the meeting, I came upon Carmichael in the corridor. I asked him if he had considered the proposal I had made to him more than a month earlier. He impatiently shrugged me off, saying he had not yet decided. I had my answer. Early Monday morning in December 1964, I telephoned Lee Hornbake to accept the Maryland offer.

LEFT: In Brittany, France while on weekend pass in April 1945.

BELOW: On leave from the U.S. Air Corps in February 1944. Seen with parents and sister Marilyn.

Working on the 83rd Infantry Division Newspaper, The Thunderbolt, *in Linz, Austra, December 1945.*

With children Jacqueline and Steven in Ithaca, New York, with Cornell University in the background in 1955.

LEFT: *One month after founding the Maryland Library School Program. Seen in the school's office in McKeldin Library in October 1966.*

BELOW: *With John Rizzo and program participant during the first Maryland Library Administrators Development Program at the Donaldson Brown Center, Summer 1967.*

ABOVE: With David Batty and Claude Walston in San Jose dos Campos, Brazil, in January 1975, while conducting a seminar at the Brazilian Institute for Space Research.

ABOVE: In Mexico City in February 1975 seated between Krystyna and Guadalupe Carrion. Also seen in the photo are Guillermo Fernandez de la Garza, Jacques Tocatlian of UNESCO, and Ricardo Gietz, President of FID.

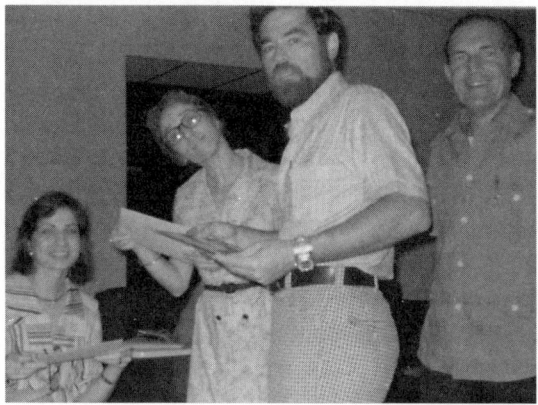

ABOVE: Standing next to John Rizzo, Delia Torrijos, and a program participant during the 1976 UNESCO Regional Management Seminar for Southeast Asia held in Tagaytay City, the Phillippines, in June 1976.

LEFT: With Rocio Marban, Paul Vassallo, and a program participant during the Organization of American States seminar held in Managua, Nicaragua, in August 1976.

ABOVE: With the other delegates during the conference of the FID, IFLA, and the ICA on cooperation and collaboration held at the Rockefeller Center in Bellagio, Italy, in May 1980.

LEFT: Seated next to Joachim Freiherr von Ledebur of the German Foundation for International Development during a meeting in December 1980 on training issues for developing countries.

ABOVE: During the August 1980 International Federation for Documentation Conference in Copenhagen. The American Delegation included Ed Walker, Judy Werdel, Paul Wasserman, and Irene Farkas Conn, who appear in this photo.

At the University of Ibadan, Nigeria, in May 1981 during a conference of the Education and Training Committee of the International Federation for Documentation.

With Wojciech Pirog from Poland's Central Institute for Scientific and Technical Information during a late 1982 visit in Baltimore.

ABOVE: At home in 1984 with Effie and Bob Knight.

ABOVE: With Danuta Nitecki, the author's last doctoral student at the University of Maryland, December 1995.

ABOVE: *Seated with student participants while lecturing at the Institute for Scientific and Technical Information of China in Beijing, January 1996.*

RIGHT: *Newspaper account of the Beijing seminar at ISTIC published in the Chinese newspaper,* Science and Technology Daily, *January 23, 1996.*

Chapter Eleven

When I announced my decision at Cornell, McCarthy and Carmichael agreed to reduce my time and compensation at Cornell to fifty percent from January through June. My classes would be held from Thursday to Saturday, which permitted me to fly to Washington on Sunday evenings. I would return to Ithaca at the end of the day on Wednesday. My children would be able to complete the school year in Ithaca before moving. Commuting arrangements were less than ideal. I had to fly to Washington National Airport with Mohawk Airlines. The first leg was between Ithaca and Newark, where I got a connecting flight to Washington. It was an hour-long taxi ride from National Airport to College Park. Taxi service was highly unreliable. I finally engaged a Maryland student employee at the Center for Adult Education. He came to meet my flight and drove me to the airport on a regular basis. The center had been constructed recently at the edge of the campus, affording not only conference and teaching spaces, but also comfortable hotel accommodations and dining facilities. The center became my home away from home. I was one of its first long-term occupants. The center was situated so distant from my office in the McKeldin Library that I remember trudging in the dark at day's end across muddy fields before reaching my destination.

Between January and September, I needed to establish the school's presence and make it known that students would be accepted for admission beginning that fall. A first order of business was to establish a secretariat. This proved less easy than I had hoped. Following several weeks of innumerable interviews, I settled on someone who had been employed elsewhere on the campus, Beulah Rybon. The University Senate almost immediately required a curriculum that could be approved to permit the school to launch a degree-awarding program by the academic year of 1965-1966. The ideal way to design the curriculum would be through faculty deliberation, but I had not yet recruited any. I was obliged to work alone and very quickly to construct the curriculum. I drew elements from conventional library school offerings and incorporated newer features, which I viewed to be essential to any forward-looking master's degree offering. I selected as the name of the new entity the School of Library and Information Services.

The proposed thirty-six hour Master of Library Science curriculum was presented to the new programs and courses committee of the University Senate. It was approved in record time. Once authorized, we announced through news releases to the regional news media that students were invited to apply for admission for the fall term. We swiftly prepared application forms and admission procedures. Because of the long pent-up demand for library education in Maryland, there was an immediate flurry of applications received in early spring. Necessary faculty had been uppermost in my mind from the moment I accepted my post. By early January, I was in constant communication with attractive prospects whom I hoped would form the nucleus faculty of the school. I sought to steamroll the process of campus interviews, to negotiate the conditions of their appointments, and to extend concrete offers. Hornbake and Elkins would ratify my selections.

Careful attention was paid to the local professional constituencies that had been instrumental in the process leading to the Maryland state legislature's authorization of the establishment of the school. Numerous meetings were held with librarians in the area to elicit their opinions about the new degree program. The meetings also offered them the opportunity to hear me and to learn my views. From the outset, strong links were forged with the Maryland Department of Education's Division of Library Extension. Nettie Taylor was for many years its forward-looking director. Associations were developed through visits and discussions with officials of the three national libraries located in the environs of College Park: the Library of Congress, the National Agriculture Library, and the National Library of Medicine. We kept these institutions abreast of plans for the program. Relationships were also established with other professional schools and academic departments on the College Park campus. Meetings with officials and faculty members were intended to foster university-wide visibility for the emergent school. The physical location of the program, within the confines of the McKeldin Library building, militated cordial working relationships with the director of the university library, Howard Rovelstad, as well as the library staff.

Each half-week that I spent in Ithaca was meant to take up my full concentration. In reality, however, my energies centered only on my classes, rather than other Cornell concerns. Between telephone calls, correspondence, and planning for the Maryland school, I had little free time for anything else, including family. A great deal of effort went into the sale of our house and the planned move to the Washington, DC, area. I spent my commuting hours between Ithaca and Washington working through papers in my bulging briefcase. By June, we moved to a community near the campus called College Park Woods. Our new home was located within a half hour's walk to my office. Much of the distance went through the wooded outer edge of the University golf course. The necessary pieces were falling into place to ensure the school's opening in September. All of the school's working and classroom areas were on the two top floors of the McKeldin Library, with only eight-foot-high ceilings. In July, I felt the full force of the summer's heat and humidity in my non-air-conditioned office — and realized that it would be impossible to conduct classes and school affairs in the summer months. Lee Hornbake listened to my concerns and promised to arrange the installation of air conditioning by the summer of 1966.

When Hornbake made his inaugural speech to the school's students and faculty in mid-September, I realized that several of my aspirations for the program had been realized. Many more were in abeyance. From the outset, I had envisioned an ideal center for the educational preparation of librarians. In discussions with university officials, library groups, prospective faculty members, and students, I always sought to articulate my objectives. Some elements could be in place from the outset. Others would have to wait for further development once the faculty was in place to deliberate my ideas. Endorsement from the University Senate and continued, adequate budgetary provision from a favorably disposed administration were also necessary. For these reasons I told Hornbake when I took the position that I would assume the deanship for a five-year term. If the exemplary program I was seeking was not in place by then, it would still be time for me to step aside and allow leadership responsibility to pass to another candidate.

Librarianship is fundamentally an applied pursuit. In comparable fields I had observed that education frequently incorporates operational elements through which students learn by doing — internships, for example, which offer supervised, planned study in a real setting, such as a hospital for a medical residency. Teaching and social work are other disciplines that offer laboratory work or field experience linking classroom education with the world of practice. This type of learning had disappeared from libraries once library education gravitated from on-the-job training to formal preparation in universities. I believed that a professional school library should serve as both a training ground and a laboratory linked to the classroom. The means for faculty to supervise student efforts could be incorporated as an element of the pedagogic experience. A hallmark of distinctive professional schools — in medicine, business, law, or engineering — was the existence of a professional school library attuned to the needs of its special constituency. The librarian of our professional school library would be identified with the faculty and the student body of the school. To fortify the association, the librarian would enjoy faculty status, would participate fully in the school, and would be invited to teach regularly. Having the resources for development of a library school library, directed by a librarian who would also be a faculty member, was one of the stipulations of my appointment.

Frances Thackston came to Maryland from Duke University, where she had been a member of the library's technical services division. She accepted her new appointment as librarian and lecturer in the summer of 1965. Thackston had already begun to build a collection in the space that was allocated for the library. A budget had been earmarked for acquisitions, and Thackston arranged for materials in the principal subjects of the school's library holdings to be transferred from the university library.

It was important to create tangible associations between students, faculty, and the world of library practice. A weekly colloquium was offered, and attendance was obligatory for all students. Invited speakers, during the spring and fall semesters, were selected from academic, public, and special libraries. They also included library researchers, scholars, and publishers. The lectures were one hour long. Each lecturer was urged to transcend the conventional litany of personal experiences to treat, instead, the political, philosophical, or conceptual issues bearing upon their work. The series was intended to provide students with an overview that would help them learn about different avenues they might pursue later in their careers.

Library education was viewed by many as a pedestrian, if necessary, rite of passage into the professional ranks. University courses were seen as largely irrelevant to the concerns of real-life practice. These classes could lead to entry-level credentials for a professional appointment, but students didn't expect them to offer substantive content. The real knowledge base was to be found in the practical world of library operations. Prospective entrants to the field were advised not to take library school too seriously. The prevailing wisdom was that library school was something to endure. Once students had acquired the master's degree, they could get on with their life's work. Maryland University had higher aspirations for its master's degree offering: if librarianship were to achieve parity with other professions, it was essential that students acquire self-respect through a rigorous, intellectual introduction to the field. Librarians themselves were scornful of the traditional library school curriculum; if they demeaned their own course of study, how would others ever take the field seriously? There seemed to me no reason why graduate education for librarianship should be held in less esteem than education for business or law. To achieve a higher standard, it was necessary to create an appropriate mix of excellent students, rigorous course content, and first-rate faculty.

From more than 250 applicants, 82 students — 35 full-time and 47 part-time students — were admitted to Maryland's new library school program. By the end of the first semester, the student body had shrunk to seventy. Admission to the school required an undergraduate performance record of high standard; a year of foreign language study, or its equivalent; and a satisfactory score on the verbal and quantitative aptitude tests of the Graduate Record Examination. While part-time students were accepted, courses were offered during normal daytime hours. Those who chose to work needed to arrange their schedules to accommodate the hours when the courses and the weekly colloquium were offered. The entire thirty-six-hour degree program needed to be completed within three years. Full-time students could obtain the MLS degree following two semesters and a summer session. The program sought to bridge the best elements of traditional library study with newer insights derived from the behavioral and technological advances that were affecting libraries and information services.

The original curriculum offered a core of eight required courses. Some of these were uncommon offerings, such as Introduction to Data Processing for Libraries. This course surveyed and analyzed the potential of machines, punch cards, computers, and systems analysis in relation to library procedures. Communication and Libraries reviewed and analyzed communications processes and explored the library's role as part of a larger social context. History of Libraries and Their Materials tracked the development of published forms and institutions within the context of the history and cultural forces that brought about advances in the field. Library Administration gave an introduction to administrative theory and principles and looked at their implications and applications to managerial activity in libraries. Elective offerings were incorporated into the curriculum across a range of subject areas. These courses were taught by regular faculty and by adjunct lecturers who were specialists from various institutions in the Washington, DC, area.

Maryland's curricular content differed from customary library school fare. Each student had to take an introductory semester-long course in library automation and computer technology. In 1965, this requirement was not met with universal acclaim. Students who came to the school were predominantly from liberal arts backgrounds. Anything that smacked of technology was anathema. In a quest to educate for the future, rather than the past, such courses were timely and relevant. Communication and Libraries was seen as an experimental offering. It placed librarianship and libraries within a contemporary cultural framework. The function of libraries in our culture was to be viewed within the context of other agencies, institutions, and media outlets that were part of society at large. History of Libraries and Their Materials reflected my own desire to impart to students the rich heritage of libraries. My doctoral experience at Michigan had been pivotal in bringing about the development of this course. Understanding the continuously changing artifact forms and institutional characteristics of libraries and how they evolved was an important area of study. Library administration was taught widely. The intent of the Maryland course was a departure from conventional practices. It proceeded along comparative lines. The library was portrayed as one type of institution among others in which administrative theory and principles are applied. The basic hypothesis was that managerial characteristics are common to all kinds of organizations. One of the primary purposes of the course was to identify these similarities. Course content was drawn from the literature of management and organizational behavior. Insights from other management areas were related to organizational behavior in libraries. Key concerns, such as change and professionalism, were also taken into consideration.

The school's first class was drawn almost exclusively from the Maryland and the Washington, DC, region. The program was new and not yet accredited. It was not until later that entrants represented a wider geographic radius and incorporated a number of foreign students. The racial composition of the school early on was homogeneous: It was virtually all white and middle class. It was also eighty percent female. The original class in 1965 included an unusual number of outstanding people who later distinguished themselves in their careers.

It was paramount to the school's success that an appropriate level of intellectual discourse be maintained in the classroom and among the instructional staff.

The limited number of faculty posts to be filled had to be of a very high caliber. Faculty members were chosen with a view to their prospective classroom performance as well as their potential for contributing through research and publication. Proper working conditions were of the essence. With the support of the university administration, the prescribed teaching load was set at a maximum of fifteen hours in the classroom. Faculty taught two courses in one term and three in the other. This arrangement was highly unusual for library education at that time. It placed the responsibility squarely on the faculty for significant professional service and regular scholarly and research contributions.

Left to its own traditions and conventional course content, academic programs tend to become ossified. Without the stimulus of fresh perspectives drawn from related disciplines, new instructional and research initiatives are infrequent. Pedestrian classes become commonplace. Poised on the threshold of a new technological era in 1965, librarianship was a field ready to profit from an interdisciplinary orientation. Important social science findings that illuminated the understanding of human and organizational behavior needed to be incorporated into the professional preparation of students. Therein lay the case for building an interdisciplinary instructional cadre at Maryland. The result could be seen in the choice of regular faculty appointees, adjunct lecturers, and joint appointments with other campus facilities. Outside organizations and research institutions were also enlisted from the plethora of international agencies that operated in the Washington area. Fostering an instructional and research climate favorable to international concerns was inevitable, especially given that librarianship is an occupation of universal scope.

Other than Frances Thackston, the original faculty choices included Daniel Bergen, an assistant professor who came from the School of Library Science at Syracuse University, where he had been assistant dean. Bergen was educated in the social sciences as well as librarianship. He brought an all-encompassing view to his analytical study of communication. Associate professor Mary Lee Bundy had most recently been on the faculty of the Library School at the State University of New York at Albany, where she focused on the public library. Her appointment at Maryland called for dividing her time equally between teaching and conducting research on public library issues, which were supported by the Maryland Division of Library Extension. John Colson, an assistant professor, came from the Wisconsin State Historical Library. He became responsible for course work in library history. Jack Mills accepted a one-year appointment as visiting lecturer.

He had been a faculty member at Northwestern Polytechnic in London. More recently he had been a research officer at ASLIB, the British counterpart of the Special Libraries Association. Mills offered course work in classification theory and research that was based on his work with the internationally celebrated classification research group, of which he was a founding member. Jean Perreault came from Florida Atlantic University where he had been chief of information retrieval. He was hired as a lecturer, teaching cataloging and retrieval courses. Under the terms of an agreement between the school and the IBM Federal Systems Division, where he had been manager of the Systems Development Department, Claude Walston taught classes in library automation and data processing.

Adjunct lecturers offered classes on a part-time basis during the first two semesters. Among them was Henry Dubester, associate director in the Office of Science Information Service of the National Science Foundation. Formerly with the Library of Congress, he came to Maryland to teach reference and bibliography. Children's library service and storytelling were taught by Anne Pellowski. She had been assistant director of storytelling services at the New York Public Library before coming to Washington. Frances Kenner offered courses in school librarianship. She had been with the D.C. Action Committee for School Libraries. Josephine Fang, then a research staff member of the New Catholic Encyclopedia, taught cataloging. One who was to have been in the original adjunct faculty was Mortimer Taube. He was president of Documentation, Inc., a pioneering library consulting and research firm. Taube had invented the concept of coordinate indexing. Tragically, he died unexpectedly of a heart attack just weeks before the first semester began.

Important elements of the vision for the new school were put on hold until a more propitious time. One component called for more spacious housing for the program. An early order of business was the design of research projects by the faculty that would be supported by non-university funding sources. The next logical step would be deliberations leading to a doctoral program. A keen personal interest of mine was the implementation of an executive development program for managers of all types of libraries. The highest priority on this crowded agenda, however, was the attainment of accreditation from the American Library Association for the master's degree.

The first year of the experimental program was exhilarating. It was a time when everything seemed possible. Everyone was caught up in an atmosphere of experimentation and change. A novel mix of faculty, unconstrained by rigid procedures, sparked debate. The principal provocateur was often Mary Lee Bundy. She could always be counted on to stir up passions as she ardently espoused unorthodox, yet original, ideas. Her input often incited outrage, but always deserved a hearing. If the faculty was caught up in the ferment of ideas bearing upon educational issues, the students were the guinea pigs. They had come in quest of a library degree. They had not expected to spend their entire time in poorly ventilated and stifling hot lecture and seminar rooms. They had not bargained for teachers with such a melange of personalities, perspectives, and alternative ways of seeing the world of libraries.

There was no fixed convention at Maryland about whether or not deans would teach. The choice was clear. I was loath to relinquish the classroom for an exclusive role as campus bureaucrat. I did understand, however, that demands on my time, such as unanticipated meetings on or off campus, might conflict with scheduled class hours. I compromised by team teaching the library administration course with Mary Lee Bundy. By the fall of 1965, I had known Mary Lee five years and I appreciated her intellectual incisiveness. When I suggested we share responsibility for the course, I simply assumed we would follow the outline and syllabus I had prepared at Michigan and Western Reserve. I planned to lecture in this course, which was required of all students. Mary Lee would substitute when I was absent and cover the occasional topic that was of special interest to her. I assumed incorrectly. I should have realized that she would never accept such a passive role.

During the very first lecture, Mary Lee sat by my side constantly questioning, interrupting, and disagreeing. At first, I tried simply to brush her aside and go on. She continued to interrupt me until she was satisfied that I had responded adequately. This became the rhythm of the class session after session. I spoke. Mary Lee challenged me to explain and defend my position in rejoinder. Ultimately, I understood that her perpetual assaults helped me to sharpen and refine my reasoning. Not only did she question my ideas; she sometimes assigned alternative reading for the students. A by-product of this lively interchange was the first volume in a new series of readers for the field. The first volume co-edited by Mary Lee and me was called the *Reader in Library Administration*. It was published in 1968.

The interpersonal fireworks of the class constituted a stormy sideshow for our students. I explained that our differences reflected the ambiguities inherent in an organizational society that was fraught with conflicting values, political orientations, and beliefs. My propensity was to orate while Mary Lee's was to engage. When I was not lecturing, she could bring the class into discussion and debate far more often than when we were forcefully interacting with each other. The students seemed to divide into two camps. Those with high tolerance for ambiguity seemed to be amused and perhaps even edified by our antics. Others were upset and embarrassed by the spectacles we made of ourselves. One charitable student of that period wrote an anonymous evaluation characterizing me as a pretty fair lecturer and Bundy as a great teacher.

Just as I had decided not to give up teaching, I was equally determined to sustain my publishing efforts. Before leaving Cornell, I had identified a gap in the information structure of the business management field and had initiated effort on a reference work that the Graduate School of Business and Public Administration at Cornell agreed to publish. It was to be the first comprehensive directory of consultants and consulting firms. I began work on the compilation of the book's content and, after arriving at Maryland, I engaged student assistance in the editorial process. Effie Knight joined the staff as a secretary in the 1965-1966 school year. She was a young woman from Scotland who had moved to Maryland with her husband and two children. Her formal education was limited, but in Kirkaldy, Scotland, she had worked for several years as a legal secretary. Her office skills were formidable and her native intelligence was exceptional. She approached every assignment with high efficiency and tenacity. Effie Knight's excellent skills earned her a promotion to secretary to the dean. This caused some awkwardness, as the dean's current secretary, Beulah Rybon, was clearly not in the same class as Effie. To avoid a potential conflict, Rybon was made office manager, without losing classification status or salary. My friendship with Effie Knight endured twenty years. She soon became involved in helping me to manage editorial projects. *Consultants and Consulting Organizations* was published by Cornell in 1966.

Before I accepted the deanship, I received assurances that the university was ready to support the new school's rapid growth and development. The library school was never more than one small program in a large university. Each dean and director competed aggressively for a fair portion of what would always be less than an ideal appropriation for every need. An inordinate amount of time was spent building a powerful case for the provision of funds. Lee Hornbake was always a resolute advocate on behalf of the school and its growing needs.

THE BEST OF TIMES

As that first academic year progressed, plans were underway to expand the student body and faculty. For the summer session of 1966, additional adjunct and summer school instructors needed to be hired in order to enable the school's first class an opportunity to pursue elective courses. Negotiations were also in progress with the budget committee and the university administration to make possible the admission of one hundred additional full-time students for the 1966-1967 academic year. At the same time, an effort was being made to increase the size of the faculty. By spring, authorization was given to recruit several new faculty members. Without the addition of this new faculty, it would not be possible to reach the critical mass needed to achieve the level of distinction in teaching and research that the school required. We wanted to avoid the fate of so many library schools — understaffed and struggling to provide only a bare minimum of subject matter.

Early recognition of the school as a vigorous new center of education for librarianship depended on the seal of approval from the American Library Association. In order to maintain momentum and to ensure students that a degree from Maryland would be universally recognized, the faculty agreed to press for acceptance from the Association's Committee on Accreditation at the earliest possible time. Customarily, schools did not apply for accreditation until several years after their debut. We wanted accreditation immediately after the graduation of the first class in August 1966. Administrative approval from the university was needed. Hornbake advised that this decision was solely the prerogative of the president. President Elkins suggested that we defer the application for a year or two; a negative decision would be a devastating blow. A denial from the association might preclude making a reapplication for several more years. I explained to Elkins that all the ingredients were in place to ensure a favorable outcome. Receiving accreditation in record time would catapult Maryland into the forefront of the field. Elkins deferred to my judgement.

The arduous and time-consuming process of preparing the documentation for accreditation was completed in the spring. The ALA Committee on Accreditation appointed as chairman of the visiting committee Lester Asheim from the University of Chicago. The date for the committee's visit to the campus was scheduled for three days in the fall of 1966. With the exception of recommendations for improvements in the school's physical plant and space, the committee voted for the school's accreditation during the ALA meeting in January 1967.

The Best of Times

By the spring of 1966, the new school introduced several innovative initiatives. The school's first contractual grant was received from the United States Office of Education's Educational Research Information Centers Training Program. The terms of the contract stipulated the development of programmed learning materials for use in the training of indexers in education. Jack Mills of the classification faculty spearheaded the effort. The results would become a basic component of the Office of Education's Educational Research Information Centers program. The deadline for completion was summer 1967. The International Symposium on Classification Research was a corollary activity that was undertaken during the summer of 1966 by Jean Perreault. The symposium brought together a group of experts from many parts of the world to report on recent trends and new directions.

By far the most ambitious research activity undertaken by the school during that time had its genesis in a conference convened in April 1966. With funding from the United States Department of Labor's Office of Manpower, Automation and Training, a group of librarians, social scientists, and information specialists met at the school to consider a pressing problem facing the field at that time: manpower requirements. Deliberations about personnel issues during this three-day seminar, resulted in a report prepared by Mary Lee Bundy and me entitled *Manpower for the Library and Information Professions in the 1970's: An Inquiry into Fundamental Problems*. It was issued in September 1966. The document served as the basis for formulating a comprehensive blueprint completed in April 1967. The final proposal was submitted for funding to the U.S. Commissioner of Education for collaborative support from the Office of Education, Bureau of Research; the National Library of Medicine Extramural Program; and, the Office of Science Information Service of the National Science Foundation. The project was titled "A Program of Research into the Identification of Manpower Requirements: The Educational Preparation and the Utilization of Manpower in the Library and Information Professions." We received a very substantial $400,000 grant.

The research encompassed a group of interrelated studies to be conducted by a team of investigators from different disciplines and from a number of universities. I served as project director, and Bundy as associate director. The overall direction and coordination of the project came from Maryland. The studies to be carried out included: "Economics of the Library and Information Professions," by August Bolino from Catholic University; "Personality and Ability Patterns

Related to Work Specialties in the Information Professions," by Stanley Segal from State University of New York at Buffalo; "Image and Status of the Library and Information Services Field," by Hart Walters from George Washington University; "Role Concepts and Attitudes Toward Authority Among Librarians and Information Personnel in Varying Environments," by Robert Presthus from University of Oregon; "The Sociology of the Information Professions," by Rodney White from Trent University; "The Executive in Library and Information Activity: An Inquiry into the Background, Attitudes and Behavior of Administrators," by Paul Wasserman and Mary Lee Bundy from University of Maryland.

The project consumed a considerable portion of Bundy's and my attention for three years. The funding made it possible for us to enlist graduate assistants and administrative staff support for some of the more time-consuming tasks associated with the research. Even so, the need for periodic team conferences, regular reports to the benefactors, and continuous communication with the members of the research team remained demanding. There was also a flurry of related activity beginning with a speech I gave at the Pacific Northwest Library Association Conference in Portland, Oregon, on August 26, 1966. "The Library and Information Professions in a Time of Change," was published in *PNLA Quarterly* in 1967. Bundy and I co-authored a *Library Journal* paper entitled "Manpower Blueprint" that appeared on January 15, 1967. I was invited to lecture at the Conference of the Southwestern Library Association on October 17, 1968 in Tulsa, Oklahoma. My remarks appeared in the May 1969 *ALA Bulletin* as "Elements in a Manpower Blueprint — Library Personnel for the 1970's."

Ever since her appointment to the faculty, Mary Lee Bundy had systematically and resolutely spoken out about the necessity for the transformation of librarianship. She saw the public library as an intrinsically white, middle-class institution that was oriented exclusively to the purposes and needs of the same cultural and social class. In a seminar she conducted in the spring of 1966, Bundy's class focused its discussions on library services for previously ignored constituencies. Outside speakers came to offer their insights. The seminar debated the need to create a new form of public library — a laboratory for use by people in economically deprived communities. Her concern was not part of my original agenda for the school. I did hold the conviction, however, that library education needed to actively foster interactions with library operations. I envisaged that the means needed to be found for students and instructional staff to straddle between the classroom and the world of practice. Bundy's values were clearly congruent with the times. We were at the threshold of dramatic social and political change. Redressing longstanding cultural inequities was one ingredient in this climate of upheaval. It was Bundy who led me — perhaps not quite kicking and screaming, but certainly not overflowing with passion for societal transformation — to understand that what she professed was appropriate and necessary for any forward-looking professional school.

Laboratory and applied research by library education that dealt with the problems of a culturally deprived population elicited widespread interest in the field of library education. There were some reservations about the project, but there was far more enthusiasm. The Prince George's County Public Library volunteered its support — the laboratory would take place in a building that the school rented and equipped, which would be affiliated with the county library system. The Maryland Department of Education's Division of Library Extension and Research Divisions also provided their support. Additional financial assistance came from the United States Office of Education. The end result was the creation of the High John Library, which was named for a black folk hero. The library was directed jointly by Mary Lee Bundy and Richard Moses. Moses had been a staff member of the Enoch Pratt Free Library's Community Action Program in Baltimore's inner city. The program began in October 1967. The classroom segment comprised three courses. There was a seminar in library service to the disadvantaged that consisted of classroom discussions and field experience. A seminar in research methods required students to design a project that was related to the program and the objectives of the demonstration library. Finally, an independent study was offered, in which each student would pursue a research topic and develop it into a full-scale report under faculty supervision. By operating the High John Library in a predominantly underprivileged black community, this school project was a magnet for socially committed students. It served as a lead-in to many initiatives that the school, its faculty, and its student body were to carry forward. Maryland was taking its place in the vanguard of the movement for change in librarianship. The implications for library education and public libraries raised by the High John program were described in an article by Mary Lee Bundy and me. "A Departure in Library Education: A Report of an Experimental Project" ran in a 1967 issue of the *Journal of Education for Librarianship*.

Chapter Twelve

During my Cornell years, I was invited on occasion to lecture on information for decision making for the Graduate School of Business and Public Administration's annual summer institute for managers from corporations and government. Many of the institute's participants had been working in technical and specialized roles. Having recently assumed managerial assignments, they were sent to Cornell by their organizations in order to learn the requisites of administrative performance. During the post-World War II era, libraries, like other organizations, had expanded. They had grown from small operations into agencies that employed large staff and required far greater financial resources. Professional preparation conventionally equipped people for entry-level posts in reference work or cataloging. Few in librarianship had been educated to assume management roles. As librarians moved up the hierarchy, their management responsibilities far outweighed their purely library responsibilities. If intensive executive training made sense for business and government personnel, certainly librarians could benefit from similar programs. In the mid-1960's there was a plethora of institutes, short courses, and workshops that librarians attended annually at the local, state, and national level. None of these centered on management, however.

The concept behind the Library Administrators Development Program was quite simple. Instead of concentrating on library matters, the two-week institute would reorient those attending from seeing themselves as librarians to seeing themselves as managers. Organizational issues like decision making, leadership, organizational behavior, budget, and financial controls would be taken up. Libraries would be seen merely as the case in point. The instructional cadre would come from management education, behavioral science, and management consulting. The course would be conducted in a remote rural setting without distractions. Complete immersion and separation from usual organizational pressures would be ensured.

Plans for the program were formulated during academic year 1966-1967. The Maryland Library Administrators Development Program would be held in the summer over a two-week period at the Donaldson Brown Center. This was a family estate that had been transformed into a residential study retreat. Situated on the north bank of the Susquehanna River in northern Maryland about an hour from Baltimore, the property had been bequeathed recently to the University of Maryland. The resident director would be Henry Tosi, a professor of management in the Maryland Business School in College Park. Tosi and I worked together to select the topical content and to identify the instructors we would invite. Once the program had been drawn up and arrangements for faculty participation concluded, the program was announced in the library media. The fee for attendees was set at five hundred dollars. At that time this was a fairly high cost for a library institute, but modest compared to comparable offerings in business schools around the country. This charge covered instruction, lodging, and accommodations. It also included airport pickup and return in Baltimore.

During its first offering, the program garnered thirty-eight participants. They came from all across the United States and Canada. The content of the 1967 course was as follows: The Factors of Management; The Librarian as an Administrator in Complex Organizations; Inter-Organizational Relationships (Conflict and Dealing with External Groups); Characteristics of Large Organizations; The Individual in the Organizational System; Leadership Theory and Styles; Theories of Motivation and Behavior; Communication Processes in Organizations; Problem Solving; Human Relations Laboratory; Objectives and Objective Formulation; Performance Appraisal; Managerial and Subordinate Development; Financial Planning and Budgeting; Collection and Analysis of Cost Data; Accounting Systems as Performance Measures and Control; Work Analysis; The Impact of Technology on Information Organizations; Implementation of Change in Organizations. The faculty included: Henry Tosi, Allan Nash, Roger Hermanson, and Stephen Carroll from the Maryland Business School; Charles Goodman from American University; Victor Thompson from the University of Illinois; Mary Lee Bundy and Paul Wasserman from the School of Library and Information Services. The program received a favorable evaluation and became the first of an annual series that went on for twenty-four years. Henry Tosi left Maryland by the next summer and was replaced as residential director by John Rizzo of George Washington University, and later at Western Michigan University in Kalamazoo. Rizzo served as residential director and I continued as the Maryland advisor and faculty lecturer for the life of the program, which ended in 1990.

Collaborations between Mary Lee Bundy and me sparked countless discussions, debates, and heated arguments. When we did reach agreement, the result took the form of a joint article, research proposal, or scholarly symposium. Ideas put forward in the library administration classes and in the manpower study deliberations led to a controversial article, which we had difficulty getting published. The article closely examined librarian behavior from three perspectives: the librarian-client relationship; relationships of librarians within their own institutions; and the role of library education and library associations in influencing professional performance. "Professionalism Reconsidered" by Mary Lee Bundy and Paul Wasserman appeared in *College and Research Libraries* in January 1968. It provoked impassioned assaults as well as support. Neither one of us had ever experienced this degree of response to our writings in the past.

From my first days in academia, I had observed that books appeared in many disciplines that brought together selections from a wide range of published articles, book chapters, and research reports. These works, which were compiled, arranged for publication, and edited by a teacher, were intended to be used as a substitute for, or supplement to, a textbook for a course. Such publications were widely used in universities. Library school students, however, did not constitute the mass market for these publications that existed in other academic fields. It was my impression that librarianship, as a growing field of university study, could take advantage of this form of publication. When Bundy and I taught library administration for the first time, the reading list was very extensive. The class drew its reading from the periodical literature of business management, public administration, and the behavioral sciences and included chapters from a number of books. In order to get these forty separate selections to students, the school library had to gather them and place them on reserve for use in the library. The first semester demonstrated that, even with multiple copies available, access was limited. The inability to take the materials out of the library compounded the problem. The second time the course was offered, we decided to copy and distribute all the required reading to each student enrolled. The preparation and distribution of the several-hundred page package caused a severe drain on the resources and energies of the school secretariat. It was a violation of copyright law to charge students a fee for these copies. There had to be a better way. The publication of a reader for the course would meet the students' needs. I also realized that readers of this sort would work in other teaching areas in librarianship just as well. While the publication of this type of book had proved successful in other fields, it had not yet been tried in librarianship. We needed to find a publisher who would take on this new project.

The search for a sympathetic, entrepreneurial ear led to Albert Diaz, the director of the Washington office of Microcard Editions. Microcard was a publishing firm that specialized in "microprint" forms. Diaz had already brought forth two printed book products. While he was not highly optimistic about the prospects for readers in librarianship, he was prepared to launch the series, and asked me to serve as series editor. Bundy and I worked together on the first book. It was a time-consuming task. Agreeing on selection criteria, eliciting and arranging permissions and recompense for copyright holders, and the editorial integration of our choices created endless frustrations. It was more than two years before the *Reader in Library Administration* was published in 1968. The successful market acceptance of the first volume led to a second printing in 1970. Diaz was sufficiently heartened by the sales to encourage me to identify a number of other editors who might prepare subsequent volumes based on the pattern used in the first book. Each volume in the Reader Series in Library and Information Science was prepared by a specialist versed in the topic to be covered. It embraced materials from many sources within and outside the literature of librarianship. The aim of each publication was to draw into focus essential knowledge for study, and to contribute intellectually to the furtherance of library education and practice. From 1968 to 1977, twenty-four different subject areas were covered in the series.

After the publication in early 1966 of *Consultants and Consulting Organizations*, which I had begun working on while I was still at Cornell, people in management consulting practice suggested that a corollary reference work would be useful. *Consultants and Consulting Organizations* provided coverage about the firms and their characteristics, but there was no source that gave biographic information about the consultants. The Graduate School of Business and Public Administration at Cornell also supported the compilation of a complementary volume. Once the criteria for inclusion in this biographical directory were determined, a questionnaire form was prepared. Several graduate assistants at Maryland assisted with the mailings and edited the responses. The first edition of *Who's Who in Consulting* was published at Cornell in 1968.

The Best of Times

By the time the school was into its third year in 1967-1968, ALA accreditation had been received. We had two years' experience behind us with the master's level program, and the number of regular faculty and adjuncts had grown to twenty-four. Of this number eight held doctorates. External research support had grown dramatically as well. Interdisciplinary links had been forged across the campus with the computer science, social science, and history faculties. It seemed a propitious time to seek authorization for offering a Ph.D. degree. Mary Lee Bundy chaired a committee to prepare the documentation supporting our representation. The process involved a review of our proposal by the Senate Committee on New Courses and Programs. A favorable decision from this committee would lead to a referral to the University Senate for deliberation. A supportive vote by the Senate would need to be endorsed by the President and then by the Board of Trustees. When the proposed curriculum for the master's degree went to the Senate for approval in 1965, the state legislature had just authorized the school's program. There could scarcely be any objection from the University Senate to granting authority for the school to offer course work leading to the MLS degree. Approval of the Ph.D. was another matter. A highly self-conscious Senate zealously and jealously guarded against offering the Ph.D. by any discipline or professional school that might be even remotely suspected of lowering the substantive academic standard.

We embarked on our hazardous political journey toward approval in Lee Hornbake's office. From the outset he had been the school's trusted advisor and friend in high place. His advice was that we be sure to explain thoroughly to the widest possible number of departments and faculty members our justification for the degree offering and its unquestioned scholarly rigor. This should take place well before the matter came to discussion and vote in the Senate. The doctoral proposal underwent a long and arduous preparation. Individual faculty members explained and discussed it across the campus, wherever they could get a hearing. The presentation was revised and edited, taking into account the advice and criticisms it had received from many quarters, until our faculty was confident that the proposal was in its best possible form. It was submitted to the Senate Committee on New Courses and Programs, where it was reviewed before being endorsed and forwarded to the full Senate for discussion at its next meeting. The Maryland University Senate in 1967-1968 was both an elected and an appointed body. Elected members represented the university's teaching and research faculty. Appointed members included deans of schools and colleges and a limited number of other senior administrative appointees. As the dean of the

School of Library and Information Services, I had a voice and a vote in its deliberations. The school also had one elected senator. Even though we had received a favorable endorsement from the Committee on New Courses and Programs, there was considerable apprehension about what might transpire during the public discussion and subsequent vote. Rumblings had been heard of some strong opposition. There were those who feared the debasement of Maryland standards should such a practice-driven, professional school faculty be empowered to offer the sacrosanct Ph.D. degree.

The debate in the Senate began politely. Spokespersons on either side of the debate stated their positions briefly and succinctly. Supporters were about equal to opponents. Colleagues from disciplines where we had close relations expressed favorable views. Skepticism was generally expressed by the sciences, whose members did not even know of our existence. The debate went on for about twenty minutes before growing more rancorous. I had not yet spoken to defend our proposal. The final speaker antagonistic to our goal was Professor Barbara Bergmann of the economics faculty. She rose and decried the awarding of the university's highest academic designation to a "Mickey Mouse field like librarianship." I spoke next. I said that I found it interesting to hear our scholarship so denigrated when our on-going research supported by reputable, peer-reviewed processes at the National Science Foundation, the Office of Education, and the National Library of Medicine amounted to more than $500,000 in funding since our inception. I added that I wondered how much external funding the Economics Department had received during the same period. My rebuttal seemed to allay any further concerns from the hard science contingent. The vote was called. The resolution to authorize the doctoral program was favorably supported by a wide margin.

The school's location in McKeldin Library during its early stages had been very trying. Lee Hornbake sought valiantly to ensure installation of air-conditioning in offices and classrooms before the summer session of 1966, but his efforts had not been successful. Classroom space had to be found in surrounding campus buildings. The school office and library staff were even more disappointed and demoralized than the faculty and students. By the summer of 1967, air-conditioning was installed in the school's offices, classrooms, and library. This did little, however, to alleviate the overcrowding in a building used by more than twenty thousand members of the student body and faculty. Elevators worked poorly, bathrooms were insufficient, and the students, lacking adequate study space, made do with the staircase steps between floors. Conditions would only worsen. The school clearly needed more space. As a new school, it would be impossible for us to win early priority in any long-term capital improvement campaign. Our only hope was to find external funding.

Undergraduate libraries were in vogue in the 1960's. The trend began when the University of Michigan built the first library building dedicated exclusively for use by undergraduate students. Soon the practice was being emulated elsewhere on other campuses. McKeldin Library served the entire Maryland campus population. The School of Library and Information Services was taking up more and more of its limited space. My relations with Howard Rovelstad, the library director, were severely strained. We competed for every square foot of unoccupied space. I proposed to Rovelstad that I discuss with officials of the United States Office of Education the possibility of receiving support for a building that could house both the School of Library and Information Services and a Maryland University undergraduate library. The Office of Education was responsible for the administration of its Library Services and Construction Act funds. With the concurrence of Hornbake and the university administration, I arranged a meeting in Washington with the appropriate Office of Education staff. I learned that, while they had not supported the construction of any structure earmarked for joint occupancy by an undergraduate library and a library school, there was no official limitation to preclude such a venture. Over the next couple of months, feverish efforts were set in motion. We rapidly prepared an application for the Office of Education before the deadline for submission. The application was approved conditional upon a shared level of support from the state, which the university administration was ready to assure. The building would not be complete before the early 1970's. By then I would no longer be serving as dean. The promise of new quarters had an uplifting effect on faculty and staff morale. Even the students, who would be gone by the time the building was ready, were buoyed by the prospect of improved conditions for those who would come after them.

In February of 1968, I received an invitation to serve as advisor to the Graduate School of Librarianship at the University of Denver. I was to be the first lecturer in the Isabel Nichol Lecture Series. This weeklong visit resulted in the University of Denver publication of *Trends and Directions in Library Education and Library Practice*. My remarks underscored the overriding issue facing the field: the need for change in the classroom and in practice. I saw innovation and adaptation as the means for occupational survival in a time when there was growing competition for the information function. My Denver lecture characterized the main ingredients of the Maryland educational offering, linking it to the need for questioning the conventional shibboleths of librarianship.

By that spring the contagion of social revolt in the wider society was being felt on college campuses. Maryland did not escape the confrontational storms that raged across academia during the remaining months of the 1960's. The High John project and Bundy's demands to alter the racial composition of the student body, in addition to the heightened level of societal demands, began to influence the Maryland program. A unique course sequence was designed to appeal to minorities and to the socially committed. It was incorporated as a special track in the master's degree offering. With financial support from the Office of Education, scholarships were made available to recruit students from the disadvantaged, predominantly black, community to attend the program. New methods were employed to equate experience with some of the conventional academic requirements, thereby making admission barriers less formidable for the most promising of these prospective students. The specialty included classes and field experience intended to prepare graduates for public library positions. They would be ready to serve as advocates for the underprivileged, functioning within the framework of the institutions as vanguards of change. Mary Lee Bundy was the program's faculty advisor. Federal funding made it possible for us to rent a small, unused campus building as our project headquarters and secretariat. The building sometimes also afforded temporary housing for needy students.

The Maryland student population constituted a far more diversified group than could be found in any other library school at that time. In addition to students in the Ph.D. program and the special track master's degree program, there were many more students coming to Maryland from outside the United States. Internal stresses and strains among some students and within the faculty surfaced during this time. Attempts to accommodate competing priorities often led to vehement and hostile, private and public expressions of differences. The heightened passions and stormy debate contributed to an academic climate that was universally recognized to be at the cutting edge of librarianship.

I became a member of the American Documentation Institute in 1965. (The organization was at that time in the process of changing its name to the American Society for Information Science.) I attended its annual conference in Santa Monica that fall. The president at the time was a psychologist doing research in information retrieval. His name was Harold Borko. He was with System Development Corporation and went on to join the faculty of the University of California at Los Angeles Library School. I wanted to meet members of this interdisciplinary organization and to familiarize myself with its work. In 1969, I was appointed to the association's Education Committee. In that same period I accepted the invitation of Carlos Cuadra, editor of the *Annual Review of Information Science,* to prepare a chapter for the 1969 volume. I worked with Evelyn Daniel, a Maryland MLS graduate and Ph.D. student who later became a library school educator and dean. Together we published the chapter on Library and Information Science Management.

Pressing occupational obligations thwarted my earlier desire to pursue further international travel. In 1969 something happened to change this. It was in a tangential way brought about when I was a candidate for the Special Libraries Association presidency. My opponent, Eugene Jackson, defeated me. I often felt that, whenever I encountered Jackson at conferences, he seemed embarrassed about having defeated me so decisively. By 1969 Jackson had left General Motors and was director of libraries for the IBM Corporation. He also served as chairman of the United States National Committee for the International Federation for Documentation (FID). The FID was, and remains, an international counterpart of elements of the American Society for Information Science and the Special Libraries Association. For several years, the representative for the United States on the FID Education and Training Committee was Charles Shilling. He was a retired naval officer and medical doctor, who was also director of the Biological Sciences Communication Project at George Washington University in the District of Columbia. The United States National Committee, the body governing American participation in FID, decided it was time to select a successor to Shilling. Eugene Jackson telephoned to ask if he could recommend me as a nominee to fill Shilling's post. Early in the fall of 1965, shortly after the school's opening, the FID held its biennial conference in Washington. I attended several sessions, but I knew nothing about the organization. I told Jackson this. His reaction was that I would learn quickly. I agreed to let Jackson nominate me. At the close of the next meeting of the U.S. National Committee, he called to congratulate me on my appointment. The die was cast. The future of my personal and professional life was to change profoundly.

In 1969 I completed another reference book. It came about as a result of my trying to locate information. In this case, I wanted to know the criteria used in

The Best of Times

selecting the recipient of a particular scientific prize. A thorough library search failed to lead to a source. I resolved to compile a compendium myself. I devised the strategy for amassing information about awards given in all fields and the details for each entry. My work began in early 1968. I took on overall editorship. Janice McLean, the associate editor, edited the entries. She had been an early alumna of the Maryland program. The resulting volume was the first edition of *Awards, Honors and Prizes: A Source Book and Directory*. It was issued by Gale Research Company.

Figuring out how best to disseminate the scholarly research, monographs, and symposia proceedings that were the result of work by faculty and students engaged my thinking from the time I came to College Park. There was no university press at Maryland. I served as a member of a campus committee to explore the possibility of establishing a university publishing entity during my early months on campus. Unfortunately, it was clear that this would not happen. The school faculty decided to begin a publication program of its own. The Student Contribution Series was launched. It was intended to broadcast the results of experimental courses, in which student essays beyond article length that deserved a wider audience could be printed and sold at a modest price. Responsibility for the series's editorial preparation rested with Esther Herman, an early alumna who had become a member of the school's administrative staff upon graduation. More than a dozen publications were made available as part of this program during the first decade of the school's history.

Initiatives undertaken during these early years gained Maryland a reputation for being a leading center for spearheading change in librarianship. Dick Moses, for example, drove a racially mixed group of Maryland students in a truck labeled, "Maryland's High John Project," into the Deep South to participate in protests against racial discrimination. Maryland students, led by James Welbourne, formed the vanguard of the activist movement by demanding social responsibility from the American Library Association. With Mary Lee Bundy as inspiration, societal concerns were examined at the scholarly level during the Change Institute on Frontiers in Librarianship, convened at the University of Maryland's Center of Adult Education in August 1969. The conference was planned and directed by Gilda Nimer, an alumna and a research assistant in the manpower research project. She prepared the proposal that led to Office of Education funding for the six-day event. She also managed the day-to-day program. Bundy and I served as advisors and contributed to the discussions. Lecturers and panel participants came from many different branches of public life, media, academia, publishing, technology, and librarianship. The loosely structured discussions, lectures, and panel sessions probed a variety of issues including the city in flux and the special problems encountered by urban libraries; ways of making libraries relevant and putting them within reach of the urban disadvantaged; how the public library could meet the needs of estranged school and community elements; the shifting philosophical perspectives in public education; the feasibility of following cues from other fields to cope with modern trends; changing aspects of the publishing industry and its impact on the library; advantages and disadvantages of new methods of information transfer and dissemination; and the dynamics and ills of the library profession and its professional groups. Underlying all this was the notion of the library as an instrument of social change. The proceedings were tape recorded, transcribed, and carefully edited before publication by Greenwood Press in 1972. *Frontiers in Librarianship: Proceedings of the Change Institute 1969* survives as testimony to the debates and passions engendered in a time when Maryland was striving to bring these issues into focus for librarianship.

The height of my enthusiastic efforts to influence change in library education came in 1969. That year I accepted an invitation from the Board of Regents of the state of Ohio to consult by preparing a study and report on library education needs in the state of Ohio. The shortage of librarians was acutely felt in many regions of the country. Following site visits, discussions with library leaders and officials at several universities, and analysis of projected statistical library growth rates and levels of anticipated personnel needed during the next decade, I submitted a report. I concluded that, rather than creating yet another ineffectual study center for the preparation of new entrants, it would make more sense to strengthen existing public institutions that were engaged in library education programs. This would have the effect of not only enhancing their capacity to add to enrollments, but it would also work to upgrade the academic standard of their offerings and bolster their stature among peer institutions. In September 1969, I lectured at Long Island University. I was there to advise the library school on program planning. The edited version of my remarks was published in *Library Journal*, April 1970, as "Professional Adaptation: Library Education Mandate." The proselytizing article avowed the need for library education to chart the way to redirect the field's philosophy and its agenda.

The *Reader in Library Administration* had proved to be commercially viable, so Bundy prevailed upon me to work with her to prepare a similar work dealing with research methodology. She acted as lead editor, using many of the selections drawn together for use in her research methods seminar. My role was principally supportive. Work on the volume was begun late in 1968. The book took only a year to complete. It was ready by the end of 1969 and was published in early 1970 as the *Reader in Research Methods in Librarianship*.

Once I had been designated the United States member of the FID Education and Training Committee, I learned that the committee convened at least once a year. The secretariat was in Warsaw at the Polish Central Institute for Scientific and Technical Information. The Secretariat distributed information to committee members well in advance of the committee meetings. Judith Werdel, who was with the United States National Academy of Sciences — the seat of the United States National Committee for FID — served also as secretary of the United States National Committee. She reported to Warsaw early in 1969 that I was replacing Shilling as the United States Representative to the Education and Training Committee. All future communications were to be addressed to me. I was supposed to hear in the spring from the committee about the 1969 meeting. I phoned Judy Werdel to inquire why I hadn't heard from anyone. It seemed that although the Warsaw Secretariat had been informed that I was replacing Shilling, notification of the April meeting in Lancut, Poland was sent to him anyway. I learned this too late to arrange to attend the April session. Werdel said she would write on behalf of the U.S. National Committee to admonish the Warsaw Secretariat and to instruct them in future to communicate with me, not Shilling, about all committee matters. I did not take part in an FID Education and Training Committee meeting until 1970.

The Manpower Research Project was actively underway from 1967 on. The studies were to be completed by 1970. Final reports were to be ready for submission to the supporting agencies at that time. Coordinating the different studies, each of which had been undertaken by a different scholar, made for a stormy sequence. No one was willing to submit to a central authority. Meetings and conferences were volatile. Relations between the investigators and Eugene McCarthy, the lead official at the Office of Education for the three agencies funding the studies, were strained. McCarthy sought to impose standard bureaucratic controls on the researchers. In turn, the researchers felt that the submission of vouchers for authorized expenditures, along with quarterly progress reports, were an intrusion on their domain. They wanted no bureaucratic interference at all. The more belligerent the tone from Washington, the more the researchers dug in their heels.

I was caught in the middle. Maryland held ultimate responsibility for the successful prosecution of the entire effort. The grant had been made and the contract executed with the University of Maryland. Participating scholars at other universities were categorized as off-campus researchers with sub-contracts.

The three years of the project seemed like a lifetime. During these months McCarthy received a liberal education in the vicissitudes of trying to ride herd on a recalcitrant and cunning collection of independent-minded behavioral scientists. The researchers, on their part, learned that failure to meet procedural requirements of the federal bureaucracy would hold up financial support. At Maryland we were assiduously pursuing our own research as part of the overall project. Negotiating between all the conflicting parties and interests took up far more energy than we could possibly have imagined when we began the enterprise. The research studies somehow continued to progress. In 1969, Bundy and I completed the data-collection phase of our study of the administrators of academic, public, special, and school libraries. We began the task of preparing reports of our findings. We received invaluable assistance from Jeanne O'Connell, an alumna of the school and a staff member of the Manpower Research Project.

To augment the evidence of our questionnaire study of library administrators, I conceived of conducting two case studies to demonstrate the administration of change in library leadership. Two large and important libraries that were in close geographic proximity to each other had appointed new directors in 1968. One was the University of California at Berkeley. The other was the San Francisco Public Library. In 1968, I wrote to the directors of these libraries and inquired if they would permit me to visit and conduct discussions with them over a period of eighteen months. I wanted to follow the progress in their organizations from the time the directors first assumed office. Both James Skipper at Berkeley and John Anderson at the San Francisco Public Library agreed to my proposal.

I traveled for the first time to the San Francisco Bay area for this project. I hoped to schedule quarterly meetings with the directors and senior officials of the two libraries I had chosen to study. Each of my visits would last for one or two days. I wanted to learn from each director and his staff what basic organizational problems had presented themselves and how the new manager would go about introducing change. Our talks would be informal, but I wanted to tape record them for later study. Of course, anything that was said would remain confidential. I met first with the director of the library at Berkeley. We spent more than an hour together. I met also with two high-level members of his staff. At the end of the day, I met again with the library director to thank him for his cooperation. I hoped to return at a mutually convenient date three months later. The next day, I went to the San Francisco Public Library. From the start, John Anderson expressed enthusiasm about my plans. He took me at once to meet his associates and encouraged them to be forthcoming with me during the course of my visits. He agreed that the talks would be a useful exercise, helping him to articulate his initiatives and approaches to problem solving. He explained that he had studied public administration and understood the usefulness of periodically reviewing the opportunities and obstacles he faced in leading the library. I left San Francisco heartened by my experiences. Within a few days I received a letter from Skipper at Berkeley informing me that upon further reflection he had decided not to continue with the interviews. He gave no further explanation. John Anderson did not change his mind.

Every three months I visited the San Francisco Public Library. I made six trips altogether. I met with Anderson, other members of the senior library administrative group, and three library board members. John Anderson used me as a sounding board for his doubts, his confusions, and his high hopes. He was candid in his descriptions of the dilemmas he faced with personnel, programs, buildings, board members, civil service, and Friends of the Library. He expressed his dreams for the library, as well as his uncertainties and misgivings. I heard from Anderson, and from those working with him, about every victory and every failure. Their perceptions were often dramatically at variance. By the end of the eighteen months, I had amassed a number of case studies of decision making in a public library under a new administration. The transcripts of the discussions ran to hundreds of pages. They provided a rich sequence of colorful, graphic accounts of the conflicts and ambiguities inherent in the problems bedeviling the administrator of a public institution. Long after John Anderson had left San Francisco, I thought that some of the material drawn from the interviews might contribute to the literature of library administration. I wrote to Anderson to request permission to publish some of this material. I assured him that I would change names and details so that the monograph's content could not be attributed to him. He refused. He felt that it would be too easy for readers to identify the San Francisco Public Library and its director, regardless of any superficial changes I might make. The edited transcripts were used only for teaching library administration classes. Over the years, countless students learned from these accounts the dramatic perils and pitfalls faced regularly by a director working in the public library of a major city.

Informal discussions with research-oriented students and faculty in the school made clear that there was no resource available to provide details about research and development underway in library and information science. The possibility of discovering a remedy for this problem seemed a good reason to conduct a summer seminar. The participants included six formally enrolled students in addition to several other students and faculty who made informal contributions to the discussions. At the seminar's conclusion, an information-gathering strategy was designed for building a database of research and development in progress. Questionnaire construction and testing had been completed and procedures for managing the database prepared. By the fall of 1969, some members of the original seminar had departed; others had taken their place as the work went forward. During the fall, the group developed the form which entries would take, the arrangement of content, and the creation of a mailing list. Worldwide distribution of questionnaires would take place by late 1969. The questionnaires were sent to 2,600 individuals and organizations. Editorial questions were resolved and the indexing format was determined. By the end of December a publisher had been identified. What began as an experimental seminar blossomed, by the spring of 1970, into a new and fully realized product. The exercise demonstrated that a seminar in librarianship could serve to transform a theoretical inquiry into practical achievement. *Library and Information Science Today: An International Register of Research and Innovation* was published in 1970 by Science Associates. It was updated, revised, and issued in a new annual edition for five years. After the first three years with Science Associates, Gale Research Company took over publishing this compendium. An article describing the project's development appeared in *Library Journal* on November 15, 1970. Its title was "The Birth of LIST: Report of a Seminar that Linked Library Education with Product Development." Its authors were Paul Wasserman and Evelyn Daniel.

During the 1968-1969 academic year, I was beginning to feel stretched across too wide a range of activities. Many responsibilities were self-imposed as I sought constantly to do too much. Funding for the Manpower Research Project enabled me to hire Paul Vassallo from the Library of Congress as an administrative aide. The assignment made it possible for him to work toward a doctorate in political science. For the first time since coming to Maryland, I finally had someone I could rely on completely to relieve me from the minutia of university bureaucracy. He also cheerfully handled many details for the planning of the new building. He made it possible for me to plunge forward into new areas.

The Best of Times

The Manpower Research Project was due to conclude with final reports from each of the studies by 1970. It was necessary to reconvene the investigators and to prod each of them to bring the research to a close. The data that Bundy and I collected also needed to be prepared in a series of reports about managers working in different types of libraries. The final reports in the series were: "The Academic Library Administrator and His Situation" (May 1970); "The Public Library Administrator and His Situation" (June 1970); "The School Library Supervisor and Her Situation" (August 1970); and "The Administrator of the Special Library and Information Center and His Situation" (September 1970). Jeanne O'Connell worked with us through the study, and helped with writing the reports. She also served as associate editor of *Library and Information Science Today*.

Bundy and I had long felt that, in order to understand better the leadership cadre in librarianship, it would be helpful to gather data revealing who they were and what traits they shared. A clear picture of library administrators was seen as a way to gauge more clearly the potential for leadership in librarianship. When the Manpower Research studies had begun, library administrators were viewed as those who might direct a fundamental reorientation of the field. The profiles of this administrative class could be understood best in the context of their responsiveness to adapting their organizations to a culture that was striving for innovation. Against this backdrop, the research sought to understand and to explain the nature and behavior of library administrators. The range of details gathered about the managers included personal history and attitudes, perceptions of basic administrative and professional issues, their organization's characteristics, and their record of adaptation in individual organizations. The research attempted to discern a propensity for change among managers. The motif of change was the cutting edge of the analysis.

Scrupulous analysis of the questionnaire responses revealed that, with the possible exception of schools, libraries of each type could be expected to continue along traditional lines. Nothing in the origins, education, work background, personal orientation, or behavioral tendencies of those studied suggested that these individuals were likely to be change agents. There was very little prospect that the leadership class would initiate major adaptations in programs and services in anything but the long run. Perhaps these conclusions should not have come as such a surprise. Library managers had selected a field that they must have anticipated would be less competitive, more secure, less risk-taking. Bundy and I had been actively engaged in the profession for a number of years. Seldom did we come upon highly innovative or iconoclastic library directors. We were naive to expect to discover Quixotes in our midst. Still, we were sorely disappointed. In our teachings, writings, and public expression we tried to spread the gospel of change. If the leadership class comprised indifferent managers, could there realistically be any prospect for anything more than continuing the business of librarianship as usual? The survey's results only served to strengthen my resolve. I decided to write a book setting forth the intellectual basis for change in the future of librarianship. I invited Mary Lee to join me in writing it.

The school's history did not represent a straight path of continuous successes. Some faculty and adjunct appointments had been mistakes. We also had our share of other gaffes. Two remain vivid in memory. As the first director of admissions for the school, we hired George McDonough from the state of Washington. Our admissions policy stipulated that prospective students be screened on the basis of transcripts and Graduate Record Exam scores. Personal interviews might take place, but they would be only for the purpose of imparting information, not in order to evaluate candidates. Our aim was to avoid bias based upon appearance. During our second year, I received a call from the dean of another campus unit. He wanted to know why we had rejected someone he thought would make a very promising student. I did not know the case and assumed the person in question had not met our criteria. My colleague insisted that the individual in question was exceedingly intelligent. He knew this candidate from her outstanding performance as president of an organization to which his wife belonged. I said I would look into the matter.

When I reviewed the applicant's file, I discovered that she was in her early fifties. She had completed her undergraduate studies at a prestigious women's college thirty years earlier. Her grade point average was impressive; her Graduate Record scores were well above our normal cut-off; and her record of experience during the last decade had been notable. I confronted McDonough and asked why this prospective student had been rejected. He told me that she had looked over the hill to him. I exploded. We had no age limitations. I strongly berated McDonough for violating our ground rules and instructed him immediately to notify the applicant that an error had been made. I called my university colleague to report that there had been a mistake, and that the woman would be notified of her admission. I wrote a personal letter welcoming the new student to our school. The experience led us to revise our admissions procedure to include a faculty committee. The student in question graduated two years later with an excellent level of achievement. She went on to a highly successful record of career accomplishment. McDonough left the school to return to the Pacific Northwest at the end of that academic year.

Another incident occurred with a young man who was hired as an office assistant during his freshman year at Maryland. Fred Liese was a favorite from his first day on the office staff. There was no chore that Fred wouldn't carry out cheerfully and competently. He was a particular favorite of Effie Knight. She relied upon him in countless ways to assist her. Over time, Fred assumed greater responsibility; everyone had full confidence in his ability to perform his job well. When the Manpower Research Project was set to begin in mid-1967, there was a need for a part-time project assistant to supervise the accounts and financial record keeping. A main requirement was to oversee expenses as the project proceeded, so that we stayed within the amounts allocated. Fred announced that he wished to be considered for the position. He had taken a course in accounting and planned to go on to graduate school to study arts administration. He felt the experience would add notably to his record. Fred got the job.

As the project progressed, I periodically asked Fred where expenditures stood in relation to the money we had available. Fred assured me that our accounts were in line. He zealously stayed abreast of these matters, regularly monitoring the financial reports that we received from the comptroller's office. During the final months of the project, I ceaselessly hectored Fred about our financial situation. He reassured me that everything was fine.

One day in December 1969, with six more months of work ahead, I received a call from the comptroller's office. We were very close to exhausting our funds. Frantically, I confronted Fred. He insisted that there must be some mistake. His information showed that our accounts were in excellent shape. With Fred in tow, I made a visit to the university's financial office. It was only then that I learned that we had not taken into account that part of the grant intended as university overhead expense. This amount needed to be subtracted from the level of funds appearing in our regular account reports. Fred turned ghostly white. He had been instructed about this by the comptroller's office during his original orientation. He had completely forgotten this instruction. There was no way for us to avoid incurring a deficit of thousands of dollars by the end of the project. Fred recited his apologies, on the verge of tears. I was very concerned about how we would set things right. I was also furious with myself for having delegated such an important responsibility to a student. I should have been supervising Fred's work. Finding a solution to the situation was awkward and embarrassing. I made profuse apologies orally and in writing to the various officials who oversaw the university's financial affairs. Finally, a decision was reached to absorb the deficit without garnisheeing Fred's salary or mine long into the future. My penchant for eager delegation to trusted associates had received a staggering blow. I promised myself that I would be more prudent thereafter. After a short period of quiet humility, Fred reverted to his usual supreme self-confidence. When last heard from, he was directing one of New York City's premier centers of the performing arts. I could only hope that his responsibilities did not extend to handling financial accounts.

With Krystyna during the September 1982 Hong Kong Conference of the International Federation for Documentation.

Chapter Thirteen

The start of 1970 seemed a good time for taking stock. It had been exactly five years since I began to commute to College Park for the school's opening. Since that time, my targets had been met. The full-time faculty had grown to eighteen, with ten others serving as adjunct members. The student body, including Ph.D. students, reached almost three hundred. I took great pride in what had been achieved in so brief a time, yet I was weary of juggling the demands of the dean's office in addition to researching, writing, and teaching. The long hours of work, the short shrift given to personal and family life, and the absence of pure relaxation had taken their toll. Something had to give. I never envisioned myself as an academic administrator for the long term, even though organizational behavior fascinated me as a subject for scholarly analysis. When I assumed the deanship, I alerted Hornbake and Elkins that I planned to hold the position for only five years. June 1970 marked the end of that time. It seemed a logical time to tender my resignation.

Lee Hornbake was the first person I informed of my decision. He was surprised. I explained to him my frank preference for teaching and research. He may have thought this odd, but he did not question my judgement. Others were equally incredulous. My explanations were not taken at face value. There was the typical speculation that I had been asked to step aside. I cared little what others thought. I felt relief and anticipation. During the spring of 1970, I began to divest myself of administrative duties. I planned to revert to the role of professor. My appointment was altered from a twelve-month year to a ten-month term that was more consistent with teaching norms. This permitted me to teach summer sessions, or not, as I chose. I was free to pursue other options. I wanted to chart a new agenda centered on personal rather than organizational goals. There were concerns about who would succeed me as dean, but I was reluctant to put my support behind any choice.

Concluding efforts on the Manpower Research Project still loomed before me. As deadline dates approached, I was pleasantly surprised by how each scholar brought his study to a close. Before the end of 1970, every one of the reports was completed and submitted to the sponsoring agencies. My thinking shifted to the book I envisaged. I wanted it to encompass the sum of my views on leadership, distilled from the insights gained during the Manpower Research Project, as well as the years of study and reflection on the management of libraries. As I began to outline the framework, I invited Bundy's input and collaboration. She was willing to work with me, but only very grudgingly. She never explained her reluctance to participate. I suspect there were two reasons. Bundy had always been intellectually restless. She found it difficult to focus on any task that demanded staying power. She was at her conceptual best during a concentrated effort over successive days and nights of ceaseless application. Her most brilliant insights normally found expression in writing journal articles, position papers, and research proposals. She was likely put off by the idea of spending months with me writing, discussing, and debating. To continue the collaboration we had sustained through all our intellectual bouts may have lost its appeal for another reason. She was disappointed and annoyed by my resignation of the deanship.

As the sixties were ending and the new decade was upon us, Mary Lee Bundy grew more and more frustrated with the slow pace of change in the country. Adaptation in the library world came at an even more snail-like pace. The High John project was only the opening salvo in the personal war she waged against recalcitrant librarians who refused to accommodate the movement for social justice. Whatever her agenda — experimentation and novel course arrangements; minority recruitment; demonstrations for revised library priorities — she remained secure as long as I was dean. She counted on me to safeguard her prerogatives with faculty and administration and to protect her speech and her actions. In abdicating my role, she may have felt I had betrayed her. From the time I announced my resignation as dean, Bundy and I moved in different directions.

By this time, my marriage and my family life had begun to disintegrate. My daughter Jacqueline, following her graduation from high school in 1967, had chosen to go to work instead of pursuing a college degree. After a couple of jobs had proved disappointing, she relocated early in 1971 to the Los Angeles area.

The Best of Times

Her cousin's family offered to help her find housing and to adjust to the region. Steven was starting his senior year in high school. My wife waited for him to begin the school year before following Jacqueline to California.

The part I played as the United States member of the FID Education and Training Committee, thus far, had been negligible. Unable to attend a meeting of its members, I did not yet understand the dynamics of the program and its workings. I was unclear about what role I might play in its activity. When information was disseminated about a meeting in April 1970 in Frankfurt, I applied for financial support from the United States National Committee to attend. There was keen interest in the National Committee in having an American voice expressed through the active involvement of the new representative. My travel plans coincided with the university's spring break. I made plans for a two-day stopover in Denmark en route to the meeting and for a weekend stay in Nice, before returning to the States.

The meeting was held in the offices of the German professional association secretariat, the Deutsche Gesellschaft fur Dokumentation. Twenty countries were represented in the committee. Normally, only a dozen delegates from different countries would contribute regularly to its programs and conferences. I was invited to present a paper on the state of library education in the United States. The common language of discourse in all FID sessions was English or French. The Committee's Polish chairman, Adam Gorski, spoke neither. The burden of handling all the arrangements, planning, and discussions fell to the secretary. I was expecting this person to be a grizzly and humorless old battle-axe based on my earlier experience, when she had sent letters meant for me to my predecessor. To my astonishment I found a young, attractive woman named Miss Krystyna Ostrowska. Here was the culprit I had vilified to the National Academy of Sciences for her incompetence. I made amends by spending much of my time during the three-day meeting in her company. Whenever sessions were not in progress, I was with her. When I could, I lured her away from other obligations, inviting her to join me for dinner. When it was time to leave Frankfurt, I promised to visit Krystyna in Warsaw in the fall.

Working on the Education and Training Committee proved pleasurable. The United States was universally recognized to be in the forefront of professional development. The members seemed genuinely interested in the views I expressed. My colleagues came from countries representing both Eastern and Western blocs. The sessions were an exciting first exposure for me to cross-cultural relationships. As the United States delegate, I felt a warm sense of fellowship with my professional associates, which far transcended any political differences. That is not to say that there were no political differences. As the United States representative participating in the work of a non-governmental organization supported by American government funds, I received no instruction from anyone. I was not obliged to make my presence or purposes in a foreign land known to the American embassy. The same was never true for delegates from Eastern Europe. They were subjected to government scrutiny and control at all times — from obtaining permission to travel abroad to reporting on one's activity during time spent in a foreign land on professional business. The values, interests, and occupational convictions of committee members, however, were widely shared; they transcended national boundaries and political differences. It was highly uncommon for disagreements on any substantive question to arise among the members based on political calculations. Occasions did occur when decisions had to be made about where to convene a biennial FID conference or how to ensure the participation of delegates from countries that did not have regular diplomatic relations with a host country. Such matters were hotly contested. At the level of the working committees, however, substantive issues were the exclusive concern. My first FID meeting resulted in friendships and associations that continued for many years. Among them were Jean Meyriat of the Fondation Nationale des Sciences Politiques in Paris; Erich Pietsch of Frankfurt Universitat in West Germany, and director of the Gmelin Institute; Herbert Schur of Sheffield University in England; and Janos Szentmihalyi of Eotvos Lorand University in Budapest.

In my report to the U.S. National Committee, I proposed that the United States make a major commitment to the work of the Education and Training Committee. In no other aspect of this key international body's activities was there such a clear opportunity to exercise a leadership role. I described the climate of respect and hospitality I had found for American pedagogical practices and educational ideas. Nowhere else could we hope to influence so dramatically international development in the discipline. My position received the unanimous endorsement of the United States National Committee. I decided that the committee's activities thenceforward should continue to receive my committed and sustained involvement. I also planned to continue the scholarly writing and preparation of new reference works and new editions along with my other editorial responsibilities. Relieved of administrative burdens, I felt that I was free to concentrate exclusively on matters that I personally cared about.

The Best of Times

As dean, I had come to rely heavily on Effie Knight. She was the highest ranking and salaried administrative employee in the school. I couldn't expect to have her continued assistance. Losing her services was a grim prospect. Michael Reynolds, a professor in the faculty, was appointed acting dean while a search committee took on the task of choosing a permanent successor. Soon into Reynold's tenure, however, a number of things went awry. It rapidly became clear that the chemistry between Reynolds and Effie Knight was not working. She felt obliged to resign as dean's secretary and head of the administrative office. She had worked with me in the planning and administration of the Library Administrators Development Program, so it seemed reasonable for her to continue working with me in handling the project's paper flow and administrative arrangements. Effie carried out this work throughout the year in preparation for the annual two-week offering. In this capacity, she continued as a school staff member on a one-third appointment. The other two-thirds of her time would be devoted to working with me on various publishing projects. The need to fund Effie's time with outside, commercial sources motivated me to step up the number of reference books we could bring to publication.

I had already decided to work on the book that would be the product of my thinking, theorizing, speaking, and manpower studies since my move into library education. Originally, I envisaged the appearance of a series of inter-related works written by the investigators who worked on the Manpower Research Project. I talked with officials at Columbia University Press about the possibility of publishing the volumes. They expressed interest, but the researchers could not be pinned down. As work progressed through the research, I realized that riding herd on the research projects was one thing. Serving as monitor and goading and cajoling independent-minded investigators to author a book, after concluding their preparation of the final technical report, was another. I decided to leave them to their own devices and publish my own volume. I cast about for a commercial publisher with a wide following in the library field. The R. R. Bowker Company, publisher of *Library Journal* and *Publishers Weekly*, offered a line of professional books aimed at the library market. They expressed interest and I signed a contract with them. The deadline was January 1, 1971. The work dragged on until the early spring of 1971. The book was not published until the start of 1972.

The New Librarianship: A Challenge for Change was, in part, an outgrowth of the comprehensive research program on manpower issues. In the preliminary matter, I identified the titles of each of the final technical reports that had been submitted to the Office of Education. These were "Supply and Demand Analysis of Manpower Trends in the Library and Information Field," July 1969, by August Bolino; "A Study of the Executive in Library and Information Activity," September 1970, by Mary Lee Bundy and Paul Wasserman; "Interlibrary Cooperation," September 1970, by Edwin Olson; "Technological Change and Occupational Response: A Study of Librarians," June 1970, by Robert Presthus; "Personality and Ability Patterns of Librarians," October 1970, by Stanley Segal; "Image and Status of the Library and Information Services Field," July 1970, by Hart Walters; and "Education, Careers and Professionalization in Librarianship and Information Services," October, 1970, by Rodney White and David Macklin.

In the course of studying library administrators with Bundy, my conceptual and philosophical perspectives had shifted from a focus on the administrator, himself, to the broader questions of leadership and of leadership potential within the discipline. I acknowledged my intellectual debt to Mary Lee Bundy, as catalyst and imaginative contributor to my thinking, in the book. Jeanne O'Connell's editorial and bibliographic help, and Caroline Forsman and Gayle Araghi's tracing of citations were also acknowledged. I thanked Effie Knight for her contribution to the manuscript's preparation and for the responsibility she assumed during the Manpower Research Project.

The book was divided into three parts. The first, "A Theoretical Analysis of the Change Process," looked at the need for change; the dynamics of change; bureaucracy and professionalism as change issues; strategies for change; and the leadership role and responsibility. "The Real World of Librarianship" analyzed institutional administration; the influence of education and library literature; governmental, economic, and professional leadership influences; and prototype forms of librarianship. The final portion, "Toward Leadership for Change" focused on problems and issues and offered an agenda for changing librarianship. The monograph articulated the arguments and the need to redirect the field. Its stated intent was to appeal for the transformation of librarianship and libraries from being reactive institutions into becoming pro-active ones. The book argued for a different future. It explained why change was necessary and through which means it could be achieved. Its ideas were addressed primarily to younger elements in the profession, to those who had fewer ties to the status quo of librarianship or to the other institutional forms of the culture. The book's audience was perceived as those whose personal and group loyalties would engender, rather than inhibit, change.

The Best of Times

In September 1970, I assumed regular classroom duties. I taught two courses each semester. Bundy and I were no longer team teaching library administration. The course was a requirement for all students, so I taught it each semester to a sizeable number. During one semester, I offered the course in business information services. In the other term, I began to give a seminar in international and comparative librarianship. It wasn't until the summer session of 1971, however, that I introduced an experimental course inspired by my experience in developing the LIST Project. By then I had been engaged for a number of years in publishing new reference works. The seminar was consistent with ideas I had long espoused and with a basic tenet of *The New Librarianship* — shifting the emphasis in professional service in information work from a reactive to proactive stance.

I called the course a Seminar in the Invention and Design of Information Products and Services. It was a formal attempt to inspire students to fashion and create information tools where they were needed. The seminar equipped students to pursue the development of new reference sources. My role was to serve as consultant and resource person, offering examples and illustrations. I gave encouragement and used personal contacts to invite specialists to join the class, where they could shed light on specific questions under discussion. The students were sounding boards, reactors, and critics. They encouraged, reinforced, or discouraged the product ideas offered. Out of these interactions and practical trials and errors, students could gain a greater understanding of new information product design and development. Sometimes projects would be brought to a successful conclusion during the semester. Sometimes, they would not be completed until long afterward. Every participant would develop into a sophisticated and analytical critic of reference sources. The results of the first offering were very encouraging. In November 1971, at the Denver meeting of the American Society for Information Science, I gave a one-day tutorial on the subject for members. In later years, I offered this seminar as a regular elective offering in the curriculum.

By the fall of 1970 my publication activities continued at an accelerated pace. Effie Knight became involved in all phases of book development and production. In 1971, the second edition of *Awards, Honors, and Prizes* was being prepared. Based on the success of the Management Information Guide Series, Fred Ruffner decided to publish bibliographic guides in other subject fields using MIG books as the model. He asked me to serve as overall coordinating editor and to select and invite individuals to act as editors in their particular subject area. I would assist them in creating their own series. The series came to be known as *The Gale Information Guide Library Series*. The series grew into the largest scale collection of subject bibliographies ever available from a single publishing company.

In 1970 and 1971, I held discussions with officials from Greenwood Press. Herbert Cohen and Herbert Johnson were executives of this relatively new publishing firm. They felt that the professional readership in the library field needed continued publications of books that shed light on new approaches to understanding. They had seen the books in the Reader Series in Library and Information Science and felt a series of original monographs would be of even more value. They invited me to assume the editorship of what would become the series Contributions in Librarianship and Information Science. By the time the first volume appeared in 1972, Cohen and Johnson had left the firm. Robert Hagelstein became president of Greenwood.

From the outset, my purpose for the series was to influence for the better intellectual currents in the field. For the Greenwood Contributions series, I encouraged colleagues to consider preparing new works of substantive merit that could help elevate professional discourse. I sought out authors who would add to the ideological, theoretical, pragmatic, or problem-solving approaches of the field. I wanted to attract those with an imaginative approach to issues in need of thoughtful discussion, analysis, and elaboration. There would be monographs, research material, advanced texts, essays, and symposia on topics of concern. Making a genuine contribution to the field's knowledge base was the only criterion for publication. The first volume appeared in 1972. Ninety-one volumes were issued during the period while I served as series editor, through the close of 1998.

I had told Krystyna in Frankfurt that I would come to see her in Warsaw in the fall. My teaching responsibilities, along with my feverish concentration on completing the manuscript for my book, kept me from making the trip until mid-December. I had a visa, but it appeared that I might not be permitted to enter Poland. In December 1970, the Gomulka government was about to fall. Foreign passengers were finally permitted to board a connecting flight from London to Warsaw. Upon landing, the airplane was immediately surrounded by soldiers. The Warsaw airport was teeming with military, and the downtown area had the appearance of an armed camp. Fortunately, the government transition was carried out without incident. A veil of secrecy enveloped much of Polish society in that period, but the city was calm. This was my first trip to an Eastern European nation; the things I saw and experienced were a revelation. The city's buildings were drab and monotonous looking. People's attire was equally plain and colorless. Ubiquitous shortages caused long lines for every consumer purchase. I felt profound sympathy for Warsaw's luckless inhabitants. At Christmas time, Krystyna and I traveled to the picturesque city of Krakow. Unlike every other major Polish city during World War II, Krakow had remained virtually untouched. The celebrated town square was blanketed with newly fallen snow.

The FID biennial Congress was going to be held in Budapest in 1972. During the Education and Training Committee meeting in Frankfurt, a sub-committee had been formed to design an international seminar on education in information science. It would convene in conjunction with the Congress. I was asked to serve as a member of the planning group. I planned to meet with the committee chairman, Szentmihalyi, right after the first of the year in Budapest. The Education and Training Committee secretary, Krystyna Ostrowska, was also expected to attend the meeting. Krystyna and I returned from Krakow to Warsaw before the end of December and flew to Budapest. We spent a memorable New Year's Eve in Hungary.

Upon our arrival in the city on December 31, we scarcely had time to get our bearings before the holiday evening began. I had arranged for us to go along with an organized group to a restaurant in the old quarter of Pest. There we would dine to the strains of gypsy violinists and drink wine to usher in the New Year. At eight o'clock we boarded a bus that deposited us in the basement of a picturesque, stone-walled establishment, where we were shown to our tables. A cosmopolitan gathering of revelers from different countries had come to celebrate New Year's Eve in Budapest. The only problem was that the Italians spoke Italian to other Italians; the Greeks and the Romanians did likewise. No one was willing, or able, to speak English, French, or German. The goulash was excellent, as was the *Egri Bikaver* (bull's blood red wine). The gypsy violinists looked right for their parts. They were corny but animated, and kept repeating the same repertoire of songs over and over. We had fun for a while, but then grew bored. We had already dined and drunk a good deal of wine, and there were still two hours until midnight. I decided it was time to leave. Krystyna was confused. We had come to celebrate the New Year. How could we simply leave when we were expected to remain until after midnight before returning to the hotel? I assured her that we could do as we liked. When we left the restaurant, snow was falling heavily but we succeeded in locating a taxi which took us back to the hotel. Somewhat annoyed,

Krystyna wanted to know what we would do now. As we strolled the corridor, deep in conversation, we were accosted by a well-dressed, older woman. She asked if we were Americans, and I explained who we were. She invited us to join the New Year's celebration already underway in her hotel suite.

We later learned that this woman, Tullah Hanley, had been a young Hungarian showgirl when a wealthy American had discovered and married her. He whisked her off to San Francisco, where she had lived for a number of years. Her husband had since died, making her a well-to-do heiress and a celebrated benefactress of the arts — particularly of the San Francisco de Young Memorial Museum. Each year she returned to Budapest for the New Year and rented a suite at the old Hotel Royale. She lavishly entertained hordes of old friends and other people whom she found interesting enough to invite to her party. There, we met innumerable charming and attractive Hungarians and party guests from other European countries. The gathering included members of Budapest's arts and media community. Like the champagne, the scintillating conversation flowed ceaselessly in several different languages. The main attraction of the soiree came just before midnight; the hotel staff turned loose a greased pig that was scrambled after by the inebriated throng. The party continued into the early morning hours.

The next day was a murky haze. Szentmihalyi took us to lunch on January 2nd, at the very same restaurant where we had begun the New Year. We never let on to him that we had been there before. During the stay, we managed to resolve with Szentmihalyi questions relating to the program and its content elements for the three-day seminar. Before leaving Krystyna, I promised to arrange a formal invitation for her to visit the United States. She would need this in order to apply for an American visa. She arrived in New York in August 1971.

In the time that I withdrew from the deanship, most important elements of my hopes for the new school had been realized. The school's culture had always been volatile. Various points of view competed for a plurality in academic debates, but free and outspoken expression of differences had been cultivated to foster democratic choices. The school was a reflection of society at large. Frequently positions were divided between administrative values, faculty perspectives, and the will of the students. In a time when belligerent utterances and behavior characterized the state of affairs in many university departments, the library school seemed far more tranquil, despite its factional splits on many divisive questions of that period.

When I resigned the deanship, I looked forward to a relatively brief and orderly interregnum before the search committee would invite a successor. As it happened, Reynolds' performance as acting dean evoked sufficient ill will among faculty and students to lead to his early replacement by a second acting dean, James Liesener. I did not want to be a partisan in the political drama of choosing a new dean, and I resisted appeals from my colleagues to speak out. Instead, I concentrated on teaching and scholarly interests. Mary Lee saw me as a traitor for not marching loyally behind the banner of her crusade. The problems multiplied. There was also confusion in the upper administrative echelons of the university. Student unrest led to a restructuring; President Elkins was relegated to an off-campus post as president of all higher education institutions in Maryland. His successor as chancellor at College Park, Charles Bishop, was expected to be more adroit in avoiding potentially explosive student actions. He came with considerable experience in student affairs and public relations. Unfortunately, Lee Hornbake, our staunchest supporter, followed Elkins to become a vice-president at the state level.

Following Bishop's arrival at College Park, a well-orchestrated campaign was mounted by Thomas Day, Vice Chancellor for Academic Planning and Policies, to reorganize the campus administrative structure. The library school's place in the hierarchy called for the dean to report directly to the Vice President for Academic Affairs. A gullible Senate of vociferous faculty and student believers voted for the new administrative division structure. This had the effect of adding a whole new layer of bureaucracy. Each division director would now report to the campus administration, while the academic units, which formerly enjoyed freedom from such control, would be under the governance of the division heads. The library school would become a minuscule unit of Division Five — a catch-all for units such as the College of Education, Home Economics, and Recreation Management. Our identification was to be altered ignominiously from the status we had enjoyed from our inception as the School of Library and Information Services to a designation as College of Library and Information Services. I watched this drama unfold with disgust. In my view, the cumbersome administrative apparatus would soon be toppled by its own weight. I was wrong. It took until 1986 for the damage to be undone. Ironically, Vice Chancellor for Academic Affairs Brit Kerwin was quoted as saying in the September 15, 1986 issue of the *University of Maryland Outlook,* "One very important benefit is that with an administrative layer removed, I now have direct contact with the deans. This has had the positive result of shortening the lines of communication."

The Best of Times

In the spring of 1971, I worked to get on with the publication of the *New Librarianship*. Effie Knight and I also concentrated on bringing consistency and uniformity to the contributions of several associate editors, who had accepted assignments for portions of the *Encyclopedia of Business Information Sources*. They included Eleanor Allen of the Lippincott Library of the Business School of the University of Pennsylvania; Charlotte Georgi, at the UCLA Graduate School of Business Library; Betsy Ann Olive of Cornell; and James Woy of the Business Library of the Free Library of Philadelphia. The material identifying the range of sources on hundreds of subjects resulted in a three-volume set. Published in the fall of 1971, it found quick acceptance and widespread use in many academic, public, and special business library collections.

In the spring, I also offered, for the first time, the seminar in international and comparative librarianship and information science. This course provided an occasion for me to organize my thinking on the subject and to plan the structure, reading list, and strategy for leading the seminar sessions. The classes were intended to analyze the information field by treating both comparative and international issues. The course would also evaluate the direction of library institutions and library practice from cross-cultural, political, sociological, and economic vantage points. The students in that first class, and in subsequent offerings, constituted a colorful blend of native and foreign students. Many American students wanted to study library issues outside the United States because of their own experiences working or studying abroad. Some of them had undergraduate majors in foreign languages or foreign studies. Foreign students came to take advantage of the only curricular offering that paid attention to the world's libraries, instead of concentrating exclusively on American values and practices. This student melange gave the seminar a more exotic flavor than would ever be found in a more conventional class.

Krystyna arrived in the heat of August at Kennedy Airport in New York with permission to visit the United States as a tourist. I had arranged housing for her in a furnished apartment in Brooklyn Heights. She had scholarship support from the publishing firm of Science Associates to attend Pratt Institute's Library School. First, she needed to pass the English language proficiency exam. She passed with flying colors and began her study in September.

My son Steven was to graduate from high school in June 1971. His academic performance made him a questionable candidate for the University of Maryland, so we considered a number of Midwestern universities that might be somewhat less rigorous than Maryland. He and I traveled to Northern Michigan University for a two-day visit. The ground remained covered with snow, and the temperature hovered in the low twenties. Steve immediately rejected the frozen North. While I was in Europe for the FID meeting in Frankfurt, he made the trek alone to New Mexico State University in Las Cruces. A lifelong Easterner, Steven was fascinated by the desert terrain and expansive, sunny skies of Las Cruces. The university was only a short drive from El Paso, and Mexico was just across the Rio Grande. The study program also appealed to him. He enrolled there as a freshman in September. I lived alone in College Park and spent frequent weekends in New York City to see Krystyna.

The 1971-1972 academic year was less contentious. A new dean had taken office, following a succession of temporary occupants. Margaret Chisholm had been chosen from the Maryland faculty, where she had been a professor of school librarianship. Her selection was seemingly made by administrative fiat during the summer lull, when few of the faculty members were in residence. Endowed with personal charm and physical presence, Chisholm worked hard to create a climate of tranquillity. The program appeared, at least superficially, to return to normality. I took part in faculty discussions but maintained a low profile, concentrating my attention on working with the master's and doctoral students.

Chapter Fourteen

After I had resigned the deanship and then completed my book, I shifted my focus to the international scene. I had made my statement by then to American librarianship, and I saw a whole world of librarianship beyond America. I felt that international libraries might hold out more promise for change than the indifference I felt characterized so much of American librarianship. I thought that by working through the Education and Training Committee of FID, I could influence choices and effect change. Maryland had the potential to be an important center for international study in librarianship. Its location put it close to the seat of numerous international organizational headquarters. United States government libraries engaged in foreign programs and exchanges. The proximity of foreign embassies and consular offices also reflected the Washington area's distinct international character. My work as the American representative to the Education and Training Committee of FID provided the scaffold from which the college might develop further elements of international engagement.

One avenue toward reinforcing an international orientation was to hold a summer institute. International specialists from Washington could lecture in their own fields of expertise and experience. Advance planning would be needed to mount such an ambitious undertaking. Work began during the fall of 1971 for the offering of a summer institute in 1972. By early 1972, the dates were set. Conference space was reserved at the Center for Adult Education and an outline of the program, along with invitations, were sent to the projected instructional team. A descriptive brochure for prospective participants and a press release detailing the offering were ready by early spring. It was around this time that I was appointed as a member of the Committee for International Library Education of the American Library Association's Library Education Division, for the 1972-1974 term. I became the Committee's chairman from 1974 to 1976.

The Best of Times

The second librarian in the school's history was Robert Haro. In 1972 he left; the search was underway for his successor. I had very strong feelings about the qualities needed in the new librarian, who would also assume the role of lecturer in the faculty. We needed a first-rate special librarian who would identify strongly with the research and teaching requirements of the faculty and with the substantive content of the collection: library and information service. The leading candidate was then in a middle management position in an academic library. A review of his dossier and personal discussion with him during a campus visit convinced me that while he seemed ambitious, he did not strike me as someone who would dedicate himself to the unique purposes of a special library and its student and faculty constituency. I saw no point in engaging someone without a serious interest in the literature or scholarship of librarianship. He would view the post more as a platform to propel himself up to the next administrative opportunity that beckoned.

I expressed my negative views vehemently. The consensus was strongly on the other side. As it turned out the prevailing forces were right; I could not have been more wrong. The appointee was Bill Wilson. As I reflect on the history of the program and those who have had the most profound influence on its development, Wilson stands apart. Not only did he epitomize the ideal special librarian in his passion for energetically and intelligently serving his clients, but he also brought a humane and caring approach to his work and to everyone he dealt with. Bill Wilson understood that a library was not simply about artifacts or procedures, but a means of helping human beings with their personal needs. His sensitivity has distinguished him to many generations of students and faculty. He is a revered person within and outside the university. He has given of himself to countless civic, social, and human causes and has won the same loving admiration from the librarians statewide who elected him president of the Maryland Library Association. I have been wrong about any number of things during my career, but never have I been more seriously mistaken than I was in my initial assessment of Bill Wilson.

By January 1972 I had been with the university for seven years. During the fall of 1971, I began to make plans for a sabbatical. The fall semester of 1972 seemed the logical time. The biennial FID Congress would be convened in Budapest in September, followed immediately by the International Seminar on Education in Information Science in Veszprem. I was to present a paper there. After that, I planned to tour European education and research centers. I would be able to meet with associates and learn about their work in library and information science in their institutions. I planned to lecture whenever I was invited to do so. I wrote an account describing the study tour and its objectives and submitted it to Margaret Chisholm. She quickly endorsed my proposal and sent it forward for higher approval. In a matter of weeks my sabbatical was authorized. I would leave in the fall as planned. There still remained the time-consuming process of securing visas and of corresponding with colleagues to alert them to the dates of my visit. I thought I would use the time in Budapest and Veszprem to meet new colleagues and hopefully elicit invitations from them to come to visit their institutions and centers. My plan was to leave Budapest the day following the Veszprem seminar and fly to Sofia, Bulgaria. Other stops included Bucharest, Moscow, Leningrad, Helsinki, Oslo, Stockholm, West and East Berlin, Prague, Zagreb, Rome, Paris, and London. I would return to the United States in early December.

During this time, I was invited to be a member of the editorial advisory board of the Institute for Scientific Information's Social Science Citation Index. It became an affiliation that I held for many years. In March of 1972, I participated in the Louisiana State University Library Lecture Series, where I offered the twentieth lecture in the series. In the presentation, "Engineering Change in Librarianship: From Revised Paradigm to Prototypes for the Future," I spoke publicly for the first time about many of the ideas that I had elaborated in *The New Librarianship*, which was about to be published. I drew upon the model of scientific progress advanced in Thomas Kuhn's seminal study, *The Structure of Scientific Revolutions*, applying its conceptual logic to the field of librarianship.

The Institute on Comparative and International Library and Information Science, which I directed that summer, included forty participants. Among them was Krystyna; it was her final course toward completion of the Pratt MLS degree. A number of distinguished internationally recognized information specialists led the sessions. Melvin Day and Scott Adams were among the best known.

About the time I left for Budapest, Krystyna moved to the East Village of Manhattan and was hired as a library staff member by Burton Adkinson, the director of the American Geographic Society. He had formerly been with the National Science Foundation, where he had headed the Office of Science Information. Krystyna's work status in the United States was subject to question by the Immigration and Naturalization Service. Adkinson, a colleague from her Warsaw days, when he had been an International Federation for Documentation president, went to special pains to make the case for her. He pointed to her Eastern European language competence as the basis for special qualifications that could not be found in a comparable United States national.

My application for a visa to the Soviet Union had been denied since I did not have a confirmed hotel reservation in Moscow. I had tried, unsuccessfully, to reserve a hotel room through a travel agency in Washington that specialized in Soviet travel. The problem, as it was explained to me by experienced observers of Soviet bureaucracy, was that I wanted to travel by myself to Moscow and Leningrad. This would place me outside the customary structured supervision and control of foreign travelers. I had planned to visit VINITI, the large centralized Soviet documentation and information system. Professor Mikhailov, the highly placed and politically well-connected director of VINITI was expected to be in Budapest for the FID Congress. I hoped to prevail upon a mutual colleague to enlist Mikhailov's help in getting a visa.

The FID Congress in Budapest was the first I had ever attended. I had registered for the conference in advance and reserved a room at the Hotel Royale. I learned that there was a shortage of hotel rooms in the city. Many attendees were descending upon the city, and available space had been overwhelmed. A pleasant appearing, English speaking information scientist from the Academy of Sciences in Warsaw described to me his desperate hunt for accommodations. I had a spacious room with two beds, so I invited this gentleman to share my room. I told him where I was staying and suggested he inform the hotel desk that I had asked him to share the room with me. He was profusely grateful. We expected to see each other in the hotel room that night. After a long day of meetings, discussions, and a leisurely dinner with friends, I made my way back to the hotel. As I walked down the quiet corridor to my room, I heard a sound that grew louder and louder. It was someone snoring; I realized in horror that the thundering roar was coming from my room. Mr. Leski was obviously fast asleep. I went to the bathroom and purposely created a racket, hoping the noise would waken my roommate before I got into bed. It didn't work. I got into bed and put my head between two pillows in an attempt to muffle the sound of Leski's snoring. The incessant buzzsaw continued. I lay quietly trying to figure out a way to sleep. I dropped a heavy pile of papers on the floor with a thud. No response. I turned on my bed lamp. Not a stir. In my desperation to sleep I began to sweat. I decided to take action. I strolled over to Leski's bed and shook him vigorously until he was awake. He looked at me blurry-eyed while I apologized for waking him. I explained that he was snoring so loudly that it was not possible for me to sleep. Would he, could he, try to stop snoring? Deeply embarrassed, he said he was very sorry; he would try to refrain from snoring. I went back to bed. The room was silent. Anxiously, I tried desperately to fall asleep before my roommate; I was not successful. Leski fell asleep first. A few minutes later the constant droning resumed. The next morning I had a short, polite conversation with Leski. I explained that his loud snoring made sleep impossible for me and that I had to rescind my invitation for him to share the room with me. Apologetically and graciously he agreed to seek out an accommodation elsewhere before the end of the day.

During the Budapest meeting I was introduced to the deliberations of the Congress of the International Federation for Documentation, the legislative decision-making body of the organization. This group, with delegates representing the national committees of the fifty-seven member nations, was arranged in United Nations fashion. A voting representative from each country was seated behind the country's placard. Fellow nationals served as advisors. The key political judgements had already been decided during discussions of the FID executive board. The resulting resolutions were presented for acceptance and passage without much discussion. Representatives from most countries had little interest in what was discussed. Nevertheless, it was impossible to predict when some spontaneous or even carefully plotted, unanticipated resolution might be proposed. As in the affairs of international governmental bodies like the United Nations, many of the political concerns of the non-governmental FID had to do with the differences between developed and developing countries, Eastern and Western bloc views, and coalitions based on language compatibility. No fireworks erupted during the 1972 Congress.

I asked Wojciech Pirog from Poland early in the meeting to introduce me to Professor Mikhailov, and to help me explain how I needed help obtaining a Soviet visa so that I might visit VINITI. Mikhailov suggested that he would arrange a hotel reservation for me and would clear up my visa problem before I arrived in Moscow. He made careful note of my itinerary and timetable. He would be in touch with Moscow about my situation while still in Budapest and follow up once he had returned home. He indicated that I should have word about the visa either before I left Hungary or in Sofia. If not, I would have it in Bucharest, my last stopping point before Moscow. With this assurance, I dismissed the matter from my mind. I assumed that I would have a Soviet visa by the time I arrived in Moscow.

The Best of Times

At one of the technical meetings, I met a Madame Micou who turned out to be the director of a research institute on social science and political science information in Bucharest. She spoke no English, but was fluent in French. She was pleased to find that we could converse. She invited me to visit her institute in Bucharest. I had already corresponded earlier with the head of another research center there, Victor Taraboi, the Romanian member of the Education and Training Committee. He had written to invite me to visit and lecture at his center. Another person I met in Budapest was Adam Wysocki, the director of UNESCO's Division of Libraries, Documentation and Archives. I explained to him that I would be visiting Paris in November as part of my sabbatical. He invited me to meet with him then to continue our discussions of library administration. Beyond the intrinsic value of the meetings, Budapest in September 1972, with its fine sunny days, renowned restaurants, lively and colorful streets and shops, and an excellent exchange rate for the U.S. dollar, was a very attractive conference venue. At the close of the Congress, forty-five participants boarded buses for transport to Veszprem, where we attended the International Seminar on Education in Information Science.

The United States contingent included Eugene Jackson, who had by then left IBM for a teaching post at the University of Texas in Austin, and Harold Borko, who had left System Development Corporation to become a library educator at UCLA. Derek Langridge was there from North London Polytechnic. He had earlier been a visiting lecturer at Maryland. Douglas Foskett from the University of London, who had taught with me one summer session at the University of Michigan, was also present. The French contingent included Jean Meyriat, from the Sorbonne and Michel Menou, an independent library consultant also from Paris, who worked on consulting assignments for international organizations in various regions of Africa. In Veszprem I was to meet Kjell Samuelson, a medical doctor who did research and lectured on information science at Stockholm University and the Royal Institute of Technology. He invited me to lecture to his students during my stopover in Sweden. Gernot Wersig represented West Germany from the Freie Universitat in Berlin. Felix Weber of the Technische Hochschule in Ilmenau came from the German Democratic Republic. The man who would later take over as FID president, Ricardo Gietz, was there from the Centro de Documentacion Cientifica in Buenos Aires. Guillermo Fernandez de la Garza of the Consejo Nacional de Ciencia y Tecnologia in Mexico was the other Latin American attendee. Wojciech Pirog, who had replaced Gorski as chairman of the Education and Training Committee, was also present. In Veszprem I met two Italian colleagues from Rome: Ms. B. Farina from the National Research Council and Mrs. G. Lubbock of the Istituto Nazionale de Informazione. Both invited me to visit their organizations. The conference of delegates from eighteen countries convened at the Technical University of Chemical Engineering. It was composed of four sessions. The papers and panel discussions on information science as an emergent discipline that were taken up during the conference included research and development in education for information science and the future of education in information science. My presentation, under the rubric of education and research, was titled "Educational Issues in International Information Systems Development." The proceedings of the seminar were published in Budapest by the Hungarian Technical Library and Documentation Center in 1974.

Our Hungarian hosts had arranged excellent meals and receptions during the meeting days, but nothing rivaled the festivities held in Budapest on our last night. A book by Douglas Foskett had been translated into Hungarian and published in Budapest several years earlier. Hungarian money was not convertible to Western currency, so all the royalties accruing to the author could only be spent in Hungary. That final night in Budapest, Foskett arranged to spend every last *florint* in his account. He invited everyone to a lavish banquet. The dinner menu included wild game and every imaginable type of alcoholic beverage. A large orchestra of gypsy violinists accompanied the meal. The celebration went on until daybreak. I left for Sofia that morning.

I had no word before leaving Budapest about my Russian visa. The first thing I did on my arrival at the hotel in Sofia was to inquire if there were any messages for me. There were none. I was in Sofia to visit Mrs. Kostadinka Kalaydzhieva, director of the National and University Library. Library educators rarely traveled so deeply into Eastern Europe in those days. I was introduced to all the members of the professional staff during an evening reception. Before that, I had spent most of the day being shown through the library's various departments. My foreign counterparts asked me many more questions about living conditions and politics in the United States than they did about library or educational matters. I was astonished to find the equipment they used to be so antiquated. There were no copying machines. Technology had not yet advanced beyond the use of ancient-looking manual typewriters. The staff members, at least those I was able to communicate with, seemed hopeful about the future. The library director was eager to establish an association between the Maryland library school program and the training courses offered at the National Library. I promised to remain in touch.

The Best of Times

The city of Sofia in 1972 seemed to be unchanged from some time in its distant past. The wide, tree-lined boulevards were quiet, with only an occasional Communist party or military vehicle driving slowly along. The air was clean and fresh. On a leisurely stroll through the city's center I found my way to a large, old-fashioned hotel. In the café, with its glittering chandeliers, I had tea served in exquisite bone China. A tuxedo-clad pianist played Chopin. In the evening, the sidewalks were quiet. In the glow of the street lamps, Sofia assumed a romantic aura that seemed to belong to another era. My visit was too short. I left with the hope that I might return someday.

My stay in Bucharest was to be for only two days before flying on to Moscow. When I learned that there was no message at the hotel from Mikhailov or the Soviet consulate about my visa, I realized something had gone wrong. I decided to wait a day or so before rearranging my flight schedule. If I couldn't enter the Soviet Union, I would simply extend my stay in Romania before going on to Moscow, where I would connect immediately with a flight to Helsinki. In Bucharest I visited the Center for Scientific and Technical Information where Victor Taraboi, my fellow member of the Education and Training Committee, was expecting me. I met with Taraboi late in the morning. We went on to lunch at the cafeteria, and in the afternoon I gave an informal seminar to a dozen or so department heads on trends in information science education in the United States.

Early in our discussion, Taraboi told me that he had heard that I would also be visiting the Social Science and Political Science Information Center. I explained that I had met Madame Micou at the Conference in Budapest. This information seemed to elicit a measure of coolness in Taraboi's manner toward me. I wondered what could have provoked his standoffishness toward me. Perhaps it was simply a matter of professional jealousy between rival institutions. I had no clue about the nuances of behavior in this alien culture, so I really could not speculate about his behavior. When my visit was over he stiffly thanked me for coming and for talking so candidly to his staff on professional matters of mutual interest. On leaving, he told me that he hoped I would enjoy the rest of my stay in Bucharest and that he hoped to see me at future meetings of the Education and Training Committee. I returned to my hotel and dined alone.

I received no word from Moscow by the next morning. When I telephoned Madame Micou, she sounded delighted to hear from me. She sent a car to pick me up at the hotel and take me to her institute. An hour later, I was sitting in her comfortably furnished office sipping coffee and having a relaxed chat. She seemed fascinated by the notion of my sabbatical and asked me to describe my entire itinerary. When I explained to her about the problem I was having with getting a Soviet visa, she saw it as a stroke of luck; I would be able to spend additional time in Romania. I told her that both my parents had been born near Jassi around the turn of the century. To this she announced that she would make plans for me to fly to Jassi for a visit. When I asked if this might not be a problem on such short notice, she smiled reassuringly and said it would not be any problem at all. It was not until that evening that I learned why.

Madame Micou asked if she might help arrange my time during my stay in Bucharest. She wanted me to meet some of her staff and to give a public lecture, but she also wanted to be sure that I saw something of Bucharest. Would I mind if a staff member took me to see the sights? I said that I would be delighted. I spent Thursday afternoon in Bucharest, and was Madame Micou's guest for dinner. She told me that she had booked me on a Saturday morning flight to Jassi, where I would spend two days. After that, I would see the region's celebrated painted churches and monasteries before returning to Bucharest. The following Friday I was to return to the Social Science and Political Science Information Center to deliver a lecture. After lunch with the professional staff, I would be driven to the airport for my Moscow flight — one week later than my original schedule. Would this itinerary be agreeable? My immediate response was an enthusiastic *oui*!

At half-past one o'clock a young staff member from the Center arrived at my hotel. He identified himself as my guide in halting, embarrassed English. Outside a car and driver from the Center awaited us. The car, the driver, and the guide were at my disposal for the rest of the day. After a few minutes, once he overcame his shyness, my guide began to speak English more easily in a British accent. I enunciated slowly and clearly to ease the strain on his Romanian ears. We spent a marvelous afternoon driving around the old city glimpsing at parks, Soviet-style structures, residential suburbs, and overcrowded tenements. We spent some time at the National Museum, visited the Opera House and the National Theater, and concluded the warm September afternoon sipping cool drinks at a chic outdoor cafe in the city center. I gave my guide a shiny, new Kennedy half-dollar, one of many that I brought along to distribute as mementos during my travels.

That evening, the driver returned to take me to Mme. Micou's house for dinner. We drove through a large, wooded park. Mme. Micou's house was in the middle of it. Her home was spacious and contemporary; it was furnished impeccably with modern furniture and artwork. Her house was in marked contrast to the general shabbiness of the city. Mme. Micou was a gracious hostess; she seemed pleased to be in my company. She enjoyed speaking French, a language she loved, but one that she had only infrequent occasion to use.

Over aperitifs before dinner, I learned her story. Her husband had been a committed member of the Communist party early on and had spent much of his life in prison for his political convictions. It was not until after the war that he was rehabilitated and rewarded with high-level government appointments. Long years of incarceration, torture, and deprivation had taken their toll; he finally succumbed to poor health several years earlier. As his widow, Mme. Micou enjoyed preferential treatment. The post of director of the Social Science and Political Science Information Center was offered to her. She had an academic background in the subjects, although she did not have experience in information work. The state continued to allow her to live in her husband's house. She remarked softly that, after all, she did not have many years before she would be joining him. Dinner was served by candlelight. The main course resembled *boeuf bourguignon*. This was certainly a luxury in a city where any kind of meat was strictly rationed. The wine was a French burgundy. We concluded the evening drinking fine cognac. Mme. Minou remarked that she hoped I would take away only good memories of her country. She reflected that perhaps my parents had been lucky to leave Romania for America before the turbulent years of the century had descended upon Europe. The evening had been uncommonly pleasurable.

Early the next day, I was at the airport for my flight to Jassi. Security arrangements for this internal flight were more stringent than I had ever experienced before. Under the sharp-eyed scrutiny of soldiers, passengers underwent a full body search and the identification of each piece of luggage before boarding the plane. During the flight, I realized just how ubiquitous the English language had become. On that short flight between two Romanian cities, every announcement was made first in Romanian, then in English. When I disembarked in Jassi, a man holding a sign with my name on it was waiting for me. In a few minutes I was in the back seat of a black car flying a large red banner and speeding toward the city. I was astonished. Mme. Micou had arranged for a party official to be available to help me for my entire trip.

Jassi turned out to be a beautiful city. It was there that I experienced *mamaliga*, a yellow cornmeal or polenta, which was served at every meal. This dish came prepared in innumerable ways. It went with eggs, meat, cheese, chicken, or any other imaginable dish. As a child I remembered *mamaliga* being served only on rare occasions as a special treat. We had eaten it then with *brinza*, a sharp goat cheese, much like feta cheese. In Jassi I consumed *mamaliga* like a bear eating his full before hibernation. I wasn't sure of the town my mother's parents had lived in before coming to America. I remembered my grandmother speaking of a place that sounded like Pudoloy. I asked about it at my hotel. No one seemed to have heard of it. When I mentioned it to the party functionary who assisted me in my travels he thought that what I said didn't sound right. He pronounced another name phonetically that sounded like, Pu-dwa-yee. Could that be it? I had no idea. He suggested we go and have a look. Back in the car with its red flag flying, we sped out of the city for half an hour before stopping at a sorry looking road crossing where a boy was playing with a dog. A cow stood nearby looking at us forlornly. A conversation ensued. The boy nodded, then he shook his head. The talk went on for only a couple of minutes. It seems that the town "Pu-dwa-yee" used to be there, but everyone had moved away. Only the boy and his family still remained. "When did all the people go?" I asked. There was more discussion, but the boy didn't know. He only knew the name of the place from his parents. As we drove back to Jassi I reflected that the fact that the town no longer existed didn't really matter. The people I had heard about who once lived there did not exist any longer either.

Over the next few days I took an overland trip through the region to see many of the still-standing church walls that dated back to the 12th and 13th centuries. A party official accompanied me as my guide. We drove many miles and stayed at modest houses or monasteries along the way. These walls, some connected to active monasteries, were still covered with religious decorations so sharp in their lines and colors that it seemed impossible that they could have been painted so many hundreds of years ago. These priceless historic structures are now part of a historic trust overseen by UNESCO. I returned to Bucharest on Thursday evening. Friday I would give a lecture at the Center.

Madame Micou introduced me to a large audience from her institution and from other Bucharest organizations. She spoke first in Romanian and then, for my benefit, more briefly in French. She explained that headphones were available for translation of my remarks into Romanian. When I rose to speak, I began in slow practiced phrases of Romanian. They were words that my guide had translated and written out phonetically. He had patiently coached me in their pronunciation. In translation I had said: "It is a great honor for me to speak to you. Romania was the birthplace of my parents. My visit to your country is therefore one of the great experiences of my life." The group seemed delighted and applauded for several minutes. Afterwards several people wondered why, since I knew their language so well, I hadn't given the entire talk in Romanian. The morning and luncheon went by with animated discussion of what I had said about education in library and information science. Then it was time to bid farewell to Mme. Micou. I expressed my gratitude for all she had done to make my stay in Romania so very memorable.

I had by that time changed my travel arrangements; I was scheduled to leave Bucharest exactly one week later than originally scheduled. At the airport my problems began. The Romanian Tarom Airlines flight was expected to be three hours late arriving in Bucharest. I would be in Moscow too late to make my connecting flight to Helsinki. There was a flight to Copenhagen; from there I could catch a connection to Helsinki. When the agent checked my ticket, she found that the change would cost me two hundred American dollars. My pleas that the fault lay with Tarom Airlines for making me miss my Moscow connection were unavailing. I inquired about the next connecting flight from Moscow to Helsinki and was told it would not be until mid-morning on Saturday. In that case, I said I would fly to Moscow and take the Saturday morning flight. The desk agent wanted me to be sure I understood that the Romanian carrier would not assume any responsibility for me missing the connecting plane in Moscow. I agreed and signed a form to this effect. When I finally boarded the plane, I thought it might be an interesting experience to spend a night at the Moscow airport.

My flight was uneventful; it was night before we landed at Sheremytov Airport. When it was noted on arrival that my connecting flight had long since departed, I was permitted to retrieve my suitcase and was then shunted aside. Half an hour later, I was taken to a desk where a Soviet Intourist agent examined my ticket. In excellent English she told me to wait a little while. I would be taken to a hotel close to the airport where I could spend the night. I would be brought back the next morning. This certainly sounded more civilized than sleeping on an airport bench. Two hours later another Intourist person approached me accompanied by a soldier. The soldier was to take me to the hotel. My passport would remain at the passport control desk. Carrying my suitcase, I followed the soldier about one block and entered a three-story, unmarked building. We walked up the stairs; on the third floor the soldier knocked on the door. Another soldier on the other side of the door let me in. He then locked the door from the inside and led me to a cell-like room with a bed and a chair. I had noticed a communal bathroom on this floor a little way down the hall. It was around 10:30 at night and the building was very quiet. I went to bed thinking about what an interesting adventure this was to be staying in a locked and guarded detention center in Russia.

The bed was a hard, thin mat on a wooden base. I was very tired and slept soundly. The next morning I awoke early. I was washed, dressed, and ready with my suitcase when the soldier came to escort me back to the airport. At the Intourist desk a different young woman was on duty. I told her I had missed my connection the day before but wished to take the plane to Helsinki that morning. She examined my ticket. Then she spent a little while talking on the telephone before turning to me again. She informed me, albeit regretfully, that the schedule had been changed. The Soviet airline Aeroflot had cancelled its Saturday flight to Helsinki. The next flight would not be until Monday. Unfortunately, it was fully booked. I was stunned. I asked if there were some way I could get a temporary visa that would allow me to go into Moscow and stay at a hotel. She apologized and said that this would not be possible. I asked her if I could call the United States Embassy for assistance. She checked the number and dialed it before handing me the phone. After it had rung for a few minutes, the Marine sergeant on duty answered the phone. I quickly told him my problem. His response was immediate. "Sorry, Mac, there's nobody here but me. Call back Monday morning."

In abject resignation, I turned again to the Intourist agent and asked what I could do. She explained cheerfully that I would simply remain at the airport hotel until I could get on the first available flight to Helsinki. She had already reserved me as a standby passenger on the Monday flight. I would not have to pay for my accommodation or meals. Tarom Airlines would be billed for my expenses. She handed me a set of coupon vouchers, one for each meal from breakfast on Saturday to lunch on Monday. In order to go to the restaurant I would simply identify myself at the station where my passport was being held, then I would be permitted to enter the flight departure area where the restaurant was located. When I asked how I could communicate with the people in Helsinki about my whereabouts, she told me where I could go to send a telegram.

Everything worked exactly as the agent had described it. My voucher permitted me to order anything from the menu up to a stipulated number of rubles. If what I selected exceeded this amount, I could pay the difference in Western currency. After breakfast, I passed back out through the control point and went to the telegraph desk. It took some effort before the clerk, who spoke Russian only, could understand where I wanted to send the wire and what I wanted to say in it. My wire went to the Finnish person in charge of planning the lecture I was to give on Tuesday. I explained that I was hopeful to be in Helsinki on Monday. I then returned to the Intourist desk where I had left my suitcase. A soldier was summoned, and I was escorted back to the hotel to my room.

By then it was mid-morning. An old woman in the corridor was pushing a wet mop over the floor of ancient cracked linoleum. She rinsed the mop frequently in a bucket of dirty water. At the end of the hall I discovered a lounge filled with battered, plastic-covered sofas and armchairs. Shelves contained copies of magazines and brochures. They were all in English, and they extolled the virtues of everything Soviet from youth activities to gymnastics to agriculture. In the corner there was a large color TV broadcasting a Russian soccer match. While I sat there examining the publications, three men came into the room. Two of them were from India, the other from Pakistan. They explained to me exactly what my ostensible hotel accommodation was about. The Soviet airline Aeroflot was promoting cut-rate fares from Asia to London, with a change of planes in Moscow. Whenever the Moscow to London flight was over-booked, as it apparently was regularly, travelers were delayed until seats became available — as little as a day, or as long as a week or two. Men occupied the "hotel's" third floor, while women stayed on the second level. Whenever we were in the building we were detained under lock and key. At the airport, however, the system was quite lax. It was possible to wander around anywhere as long as one didn't leave the airport. Passports were always kept at the passport control point. The men I spoke with seemed far more relaxed about the state of affairs. I could only hope that Monday would be my departure day.

When lunchtime came, six or seven of the men on my floor asked to be taken to the airport, where we all went to sit at the same table in the restaurant. What ensued was a battle of wills between the diners and the waiter. Success was achieved by ordering food from the menu for the precise amount of the voucher, not a ruble more. The waiter tried to foil our efforts by announcing that certain items were not available. He would point to the menu and say, *"nyet."* We would move on to other choices. The contest went on like this until either side had exhausted their energies. Negotiations would end with a shrug when one or the other side would grudgingly give in.

The Best of Times

On Sunday morning I started the day expecting little. At the Intourist desk the agent on duty informed us that the staff wanted to provide some diversion for the detainees. They had arranged a bus trip to take us into Moscow to see the sights. It would be leaving at ten o'clock. All the men and women from the hotel waited eagerly to start out. It was not before eleven o'clock that all twenty of us were herded into a bus. An Intertourist agent came along as our guide. A soldier guarded against our escape in the city. We headed toward Moscow, looking forward to seeing the Soviet capital.

Our first stop was a downtown hotel. Here, we waited another half an hour while another group of detainees joined us. We then proceeded toward city center. A heavy rain began to fall. "On our right," the guide announced, "is the celebrated Gum Department Store." The continuing downpour made visibility impossible. The rain subsided to a drizzle, and when we reached the Kremlin, the bus came to a stop. The Intourist guide asked the driver to open the bus door so we could get out to walk near the celebrated Soviet headquarters. Then the soldier spoke. There was a heated argument between the soldier and the Intourist agent. She looked as if she was about to cry. The soldier barked out a command to the driver. We peered out the fogged over windows for a fleeting glimpse of the Kremlin as the bus drove away. We went back to the downtown hotel, where the first group of Moscow tourists got off. Then we drove back to the airport. The tour was over. We did not understand what had caused the problem, but clearly our Intourist guide was in distress. She spoke to no one and fled when we stopped to let her off. That evening, the battle of wits with the waiter at dinner became a blood sport. On Monday, by a stroke of luck, my standby status was transformed into a reserved seat. I departed Sheremytov Airport mid-morning for Helsinki. For the first time in my experience as an air traveler I was part of a planeload of passengers who spontaneously cheered when the aircraft took off.

Helsinki was all shining steel and modernity. It was interesting to compare how this small country in the cold north could bear such an aura of prosperous good fortune, when everything I had seen in Russia seemed so seedy. My telegram had apparently never been sent or received. I learned that previous arrangements had been suspended when I had not been heard from, but everything would go forward as planned for the next day's program. I would be speaking to a meeting of Finnish special librarians. This group had the strongest reputation of any in the library community, in a country recognized for being way ahead industrially and technologically. Many of the special librarians occupied high-level managerial posts in their companies. They enjoyed far higher status in the business sector than did their counterparts in the United States.

Sinikka Kosciala was my contact person in Helsinki. I had first known her in 1964, when she was a student in the library administration class with me as a master's student at Western Reserve University. Later she went on to become one of our early Maryland Ph.D. graduates. By fall of 1972, Sinikka was directing a major technical university library in the Helsinki region. She had arranged my visit to Finland. I had no time for tourism, only time for a short walk in the smart and sleek central district of Helsinki. I left for Oslo the next day.

I arrived in Norway in October when the natives of Oslo felt they were experiencing an extraordinary heat wave. The temperature was around seventy degrees Fahrenheit. My visit included a stop at the Oslo University library. I was cordially received there by the director, Ben Rugaas. Rugaas and I had met at a conference earlier. He was about to leave for a trip when I arrived. He assigned a staff member to show me through the operations of the library and all its departments. The weather was so agreeable, I concluded my official visit to allow time to wander the city. I visited the Kon-Tiki museum, where I was awed by the exhibition and a lecture about Thor Heyerdahl and how he had sailed the ocean to retrace the presumed intercontinental sea travel centuries ago. By nightfall, the weather had returned to normal — a brisk thirty degrees. On the second day the wind, with its frequent blasts of frigid air, made the day fit only for a museum visit.

In Stockholm I had arranged to see the new and modern central public library at the invitation of its director of public relations. She and I had corresponded in the late 1960's about the High John project. She devoted the better part of a day driving me around the city to see several new branches of the public library. They surpassed anything in the United States. They combined in one modern, functional setting library arrangements, areas for art exhibitions, attractive conference rooms, and public auditorium facilities. The Stockholm public library's central building was a model of dazzling Scandinavian architecture. It afforded well-designed spaces for book display and well-lighted reading tables and study carrels.

That evening, Kjell Samuelson took me to dinner at a fine restaurant before we went to the University of Stockholm for my presentation. The food and wine were so excellent I felt more inclined to go to sleep than to accompany him to the lecture hall. My talk had been announced publicly. In addition to Samuelson's regular class, interested people from information and research centers in the city filled the large room to capacity. I talked for about forty-five minutes about education and practice in the United States in library and information science. The question-and-answer session did not conclude for another hour. There was high interest among those present in how information organizations were evolving in North America as the pace of technological breakthroughs quickened. From the tone of the questions, it seemed to me that there were more pronounced differences between information scientists and librarians in Sweden than in the United States. I explained how some library education programs were incorporating data processing and retrieval elements into their curricular offerings. I also discussed how the former American Documentation Institute had undergone a name change, if not a complete metamorphosis, into the American Society for Information Science, and how its membership included as many librarians as those from other disciplines. I left Stockholm feeling that this city clearly could hold its own in any comparison with the best the United States had to offer in the library and information field.

West Berlin was my next stop. I had not been in Germany since the grim post–World War II days. I was astonished by the opulence I saw displayed in the windows and on the counters of the fashionable shops. The restaurants and cafes were crowded with well-attired and well-fed West Berliners. It was a striking contrast to the rubble-strewn streets, demolished buildings, and bedraggled human beings I remembered so vividly from twenty-five years earlier. Gernot Wersig met me for lunch in a cafe near my hotel in order to discuss FID Education and Training Committee business. Wersig, a professor at the Free University of Berlin, had become the West German member replacing Eric Pietsch upon his retirement. Wersig had a reputation as a self-assured, young iconoclast. It was during this period when Helmut Arntz, the FID president from West Germany, was seeking to move the seat of the Education and Training Committee from Warsaw to West Germany. Wersig was seen as the likely choice for committee chairman if the switch was made. Wojciech Pirog had assumed the role of committee chairman following Gorski and was waging a tenacious political struggle in the International Federation for Documentation Board to retain the secretariat in Warsaw. I liked and respected Pirog very much, and my sympathies were with the Poles.

During lunch, Wersig was cordial and friendly. He described his teaching and research and regretted that he could not invite me to lecture at his university; the fall term had not yet begun. He suggested that he thought the Education and

Training Committee needed fresh ideas and new program initiatives. He thought that he and I would be able to accomplish a good deal working together on needed changes. I was non-committal, not wishing him to report to Arntz that I favored ousting Pirog. We parted on a cordial note, both realizing that we would be working together on joint efforts, whether the committee seat remained in Warsaw or not.

Part of my Berlin stay involved a visit to the Central Institute for Information and Documentation in East Berlin. I took a train to the transfer point from West into East Berlin. With a formal letter inviting me to visit the Center from its director, Dr. B. Winde, I received the necessary day pass to cross into East Berlin. After I exchanged the stipulated amount of Western currency for East German marks, I underwent an interrogation, a body search, and an examination of my passport. Finally, I was permitted to continue by train into the eastern sector. After arriving at my station, I took a taxi to a large, gray public building that housed the Institute. My host Dr. Winde, who was said to have been a dentist earlier in his career, was very friendly and seemed interested in demonstrating the high level of his staff. Like many other centralized institutions in the Eastern Bloc, this agency carried out all the information functions for the state in economics, science, and technology. Its responsibilities included abstracting and indexing scientific and technical literature; translation activities; information storage and retrieval; dissemination of information; and training programs for documentation workers. What I saw in my cursory tour of the several-hundred person agency was a large-scale bureaucracy. Obsequious deference to those who held authority was much in evidence in every unit I visited. Sections of the building were divided by function. The poorly lit rooms reeked of tobacco smoke. Shabbily dressed men and women were seated very close to each other bent over their timeworn desks. The equipment was all of pre-World War II vintage. It was a depressing picture, lacking any vitality or cheerfulness. In the large employee cafeteria, the odor of cooked cabbage and cigarettes was everywhere. People ate swiftly and spoke in hushed tones. I was happy when it was time to leave. I retraced my steps and traveled back to the control point. I re-entered West Berlin with relief.

From West Berlin, I went on to Prague. My guide during this short visit was George Toman. He was an information specialist who had a teaching connection in library education at Charles University. His family background was in international trade, with close ties to England. Toman detested what he called the total state control of people's lives. In excellent English, he delighted in enumerating the countless ways he had outwitted the Socialist system. His chief ambition was for his college-age son to attend the London School of Economics. The University in Prague was not in session while I visited. I had to be content to learn about library education matters informally from Toman, whose view seemed heavily biased. As a city guide, George Toman was indefatigable. He made it his mission to ensure that I saw everything worth seeing and experiencing. He was well informed about the history of each section of Prague and all its buildings and public sites. He was also a connoisseur of fine food and drink. We visited a number of the city's celebrated cafes, beer halls, and restaurants. Prague was very inexpensive by American standards, especially since Toman saw to it that I received the most advantageous black market rate for my American dollars. My visit to Prague was short on professional value but highly pleasurable as a personal experience.

Yugoslavia came next. My objective was to visit the University of Zagreb's library education program. The director, Bojo Tejak was an older man, well beyond normal retirement age. He was tall and distinguished looking with a great mane of white hair. He had earned his Ph.D. in England and had received many honors for his academic achievements. Tejak was a latecomer to information science. He had distinguished himself earlier in his career as a professor of chemistry. A passionate convert to new ideas, Tejak saw information as the Holy Grail in the study of science and technology. This had led him to shift fields. His intellectual stature empowered him to build a large education and research program in library and information science at the University of Zagreb. He also received UNESCO support, which he was using to build a museum of new and old equipment and machines that were used in library and documentation activities. Tejak was a genial host, but he was under pressure with special assignments from the university president. He assigned a younger member of his staff to accompany and assist me during my stay. This man was pleased to have the occasion to use his English during my three-day stay.

This young engineer had an interesting story to tell. Ten years earlier he had received approval to study in the United States. Living in Atlanta, he completed undergraduate and graduate degrees at the Georgia Institute of Technology. His wife gave birth to their two children during this time. In his enthusiasm for all things American, he became a zealous football fan. On completing his studies, he worked for an engineering consulting firm in Atlanta. A couple of years later, the pull of family ties and his wife's homesickness led him to return to Yugoslavia. Back in Zagreb, he discovered that there was no suitable job for someone with his background. The job he currently held with Tejak in information science was the best he could find, and he was not happy in it. He looked back wistfully upon the better life he had led in America. He was pleased to be surrounded by his extended family again, but he would return to the United States in a moment if he could. Unfortunately, there was no conceivable way for him to gain government approval to leave the country a second time. Talking with me about life in America was a way for him to relive what had been the happiest years of his life. I left Yugoslavia pleased with what I had learned. Tejak had lived up to his advance billing as a towering figure in the field, even though his contributions received only limited attention in other parts of the world. A couple of years later, Tejak visited the United States on my recommendation as a guest of the American Library Association International Library Education Committee.

In Rome, I intended to visit the National Institute on Information and the National Research Council. Neither of my colleagues was available at the time of my visit, so I left for Florence to attend a meeting of the International Informatics Association. I went there by train, and spent one day attending sessions and visiting convention exhibitions. The association was principally composed of senior government data-processing experts. The meeting concentrated on large-scale computers and their applications to national information systems. I learned a good deal there about the direction that librarianship and documentation would very likely move during the next decade to rationalize national bibliographic information systems. During my brief stay, I spent a day at the Ufizzi and attempted to soak up the flavor of the city's byways and architectural treasures.

In Rome once more, I strolled to the Vatican. This was the day of the Pope's weekly audience. Great hordes of people were organized by country to take part in the occasion. Passing by one large and well-dressed crowd, I heard English being spoken. This was a contingent visiting from Milwaukee; they asked if I would like to join their number. I was swept along in the teeming assembly and soon found myself witnessing the colorful procession of resplendently attired cardinals. I was in the midst of a great multitude when the Pope addressed his remarks in countless languages to the crowd. In clear English, the Pope identified the Milwaukee throng, which immediately electrified the ranks of those around me. I was lucky to witness this unusual spectacle.

The Best of Times

My visit to Paris began when Michel Menou met my flight at the airport and drove me to my Left Bank hotel. That evening Menou took me to a restaurant where the *specialite de la maison* was reputed to be the best *andouille* in Paris. I had never tasted this dish before; I had no idea what it was. I was perturbed when I found myself confronted with a plate full of pork sausage. I slowly, methodically, and queasily chewed my way through it. I didn't have the heart to tell my host that I abhorred pork sausage. I survived the ordeal by washing everything down with many glasses of excellent wine.

UNESCO was my principal professional destination in Paris. I learned from Adam Wysocki that UNESCO had established, as a priority in its training agenda for library and documentation managers in the different regions of the world, workshops to enhance their managerial competence. I explained to him that since 1967, Maryland's Library Administrators Development Program had pursued a similar program on an annual basis with North American information personnel. Wysocki questioned whether the same experience might be relevant for professionals from other countries, particularly developing countries. I explained how the topics covered treated universal concerns: decision making; managing by objectives; and finance and budgetary control, all of which transcended national boundaries. Our conversation led to the idea of UNESCO sponsoring two or three overseas participants to take part in the Maryland program. That way, we could discern whether the Maryland model made sense for non-North Americans. Wysocki introduced me to Jacques Tocatlian, a United States national who was serving in the Division of Libraries, Documentation, and Archives. He was the official responsible for education and training. I had met Tocatlian in the United States before he joined the UNESCO staff. He was asked to arrange the contractual details that would ensure that individuals selected for a scholarship to Maryland's Library Administrators Development Program would be ready to participate by the summer of 1974. The plan was that these overseas participants would help UNESCO evaluate the usefulness of the program's content for application in different regions of the world.

I went on to London, where I gave a lecture at Northwestern Polytechnic. My colleagues — Mills, Langridge, and Chris Needham — who had all served as visiting faculty members at Maryland, invited me. Our group also included Edward Dudley, head of the library education program. Far more memorable than my talk was the evening I spent with these friends in Soho pubs and a restaurant whose name I have long since forgotten. The last leg of my tour was to Wales and the University of Aberystwyth. To reach the university, one had to travel the last miles of the journey on a single-track railroad line. This required some dexterous maneuvering and switching by the engineer in order to avoid running into a train coming along the track from the other direction. The Wales College of Librarianship in Aberystwyth was the largest library school in the United Kingdom. Frank Hogg, the principal of the college, was celebrated for spending more time traveling abroad than he spent at home. I was put up in a dormitory building looking out on a rocky beach and the turbulent sea. It was late in November 1972, and the air was cold and fresh with the smell of the sea. Strong, windy gusts blew in off the ocean. I lectured to the student body about trends in library and information science. Questions at the end focused on the political struggles being waged on the United States campuses. My message about the imperative for change in librarianship struck a chord with the student audience. Before leaving, I was awarded a placard denoting honorary membership in the Welsh Student Mafia Society. When we learned that the southbound train would not be running from Aberystwyth, Tony Foskett volunteered to drive me to the nearest operating train station. Tony drove me a long distance to the largest city where I could connect with a London train. Once there, the only train headed back to London was the all-night milk train, which stopped at every station along the way. My flight back to Washington was scheduled for mid-morning the next day; I returned to London with barely enough time to make the flight. A taxi took me to the hotel where I had left my luggage. I hastily repacked and scurried to the airport just in time to catch my cross-Atlantic flight home.

Chapter Fifteen

By the time I returned to the United States, I had decided that I would ask Krystyna to marry me. Clara was living in the Los Angeles area, and I needed to see her to discuss a divorce. Back in my office in College Park, I reviewed my correspondence and found a letter from Guillermo Fernandez de la Garza. Guillermo was then a senior officer of CONACYT (Consejo Nacional de Ciencia y Tecnologia), an agency that roughly paralleled the United States National Science Foundation and the National Academy of Sciences. He was responsible for developments in Mexican library and information science education and training. He formally invited me to come to Mexico City early in 1973 as part of a North American team that would help plan a graduate degree program in library education. I accepted his invitation and planned to spend several days in Mexico. I scheduled a stopover in Los Angeles on my return trip to see Jacqueline and to arrange matters with Clara.

During my absence from the country, publication efforts continued under the scrupulous monitoring of Effie Knight. A new reference work had been started in summer 1972. Collaborating on this work with me as associate editor was Esther Herman. The book, *Museum Media*, was a directory and bibliographic source book, which detailed publications, media, and other informational products available from museums of every type. Gale Research Company published the first edition in the spring of 1973. An article, embodying some of the findings of the manpower research, which I had written with Jeanne O'Connell, appeared in the December 1972 issue of *Special Libraries* as "The Special Library Manager: A Profile."

Work with my Mexican colleagues began in January 1973. It was the start of a professional relationship that lasted many years. The conference was held at the

THE BEST OF TIMES

Colegio de Mexico located in Mexico City. Guillermo had invited leaders of Mexican librarianship. William Summers, who was with the library education program at the University of South Carolina, and was also active in ALA affairs, and in the work of the Association of American Library Schools, joined me. The deliberations were lively and produced a set of clear recommendations laying out the necessary elements to establish a graduate degree program for Mexican librarians and information scientists. North American guests stayed at the charming and comfortable Hotel Suiza, in Mexico City's tourist section, the Zona Rosa, or pink zone. I found Mexico so much to my liking that I resolved to return in the coming months and to learn to speak some Spanish.

It proved difficult to move ahead with the Mexican education plan. Complex political difficulties in Mexico impeded progress. But, if the sessions had failed ultimately to realize Guillermo's aspirations, the conference did open the way for me to enjoy many cooperative ties and educational interactions with the people I met there. The experience may have been the reason I was later asked to serve as a member of the Bi-National Committee in Information Science between the United States and Mexico. The committee was established by the National Science Foundation. It was part of an initiative carried out during the 1970's, in which cooperation and exchanges were fostered in scientific information and knowledge transfer between the United States and nations such as India and Mexico.

In California, Clara and I discussed conditions that would lead to an amicable divorce settlement. Once back home, I engaged an attorney and began the process. My divorce was finalized in early April 1973. Later that month, Krystyna and I were married in Upper Marlboro, Maryland. By then, she had given up her position with the American Geographical Society Library in Manhattan and moved to College Park.

By spring 1973, Jacques Tocatlian at UNESCO had arranged for me to serve as a consultant on the development of a program for managers of library and information systems in developing countries. I helped plan for and reviewed applications from overseas library people who wanted to come to Maryland's Donaldson Brown Center as participants in the Library Administrators Development Program, in summer of 1974. Over the course of the next ten months, we sent out information about the offering and screened applications. These applications went to Paris first, before they were forwarded on for further review at Maryland.

THE BEST OF TIMES

Three fellowship recipients were chosen. It was also at this time that I was asked by Wysocki to accept appointment as a member of UNESCO's Advisory Council to study convertibility and standards in graduate education in information science. The effort was carried out from 1973 to 1975.

At the start of the spring semester of the 1972-1973 academic year, I resumed my normal teaching role. Once the term ended in May, I flew to St. Paul, Minnesota to deliver the Perrie Jones Lecture at the St. Paul Public Library. I spoke about future directions for the public library in an era of change. In June, I returned to Britain for two weeks as visiting international lecturer for the European Summer School offered by the Library School at Liverpool Polytechnic. Later in the summer, as part of my UNESCO consultancy and service on the Advisory Council, I traveled to Paris. In the days immediately following my work at UNESCO House, I participated in a seminar organized by the French counterpart of the Special Libraries Association. There, I led discussions about levels and specializations in the educational preparation of information professionals. My contribution was titled, "Recruitment and Utilization of Personnel: An Aspirational View," which was later published in *Documentaliste*, in March 1974.

By the summer of 1973, my attention turned more and more toward international concerns. By then I was playing a more active role in the work of the FID Education and Training Committee. In the aftermath of my sabbatical, I was often invited to participate in seminars, training programs, and conferences outside the United States. In addition to my international projects, I devoted more attention to my other major interest — the development and catalysis of information products and services. I became heavily immersed in designing and mounting projects that resulted in new reference books. My collaborators and I also prepared new editions of earlier efforts through revision and updating. I continued to encourage other librarian authors and editors to contribute to the Management Information Guide Series, the Gale Information Guide Library Series, the Readers in Library and Information Science Series, and the Greenwood Contributions Series in Library and Information Science. To juggle all these editorial activities, I relied even more heavily on the skills of Effie Knight. Without her unflagging support, the productive achievements we engaged upon would never have come to pass.

In 1973, one of these projects was the revision of the 1960 book, *Sources of Commodity Prices*, published by the Special Libraries Association. This time, in light of the frustrating experience of bringing forth the first edition by committee, we carried out the work independently, with only the assistance of a graduate student. Diane Kemmerling was the co-compiler. The volume provided references to wholesale and retail price quotations on more than five thousand agricultural, commercial, industrial, and consumer products. This was a considerably larger number of items than had been included in the earlier publication. It took only one academic year to prepare *Commodity Prices: A Source Book and Index,* which was published in 1974 by Gale Research Company. Efforts were also begun in 1973 on a new reference work that would help consumers identify where to find redress for problems they encountered with products and services. In 1974, Gale Research Company published *Consumer Sourcebook.*

At the beginning of 1974, I became chairman, for two years, of the American Library Association's Committee on International Library Education of the Library Education Division. The committee selected speakers and arranged for a lecture tour, which would feature a distinguished international educator or scholar. The tour would go to over a dozen United States library schools. I was pleased to be in a position to put forth the nomination of Professor Bojo Tejak for the lecture tour. He was selected to be the visitor for 1975. During his American sojourn, Tejak visited some of the leading centers of American library education from coast to coast. His lectures there described his experiences in furthering information science in Yugoslavia. I was gratified that he had enjoyed this exposure to the American library education community; he died soon after returning to Zagreb.

In 1974, we started work on two other reference titles. *Library Bibliographies and Indexes,* appeared in 1975 with Esther Herman as its co-editor. This was a first attempt to gather details about the unique specialized bibliographic, directory, and indexing projects carried out by public and academic libraries in the United States. It was prepared to attract the interest of librarians and readers beyond the local community where the material was produced. The second effort was an updated and comprehensive reworking of *Awards, Honors, and Prizes.* Volume two of the third edition was called *Awards, Honors, and Prizes: International and Foreign.* It was published in 1975. It provided descriptive details covering the prizes given by international bodies, organizations, and institutions in countries around the world.

The 1974 Library Administrators Development Program included three individuals from developing regions supported by UNESCO. They came from Turkey, Mexico, and Colombia. All three were fluent in English, and each took an active part in the lectures, case discussions, and informal exchanges during the two-week period. Like the North American participants, the overseas attendees were asked to fill out evaluation forms for each of the individual sessions as well as for the program in its entirety. We wanted to learn their frank observations on the suitability of the program for non-United States nationals without any American organizational experience. We were pleased to learn that all three thought that the seminar offered great value for foreigners, because so much of what was treated dealt with managerial issues that were just as applicable in their countries as in the United States. Their comments were studied carefully by John Rizzo and me before being dispatched to Jacques Tocatlian at UNESCO. We thought that the favorable reaction from the foreign attendees might dispose UNESCO to support a limited number of future overseas participants. Instead, it was decided in Paris that the Maryland program should provide the model. John Rizzo and I were asked to assume responsibility for managerial workshops to be held outside the United States. We would draw upon indigenous instructional personnel to work with us to cover subject areas outside the range of our competence. The first such effort was scheduled to take place in Mexico in August 1975.

In mid-fall 1974, I received an overture from a Brazilian Ph.D. student at Maryland on behalf of the director of the Brazilian National Institute for Space Research. Dr. De Mendonza, an internationally recognized, Stanford-trained space scientist, who led the Institute, wanted me to organize a team to offer a two-week workshop on information science in San Jose dos Campos. The participants would be officials, economists, and librarians. Preparations for the workshop took a strange turn. Telephone charges for calls from Brazil to the United States were very costly at a time when Brazilian currency was not freely exchanged on the international market. An ingenious alternative communication mode was employed. De Mendonza used an amateur radio transmitter to call a Brazilian compatriot in Long Island at pre-arranged times. Once they had established radio contact, this person telephoned me. I spoke into the telephone, while the man in Long Island held the receiver to his radio transmitter. That way, everything I said could be heard by radio in Brazil. I could hear De Mendonza by the same means. This contrivance worked well enough for us to go forward in planning the program.

I invited David Batty and Claude Walston to join me on the team. Batty was at the time on the faculty of McGill University in Montreal. Walston was with IBM's

Federal Systems Division in the Washington, DC, area. Batty was to lecture on classification and retrieval; Walston would treat data processing and automation; and, I would deal with management and organizational behavior. Negotiations and planning were concluded by mid-December. The workshop was scheduled for the 6th through the 17th of January 1975, at the Institute in San Jose dos Campos, which was midway between Rio de Janeiro and Sao Paulo. We fit in some time to tour the country. Walston's wife, Betty, accompanied him; Krystyna came with me. When I explained at the Brazilian Consulate that I would be lecturing at the Institute for Space Research, I was told that a simple tourist visa would not serve. I learned that we had to submit, with our visa applications, police clearances attesting that we had no criminal record. This annoyed me so much that had I known beforehand of this demeaning requirement, I would not have accepted the assignment.

Krystyna and I arrived in Rio de Janeiro very early in the year. We spent a few days in the lush Copacabana district, and visited the tourist attractions of the city before traveling south by bus to San Jose dos Campos. It was a quiet, late Sunday morning when we checked into the hotel. My colleagues had not yet arrived. The hotel occupied one side of a square in the center of the city's downtown area, next to the bus station. The manager himself showed us to our room on a high floor. He proudly demonstrated the perfect view of the main square from our window. We returned to our room after a long day of exploring. We were tired. From a nightclub on the opposite side of the square, loud music was blaring. The raucous sound of horns and the heavy beat of a drum continued uninterruptedly. Shutting the windows was no help. When it became clear that the racket was not going to stop, I went down to the hotel's registration desk at 11:30 p.m. to request a room change. The clerk on duty was astonished that we were displeased with one of the hotel's finest rooms, from which one could see and hear everything happening in the heart of the city. He shook his head and suggested that if we were really displeased with the room he was sure that an interior one would be available, but not before the next day. The music continued without pause until the early hours of the morning. I arrived at the first day of the seminar blurry-eyed and groggy.

The seminar participants included a number of research scientists at the Institute, as well as members of the staff of its library and seven or eight special librarians and library educators, who had been invited from around the country. There were twenty-five in all. The sponsoring organizations paid for their participation as a means for the Institute to recover some of the costs of mounting the workshop. The group convened in the mornings and afternoons. Batty, Walston, and I took turns spending two hours in lecture, discussion, and demonstrations. Between times, there were consulting sessions with Institute staff from various departments and individual conferences with the other seminar attendees. Participants were obliged to work in English. No provision had been made for simultaneous translation, but the level of comprehension was very good.

In 1975, Brazil was under the thumb of a ruling military junta. Political discourse was taboo. Batty, during one of his characteristically flamboyant lectures, cited as an instance of stupidity the way generals commit men to their death in battle because they are unable to comprehend the consequences of their decisions. Walston and I sunk deeply into our seats, cringing as we listened to his words. The participants were absolutely silent. Batty looked toward us questioningly. He observed our dismay, simply shrugged, and continued by taking his remarks in another direction.

We made a very compatible instructional trio, but for one note of dissent. The Institute felt our presence was fleeting. There were countless organizational problems relating to the application of technology in information retrieval, for which they needed more guidance. Our hours of instruction and small group sessions were simply too few. By the second day, the institute arranged evening sessions. The bus would either return to the hotel and pick up the instructors after dinner or keep them at the institute for late afternoon meetings that could run to six or seven o'clock. The demands on our time grew onerous. I suggested to Batty and Walston that this was not consistent with our contractual obligation to offer a seminar. Batty took no position on the additional demands made upon us. Walston disagreed with me strenuously. We were working for the institute. In his view, if they required our services in the evenings as part of what they needed, we had an obligation to provide this. I overruled him. My position was that we had been engaged to offer a workshop. Consulting meetings could be accommodated during normal daytime hours. We needed our evening hours to be free to relax, lest we become overtired or ill. I met with De Mendonza and discussed the matter with him. He concurred with my judgement; the after-hours sessions ended.

Two unusual episodes punctuated our stay in San Jose dos Campos. The first was during an automobile drive on the road to Sao Paulo. Several heavily armed soldiers stopped our car. Everyone was ordered out of the car and told to lean with his or her arms on the hood with our legs stretched out. We were subjected to a careful body search. The soldiers examined closely the interior of the car and the trunk. We were then told to get back into the car and were waved on. No explanation was offered. We learned from the Brazilians that this had been no more than a routine military check of vehicle traffic on the country's highways. Under the terms of our contract, Walston, Batty, and I were to be compensated at the end of the program in U.S. currency. When the time came to be paid, the paymaster tried to pay us in Brazilian *cruzeiros*. We protested that we had no use for the local currency since it was not convertible into dollars. Grudgingly, the official said he would try to get dollars for us. He paid us in American Express travelers checks in dollars, which were made out to and endorsed by Brazilians whom we did not know. It seemed strange that a reputable government research institution had to buy travelers checks on the black market. Still, the seminar had been very well received. We had made new professional associations that would continue long into the future. The Walstons remained in the country for a bit of tourism in the company of a friend, who was a medical official, and his wife. The unfortunate and ironic aftermath of the Brazilian adventure happened a month later in the United States, when Claude Walston came down with a severe case of hepatitis. His medical treatment lasted more than six months before he was fully recovered.

Planning efforts were underway during the 1974-1975 school year for the first of the management seminars sponsored by UNESCO for library administrators in different regions of the world. Wysocki and Tocatlian had decided that mounting these programs close to the home countries of the participants was most efficient and economic. UNESCO contracted with CONACYT in Mexico to assume responsibility for making all the local arrangements for the first offering. This included identifying an attractive setting with comfortable living arrangements, as well as conference and dining facilities. Plans for arrival and departure, and for the local travel needs of the foreign attendees also needed to be taken care of. Finally, the organizers needed to provide simultaneous translation of lectures, as well as suitable recreational diversions for the weekend. Rizzo and I were responsible for developing program content and instructing some of the sessions. We also selected individuals from the region to attend the seminar and identified, in consultation with the local host organization, qualified indigenous faculty to cover the subjects that Rizzo and I would not treat. Fernandez de la Garza at CONACYT designated Guadalupe Carrion as the resident director to work with us. She was one of the most highly regarded librarians in Mexico. She was well known for her professional, interpersonal, and intercultural skills.

The Best of Times

We felt that a management seminar designed for a Latin American group, that was widely announced, would attract applications from many more qualified applicants than could be admitted. This proved to be the case. The number UNESCO was prepared to sponsor could not exceed thirty, including several participants from Mexico itself. It was frustrating having to exclude many other highly promising attendees. Rizzo and I were certain that the most difficult task we faced would be to identify qualified indigenous faculty to work with. From long experience with the Maryland Library Administrators Development Program, we knew that the ability to instruct appropriately in such a workshop called for more than academic qualifications or senior managerial experience. Few seemingly highly qualified individuals were endowed with the ability to work comfortably with this type of audience. What was needed was the capacity to blend theoretical and practical instructional content with behavioral sensitivity and interpersonal skills, so that the instructor would make the lectures, case studies, and group exercises germane to the needs of library managers. By a stroke of good fortune, I had occasion to attend a meeting of the U.S.-Mexico Bi-National Committee in Mexico City, during spring 1975. While there, I took the time to meet with Guadalupe Carrion to discuss plans for the August 1975 international seminar. She arranged for me to talk with Jorge Bustamante. Bustamante was a management consultant married to a librarian who was educated in organizational behavior in North America. He was widely experienced in training efforts in Latin America. When I showed him the subjects covered in the Maryland Library Administrators Development Program brochure, he immediately understood the thrust of the workshop. He suggested that he and a younger associate could easily fit their presentations into such a framework. I was impressed with him and told him that I would confer with John Rizzo. I was confident that he would support my recommendation that Bustamante and his colleague work with us in August. Once back in Maryland, Rizzo and I agreed by phone to invite them to join us.

I hoped that the UNESCO assignment would be the first of a number of Latin American opportunities. In September 1974, Krystyna and I enrolled in a beginning Spanish class in the evening at the University of Maryland. I planned to be in Mexico in August for the UNESCO seminar. As the workshop approached, we decided to take an immersion course. We enrolled in a study program in Cuernavaca for a four-week period that ended on the Friday before the Sunday when I had to be in Mexico City. The school director was Ivan Illich, a scholar and author on education theories, quality of life, and cultural behavior. He gave occasional informal talks (in English), that expressed his outrageously iconoclastic point of view. I enjoyed the lively, and sometimes contentious, discussions we would engage in.

Krystyna and I lived and took our meals in a modest motel within walking distance of the school. We spent the better part of every day in small classes, doing language laboratory exercises and absorbing as much grammar and vocabulary as possible. We practiced our conversational skills. The other motel inhabitants were all American secondary school teachers from different parts of North America. They were polishing their Spanish skills so that they could work more effectively with Latino students. By evening, we had all become so saturated with Spanish that we didn't have the energy to converse further in anything but English. Our conversations were well lubricated by *el Presidente* brandy or gin. The weeks of study, while failing to make me a fluent lecturer in Spanish, did help me to understand questions posed by the seminar's participants. I could also understand much of what Bustamante was saying as he lectured to the group.

John Rizzo joined us in Mexico City on the weekend after the language study. On Sunday, Krystyna , accompanied by a fellow student from our Spanish class, set out on a two-week train tour of Mexico while I was working. Rizzo and I rode the bus to the Nestle Center where the course was held. The center was a spacious, luxuriously appointed conference center nestled in a wooded region off the main highway about an hour's drive from Mexico City, near Toluca. Everything conspired to make this seminar a memorable experience for all those who participated.

The group was interested and enthusiastic. They shared the exuberant zest for life characteristic of the Latin temperament. Laughter and song broke out spontaneously and often. Many of the students were very well educated. They were about equally divided between men and women, mostly in their twenties and thirties. They came from special libraries, university libraries, government libraries, and library education. The group easily blended into a compatible, relaxed collective. Meals were excellent, and the private room accommodations were spacious and handsomely appointed. The center's manicured grounds offered numerous walking trails that led through the woods.

The seminar itself went flawlessly. Guadalupe Carrion had seen to everything. The simultaneous translators were seasoned professionals. Even so, a number of participants dispensed with the headsets, preferring to practice their English.

Bustamante and his colleague were so effective that Rizzo and I concluded that they were as good as the best of our American Library Administrators faculty. One evening during the first week, CONACYT bused the group to a roadside restaurant and nightclub. We ate, drank, sang, and danced. The seminar participants fully rivaled the professional entertainers. On the weekend we were put up in a downtown hotel in Mexico City. From there we were taken to the Pyramids and the floating gardens of Xochimilco. We went to dinner at a western-style restaurant, where we enjoyed steak dinners served by waitresses in cowgirl costumes. Many lasting friendships were forged during the seminar. We all made professional ties that would continue through correspondence and personal meetings and at conferences in the United States and Latin America. Some participants later served as catalysts and originators of comparable seminars in their own countries. Rizzo and I left Mexico gratified by the results, and we looked forward to duplicating the experience in similar UNESCO offerings elsewhere in the world.

In October 1975, I accepted an invitation to prepare a paper for the Boston meeting of the American Society for Information Science. It was called "International Educational Patterns in Information Science: Characteristics and Issues." In it, I encapsulated many observations gleaned from my study tour in the fall of 1972. I also shared insights gained through my work in the FID Education and Training Committee. The paper drew together elements of traditional library study, technological components from information science, behavioral approaches to understanding client needs, and managerial principles needed to effectively administer information organizations. In November, following a meeting of the Education and Training Committee in Warsaw, I traveled to East Germany to participate in the ninth Colloquium on Information and Documentation, which was sponsored by the Technische Hochschule of Ilmenau. The occasion allowed me to witness firsthand the professional and cultural characteristics of a society reputed to be the most rigidly controlled of the Soviet satellite states. The invitation came from Professor Felix Weber, an engineer who was director of the Institute for Information Science, Inventions and Law. The institute concentrated on scientific and technical literature and was particularly strong in the field of patent literature. Weber was then the East German member of the FID Education and Training Committee. He had never received sponsorship or approval to attend sessions when they took place in the West. On rare occasions he was permitted to participate when a meeting was held in an Eastern bloc nation. We had become acquainted at one such event in Veszprem. He explained then that his graduate program sponsored a biennial conference at a resort location, and asked me if I would attend and give a paper. He followed up later, writing to invite me to the November 1975 event. I was scheduled to be in Warsaw for the FID committee meeting in the days immediately preceding, so I accepted.

The meeting was held in Oberhof, a beautiful city in the Black Forest region high in the mountains. I learned later that the large hotels in the area were visited by worker families, who were selected every two or three years to spend their holidays there. The modern buildings had large, modestly furnished rooms. There were huge dining halls where meals were provided cafeteria style. On the top floor of each hotel, there was a nightclub where entertainment and alcoholic beverages were available. The busiest place in each hotel was the government-run duty-free shop. American cigarettes, French wines, and East German-made luxury clothing were sold there. The only proviso was that anything bought had to be paid for in Western currency. This arrangement was confusing, since regulations prohibited the possession by East Germans of dollars, pounds, francs, or West German *deutschmarks*. A flourishing traffic of consumers, nevertheless, frequented the shops all during my stay.

Delegates to the conference were drawn from eight Socialist countries. The language used during the sessions was German. All those attending were supposed to come prepared to work in this language. When I accepted Weber's invitation, I told him that, while I might be able to follow some of the proceedings, I wouldn't be able to prepare my paper in German. We agreed that I would write my paper in English. A translator on the staff of the Hochschule was asked to translate it. The paper could be read for me, or I could read it to the audience myself.

Nearly eight hundred participants attended the three-day colloquium. Visitors from the West were in little evidence. Gernot Wersig from the Free University of Berlin, who had just assumed the chairmanship of the Education and Training Committee upon its transfer from Warsaw, was the only other person from outside the Soviet region. Even though Weber had received government approval to invite token representation from the deeply suspect West, Wersig and I had the feeling that political sentiment among the East German attendees was decidedly cool. I may have been seen by most as an exotic outsider. Wersig, however, aroused stronger feelings. He was viewed as a brash, know-it-all West Berliner. The East German contingent resented him. Some of the platform speakers spoke of the gulf between West and East, failing to indict anything more than the usual specter of capitalist imperialism. The connection to the field of information science was unspecified.

Despite the chilly political climate of the conference, I remember the beauty of the snow-covered mountains and forest. Oberhof and its surroundings looked like a scene out of a fairy tale. Other memories are less flattering. Mealtimes in the vast dining hall were crowded with delegates noisily enjoying their food at communal tables. The atmosphere was like that of a high school cafeteria frequented by a throng of quaintly attired middle-aged men communicating with each other in odd-sounding languages. There was also the ever-present smell of steamed cabbage. After long evenings spent drinking too much wine in the nightclub, the odor drastically curbed my appetite

My paper was delivered on the second day of the conference, which allowed me sufficient time to rehearse my talk carefully with the translator. Dr. Karl Graf was an Ilmenau lecturer in foreign languages and translation. He patiently listened to me and carefully corrected my pronunciation; by the time of the presentation, I had the text under control. It was a long twenty minutes before I doggedly concluded my remarks. I felt certain by the end that my relief could not have been any greater than that of the audience, which had suffered through it with me. The session chairman complimented me on the clarity of my reading. His polite comments indicated his pleasure that I had finally finished. The paper was titled "Trends and Developments in Education and Training in Documentation and Information Science: Issues, Problems and Proposals." It was published in German in the *Proceedings of the Ninth Colloquium on Information and Documentation (from November 12th through 14th 1975),* under the rubric of "Theme I: Criteria for Education in International Information Systems," and issued by the Technische Hochschule Ilmenau in 1976.

In early 1975, work was begun on the preparation of two new reference books. Both would require over a year in preparation. *Festivals Sourcebook* was designed to identify and characterize the hundreds of special celebratory events in all fields that were regularly held in the United States. My associate editors were Esther Herman and Elizabeth Root. The other book was *Ethnic Information Sources in the United States*. The objective of this work was to assemble details and sources of information on the many diverse peoples, from outside the country, who had come to make their homes in America. Jean Morgan, an early alumna of Maryland, collaborated as the associate editor of the second volume. Gale Research published the first editions of both works in 1976. They were revised, updated, and issued again in the mid-1980's.

As a result of the participation of a black university librarian in the 1975 Library Administrators Development Program, the offering came to the attention of the president of the United Board for College Development in Atlanta, Georgia. This led to a relationship that lasted until the end of 1978. As consultants to the Board, John Rizzo and I offered management workshops for academic librarians from predominantly black institutions on the Eastern seaboard, which were financially supported by the Board. Our task was to enhance the performance capabilities of these library directors who came to attend short, concentrated courses in Atlanta on management topics. We visited also twenty-four colleges during this time. We worked with the librarians, their staffs, and the administrative officials of these institutions to put in place management strategies including management by objectives, systematic personnel management techniques, and financial control instruments. Rizzo and I worked with more than fifty library administrators, who came from very small colleges to good-sized universities.

Chapter Sixteen

During the fall of 1975, a young Bolivian, Oscar Harasic, came to my office. He was one of a three-person team in the Unit for Technical Change of the Science Secretariat, in the Washington office of the Organization of American States. He and his Peruvian colleagues, Erwin Fetzer, the unit chief, and Miguel Tejada were responsible for starting a program to build a network of technology and industrial development centers in Latin America. All three men had engineering backgrounds and had studied at American universities. None had any experience or knowledge of the information field. Harasic interviewed me about technical information and what would be involved in setting up national information centers, as part of an Organization of American States initiative to foster a technology transfer system in the developing nations of South and Central America. Following this and subsequent discussions, I was engaged by Fetzer as a consultant. In December 1975, I worked with the three men to outline a program of seminars and workshops that would train the individuals in charge of building the centers.

In early January 1976, Krystyna and I traveled to Guatemala where I offered the first workshop. First, we spent a brief holiday in Panajachel on the banks of Lake Atitlan. From there, a bus took us to Chichicastenango, a colorful and renowned indigenous open-air market. The seminar took place over a two-week period in Guatemala City. I lectured on how to start, organize, and administer an information center. Rowena Swanson, an experienced information science educator working in the Denver area, treated information retrieval and information handling systems during the second week. The person handling local arrangements was Rocio Marban. She was in charge of Guatemala's central information center in science and technology. She was a young, technically prepared university graduate who was a newcomer to the information field. She was very well organized and spoke English fluently. Oscar Harasic came as the representative of the Organization of American States. He took part in what was the first in a series of workshops meant to prepare a cadre of well-trained information personnel. Ideally, this workshop's participants would have been sent instead for formal study in library schools. The Organization of American States, however, did not have the money or the time for such an undertaking. The workshop series was seen as the next best alternative. Twenty to twenty-five people would continue to come together every three or four months, for four or five days. These follow-up seminars, after the first two-week introductory workshop, would focus on a subject area necessary for the information center personnel to function effectively. The sessions were also intended to build collaborative, inter-country relationships among the participants, thereby strengthening the effort to construct a workable network for the Central American and South American regions. Workshop participants came from widely diverse backgrounds, including engineering, marketing, and finance. The objective was to transform them into competent information personnel through the workshop experiences.

The Guatemala seminar was designed to cover the organizational and administrative problems inherent in setting up and organizing a center. It was intended to give Harasic the opportunity to build effective links with the participants that would lead to coordinated future efforts. It was also expected to cover some of the operational requirements in systems design and information handling procedures. The participants seemed strongly motivated and participated with interest in the lectures and discussions. They began to see how the centers could interact in a fruitful way. I left with the impression that they had blended into a cohesive group and that the workshop series was off to a successful start.

It was not until several weeks later that I learned from an embarrassed Oscar Harasic that the second week had not gone so well. Harasic did not say so, but I felt that it was my fault. I had selected a colleague to teach at the workshop who had a strong background and reputation as a qualified specialist and lecturer. I had failed to inquire whether she had previous overseas teaching experience. The difficulty arose when she imposed expectations that customarily govern North American seminars. She always arrived punctually, ready to begin each session. The participants were late. Punctuality is an American trait that Latin Americans do not share. Attendees would invariably drift into the seminar room as much as fifteen to twenty minutes late. My pattern during the first week was to banter with early arrivals until enough of a quorum was reached. My colleague grew increasingly furious with the dilatory behavior. She waited a few minutes before strongly berating those present for their tardiness. The class was predominantly male, from cultural settings steeped in the macho tradition. Here was this female American lecturer scolding them for perfectly normal behavior. Matters only grew worse as the week progressed. The more annoyed she became, the more the group conspired to arrive later and later for every session. By the end of the week the tension between the instructor and the audience had made the learning climate untenable. It took me some time to draw this out of Harasic. The lesson to me was clear. I could not make the blithe assumption that good sense would work automatically in an overseas context. Before inviting any U.S. colleague to instruct in a foreign setting, it was essential to discuss the importance of cultural differences.

Two months later, Krystyna and I were back in Latin America, in Mexico City. I was there to work with a group in charge of local arrangements for the FID Conference that would be held there in September 1976. I was on the planning committee for the seminar on education and training, which was to be held immediately preceding the FID meeting. UNESCO had just begun to support the attendance of a small number of individuals active in educational efforts from developing countries. This pre-conference seminar afforded an opportunity for them to learn about new developments. It became a popular regular feature of biennial FID Congresses. During that week, I was invited by Judith Licea de Arenas, director of the library school, to give five evening lectures called "Perspectives on Librarianship." The faculty of Philosophy and Letters of the Autonomous University of Mexico, in its series on Contemporary Thought, sponsored the program. I spoke in English, while Jaime Pontigo, who had been one of the three overseas participants attending the Maryland Library Administrators Program in 1974, followed every five minutes of so with a summary of my remarks in Spanish.

By that spring, the series of workshops I had planned for the Organization of American States was moving ahead on a regular basis. They continued through 1977. My role was to identify qualified instructors on subjects deemed important in building performance competence among the staffs of the information centers. I also briefed instructors on how to work with the groups. I was also available as a sounding board for their ideas and questions on program content and the level of sophistication of the audience. Staff members of the Unit for Technical Change convened meetings periodically during this training period with the Centers' personnel to deal with questions about organizational and network planning. The workshop series included the following: Organization and Planning of Information Centers, Guatemala City, Guatemala, with Paul Wasserman and Rowena Swanson, January 1976; Marketing and Economic Problems of Information Centers, Santa Domingo, Dominican Republic, Gary Ford, July 1976; Standardization for Information Centers in Central America and the Caribbean, Managua, Nicaragua, Paul Vassallo, August 1976; Information Science, Documentation and Information Storage and Retrieval, Tegucigalpa, Honduras, David Batty, November 1976, Microform Information Systems, San Jose, Costa Rica, Albert Diaz, December 1976; Evaluation Methodology for Information Services, Guatemala City, Guatemala, Gene Palmour, March 1977. After inaugurating the sequence in Guatemala, I attended and participated in only two other offerings — the one on standards in Nicaragua, and the marketing workshop in the Dominican Republic.

By 1976, we had incorporated marketing and market research as a full-day component of the Library Administrators Development Program at Maryland. Gary Ford of the Maryland marketing faculty covered the subject during the Library Administrators Program. I had started working with him to identify marketing case studies in the information field. When I traveled to Santo Domingo to sit in on his lectures, we had begun to consider preparing an article that would introduce the marketing issues essential for library and information managers. The meeting in Santo Domingo coincided with a dance jamboree for participants from all over the Caribbean. I still remember the sight of countless lithe, young dancers cavorting in the elevators, corridors, and public halls of our hotel. Energetically yet gracefully they danced the merengue night and day to the Latin beat of music issuing from loudspeakers that were placed every few feet in the public spaces of the hotel. The local organizing institution for the workshop was the Banco Centrale. The country's central information center was located within it. Each day a bus, with the name of the Banco Centrale emblazoned on its sides, would pull up to the hotel. Participants were then transported to the bank for the day's sessions. Every day a man got on board along the way, announcing that he would exchange Dominican currency for American dollars at a rate almost double the official exchange rate. No one seemed struck by the incongruity of black market transactions taking place in a vehicle that boldly proclaimed the name of the country's official bank.

During academic year 1975-1976, a novel pedagogic project was launched. Donald Hausrath, the Washington-based coordinator of the overseas library program of the United States Information Agency, had an educational series in mind for the agency. He felt that there was a need for a training program that could help indigenous staff members in libraries around the world that were part of the United States Information Service. Hausrath had come to know the Maryland program earlier in the 1970's as a Jefferson Fellow on study leave from his agency. He audited several classes and participated in the Library Administrators Program. He proposed to me a contractual relationship with the United States Information Agency that would result in a series of learning modules on subjects normally taught in a library school. These videos and accompanying materials would be used for self-instruction by library staff abroad. As our discussions progressed it became clear that more than just interested faculty would be involved to videotape lectures. A commercial video production firm was necessary to ensure the quality of the visual element of the teaching material. The production firm would have to work closely with individuals who were preparing the learning modules. A new company, Library Training Consultants, was formed to prepare and deliver the final products to the USIA. Gilbert Herman, a Washington businessman who was Esther Herman's husband, and I, were the principals. I chose the lecturers to prepare the instructional units and oriented them to the content elements needed. I also ensured that the quality standard of the completed material met the requirements of the library system staff members for whom they were intended. Herman handled relationships with the Washington-based company where the video lectures were to be prepared. He also oversaw the scheduling of the instructors for the video sessions and the production and delivery of the final video products.

My previous experience of editing by committee did not prepare me for the trauma of trying to orchestrate the efforts of the ten different academic egos. My tactics ranged from pleading to cajoling, to reminding, to threatening faculty to prepare their learning materials. Getting each lecturer to the production studio was equally difficult, resulting in constant postponements. Gil Herman's difficulties made mine seem like child's play. He had to cope with the vagaries of a TV production company where the crises ranged from the temperamental ups and downs of the prima donna producer, to the technical limitations of a struggling and underfinanced media firm where engineering expertise was always in desperately short supply.

The first modules in the project were produced early in 1976. The entire series was not completed and delivered to the United States Information Agency until mid-1977. Each of the twelve modular units followed a common format and consisted of two basic components: the printed material and the videotape lecture. The printed material in a loose-leaf binder outlined the major topics to be covered in the video lecture and in the readings. A printed pre-test offered questions to identify themes the learner would be expected to know. The reading list included selections to be read before viewing the videotape. Further reading suggestions were given on the subject of the study unit. A post-test was provided to test understanding upon the completion of the readings, the lecture, and the exercises. Answers were provided as well. The last printed element was an evaluation form for the learner's assessment of the experience. To complete a single training unit was expected to take the user between four and ten hours, depending on learning styles based on differences in educational background, experience, and degree of unfamiliarity with the subject covered. There were twelve modules in the series. They covered a range of topics: an introduction to reference work; library administration; basic sources of American business information; science and technology sources; social science information; environmental information sources; and American governmental information systems. The learning modules were intended for individuals working independently for self-instruction. As it turned out they were, almost exclusively, used for group workshops. Experienced library school-educated moderators would direct the viewing and lead the discussion. Learners were far more willing to participate along with fellow students in a group led by a real teacher than to work on their own.

With the first regional program in Mexico behind us, UNESCO asked Rizzo and me to repeat the offering in the Philippines in June 1976. The experience in Mexico had gone so well, we hoped to replicate the experience for Southeast Asia. Before giving the course in Mexico, I had spent time in the country for other purposes. I had met Bustamante and thoroughly discussed with him the program's content, style, and perspectives. No such opportunity was possible in the Philippines. In Manila, the National Science Development Board was responsible for conference planning. Our liaison was Delia Torrijos, a Board staff member who later became a regional UNESCO official in Bangkok. We communicated through correspondence, trying to explain to her the attributes and training skills we were seeking in the indigenous faculty needed to cover topics that neither Rizzo nor I would treat. Delia Torrijos was very perceptive, but the range of her instructional talent seemed quite limited. For the most part, those selected to work with us turned out to be senior administrative functionaries of the Marcos bureaucracy. They came from government agencies where an authoritarian mode of administration prevailed. Our propensity was to seek more conceptual, behaviorally oriented lecturers. Rizzo and I encouraged group problem-solving and decision-making strategies that involved broadly based participation. Many of the local instructors offered little more than recitations about how they ran their agencies through a system of rigid controls. The best elements of the local instruction treated technical subjects like finance and budgetary control, concentrating heavily on procedures and techniques. Rizzo and I covered more than half the program content, and there was ample treatment of alternative ways of managing an information organization beyond simply employing command and control techniques.

As had been the case in Mexico, students were drawn from many other countries in the region. In spite of their diversity, the participants adopted a common festive mood through the two weeks. There was much singing and dancing in the evenings. The conference site was two hours from Manila, in Tagaytay. This was a large training facility used for the instruction of civil servants from government agencies located opposite an island, on which there was an occasionally active volcano. The quarters were comfortably furnished. The conference facilities offered a full range of audio-visual equipment, and the meal service featured regional food specialties. In the middle of the second week of the course, a severe hurricane struck the Philippines. Outside the conference center windows, day was transformed into night. In the storm's aftermath the countryside and the roads were flooded. To a foreign observer the sight appeared to be of terrible devastation and destruction. The locals smilingly shrugged it off as a routine event. The participants formed a congenial company with English as the common language. The ability to speak English had been a requirement used in the screening process. While we would like to have been more selective in choosing local faculty, our overall assessment of the workshop was favorable. The participants gave the program high marks as well. We developed a third regional course a year later in Turkey.

On the eve of my departure to attend the FID Conference in Mexico City, in mid-September 1976, the Mexican government announced a devaluation of the peso. I always seemed to find myself in countries where the exchange rate was disadvantageous. On arrival in the Mexican capital I discovered the chance of a lifetime. Single rooms at a favorite hotel, the Maria Cristina, were only six dollars a night at the new conversion rate. Everything being sold bore astonishingly low price tags. Never before, or since, have I shopped with such vigor. I bought an oversized suitcase to accommodate all my new treasures. During the Education and Training Committee's pre-conference seminar I made two presentations. I characterized the UNESCO workshops in a talk entitled "A Management Course for Administrators of Information Programs in Developing Countries: Experiences in Latin America and Southeast Asia." The second speech, "Use of Videotape in Education for Information Science," described the USIA project, which was still in progress.

My colleague, Jerry Kidd, and I worked for five days in November 1976 for the State Department Leaders Program for Policy Officials from Latin America. We planned and directed A Pan-American Seminar on Information Systems and Services: Present Status and Future Directions. Kidd and I lectured to twenty-five high-level officials who had been invited to come to Washington from many countries in the hemisphere. We arranged for the group to hear selected speakers from government and research agencies where innovative efforts in the information field were underway. Following the seminar in Washington, the participants traveled for another week for site visits and demonstrations at key information centers and academic research installations across the country.

On another UNESCO assignment, I traveled with Krystyna to Santiago in December 1976. I was there to advise the University of Chile's Department of Library Science of the Faculty of Philosophy and Letters on curriculum, teaching methods, and program content. We lived in a hotel for the month. During the second stage of the consultancy, from mid-July to mid-August 1977, we sublet a furnished apartment close to the Providencia shopping area, less than half an hour's walk to the university. With the exception of our visits to Poland, where Krystyna had family and close personal ties, discussion of political topics while traveling abroad had always been taboo. Locals were unwilling to discuss, or criticize, the government or the performance and behavior of its officials. When we were in Chile, General Pinochet and his military junta were in control. It was clearly not a time to make jokes in public about generals. We found ourselves straddling two worlds.

Amalia Rodriguez was the director of the library education program at the University of Chile. She moved from her position as director of a special library to head the library school after Pinochet came to power. The Pinochet administration had removed from office all those who had held senior positions during the Allende period. Amalia's husband was a high-ranking officer in the Chilean

Air Force and a member of the country's military elite. At a party given by Amalia, one of the wives remarked that the *toque de queda* (the curfew prohibiting anyone from being outdoors between 10:00 p.m. and 6:00 a.m.) was an excellent measure. It ensured that husbands would be home where they belonged, instead of staying out all night chasing women.

Amalia was energetically working to upgrade the level of her department's program. She asked me to share information with the teaching faculty of her department and of other disciplines, as well as the university administration and student body. I talked with them about educational methods, course content, and instructional innovations in North America. I met regularly with classes and lectured. I also worked with the staff of the university library, reviewing their procedures and management practices. From Amalia's perspective, she and her husband were working hard to do good works for their country. Others saw matters very differently.

A leading American figure in Santiago at this time was the regional United States Information Service librarian, Ann Hopping. She was responsible for the American library in Chile, and for the country library programs in several other Andean nations. During both my visits to Chile, she arranged for me to speak at public programs and to meet individuals who had once been prominent in Chilean library education. These were people with markedly different backgrounds from Amalia Rodriguez and the ruling elite. Ximena Feliu and Ana Maria Prat were two people that Krystyna and I befriended. Ximena's father had been a leading administrator at the University of Santiago before the Pinochet regime took power. Ximena, herself, had been head of the library education program at the university. Ana Maria Pratt was a fellow faculty member. Both were dismissed from their posts for political reasons. Ximena remained outraged by the way the military had swept through the offices of all politically suspect faculty and had carried out their books to burn them in a great bonfire on the campus. Feliu and Prat, who were no longer employable in the Chilean government, found refuge as library staff members with an international social science organization that had a regional office in Santiago. Their friends and colleagues told us many gruesome accounts of the reign of terror following Allende's overthrow. Countless people had disappeared. Human bodies were regularly seen floating in the Mapocho River through Santiago.

We became very friendly with Beatriz Castro, director of the National Center for Information and Documentation. She shared a close relationship with an

American man who worked in the Embassy in Santiago. As two women from different countries involved with American men, Krystyna and Beatriz felt a kinship of spirit. We spent several evenings in the company of this couple. Jim was an economics specialist with the American delegation. His experience in the U.S. seemed to have been with the State Police in West Virginia and later in Vietnam and Central America. On the last evening the four of us spent together, Jim drove us to his home in a mountain suburb outside Santiago. We enjoyed a bountiful dinner and consumed a good amount of fine Chilean wine. Krystyna took lots of snapshots of our group. Jim later drove Beatriz to her parents' home and dropped us off at our apartment. As we were saying goodnight, a tipsy Krystyna blurted out: "Jim, what are your intentions with Beatriz?" I was dumbstruck. Jim managed to mumble something unintelligible before heading home. Back in the states, Krystyna retrieved her developed film and was perplexed to find that all the photos that she had taken at Jim's house came out blank. My suspicion that Jim was a CIA agent was confirmed.

During our stay in Santiago we spent a weekend in Vina del Mar, a resort city on the Pacific coast, north of Santiago. Vina was home to one of South America's most famous gambling casinos. We went there for a holiday celebration and dressed carefully for the occasion. The weather was mild, so I donned a beautifully sewn white *guayabera* shirt that I had bought in the Philippines. I had saved it for just such an occasion in Latin America, where all the men wear them. We strolled through the balmy evening from our hotel and into the casino where we were stopped before we could go into the main hall. A troubled looking man, recognizing that we were not Chileans, but North Americans, drew me aside and whispered that I was not properly attired and could not be admitted. I protested to no avail. I was told that a suit was the required attire. My elegant *guayabera* didn't make the grade. I refused to be bullied into returning to the hotel to change. We left the casino and wandered off elsewhere in the city to enjoy a leisurely dinner. I'll never know how much money I might have won that night.

Immediately following the program in the Philippines, UNESCO invited John Rizzo and me to accept two more assignments. The first was an offering of the third regional management workshop in Turkey, in June 1977. The second was the preparation of a manuscript for those who might wish to conduct a course in administration along the lines of the Maryland program and the two UNESCO workshops. *A Course in Administration for Managers of Information Services: Design, Implementation and Topical Outline* was published by UNESCO in

December 1976. This monograph served as a guide for instructors mounting a seminar for library administrators. Chapter subjects included: General Introduction; Participants — Characteristics and Selection; Methods of Instruction; Key Roles, Qualifications of Director(s) and Faculty; Arrangements, Facilities and Program Ambience; Treatment of Program Content; and Post-Seminar Concerns. The book was later issued in French and Spanish translations.

The reference book *Consultants and Consulting Organizations* brought together information in one place about thousands of individuals and firms. By the mid-1970's, this book had gone through a couple of editions and was widely used as a lookup source for details about consulting groups in many different fields. At this time, there had been a burgeoning of organizations and firms that provided learning opportunities in many subject areas and technical activities. There now appeared to be need for descriptive information about the hundreds of non-academic organizations that offered training courses and workshops of short duration. In 1977, we began work to prepare a reference source that would include details about the organizations that made such study programs possible. We gave details of the content, duration, and other characteristics of such offerings. Janice McLean was the associate editor. Gale Research published the first edition of *Training and Development Organizations* in 1978.

Warsaw was the venue for the regular meeting of the FID Education and Training Committee in May 1977. The committee chairman then was Gernot Wersig. At this conference I described the experience of developing the teaching materials for the United States Information Agency and demonstrated their use. The paper was called "Self-Instruction Training Materials for Librarians and Information Scientists: The Use of Text and Video Learning Modules." In June 1977, the third UNESCO regional training seminar was held in Ankara, Turkey. UNESCO cast the net more widely this time to attract applicants. The result was that participants came from countries in Africa, the Middle East, and Europe. The host agency was TURDOK, the Turkish National Documentation Center in Ankara. Working again in Ankara fourteen years after my first visit was a sort of homecoming. Those I had first met when they were graduate students at Middle East Technical University — some of whom had gone on to complete Ph.D. study at Cornell — helped us to be more discriminating in identifying indigenous faculty. In the months leading up to the workshop we selected professors from Middle East Technical University and the University of Istanbul who matched our specifications for behaviorally oriented management scholars and trainers.

The Best of Times

The conference site was a luxury hotel outside Ankara where the air was clear and each meal offered appetizing Turkish dishes.

The seminar proceeded along the lines developed in Mexico and the Philippines. The last day of the two-week session was customarily left free for an open forum. The participants were encouraged then to discuss cases drawn from their home organizations. Rizzo and I, along with the participants, served as an advisory panel offering techniques and strategies for resolving organizational problems that might be raised. One participant was from Austria. This individual was a highly placed functionary in the government information structure. He arrived without having read any material about the seminar in advance. He came with the expectation that all the sessions would be devoted to discussing problems that the participants dealt with in their own work. During the first morning, he interrupted the lecturer to demand that participants be permitted to discuss their specific managerial problems. In his opinion these were more relevant than what was being covered. Rizzo and I explained patiently that the last day of the two weeks would provide such an opportunity. By then the group would have had the benefit of the lectures and exercises on the full range of subjects that would inform their understanding, before attention would be turned to situational needs. He was not mollified; he continued to mutter discontentedly. The next morning, Rizzo told me that one of the participants had complained that this man tried to incite others to join him in his demands. We had never encountered a problem like this before. I decided to confront him directly. Quietly, but firmly, I explained to him that he had become a disruptive influence and that such behavior would not be tolerated. He had a choice. He could remain and conduct himself in an orderly manner. If he did not desist in his actions, however, he would be dismissed from the program at once. An explanation for the decision would be communicated to UNESCO and to his institution. He seemed visibly upset to hear this and apologized for causing any difficulty. By the end of the two weeks he had become a stauncher and more vociferous supporter of the program than any other participant.

On the weekend between the first and second weeks, TURDOK arranged for us to make a bus trip to Cappadocia, a fabled setting deep in far eastern Asia Minor, which had been at times part of the Persian and later, of the Roman Empire. This stark, desolate area was in a mountain region of deep craters and caves that were said to have been the dwelling places for people hiding from persecution. The terrain resembled a lunar landscape. On the way there, we stopped in a large town reputed to be one of the principal trading centers for Turkish rugs. One could not spend any time in Turkey without learning about the high quality of the rugs made by the artisans in the country. A participant from a neighboring country said that if he brought anything home from Turkey, it would be a rug. I saw a *kilim* rug on the wall of a shop, which caught my fancy. Adopting customary trading practices of the region, I halfheartedly offered the merchant half the posted price. I assumed that the merchant would make a counter proposal. He did not. This surprised me. I wondered why there had been no bargaining. Later, one of our Turkish faculty explained why. He said that I must have bid on one of the better rugs in the shop. The merchant was in the unusual position of owning an inventory of valuable products, which could not be replaced. The worth of his fine rugs was continuously rising. It was actually in his best interest to sell off only enough of his fine rugs to maintain himself and his family. The longer he held onto his inventory the more valuable it would become over time.

At the end of the weekend, Krystyna arrived from Italy, where we had been before I came to Turkey. At the end of the workshop, we planned to spend several days in Istanbul. John Rizzo and several course participants were also headed there. We looked like exotic, international travelers. Our group included people from the United States, the Ivory Coast, Ethiopia, and Egypt. We wandered together through the covered bazaar and the celebrated mosques. An evening spent at the apartment of Mary Berkmen, a seminar participant from Istanbul's Robert College, and her husband, Salim, was the high point of the stay. We listened to jazz while chatting with members of Istanbul's art, literary, and academic communities. From the balcony we looked over the Golden Horn to see the sparkling lights of many vessels. Across the water on the other side of the Bosphorus, we could discern Turkish buildings on the continent of Asia.

In the summer of 1977, a master's degree student and graduate assistant, Eileen Goldstein, went to Mexico as a CONACYT summer intern. She worked with Guadalupe Carrion and Antonio Ayesteran on information problems. She also concentrated zealously on improving her Spanish. Her performance so impressed Guillermo Fernandez de la Garza — under whose administration she had worked — that he hired her after her graduation. In 1978, she became head of one of Mexico's most important special libraries at the Institute for Electrical Research in Cuernavaca. This was a government enterprise with regional offices and branch libraries around the country. Guillermo had just been appointed the director.

The Best of Times

I accepted an assignment in October 1977 to give a five-day workshop in Panama City under the auspices of the United States Agency for International Development for library and information personnel of the Panama government. This course was the first phase of a two-part offering. It dealt with the organization, management, and service programs of information centers. Thirty-five Panamanians from scientific and technical, academic, and public libraries participated. During that week, feelings were running high in the country about the control of the Panama Canal. I watched as a U.S. government automobile was surrounded suddenly by an angry mob near the city's downtown area. The passengers were forcibly ejected. The crowd set fire to the vehicle. I visited and watched the Panama Canal in operation. This sight was so impressive that when I returned home I immediately read David McCullough's inspiring, award winning account of the Panama Canal's history and construction, *The Path Between the Seas*. My second visit a year later proved far more tranquil. Krystyna joined me there, and on the evening of her arrival, we discovered *langostinas*. We returned to the same seaside restaurant several nights running to feast on these succulent baby lobsters.

With the encouragement of the U.S. National Committee, my work with the FID Education and Training Committee became more active. By 1977 education was coming to be seen as a primary avenue for influencing international information developments toward American perspectives. It was also perceived as a catalytic factor in extending the use of American information products, both commercially produced and from the U.S. government, around the world. I was encouraged to play an active role in planning the seminar, which would be sponsored by the committee during the fall of 1978, in Edinburgh. Given the high priority accorded to education, I was invited to become a member of the U.S. National Committee for FID early in 1978. It was during this same period that I was asked by UNESCO to serve as a consultant in arranging and contributing to a seminar on information planning and economic development for the African region, to be held in Accra, Ghana, in July 1978.

This conference, with attendees from many Anglophone African nations, was sponsored by the University of Ghana and was held at the University's Conference Center outside the city. The chairman was Professor Sam Kotei, head of the library education program at the University of Ghana. The role I played, along with Marta Dosa, of Syracuse University, was to serve as advisor to Kotei and to present papers during the five-day seminar. My responsibility included offering the keynote address, "Strategies of Information Management in Developing Countries." My remarks centered on four themes: information as a tool of development; technology transfer; inter-reliance and interdependence; and planning for information management. The other paper I gave was called "Techniques of Documentation for Transfer of Technology." In it I reviewed and critiqued several systems and structures, inter-relations, and activities — all of which shared the idea of information dissemination built upon models different from the conventional, passive library form. These papers were later published by the University of Ghana in the Proceedings of the Seminar, appearing in spring 1981.

Ghana was undergoing great political and economic stress at that time. Kotei, the program chairman, who was an affable and articulate speaker, seemed preoccupied as the symposium was beginning. The morning of the second day of the meeting, the daily Accra newspaper carried a detailed account of our meeting. The first sentence described Professor Sam Kotei's welcome to a large contingent of international participants at this important international scientific meeting. On the same front page, under a banner headline, the main story proclaimed that General Kotei had been placed under arrest on a charge of financial corruption. As we read this account we became aware of why Sam Kotei had been seen so little as the conference was getting underway. General Kotei was his brother. Sometime later, after the conclusion of the seminar, the general was executed. Sam Kotei and his family left the country for Botswana, where he assumed the post of director of the library education program until his own untimely death several years later.

Food service during the meeting consisted of modest meals with small portions. The most popular event during the conference, as a result, was a reception and buffet dinner given for the delegates by the U.S. Information Service. William Bennett, whom I first knew in 1963 in Ankara as the UNESCO-appointed director of Middle East Technical University Library, was at this time the USIS regional librarian for West Africa, based in Accra. He was our genial host. Before the conference attendees' departures on Saturday morning, a celebratory closing dinner was given on Friday night. Sam Kotei spoke eloquently and punctuated his remarks with a number of toasts. Frogs croaked so noisily outside the banquet hall that Kotei had to make his words coincide with lulls in this bullfrog chorus in order to be heard. The next morning participants were informed that no breakfast was available since all the food for the conference had already been consumed.

The Best of Times

From Accra I went to Dakar in Senegal. I addressed the students of the principal library education program in francophone Africa at the University of Dakar. My next stop was Casablanca, where I met Krystyna for several days of tourism in Morocco before flying to Paris to meet with UNESCO officials and to report on the Accra seminar. In Paris, I agreed to serve as a consultant for the UNESCO General Information Program. I would attend and report on a conference to take place in Madrid in September 1978, preceding the Edinburgh FID Biennial conference. The Madrid meeting was called REUNIBER-78, a Conference on National Systems Development in Scientific and Technological Documentation in Latin America. It was convened by the Spanish National Research Council and was held in its conference facility. In attendance were many of those I had worked with during the Organization of American States workshops. The Organization of American States supported their attendance in Madrid; they also funded site visits to several information centers in Western Europe. In Edinburgh I offered a paper (co-authored with Gary Ford), "Problems of Education and Training in Marketing and Market Research in Information Science." This was published in *Education and Training: Theory and Provision,* the 1978 conference proceedings issued by the International Federation for Documentation in 1979. It was also during 1978 that work began on two new reference books. The first was *Recreation and Outdoor Life*, a volume providing details on the range of organizations, institutions, and information sources that covered sports and pastimes in North America. This book was conceived by my son Steven, and he served as its associate editor. *Learning Independently*, in which the associate editor was Edmond Applebaum, identified the organizations, institutions, and companies that made available materials and media for self–study. It provided details about the content of the resources, their cost, and where and how to acquire them. The first editions of these works appeared in 1979 under the Gale Research Company imprint.

Chapter Seventeen

At the 1978 FID conference the executive board voted to transfer the Education and Training Committee to the United States for a four-year period. It would be moved from the Free University in West Berlin to the University of Maryland. I envisaged expanding the committee's role and functions to include a number of new activities. In order to implement this goal I applied for and received a sabbatical leave for the spring semester of 1979. I had earlier discussions with Kieth Wright, then dean at Maryland, and with the faculty, locating the committee at the university. This would constitute only one aspect of a plan to extend our international efforts in library and information science. I was designated professor in charge of the international education programs, and a brochure describing our offerings would be addressed to prospective master's and doctoral students. During this period two new efforts were begun under the aegis of the Education and Training Committee with support from UNESCO.

The first initiative was the issuance of a monthly newsletter that would share details about new programs, workshops, scholarships, special programs, and publications about educational activities and developments in the field. It was based on information solicited from organizations everywhere in the world. To collect the material, edit the content, and prepare the publication and its distribution, a Maryland doctoral student interested in international education was assigned to work with me. The corollary effort was the Clearinghouse on Education and Training Materials in Library and Information Science. Education and training agencies in developing regions were our target audience. The idea behind this effort was simple. In less developed countries new offerings were brought into being without benefit of earlier experiences. Our task was to seek out and collect from faculty and trainers in established institutions copies of course outlines, reading lists, exercises, and other teaching materials that had already been prepared for use in classes, institutes, and other teaching situations. We would organize and classify this material. Upon request from anywhere in the world, a copy of any material contained in our clearinghouse files would be photocopied and mailed to the seeker without charge. Contributions of material were voluntary. Some shared the products of their work generously and enthusiastically. Others were more proprietary and made nothing available. Nevertheless, the files grew dramatically in size and scope. Over the course of four years, the statistics of material received and the volume of satisfied inquiries increased at a rapid rate.

Efforts were also begun to seek to expand membership and participation in the work of the committee. When I attended my first meeting in Frankfurt in 1970 only twenty of the FID member countries had designated individuals to serve as delegates. Only a handful ever attended meetings or participated in committee projects. With the encouragement of the United States National Committee for FID, I corresponded with every national member that had not appointed someone to serve. I proposed that a qualified representative be selected to participate in the committee. To the countries whose designated members had not participated in committee efforts in five years, I wrote to suggest that they appoint someone new or that they provide greater support to the existing member. During my term, the number of national representatives to the Education and Training Committee almost doubled. The level of participation from nations that had not been involved before also increased.

To heighten American interest, I invited the committee to meet in the United States for a workshop to be held under committee auspices in Minneapolis, immediately prior to the October 1979 Annual Conference of the American Society for Information Science. This session was intended as an opportunity for the exchange of views among educators and trainers in developed and less developed regions. Participants came from twenty-four countries. The seminar theme was Education and Training for Information Services in Business and Industry in Developing and Developed Countries: the Needs, the Experience, the Newer Trends. I presented a paper: "A Formal Course in Business Information Services" and chaired the final panel and open discussion. The proceedings of this workshop were published by FID in 1980.

In 1979, I was appointed as a member of the Advisory Screening Committee in Library and Information Science of the Council for the International Exchange of Scholars. This was the body charged with evaluating the qualifications of applicants for Fulbright teaching and research awards. My appointment extended until 1981 when I was designated chairman of the committee until 1982. Late in 1979, Krystyna and I were in Cuernavaca, where I worked with Eileen Goldstein planning the staff development of the Technical Information Department at the Institute of Electrical Research in Cuernavaca. Goldstein directed a system of twenty-seven library employees and twelve engineers. The design called for an orientation series, a workshop and seminar series, in-service training, outside organizational site visits, and internships. The workshop series was conducted over a one-year period and followed the pattern used in staff development with the Organization of American States Information for Industry Centers in Latin America. Each training session was typically a four-day workshop. Subjects and instructors were Organization Structure and Services of Information Systems, and Information Resources in Business, Science, and Technology, with Paul Wasserman; Retrieval, Classification and Thesauri, with David Batty; Marketing and Market Research for Information Services, with Gary Ford; Evaluation of Information Systems and Services, with Gene Palmour; and Administration, Communication and Interpersonal Skills, with Jorge Bustamante. Eileen and I prepared a paper describing the workshop experience that appeared in *Special Libraries*, July 1981 as "Training and Development of a Library and Technical Information Staff."

Following our December 1979 stay in Cuernavaca, Krystyna and I flew to Zihuatenejo, a resort city on the Pacific. On the second day of our holiday I came down with a severe case of dysentery. I had to be admitted to a private medical clinic run by the physician who examined me. There, I was placed in a bed and hooked up to intravenous fluids. There were no nurses administering to patient needs; only two small girls were in attendance to clean and to answer the phone. The patients' families customarily saw to the patients. A pad was provided near my bed where Krystyna was to sleep that night. Nighttime brought the raucous sounds of the discotheque in the house next door. When the noise stopped around midnight, we fell asleep. In the middle of the night I noticed that the I.V. container was empty. I woke up Krystyna; she went down to the admitting desk to try to learn how the bag could be replaced. Behind the counter she found the two little girls asleep beside a pig. She woke them and explained what was needed. The girls came back to my room with her and knew precisely what to do and how to do it. The next morning the doctor decided that I could be discharged. He advised rest and a bland diet for several days. We flew back to Mexico City. Our plan to travel to Guanajuato was put on hold for another time. For the next five days I subsisted on the same dinner of *pechuga*, chicken breast, before I finally regained my strength.

Later that month in January 1980, I returned to Cuernavaca to offer the first workshop in the Institute of Electrical Research series. With Gary Ford I prepared a paper drawing on the training experiences in the Organization of American States and the Cuernavaca programs. It appeared in the spring 1980 issue of a new journal edited by John Rizzo, *The Journal of Library Administration*. The article was called "Market and Marketing Research: What the Library Manager Should Learn."

At UNESCO in 1980 there was growing sentiment to encourage non-governmental organizations to work more collaboratively. There was thought to be too much duplication and overlap in the roles, functions, and activities carried on by the International Federation for Documentation, the International Federation of Library Associations, and the International Council for Archives. UNESCO was a major financial contributor to the operations and projects carried out by these organizations. Elimination of redundancy was seen as a way to reduce UNESCO's expenditures. There were clear similarities of interest in educational matters among documentalists, librarians, and archivists. FID's Education and Training Committee scrupulously invited the participation of members from the other two organizations. The clearinghouse and newsletter projects were initiatives that already led to a greater degree of collaboration. Information was regularly disseminated, encouraging involvement and alerting those in education and training to contribute to and receive the benefits of these services by adding the names of interested members to our mailing list. The U.S. National Committee for FID strongly endorsed any moves that might encourage joint efforts.

In May of 1980, a meeting was scheduled in Bellagio, Italy, at the Rockefeller Conference Center. Representatives from all three organizations came to discuss future cooperation and collaboration. I was designated by the U.S. National Committee to attend the three-day meeting as its representative and in my capacity as chairman of the Education and Training Committee. Krystyna came with me to Bellagio. Only official participants could stay at the Conference Center, so Krystyna remained at a hotel overlooking Lake Como. On the final evening of our session she was invited to join the group for cocktails and dinner. Like Cinderella, she then disappeared to return to her hotel room in Bellagio.

The meeting attracted strong representation from all three groups. Jim Haas, president of the Council on Library Resources in Washington, DC, was present as an observer. The council had been a long-term supporter of the International Federation of Library Associations. Discussions were conducted in a friendly and informal manner. Despite a willingness to work together, it was evident that differences in history, orientation, and philosophy precluded even the simplest possible changes — such as holding annual or biennial congresses and conferences simultaneously in the same location. Consensus was reached in matters pertaining to education and training. All agreed that in this area it was possible to serve the common interests of all three groups. I was asked to convene a meeting that brought together the FID Education and Training Committee, the International Federation of Library Associations Education and Research Board, and the International Council for Archives Committee on Education and Training, as well as observers from UNESCO and elsewhere. We discussed possibilities for implementing practical cooperative measures. The meeting took place for two days in December 1980 in Frankfurt. It led to concrete plans for future collaborative efforts by the education committees of the three organizations. Immediately afterward, I went to West Berlin where the German Foundation for International Development had arranged a five-day conference on Training Materials in Library and Information Science with Particular Reference to the Needs of Developing Countries. I had been asked to chair this meeting and contributed a paper called "Transferability of Curricular Models." Universal collaboration among educators and trainers received further reinforcement at this meeting. The Clearinghouse on Education and Training Materials was underscored as a key resource for educators and trainers in developing countries.

Krystyna and I spent the closing days of 1980 in Frankfurt before flying on to New Delhi. I was to serve there as director and lecturer in a two-week-long UNESCO workshop for library and information center administrators in the Asian region. The workshop was patterned after the courses that Rizzo and I had organized in the three other regions of the world. When we boarded our flight to New Delhi, we found our tourist-class seats occupied by two passengers who had started the flight in London. We were ushered into the first-class compartment. For the first time in all our travels together, we occupied choice seats close to the flight deck. We ate gourmet fare and drank endless quantities of fine champagne. Under the influence of this regal treatment, we felt as if we had arrived in India on a magic carpet. When we debarked at the New Delhi airport we were quickly jostled back to reality. We competed in a swarming horde of people to find our luggage in a room that was too small for the large crowd. Once past the rituals of customs and entry procedures, we were relieved to be met by a UNESCO driver. He helped us maneuver our way through the many human beings jammed into the airport and led us to a vehicle that would take us to the New Delhi International Center.

The host organization for the seminar was the Indian National Science Development Board. The person designated to work with me was Major Thiagarajan, a retired military officer in his late thirties. He had strong interest and experience, but little educational background in management. During the months leading up to the conference, I had written copiously describing precisely the training skills we were seeking from the indigenous faculty. Thiagarajan succeeded in engaging a group of well-qualified and effective lecturers to cover topics in the workshop outline which I would not treat. About half the twenty-five participants were from India. The others came from other Asian countries. The International Center was a comfortable conference site. It offered good living accommodations, excellent meal service, and well-equipped seminar rooms. The center also served the local academic and professional community. It provided a good library and weekly public lectures by distinguished international speakers. During our stay, Clark Kerr, who had been the Chancellor of the University of California higher education system, addressed the audience one evening. The participants were an interesting group of predominantly male library managers who were thirty to forty-five years old. One participant came from Mongolia. In order for him to understand the lectures, we had to engage a local specialist who could simultaneously translate the lectures into Russian. Two others in the group were from Kabul. One of them was a public librarian; the other was an academic library director. Afghanistan was under Soviet domination at that time. Early in the first week, the public librarian drew me aside to speak to me privately. He explained that his countryman was a member of the Communist party who was responsible for observing his colleague's behavior for any signs of disloyalty to the government. He told me that he wanted to write to his relatives in California. He wanted to know if it would be safe to mail a letter from the International Center, without his compatriot knowing about it. I gave him my assurance that this would be perfectly safe. In spite of my reassurances, he watched his colleague apprehensively all through the seminar.

There was also a young Iranian in the group. His English was excellent; it had no trace of a foreign accent. He held a Ph.D. in science from Ohio State University and had lived in Ohio for a number of years. He was charming and friendly to

Krystyna and me, often sitting with us during meals or in the lounge reminiscing about his life in the States. It was not until after several days had passed that I learned from Thiagarajan that this man had been complaining to other participants. He was indignant about the wrong UNESCO had committed in engaging a workshop director from the imperialist United States. Thiagarajan explained to him that I was not representing the United States, but was there as a UNESCO consultant. It was to no avail. The grumbling persisted through the course, even while he maintained his courteous manner toward Krystyna and me.

Krystyna and I found the International Center to be an oasis in a great desert of human misfortune. Whenever we walked off the Center grounds we would come upon large numbers of people, whole families, living in the streets. The street served as their bedroom, living room, kitchen, and toilet. As first-time visitors to India who had never before witnessed such human squalor, we found this very disheartening. It was winter. Despite the popular notion that all of India is a tropical weather zone, the temperatures were often in the low forties. The air was raw, wet, and cold. The center was situated close to a lovely park. On one of the first days of our stay, Krystyna befriended a homeless blind woman and her child in the park. Every day during our stay Krystyna brought them food. We often reflected on how these poor souls had survived before Krystyna came and what became of them once she had left. Over the weekend, the workshop participants traveled by bus to Agra to behold the wondrous Taj Mahal. Amidst its splendors, crowds of malnourished men, women, and children in abject poverty were begging throughout the area.

On the evening of our departure, Major Thiagarajan invited us home for dinner. As a senior civil servant, he occupied a flat with several rooms in a high-rise building in a residential neighborhood. It was sparsely furnished and unheated. He and his wife were gracious and hospitable. They served us a modest dish made from ingredients that must have cost them a great deal. The highlight of the evening was when their two beautiful and dark-eyed children—a ten-year-old boy and a twelve-year-old girl — cheerfully sang, "How Much Is That Doggie in the Window?" We went by taxi from their home to the airport for a 2:00 a.m. flight to Bangkok. The terminal at this hour was as crowded as on the day we arrived. It was filled with sleeping families in every available space. Walking around the large public hall, we had to weave around to avoid stepping on prostrate bodies. Arriving in Bangkok after our flight, we felt as if we had landed on another planet, where the alien population was healthy and smiling.

The Best of Times

Krystyna and I returned to Cuernavaca in March. I gave a seminar there to the Institute of Electrical Research staff on Information Systems and Sources in Business, Science, and Technology. This time we managed to get to Guanajuato. I addressed an audience of library staff members and library school students at the University of Guanajuato. My talk covered trends in library management and information systems. In 1981, Albert Diaz, who published the Reader Series in Library and Information Science when he was with Microcard Editions, had gone out on his own. He ran a series of workshops for librarians called A. J. Seminars. I served as advisor on seminar content and helped him to identify qualified instructors. In April I taught a seminar for him on Business and Economic Information Sources. The seminar took place in Washington, DC, and then in New York City in May. Immediately prior to the June meeting of the American Library Association Conference in San Francisco, I repeated the one-day offering.

The FID Education and Training Committee held its first business and technical session in Africa in May of 1981 at the University of Ibadan in Nigeria. I chaired the conference and worked with the local organizer, Bimpe Aboyade, a professor who was head of the university's library education program. Identifying Training Needs for Library and Information Services in a Predominantly Non-literate Society was the conference theme. The Nigerian economy was thriving due to its booming petroleum production. Several delegates came from Europe, and there were a number of participants from Anglophone African. The greatest number came from different regions of Nigeria itself. Peter Lazar, a Hungarian information scientist active on the Council of the International Federation for Documentation, was serving in Nigeria at that time as a consultant to the United Nations Development Organization. He arranged for me to come to Lagos at the close of the Ibadan meeting. I gave a lecture for a workshop at the Federal Institute of Industrial Research called "Business and Economic Information."

Lagos was a big, bustling, and heavily congested city. It was reputed to be dangerous for unaccompanied Europeans, so I never left the hotel without a local person accompanying me. In order to make my presentation in Lagos, I had to extend my stay in Nigeria two extra days. Lazar arranged for a United Nations Development Organization car to take me to the airport the morning of my departure. Along the way a number of people shouted at our car and made threatening gestures. The driver explained that a national strike had begun and that many people were demanding that all work be halted, including the use of automobiles. At the airport, the driver took me into the terminal to ensure that planes were flying. If not, he would drive me back to a hotel in the city. Some flights were not operating, but my flight to London would be ready for boarding and departure in half an hour. Reassured, I thanked the driver and he returned to the Institute. At the currency exchange counter no one was on duty. I was left with seventy-five dollars worth of non-convertible Nigerian money. Still, I felt fortunate to be getting out before the whole country ground to a halt. After boarding our flight, passengers sat in the aircraft twenty minutes before being asked to disembark: the tower controllers had joined the strike.

Back in the terminal I felt cut off from the world. Telephones were out of order; I had no way to call Lazar to report what had happened. A friendly young Indian couple from my flight struck up a conversation with me. When I explained my predicament, the husband said that his firm in Lagos had arranged for someone to wait at the airport with a motorcycle, in case the flight did not depart. This driver was to be dispatched back to the city to report to the company on what had happened. I was relieved when the man told me that he would have the driver go to the Federal Institute of Industrial Research as well. Lazar would be apprised of the situation on my behalf. A couple of hours later, Peter Lazar and an official from the Institute arrived. They brought the disturbing news that the strike against the government had become widespread. An early end to the strike was not likely. If things did not clear up by the next day, a driver would take me to Togo, some six or seven hours away. From there, I could probably get a flight to Europe.

As we discussed this option a British Airways official informed the stranded passengers that our departure was postponed indefinitely. Those who lived in Lagos were encouraged to return to their homes, where they would be informed about future flight plans. Visitors like myself would be transported by British Airways to a motel near the airport. The airline would pay the first night's bill and meal charges for twenty-four hours. Beyond that, if the strike persisted, we would have to make our own arrangements. My colleagues agreed that, if the strike were still in progress by noon the next day, the car would come to the motel and take me to Togo. On the way to the motel, I sat next to an Israeli businessman who told me that he had been in Nigeria once before when the same situation had arisen. He did not get out on a flight for ten days. I settled in at the motel and had dinner. In my room there was a short-wave radio. I switched it on to hear a booming voice announcing that the government strike had been called off. Negotiations for a settlement were to begin immediately. Instead of unpacking, I stayed up reading a book and hoped to hear good news about my delayed flight.

The Best of Times

Forty-five minutes later there was a knock at my door. A British Airways staff member told me to be ready to leave for the airport in ten minutes. On arrival at the airport passengers were taken directly to the same plane. We departed at once. There was no time to alert those passengers who had returned to their homes in Lagos. The 11:30 p.m. flight to London left without them. Once we were airborne, I learned from a member of the crew what had caused the strike. Since the economy was so strong, government employees wanted the government to provide each of them with an automobile as one of their job benefits. I never learned how the dispute was settled.

By the summer of 1981 I was in Mexico City again. At the invitation of Jose Quevedo, the director of INFOTEC, I acted as an advisor to the professional staff. INFOTEC was a quasi-governmental industrial consulting organization that offered information services, technical studies, and market research for the nation's commercial and technical companies. During the five-day period I worked with staff members and gave lectures on several topics: client relationships; marketing of information products; search strategy; and information systems in science, technology, business, and economics.

Early in the 1980's, the federal government's support for international information efforts was reduced dramatically. From the late 1950's into the 1970's, the Office of Science Information in the National Science Foundation, which was directed by Burton Adkinson, had undertaken many initiatives. In the field of documentation and technical information the primary international society, the International Federation for Documentation, had been for its entire history little more than a European organization. In the early post-World War II years, the seat of the United States membership in FID had been the American Documentation Institute, which became the American Society for Information Science. The institute's president, Karl Heumann, in collaboration with Adkinson, worked to transfer the organization's responsibilities to the newly created Office of Documentation in the National Research Council of the National Academy of Sciences. With the American ascendancy in scientific and technical research, and its concomitant technical literature and information handling, Adkinson saw that it was time for the United States to take a stronger role in building professional ties to the world's scientific community. In the aftermath of the Soviet Union's Sputnik space launch, the time seemed especially propitious to advance American interests by opening a window onto scientific achievements abroad. The International Federation for Documentation was therefore seen by Adkinson as an essential avenue toward this objective, particularly in the Soviet Union.

The field of librarianship was arranged otherwise. The International Federation of Library Associations served the international community. It was the acknowledged international, non-governmental professional association working on behalf of libraries around the globe. The organization of the International Federation for Documentation was different. Its structure was based on the designation in each member country of a national member. The seat of the national membership normally resided in a government institution. Support for annual dues was levied against each national member on a scale comparable to that used in the United Nations. Funds came from a government source in each member country. These were sufficient to cover the dues, to support the costs of delegate travel to the biennial Congress, and to support participation in the work of committees. Adkinson was instrumental in allocating support from the Office of Science Information in the National Science Foundation to the U.S. National Research Council's Office of Documentation, which was the designated seat of U.S. membership. This small office was later incorporated into the Office of the Foreign Secretary of the National Research Council. The U.S. National Committee for the International Federation for Documentation was set up with representatives from leading American scientific and information organizations. These representatives directed the participation and involvement of United States nationals in the work of the International Federation for Documentation. Adkinson's commitment to U.S. participation in the work of FID had led to his election as the organization's president in the early 1960's.

By the 1980's, officials responsible for the Office of Science Information in the National Science Foundation, consistent with the retrenchment initiatives of the Reagan administration, felt that government financing of international scientific activities had been provided long enough. American support for participation in such international bodies as FID should stem from the professional community, rather than from the U.S. government. This policy shift meant that each year the National Science Foundation reduced its contribution. Support for U.S. participation in the International Federation for Documentation was cut off completely in 1982. Without support from the National Science Foundation to finance the work in the Office of the Foreign Secretary, Judith Werdel, who had handled the responsibilities for the FID secretariat since 1963, had to leave the National Academy of Sciences. In 1982, for the first time, the United States delegation to the FID Congress and Conference in Hong Kong was delinquent in paying its dues.

The Best of Times

When I went to the 1982 meeting in September, American participation in the organization was in peril. The only money remaining in the United States National Committee's account was left over from the 1965 Washington, DC, FID Congress. Twenty-five thousand dollars remained in this account in 1982. The U.S. National Committee decided that these funds should be kept in reserve and that annual payments should be suspended until another support source was identified to replace the National Science Foundation. Over a four-year period, the United States did not meet its dues obligation to FID. With funds no longer available from the National Science Foundation, the National Research Council could not continue to sponsor the U.S. National Committee. The U.S. National Committee was therefore obliged to perpetuate itself as a body independent of any institutional sponsorship. An unsuccessful effort was made to have the American Society for Information Science offer sponsorship. The society did, however, offer the committee the use of its offices in Washington, DC, where it would convene its meetings. American participation in FID activities continued unabated during this time, even though the issue of delinquent dues owed by the United States remained unresolved.

Chapter Eighteen

I had served as chairman of the Education and Training Committee of FID for four years by the end of 1982 and decided that the post should be passed on to someone else. The U.S. National Committee thought that American interests would be best served if the committee remained in the United States. I contacted a number of colleagues in library education programs who had been active internationally to consider becoming my replacement. Limiting the search to individuals engaged in information work in universities was deemed appropriate in view of the committee's basic purpose. Marta Dosa, a professor at Syracuse University, with a considerable background in overseas activity, took on the role. The transition from the University of Maryland to Syracuse University took place at the start of 1983. I continued my participation as a United States member of the Education and Training Committee.

Collaborative efforts among non-governmental organizations in the information field continued under the auspices of UNESCO's General Information Program. An advisory board was established to further such efforts, and I was invited to serve as a member. The board convened in May 1983 in Paris to plan for an October 1984 Symposium on Harmonization of Education Programs in Librarianship, Documentation and Archives. I was commissioned to prepare a report for discussion at the conference as well. The three organizations — FID, IFLA, and ICA — established a working party to serve as forerunner to the UNESCO symposium. In August 1983 Krystyna and I went to Vienna, where I attended a meeting of this working group. The Austrian government provided housing. Krystyna and I were lodged in the imposing Museum of Natural History for three days. We settled in a spacious apartment reserved for use by visiting scholars. I wondered whether being domiciled in quarters immediately adjacent to the dinosaur exhibition reflected the Viennese organization's views of the ideas I was to advance during our sessions.

I made two contributions to the Vienna meeting. The first was, "A Review of International and Regional Programs in Training Managers for the Information Professions," which was later published in *Education for Information* in 1984. This was a new journal started in 1983 by two Aberystwyth faculty members. I had accepted membership on its editorial advisory board. Following the Vienna meeting, I traveled to Munich to attend the board's first meeting. My second report in Vienna was a draft of the UNESCO study. The final paper, "The Teaching of Management as a Subject for the Preparation of Librarians, Documentalists, Archivists and Other Training Specialists" was adapted with the modifications suggested in Vienna and a critique from the UNESCO panel delegated to give me their reactions. It was accepted by UNESCO and issued in June 1984. The paper was presented formally at the International Symposium on Harmonization of Education and Training Programmes in Information Science, Librarianship and Archival Studies in Paris, in October 1984.

By end of 1983, the information for industry centers program in Central and South America, which began with my training efforts for the Organization of American States Unit for Technical Change in 1976, had been operating for seven years. In the intervening years their directors and staffs had gained considerable experience and operational expertise. When the OAS and the United States National Technical Information Service convened a workshop for more than fifty participants from the centers, the overall theme of the three-day meeting in Miami was micro-computers in technical and information centers. The level of knowledge among the participants was impressive, compared to where they had been only a few years earlier. I served as workshop director, coordinating the technical sessions and panel discussions. I also lectured on business and technical information services and management.

By the end of the 1970's, the number of publications in which I had played some role had reached proportions that I felt were getting beyond my control. My responsibility varied widely in the planning, managing, and editing of the reference books. Through the years I had enjoyed the unfailing supportive efforts of Effie Knight. By the mid-1970's, however, she began to suffer severe health problems. She had to undergo kidney dialysis three times a week and was no longer able to come to the campus on a regular basis. She was a strong-minded woman who had been active throughout her career. She was determined not to let her poor health impede her work role. The solution to the problem was for her to turn part of the lower level of her home into a business office. Her husband Bob Knight, a mechanically inclined type, was trained to administer home dialysis. Dialysis sessions three evenings a week allowed Effie to devote the rest of her time to work. If she became tired or indisposed, she could readily go upstairs to rest. Her home was equipped with a copying machine, shelves, file cabinets, and room for several desks and typewriters. Publication efforts that were separate from my university responsibilities were worked on at the Knights' house. An administrative assistant was hired to work on campus with me on the Library Administrators Development Program. The Knight house had a backdoor entrance to the business office, which was located only ten or fifteen minutes by car from the campus. I went there several times a week to conduct meetings and to work on the different reference book projects. Over time, the course of Effie's disease reduced her energy level. It gradually became clear that the office arrangement could not continue indefinitely. We decided not to add any more new projects. By 1980 I started thinking seriously about how to divest responsibility for some of the reference books that required frequent revisions and updating.

Other factors influenced my decision to cut back on my publication efforts. When the Gale Management Information Guide Series was begun in 1963, and when the Gale Information Guide Library Series was launched in 1971, the market for bibliographic works was extensive. Libraries of all kinds were growing, and collection development was expanding apace. Reference book prices were modest. At the outset, a volume in the Management Information Guide Series sold for less than nine dollars. Time and inflation played a part to influence price increases. The cost for such books became prohibitive. Bibliographic titles were competing in a library market where acquisition budgets had not kept up with inflation. By the beginning of the 1980's, Gale Research focused on high-priced directories and large compilations. To continue the longstanding Management Information Guide Series and the Gale Information Guide Library Series was no longer economically viable. No new volumes were entered into the pipeline after 1981. Authors who were still engaged in preparing uncompleted volumes were informed that, due to market conditions, no additional works would be contracted for, but that books in progress would be published unless the author himself chose not to complete the effort. By the time the last volume of the Management Information Guide Series was issued in 1982, thirty-eight volumes had appeared. At the close of the Gale Information Guide Library Series in 1983, a little over two hundred books had been issued in twenty-one subject fields.

The Best of Times

The last of the Reader Series in Library and Information Science appeared in 1979, by which time twenty-four volumes had been published. It had started with Microcard Editions as the publisher. A merger brought the series to the National Cash Register Company. It finally ended up with Information Handling Services before being brought to a close.

In 1982, Fred Ruffner and I began serious discussions about having Gale Research Company assume control of the continuing reference titles I had developed since the 1960's. I wanted to reduce my efforts and lessen demands upon Effie Knight. We held back several titles, however, since neither Effie Knight nor I wanted to desist completely. During the 1970's, my son, Steven, and daughter, Jacqueline, also became active in working with us on several of the publications. I thought it prudent to retain copyright in some of the publications. After spending his early college years at New Mexico State University and at Northern Colorado State University, Steven returned home to graduate in recreation management from the University of Maryland in the mid-1970's. He decided that he liked working on reference book projects with me. Jacqueline had relocated to Maryland from California in the late 1970's; she too had become active working in my publishing efforts.

One book we retained was *Statistics Sources*, which by then was a biennial publication. It became an annual release not much later. Another title we held on to was *Law and Legal Information Directory*. It was first issued in 1980 and was intended for biennial updating. This was a source book offering details about the activities, institutions, agencies, and programs of concern to the American law profession. A third book was a 1982 title conceived by Steven, which he co-edited, called *Lively Arts Information Directory*. This work did not capture a large enough audience to warrant republication after the appearance of the first edition.

Fred Ruffner and I wanted to ensure continuity in the preparation of future editions of the books I would no longer work on. Through the years, I had worked with a number of individuals who were experienced in the editorial requirements of putting together the reference titles. Fred Ruffner asked me to identify those I felt were responsible enough to work directly with Gale Research Company as managing editors for the titles on which they had worked. The final contract was drawn up in December 1982. I relinquished copyright to Gale Research Company for the following books and their supplements: *Consultants and Consulting*; *Who's Who in Consulting*; *Awards, Honors, and Prizes*; *Training and Development Organizations*; *Consumer Source Book*; *Ethnic Information Sources*; *Commodity*

Prices; and the *Encyclopedia of Business Information Sources*. Janice McLean, who had been associated with me on a number of publications since her student days at the University of Maryland in the late 1960's, continued on as editor of *Consultants and Consulting Organizations* and *Training and Development Organizations*. Gita Siegman, another Maryland alumna, carried on with *Consumer Sourcebook* and *Awards, Honors, and Prizes*. James Woy, director of the Mercantile Library of the Free Library of Philadelphia, who had been an associate editor of the *Encyclopedia of Business Information Sources* since its inception, became its managing editor. With the suspension of work on so many publications by early 1983, the volume of effort at the Knight house was dramatically reduced. Effie Knight could readily handle the more limited scale of the continuing residual efforts. Linda Stemmy, who had been a valued secretarial assistant on a number of projects with us during a long period, left the office to continue in a similar capacity to work with Janice McLean.

I turned my attention to my non-publishing activities. In 1982, I accepted an invitation from Thiagarajan to serve as a member of the editorial advisory board of the *Indian National Information System for Science and Technology Newsletter*, or NISSAT. At that time, I was also involved in fund-raising efforts for the United States National Committee to support U.S. involvement in FID. It was not until 1985, however, that I became chairman of the National Committee and took personal responsibility for the fund-raising necessary to keep the U.S. from being expelled from FID for delinquent dues. I increased my efforts to encourage new authors to prepare works for the Greenwood Contribution Series during this time as well. A spate of new titles was published in the mid-1980's. I remained on the editorial board of the *Journal of Library Administration* until 1989. Once a year, I offered a seminar in inventing and designing information products and services. I concentrated heavily on adapting the framework and reading list for this course.

In the early spring of 1983, I received an invitation to present a paper in Brasilia at the Seventh Annual Meeting of the International Association of Agricultural Librarians and Documentalists. I was informed that the association had authorized my travel and that I would receive a formal invitation to participate from the Brazilian planning group. The invitation would enable me to get an entry visa from the Brazilian Consulate in Washington. I prepared the paper and reserved a flight, so that I would be in Brasilia well in advance of my Monday morning presentation. Several days before my departure I still had no formal invitation from Brazil. I telephoned the functionary in Brasilia responsible for arrangements and explained that I was due to fly out Saturday morning. He assured me that I would have the invitation in my hands before Friday. By Thursday noon, it still had not come. I tried telephoning Brasilia again but could not reach the person I had spoken to earlier. By Friday morning I still lacked authorization. I canceled my travel plans and dispatched my paper to Brasilia by air courier. The authorization finally arrived Monday morning at just about the same time my paper was being read at the conference by someone who had volunteered to present it in my absence. The title of the paper was "Technological Innovation in Information Transfer: Strategies of Information Management." It was later published in the meeting proceedings.

In fall of 1984 I made two trips to Europe. I went to the FID Conference in the Hague in September, where I gave a paper during the Education and Training Committee Workshop. It was titled "The Teacher's Challenge in Curriculum Planning and Implementation" and was published in the Conference Proceedings in 1985. More importantly, I represented the U.S. National Committee for FID in the meeting of the Executive Committee, where a discussion took place about the United States' delinquency in paying its dues for the past four years. I sought to explain our difficulties, but was ashamed and embarrassed by the fact that our affluent nation was in default, while far more impecunious countries were not. The Board was reluctant to expel the United States, but it felt that if our country continued to ignore its annual dues payment other nations would follow our example, and the FID would soon face bankruptcy. I was so moved by the concern and sympathies the group expressed for our plight that I made a promise to do everything in my power to ensure that the dues payment would be made again beginning in 1985. In October, I was in Paris for the UNESCO International Conference on Harmonization of Education Programs in Librarianship, Documentation and Archives. The report I had prepared as UNESCO consultant on teaching management became the basis for a full day's discussion.

I was elected chairman of the United States National Committee in January 1985. I served for four years, until the end of 1988. I mostly remember the term being taken up with the incessant need to solicit funds. Tied to the Dutch *guilder*, the United States' annual dues to FID fluctuated each year. FID had been established in Holland and was headquartered in the Hague. Our dues ranged between $17,000 and $20,000 a year. In the absence of a single source of funds, my task was to raise this amount from prospective contributors. I turned to companies in the information and publishing industries. I wrote to the chief executive officers of companies that did business with libraries and information centers whose activities bore some relationship to the fields in which FID was most active. Each individually composed letter explained the basis of the financial need and identified the importance to the United States, and to the company, of continued U.S. participation in FID. I underscored how the United States was being dishonored in the international information science community by failing to meet its dues obligation. I appealed to the officials' national pride. In follow-up calls to these executives, I asked for contributions toward the dues payment.

Those telephone conversations were very difficult for me to make. Sometimes I would receive a written response and was spared the need to make a call. As a rule, such letters were designed to save everyone's time by simply saying no. In a few instances, a written response included a small contribution from the company of fifty to one hundred dollars, or a promise that a check would follow. Sometimes, I simply could not get through to the appropriate person. After four or five unsuccessful tries, it became evident that I was *persona non grata* and that my call would not go through to the boss. The worst situations occurred when the potential donor sounded as if he thought that I personally would be the beneficiary of any contribution. For the most part, I received a polite and sympathetic hearing. The most generous donations were from company officers I had personally known and had worked with in the past. Every year during my fund-raising tenure, Fred Ruffner offered a generous contribution from Gale Research Company. Painstakingly, I succeeded in generating sufficient revenues to meet the dues obligation during each of the four years of my term of office.

In the summer of 1985, Krystyna and I were in Varna, Bulgaria. A conference was held there for several days to bring together representatives of the education and training committees of FID, IFLA, and ICA. The weekend before the sessions began we made a stopover in Sofia. I had first visited the city in 1972. Much had changed in the interim. There were many more automobiles in the streets, and the people seemed better dressed. Finding a meal in a restaurant or hotel proved a formidable undertaking, since most places were fully reserved for organized tour groups. We ate from outdoor stalls that sold hot and cold snacks and ice cream. I was fearful of what Varna might hold in store. My apprehension proved needless. The resort area on the Black Sea, where our meeting was held, was called Golden Sands. It was a suburb of Varna. The conference participants stayed in the International Journalists Center, an attractive, state-run holiday center for the country's literary and media elite. Mme. Todora Toplova, director of the State Library Institute in Sofia, was the local chairwoman in charge of the arrangements. The area was swarming with vacation travelers from Britain and

The Best of Times

Scandinavia. They came on budget flights to stay at the countless cottages and boarding houses. Mme. Toplova's political connections no doubt ensured that the meals we were served throughout our stay were delicious and bountiful. The country was experiencing extraordinary shortages of consumer products, most notably food, but we enjoyed an abundance of meat and red wine. High-level intervention must have been required for us to eat so well.

The conference chairperson was Miriam Tees of McGill University. A professor of management at the library school, she was active in the work of IFLA. The meeting emphasized the teaching of management. Yves Courrier, chief of the section for Training of Specialists and Users in UNESCO's General Information Program, brought his organization's perspective to the discussions. He emphasized the requirements of the non-industrialized countries. Michael Cook, a British archivist, expressed the views of the International Council of Archives. My paper presented the content of my report to UNESCO the previous fall. The meeting reinforced the commitment to collaborative effort toward unifying pedagogic methods and content in the educational preparation of information managers in both developing and developed nations.

The comforts and pleasures we experienced at the Communist-party-supported International Journalists Center were in sharp contrast to the grim shortages we observed and heard about on every side. When the protective barrier that separated us from the realities of life in Bulgaria was removed, the authoritarian life endured by the native population became painfully apparent. At the meeting I met a kindred spirit from Bulgaria. Lyuben Atanasov was a professor in the faculty of library and information science at the University of Sofia. Like myself, he saw how library scholars could contribute to the development of reference works. He showed me several important, widely used Bulgarian reference publications in the humanities that he had brought into being. Before returning to Washington, Krystyna and I enjoyed a brief sojourn in Athens and several days on the island of Mykonos. Again, we experienced the stark differences between conditions in the Soviet bloc countries and in the West. Once we got beyond the suspicious and surly airport officials in Sofia, the heavy weight of state control was left behind.

In 1985, a new library periodical, *Infomediary*, featured articles on innovation and new paths for the information field. I was invited to contribute to its first issue. My piece, "Invention and Development of Information Products and Services," appeared in Volume 1, Number 1. I explained in it the conceptual basis and rationalization for revising the role of librarians from reactive performance to proactive information producer. I also spelled out the methods and processes for creating original reference tools for clients.

After Gale Research had decided to bring an end to the Management Information Guide Series and the Gale Information Guide Library Series early in the eighties, no outlet existed for the continued publication of bibliographic information sources under an open-ended rubric. I was convinced, however, that there were still many important subjects for source books that would benefit students, researchers, and practitioners. What was lacking was a publishing firm with an interest in the library audience. Oryx Press in Phoenix had just begun to publish books aimed at the library market. I discussed my ideas with the company's president, Phyllis Steckler. She decided to launch a new Business and Management Source Book Series. I would serve as managing editor on the project. I also took on the responsibility for Oryx of identifying contributing editors who would develop other similar series in different subject fields. Our efforts were modeled after the Gale Information Guide Library. These publications appeared from 1985 through 1989. Nineteen titles appeared in the Business and Management Source Book Series. A small number of works in other subject fields were brought into print as well. Although market prospects seemed promising at the outset, both these publication programs were concluded in 1989. A thorough financial analysis of revenues from sales revealed that it was not possible to sustain the publication of such an extensive and continuing bibliographic enterprise. Oryx, like Gale Research, decided to discontinue these series.

The volume of activity devoted to preparing new editions of reference books was drastically diminished by the mid-eighties. Frequently revised reference titles were by then controlled by Gale Research Company. We did take responsibility for preparing the second edition of *Learning Independently* in 1982. The second edition of *Ethnic Source Book* was issued in 1983. The second edition of *Festivals Sourcebook* came out in 1984. Only two major reference works continued: *Statistics Sources* and *Law and Legal Information Directory*. By this time my son Steven, assisted by his sister Jacqueline, took over the editorial direction for both of these publications. Work on these projects continued at the Knight residence. Effie Knight still carried on in her role as office and production manager. On August 15, 1984, Effie Knight died suddenly of a heart attack.

Effie Knight had been my colleague and friend for many years. I was devastated by her death. We had worked harmoniously together with trust, respect, and affection on virtually every task I had taken on. I could not even imagine continuing on without her competent assistance. When I spoke at her memorial service at the University of Maryland Chapel, I sought to convey all she had meant to me and to the many others whom her life had touched profoundly. Still, life had to go on. It was some small comfort to know that, at the time of Effie's death, we had already given up responsibility for many of the more demanding book products. I resolved to avoid launching many more ambitious titles.

There was one idea, however, which I felt compelled to bring to fruition. I wanted to apply the strategy behind the widely used *Encyclopedia of Business Information Sources* to several other important subjects. Four new projects, therefore, were begun in 1985. I did not plan to continue any of these efforts beyond the preparation and publication of the first edition. I sought out librarian colleagues with the necessary background and subject knowledge to help me. Four books were brought out between 1986 and 1988. They were The *Encyclopedia of Health Information Sources*, 1986, Associate Editor: Suzanne Grefsheim; Assistant Editors: Lois Culler, Elaine Martin, Karen G. Smith, and Thomas E. Smith; *Encyclopedia of Senior Citizens Information Sources*, 1987, Associate Editors: Barbara Koehler and Yvonne Lev; *Encyclopedia of Public Affairs Information Sources*, 1987, Associate Editors: James Kelly and Desider Vikor; and *Encyclopedia of Legal Information Sources*, 1988, Associate Editors: Gary McCann and Patricia Tobin. The books were assigned to Gale Research Company for the publication of subsequent editions. My son, Steven, brought forth the *Encyclopedia of Physical Sciences and Engineering Information Sources*, which was first published by Gale Research in 1989. It has since been updated and reissued in later editions.

My service on the Screening Committee for the Fulbright program in the early 1980's whetted my own appetite for a Fulbright professorship abroad. When announcements from the Council for the International Exchange of Scholars were distributed in summer 1985, for the 1986-1987 academic year, I noted that the University of Kelaniya in Sri Lanka was looking for a professor of library administration. My knowledge of this small island nation south of India was negligible. All I knew was that it was an exotic, tropical country that might prove interesting for a semester of teaching. I submitted an application, but learned in the spring that I had not been selected. I decided to give myself a consolation prize; Krystyna and I would make a private journey to the Asian region. In order to qualify for the sabbatical leave, I had to plan an itinerary of lectures and professional visits. I decided to concentrate more on meetings with educators at educational institutions, rather than on scientific and technical information centers. I wrote to colleagues at library schools and at USIS library centers to let them know when I expected to be in their area. I heard back from many people and places; I was able to organize a schedule that mixed professional purposes with opportunities for tourism. Before heading west in the fall, I spent several days during the summer of 1986 in Mexico City. I worked there as a consultant for the International Atomic Energy Agency, planning a workshop for the agency's regional information centers in the hemisphere. The program concentrated on information center development and management. The workshop was later implemented under the direction of Eileen Goldstein.

I organized lecture materials for my sabbatical trip to Asia in advance. I was prepared to discuss a range of topical areas depending upon the particular interests of the host institutions. My travel itinerary began in Sydney near the end of September. There, we made short visits to the principal cities along the southern perimeter of Australia. In Sydney, I gave a two-day seminar at the School of Library and Information Studies of Kuring-gai College of Advanced Education, which was located in a suburb of the city. I met with faculty members and advanced master's students. The subjects treated were trends in library education and research in North American library education, and library administration. The session provided a useful orientation to the world of Australian library education. I found the students and faculty easily up to the American standard. They shared a keen interest in the subjects treated, a strong analytical approach, and a ready disposition to raise penetrating questions. We had ample time during our stay in Sydney to admire the majestic sweep of the celebrated Sydney Opera House and to take in the city's other scenic splendors during a three-hour harbor cruise.

Canberra was the second stop. During a brief stay we concentrated on the National Library, the congressional buildings, and the National Art Museum. Then we were on to Melbourne. At the Royal Melbourne Institute of Technology Library School I talked to two classes. It was a wide-ranging discussion, basing my remarks upon questions the students had been invited to suggest before and during my presentation. Melbourne had the cosmopolitan character of a European city with its handsome architecture and impressive new culture center. In Adelaide the architectural style was predominantly Victorian. Tony Foskett, who had been a visiting faculty member at Maryland in the 1970's, was the head of the South Australian Institute of Technology Department of Library Studies in Adelaide. During this visit, Foskett was away in Perth as a member of an accreditation team assessing the library school program. He arranged for his deputy to host my visit in his absence. I spoke there about the evolution and characteristics

The Best of Times

of special libraries in North America. Our last stop was Perth. Patricia Layzell Ward, director of the Western Australian Institute of Technology library education program, arranged for me to give a public lecture to the city's professional community, and for me to speak to students and faculty on the campus. My lecture at the school dealt with library administration, a subject in which Patricia Ward and I shared a common interest. I spoke to the library community about general directions in American library and information science.

The bright and booming city of Perth seemed like California a century earlier — when everything was before it and nothing would be impossible to achieve. The perennial blue sky and sunshine were reflected in the friendliness of the people, who all seemed expectant and optimistic. The Western Australian Institute of Technology had already embarked on a distance education program that offered instruction to students in the farthest northern regions of the province. The program was well in advance of such comparable library education efforts anywhere else in the world. We drove with Pat Ward and her husband, Geoffrey, to a regional park. There we observed up close the antics of kangaroos and koala bears in their natural habitat.

Travel plans following Australia called for some days of pure tourism. Krystyna and I flew from Perth to the airport in Denpasar to meet my sister and her husband. We met there for a vacation in Bali. We passed an idyllic time attending music and dance performances, tasting exotic dishes, visiting picturesque villages, and marveling at the striking beauty and artistic talent of the native people. We could not resist buying many more colorful artifacts than our luggage could hold. We had to buy a huge, oversized suitcase to hold our newly discovered precious finds. The feverish buying of enticing Balinese souvenirs obliged us to check part of our luggage at each airport along the rest of our route in order to avoid dragging heavy bags to each hotel.

We flew on to Jakarta. Marilyn and her husband, Ed, joined us in Jakarta two days later. I had a speaking engagement at the American Center, and I was also expected to go to the library school at the University in Jakarta. A university faculty member drove us to see a miniature version of each of the Indonesian provinces in a large tourist complex outside the city. Dance, theater, and other native performances were presented in pavilions modeled after the architectural style of each region. At the American Center, the indigenous USIS librarian arranged for me to deliver a public lecture to members of the library community on the American library scene. After the serenity of Bali, Jakarta was something of a shock. Its teeming crowds and traffic congestion rivaled Mexico City. Highlights of our stay included the extraordinary meals and the striking exhibits on display at the Indonesian National Museum, which depicted every facet of the country's past.

By the time we reached our next stop in Singapore, I was viewing the world from behind a tissue. A heavy cold made my nose drip and my eyes tear ceaselessly. The only consolation was that we were going to stay at the venerable Raffles Hotel. When we arrived we found this landmark hotel in crumbling disrepair. It was soon to be demolished to make way for a luxury high-rise. While the other three made the tourist rounds, I nursed a disabling fever and cold. I lay propped up in a giant bed in the Somerset Maugham Suite. I remained there swilling enormous bowls of piping hot chicken soup that were delivered hourly by a doting room service waiter. He looked old enough to have served the youthful Maugham half a century earlier. I was well enough to imbibe a vastly overrated Raffles "gin sling" in the decadent, colonial lounge before our bus trip to Malacca in Malaysia. There, we peeked at historic remains from the Portuguese imperial period through heavy sheets of rain that came pouring down throughout our visit to the famous port area. We arrived next in Kuala Lumpur. This city proved a genuine surprise with its surfeit of ultramodern hotels and office complexes; the awesomely resplendent National Mosque; and the immaculate condition of its streets. The city's antiseptic modernity and seeming economic abundance were in stark contrast to the conditions that prevailed in other parts of the region. From Kuala Lumpur we flew to Penang on the western coast of the Malay Peninsula. The Eastern and Oriental hotel was an establishment with a rich storied past, but unlike the Raffles, it had been carefully maintained to retain its classic features. Our splendidly appointed room boasted a balcony overlooking the terrace with a view of the sea. We spent a couple of days luxuriating in these handsome quarters and toured the local attractions in a hired car. Our Chinese driver told us about brutal assaults on the large Chinese community during the nationalist uprisings of the past. From Penang we went on to Bangkok. Our tourist-class flight with Thai Airlines lasted just under an hour. In that brief time, we were plied with cocktails and served a delicious meal followed by after-dinner liqueurs.

The Erewan Hotel was our stopping point in Bangkok. In October 1986 this was a grand and centrally located establishment with huge lounges, wide corridors, and spacious rooms. It had a rich past but a short future. It was soon to be torn down to make way for still another modern, luxury hotel that would be indistinguishable from all the others rising across the city's skyline. Cynthia Borys, the regional USIS librarian, had arranged for me to lecture at the American Center to students and faculty from several universities. She also planned a reception and dinner at the famed Oriental Hotel. I met a dozen leaders of Thai librarianship and formed associations that I pursued during subsequent visits to the country. Krystyna and I had first visited Bangkok in January 1981. Since then, it had been a favorite place to stay. We made a three-day trip to Chiang Mai in the north. We frequented all the tourist attractions and accumulated more souvenirs to add to our already burgeoning burden. I let myself be coerced into mounting an elephant with Krystyna, who shamed me into it by pointing out an ancient Chinese woman riding atop another elephant. We wobbled along uncomfortably for a few hundred yards through dense, tropical foliage.

From Bangkok my brother-in-law, Ed, returned directly to the United States. My sister continued on with us to Hong Kong. Barry Burton, from the Hong Kong Polytechnic Institute Library, planned a full-day workshop under the auspices of the Hong Kong Library Association. An audience of sixty senior and middle managers from academic and special libraries came to hear me give an abbreviated version of the Maryland Library Administrators Development course. There was sufficient time during this stay to revisit the colorful street markets and enjoy the ethnic neighborhoods. We also took a ferry ride across the water and rode the funicular to the highest point. In Kowloon, we admired the picturesque views from the waterfront near our hotel. Cynthia Borys alerted Lynne Martin, the U.S. cultural affairs officer in the American consulate in Taipei, to the dates of our visit. She organized a luncheon at the Taiwan Library Association, where I met the directors of the university libraries and the heads of both library schools in the Taipei area. During a visit to the National Taiwan University, I learned about the library science education program from its chairman, James Hu. I also spent a day at Tamkang University, where Shih Hsion Wang, professor of educational media and library sciences and director of university libraries, demonstrated the advanced level of some of the library school's technical offerings. A special treat was a tour of the newly constructed National Library by Dr. Wang, its librarian. Lynne Martin also arranged for us to see a colorful performance of Chinese opera. In addition, we managed two trips to the Chinese National Museum to view its remarkable collection.

In Taipei we had rooms on an upper story of the high-rise Ambassador Hotel. In the middle of the night we were awakened by a strong shaking and rocking of the bed. The walls swayed. A strong earthquake had rattled the building. By this time my sister came in wearing her bathrobe. We wondered how severe the damage was and whether we were at risk on that very high floor. Fearful of taking the elevator, we walked down twenty flights of stairs to the lobby. No one was there, only one man calmly mopping the entry hall floor. When we approached the registration desk to make inquiry a clerk appeared to inform us in a very relaxed manner that, yes, it had been an earthquake, but this was a common occurrence and nothing to be alarmed about. Sheepishly, we returned by elevator up to our rooms and tried to go back to sleep. During breakfast at a restaurant near our hotel several hours later, there was more shaking. The floor beneath our feet and our table rocked as Taipei experienced the aftereffects of the first quake. No one in the restaurant seemed concerned. The effect of this incident, however, was to make the weather during the rest of our stay highly unstable. There were high winds and ceaseless, torrential rain during the remaining days.

In Seoul, Myung Soon Park arranged my professional program. Myung Soon had been a visiting scholar at Maryland from the Ewha Womens University Library School, where she was a faculty member. Another Korean colleague was Pongsoon Lee, from the faculty of the Korean Women's University. She served with me as the Korean member of the Education and Training Committee of FID. Both women planned occasions for me to address the student bodies of their schools. Myung Soon arranged several social events, including dinner at Korea House on our first evening, where we were introduced to Korean cuisine and folk entertainment. She also assisted us in planning an excursion to the picturesque city of Kyonju. We were introduced to the spicy national dish, *kimchi*, and to ginseng, an herb believed to ensure enduring health and well-being.

On our way home, we made a short stopover in Hawaii. In Honolulu we stayed in the heart of Waikiki's tourist district near the sea. Lee Putnam, who had been my Ph.D. advisee, was an administrative staff member of the University of Hawaii library. She arranged for me to visit the University's Library School. I gave a lecture on library administration to the student body. Miles Jackson, dean of the school, suggested that I might like to teach in the school's summer session. I would later take up this invitation.

Chapter Nineteen

We returned to Washington at the end of November. Awaiting me was a letter from the Fulbright Commission informing me that my application for a Fulbright professorship to Sri Lanka, which had not been approved for fall 1986, was granted for the spring term of 1987. It took some scurrying about to have my sabbatical leave extended for the full academic year. I was ready to leave in January 1987. This time I traveled alone. Krystyna was in the process of shifting from part-time duties to a full-time role as director of the Library and Research Center of the National Museum of Women in the Arts. The museum was scheduled to move into its new building in the spring. En route to Colombo in early January I stopped overnight in Paris. I planned to see the new Musee d'Orsay, which had recently opened on the Left Bank. A winter snowstorm that crippled Washington just after my departure had already left the Paris region buried under deep snowdrifts. I spent the night at an airport hotel; there was no chance of getting into the city before I had to fly to Sri Lanka.

My assignment in Sri Lanka was to serve as professor in the library education program of the University of Kelaniya. This large institution was located in an outer suburb of the capital city. I was to offer instruction in library administration and other subjects as needed. I arrived on a Friday and was met by a chauffeur from the United States Center, where the Fulbright program was headquartered. He drove me to a modest hotel where a reservation had been made for me. I was on my own until Monday morning. I was weary from my long trip and disoriented by the time difference — Colombo is almost exactly half way around the world from Washington. It was not until Saturday that I ventured forth to explore my environs. My temporary quarters had been chosen for their inexpensive rates. I resolved to move elsewhere as rapidly as I could to escape the close space of my room, which was damp and pungent. Along the city streets I came upon colorful shop fronts and busy throngs. The people were strikingly attractive, slim and brown-skinned. I spent most of Saturday walking everywhere. I covered two miles along the main thoroughfare, alongside the sea, to the central downtown district. I took my meals in restaurants at the larger hotels facing the ocean or in the numerous eating establishments along the main street. The native languages were Singhalese and Tamil, but virtually everyone understood and spoke English as consequence of the more than a century of British rule. I ventured into the great municipal market district and walked the long stretch of sandy oceanfront, where local families relaxed by flying giant kites that were shaped like birds or other animals. The weather was warm and humid with a slight breeze off the water. The sky was a cloudless blue, and the sun shone brightly. The pace was unhurried and languid. I had the pleasurable feeling of having found my way to a south Asian version of Latin America.

At the United States Center on Monday, my main concern during discussions with Bogoda Premaratne, the Fulbright director, was to find a suitable, furnished accommodation. By a stroke of good fortune, another American Fulbright professor had just vacated an apartment to move down the coast. The apartment was on the upper floor of a private house owned by one of the secretaries at the center and her husband. It was located in a good neighborhood. It had been constructed as an addition to the house and was expressly intended for rental to foreign visitors. It was described as being fully furnished with a modern kitchen and a bathroom with a shower. There was a living room and a bedroom with air conditioning. The apartment had its own private entrance. The rent was expensive by Colombo standards, but it sounded ideal, and after a weekend in an uncomfortable hotel room, I was keen to see it and move at once. The secretary said that I could see it right after my talk with Mr. Premaratne.

During my talk with Premaratne, I learned that Kelaniya University, like several other major academic centers in the country, was undergoing marked unrest. The students were boycotting Kelaniya University, causing the temporary suspension of classes. I was supposed to meet the next day with the Vice Chancellor and Professor Jaya Lankage, head of the library education program and director of the university library. Following that meeting, Premaratne and I were to drive to Kandy to see Cyril Ponnamperuma, director of the Institute for Fundamental Study. I had met with Ponnamperuma in 1986 on the Maryland campus, where we first discussed the possibility of my Fulbright professorship. A perpetual world traveler, Ponnamperuma divided his time between the University of

Maryland, where he held an appointment as professor of chemistry and biochemistry, and Sri Lanka where he served as science advisor to the president and director of the Institute for Fundamental Study. Were I to come to Sri Lanka, he hoped I would accept an appointment as visiting scientist at the institute. I would serve as a consultant to help develop an advanced scientific and technical information center at Kandy. The center would be a model for developing regions of the world. When I accepted the Fulbright for the spring term, I called to inform Ponnamperuma of my anticipated arrival in January.

By Monday evening I had moved into an attractive and comfortable new apartment. My favorite furnishing there was a high-powered short-wave radio, which brought in BBC, Voice of America, and Radio Moscow. The apartment had a modern kitchen where I could prepare my breakfast. On the days when I was in Colombo, the friendly secretary who had become my landlady agreed to send up dinner for me for a modest amount. The household servant, who brought my dinner, also cleaned the apartment. I was able to buy fresh pineapples, bread, juices, and bottled water at a quaint looking corner shop nearby. Fulbright professors enjoyed shopping privileges at the United States Embassy's duty-free store. There, I could buy packaged foods, bathroom products, and wine. Colombo also boasted a couple of large, Western-style supermarkets that stocked American, Japanese, and German products. Transportation posed some problems. Most Fulbright professors who had come in the fall bought or leased cars to use during their stay. I was reluctant to drive in Colombo's melee of bikes, motorcycles, cars, trucks, and buses and I was still uncertain about my specific travel needs.

On Tuesday Premaratne and I spent over an hour in heavy city traffic before reaching the University of Kelaniya. The Vice Chancellor and Lankage greeted me warmly. They expressed pleasure to have me at the university and apologized for the disarray on campus. The student unrest was explained as a manifestation of the general malaise sweeping through the country, the result of the years-long struggle going on between the country's military forces and insurgents in the northern and eastern regions. I learned a great deal about the conflict between the majority Singhalese Buddhist community and the Tamil Hindu minority. Tensions between them were tearing the country apart. It was not clear whether the differences between students and administration would be resolved to permit the early resumption of classes. I was encouraged to go to Kandy where I could contribute more usefully to the institute's program. I would return to the campus late in the week and meet with Lankage to plan my teaching program.

The Best of Times

The drive to Kandy took us from the coastal plain over one hundred kilometers of a winding, two-lane highway. We made our way through towns, farmland, and tea plantations at the lower elevations, and then up into the hill country, where the city of Kandy was situated 1,700 feet above sea level. Two centuries earlier Kandy had been the capital of the indigenous people of Sri Lanka. The town surrounded a small artificial lake. The Institute for Fundamental Study was made up of a complex of buildings that housed offices, laboratories, and a limited number of living quarters. It was located high on a hill overlooking the city. The staff of well-qualified researchers from Sri Lanka and a number of other countries was augmented by visiting scholars who came for shorter stays to lecture, do research, or consult. The center was a community unto itself, supported by a staff of office personnel and building and grounds keepers. There were dining facilities, a small technical library, and a motor pool. There was a plan to reconstruct some space into hotel rooms for visitors. This work, however, would not be completed during my stay. I stayed on an extra two days to meet and talk with the scientists in residence. Premaratne returned to Colombo. I took a room at the historic Queens Hotel, which was near the site where the supposedly authentic tooth of Buddha was kept on public display. This relic was carried through the streets during the annual ceremonial procession of the Perihera on a mid-summer night of the full moon. Ponnamperuma was happy to have me spend several days each month at the institute working toward the establishment of an advanced information center. This library facility would be planned to take advantage of the latest technological advances in information retrieval. Its director would be an information specialist with a background in science and someone who would be seen by the center's scientists as a professional peer. While I was in the country, Ponnamperuma hoped I would inform the academic and research community on the latest developments in information retrieval in the sciences. He asked me, therefore, to deliver a public lecture in March in Colombo under the sponsorship of the Sri Lankan National Academy of Sciences. I enthusiastically accepted this invitation, especially in light of the fact that my teaching role at the university was likely to be limited by continuing student unrest.

Back in the capital, I spent some time at the United States Center, where the USIS library, directed by an indigenous librarian, formed part of the complex of offices and buildings. I kept in touch with Lankage by telephone and made two or three visits to his office at the university, where the library operation continued even while classes were suspended. Together, Lankage and I visited the major libraries and information centers in the Colombo area. These were university libraries, special libraries, research centers, and the Congressional Library. I also indicated my willingness to talk with professional library groups, if suitable programs could be arranged. Without regular classes to teach, I informed Premaratne that I was available to serve as a consultant to the directors of libraries who might find my background and experience useful. I ended up with an active schedule of special programs, conferences, and seminars. These took me to different sections of the country where I was able to work with a wide cross-section of the library community. Lankage's ambition was for Kelaniya to offer the first graduate program in library and information science in the country. I worked with him to prepare the design and then to participate in its formal presentation to the governmental body that would consider it for approval.

Finally, two weeks after my arrival, it looked as if I could begin offering instruction. There seemed to be a lull in the administration/student conflict. The library school students were more concerned with their professional study than with any political agenda, so Lankage announced the start of the course in library administration. At the first session I found myself in a large lecture hall with only forty students. Just as I was ready to start, a young man came into the hall. He beckoned me to one side of the platform. In a polite, quiet tone he told me that if the class were to continue, I would be putting everyone at risk of a bomb being thrown into the room. Then he left. Lankage was sitting in the audience; I told him what had been said. He shrugged, arose, and resignedly informed the audience that class was being canceled because of a threat from the student movement. The students slowly shuffled out of the room. This was the last time I spent time in a university class during my entire semester in Sri Lanka.

As the weeks went by, my days were spent working with different library groups in Colombo and in nearby regions. Transportation was usually by inexpensive motorbike taxi, very much like those that scoot around the streets in Bangkok. I could walk to the U.S. Center in half an hour. To reach the city center, I took the bus. When I needed to travel to institutions near the city, Premaratne's driver would take me. My visits to Kandy were arranged with the Colombo office of the Institute for Fundamental Study. A car for the institute went back and forth several times weekly. I got used to the spicy Sri Lankan food and delighted my landlady when I told her how much I enjoyed the meals she sent up to my apartment. Parts of the country remained in a state of violence during early 1987. There were frequent military skirmishes that continued regularly in the north between the army and the armed separatists known as the Tamil Tigers.

Atrocities were committed by both sides; torture, bombings, executions, even the massacre of whole villages were a regular occurrence. This had little visible effect on the population of Colombo. For them, the terrors seemed very distant, but student unrest and lockouts continued. The BBC accounts conveyed a truer sense of conditions in the country than did the optimistic, government-controlled stories in the Colombo newspaper. Life proceeded as usual. Security measures, however, were everywhere in evidence. Each vehicle entering the U.S. Center compound underwent a thorough examination of its interior and undercarriage.

By mid-March I prepared my paper and presented it in Colombo to more than one hundred members of the scientific community from academic and research institutions. It was titled, "Information Transfer in Science and Technology." In it, I examined the evolution of scientific communication methods, provided a framework for understanding the different elements of the primary and secondary reporting mechanisms for new research findings, and characterized the advantages and disadvantages of traditional and newer information technologies. I explained the direction that new retrieval systems were taking and how they could open public channels to propel scientific and social progress. I suggested that an important consequence of the newest electronic retrieval tools would be greater parity in access to current research intelligence between developed and developing regions of the world. A somewhat revised version of this paper appeared in *Asian Libraries*, September 1991, as "Information Transfer in Science and Technology: An Overview."

In the absence of regular classroom teaching, I made frequent trips to Kandy to plan the model information system for the institute. I also corresponded with foundations and inter-governmental bodies to solicit financial support for this enterprise. These obligations left me with quite a bit of free time. I read many books from the U.S. Center library collection and spent the weekends absorbing the colorful spectacle of Colombo.

In New Delhi, Donald Hausrath, who was during this period director of the USIS library program in India, proposed that I take part in a lecture tour in the spring. The tour was to be sponsored by officials of the Speakers and Artists Program in the American Participants Program in India. While his recommendation to the program was being reviewed, he faxed me to suggest that I seek approval from the U.S. Cultural Affairs Officer in Colombo for the trip to India. It was unclear whether classes in Colombo would resume when I made my request in early February. A long spring recess customarily took place in Sri Lankan educational institutions, so I arranged my dates for this holiday period in early April. Immediate approval was granted. There were concerns about exactly what the Fulbright professors were accomplishing while their universities were shut down — a lecture tour was viewed as a positive contribution that would be credited to the Sri Lankan Fulbright program. Support came soon thereafter from USIS India and I immediately faxed Hausrath a list of topics on which I would be prepared to speak. The most formidable barrier came when I attempted to obtain a visa from the Indian consulate in Colombo and made the mistake of identifying the specific purpose of my trip. To gain admission to India I was obliged to misrepresent myself. I withdrew my original application and resubmitted the visa request stating that my purpose was tourism. I received my visa approval only one week before my scheduled departure.

As soon as my plane landed in Madras, I knew that the vacation was over. Hausrath had arranged such a tightly scheduled program, I felt as if I were in perpetual motion. Nevertheless, the Indian tour turned out to be one of the most stimulating overseas professional efforts I had yet experienced. On my first Indian assignment in January 1981, I had constantly witnessed the undernourished and sickly people. This time I was insulated from the sight of such desperate scenes. As a State Department sponsored lecturer, I received VIP treatment. A succession of public affairs and program officers of USIS carefully sheltered me, virtually every step of the way, from seeing the abject misery. I was met at airports, escorted to speaking engagements and meetings, and spent little time walking about. I mostly traveled in an oversized American car. Reservations had been made for me at some of the most attractive hotels in the country. I took almost every meal in the company of USIS officials, local librarians, academics, or other interesting people.

My itinerary took me on a circular route to the four USIS posts: Madras, Calcutta, New Delhi, and Bombay. Each group, center, association, and academic institution that I addressed along the way requested lectures, seminars, or informal presentations based on their particular area of interest. Their choices formed the basis for the subjects I would treat. The topics I proposed were: Management Issues and Trends in Information Science; Invention and Design of Information Products and Services; Business and Economic Information Systems; Trends in Library and Information Science Education; and the Information Communication and Transfer Process in Science and Technology. In Madras I spoke at the

The Best of Times

Department of Library and Information Science of the University of Madras and at the American Center. In Bangalore, I lectured at the National Aeronautical Laboratory. In collaboration with the faculty of the Documentation Research and Training Center, directed by Professor Bhattacharya, I participated in an all-day seminar. In Calcutta, I spoke to the student body of the Department of Library Science of Jadavpur University. At the National Library in Calcutta, I also addressed the membership of the Bengal Library Association. I spoke at the American Center there as well. While in Delhi, I addressed the students and faculty of the Department of Library and Information Science of the University of Delhi, and gave a seminar to the Indian National Scientific Documentation Center.

From Delhi, Hausrath and I traveled to Chandigarh. I offered a two-day workshop at the University of Chandigarh for students and faculty at the invitation of Mrs. A. K. Anand, the director of the university library. After returning to Delhi, I flew on to Bombay to speak at the U.S. Center before going by train to Poona, where I gave a two-day seminar for local librarians at the University of Poona. I flew the next day to Madras where I boarded my return flight to Colombo. When I returned from Poona to Bombay, I read a gruesome account in the newspaper of a bombing of the central market in Colombo that had occurred the day before, on Wednesday. The explosion killed an untold number of people estimated to be in the hundreds. The disaster was attributed to Tamil insurgents as a tactical device to draw some of the military forces away from the north and back into the capital city. Colombo was under martial law, and a curfew was in effect from dusk to daybreak. This was upsetting news to learn on the eve of my return to Colombo. My arrival time was eight o'clock in the evening. I was uncertain whether or not, under the changed circumstances, the limousine I had arranged for would be at the airport. Armed soldiers surrounded my plane as soon as it landed. It was clear that routine security measures had been ratcheted up several notches. Fortunately, the driver was waiting for me. He was very apprehensive about being abroad in the city after dark. My words of reassurance about how essential travel could not be viewed as an infraction against the curfew did little to mollify him. As we drove into the city we were waved down and scrutinized twice by nervous young soldiers. When we reached my apartment at around eleven o'clock, I suggested to the driver that he could sleep in my living room until morning. He declined the offer. He was afraid that his family would become too distressed if he were gone for so long. My overly generous tip was not enough to buoy his spirits when he left.

The Best of Times

That weekend, the city was exceptionally quiet. Most people remained in their homes. My landlady informed me that at the American Center there was grave concern about whether any United States nationals had been in the market when the bomb went off. Attempts had been made by the embassy staff on Thursday and Friday to contact every American known to be in the country. My absence was a source of consternation, until the Fulbright director reported that I was in India. When the final count was completed, it appeared that no known United States citizens were among the missing. Early the next week, the embassy invited all the Americans working in the Colombo region to a meeting. We were informed of contingency plans to evacuate all U.S. citizens on an American naval vessel if the situation were to deteriorate into armed insurgency. For several more days, Colombo remained in a dazed state as the estimates of the dead and missing from the bombing mounted. After a week, the military occupation and curfew were lifted. Life returned to a more normal state. I had once taken a scenic rail journey through the hill country between Kandy and Colombo before the bomb blast. Several weeks later a bomb went off on the tracks, causing the train to derail. A number of passengers were killed and injured. Non-natives were not the targets of this random violence, but it seemed highly advisable to stay clear of obvious targets and crowded areas.

In early May, Frank Hogg from the University of Aberystwyth, arrived in Colombo for a ten-day assignment as a British Council consultant to the National Public Library Board. We took advantage of his stay to organize together a two-day conference in Colombo for the country's public and academic librarians. The conference was held under the auspices of the Sri Lankan Library Association. The subject of the symposium was library administration. It drew a large audience to the Colombo Conference Center. Before leaving Sri Lanka, I joined Premaratne to travel south on a tour. I visited with several university library directors and university presidents.

My tour of duty in Sri Lanka ended in May. I had managed to work with many members of the library community, even though my Fulbright assignment to offer university classes had proved impossible. My efforts on behalf of the Institute for Fundamental Study in Kandy became the basis for a continued association between the institute and the College of Library and Information Services at Maryland. The planning I carried out with Lankage in Colombo yielded a framework for the graduate education offering in library and information science at Kelaniya. Strong ties had also been formed with many special and academic librarians in the country. In spite of the depressing effect of the continued violence, I came away with a deep respect for the quality of Sri Lankan intellectual discourse, and for the high level of its cultural and artistic attainments. The only sorrow of my sojourn was that such a lush and enchanting island nation of well-educated, attractive people was becoming so hopelessly mired in a ceaseless armed struggle.

On my return journey to the United States I stopped long enough in Bangkok to take off on an eight-day tour of Burma. Arthur Vespry, librarian of the Asian Institute of Technology, helped to arrange the trip for me while I had been in Colombo. Burma was under the control of an authoritarian military junta. The repressive hand of the rulers was everywhere in evidence. The country appeared to be in a time warp. All the buildings I saw looked as if they had been built many decades earlier during colonial rule. They were in a state of neglect and decay. The nation was totally isolated from the outside world. Personal freedom and human rights were non-existent. Yet the people were among the most beautiful I had seen anywhere in Asia. The splendors of the pagodas were unrivaled. The celebrated Shwedegon Pagoda in Rangoon, with its world-famous golden *stupa*, was especially breath-taking.

My itinerary included Rangoon, Pagan, Mandalay, Heho, and Taunggyi. The sorrowful conditions of life in Burma reminded me of wartime and early postwar Europe. There were severe shortages and a ubiquitous black market. The travel agency literature suggested that: "You should be aware that everything is marketable in Burma." It even set forth the black market prices for cigarettes, scotch, a bar of soap, and a package of aspirin. I eagerly looked forward to viewing the fabled sights of Burma, but left saddened by the plight of its people. Back in Bangkok, I stayed on the campus of the Asian Institute of Technology in the city's suburbs. I lectured there for five days to librarians in residence for a several-week-long regional workshop for information personnel. Vespry was offering the workshop on a regular annual basis. I used the same repertoire of topics as I had in India. Twenty individuals from special libraries in countries of Southeast Asia participated. From Bangkok, I returned to Washington with a brief overnight stay in Hawaii to ease the shock of the time change.

I had been back in my office only a couple of weeks when John Sherrod invited me to collaborate with him on a project with Volunteers in Technical Assistance (VITA). The United States Agency for International Development (AID), sponsored the project. Henry Norman, president of the organization, wanted an outside evaluation of the effectiveness of VITA's work, to be prepared by end of September 1987. VITA had been serving as a private, voluntary organization providing development assistance for nearly thirty years. A combination of information services, consultancies, training programs, and publications were offered at no charge to recipients throughout the Third World. AID wanted VITA to decrease its reliance on government support and to seek funding from outside sources. Sherrod and I were appointed as an external evaluation team to carry out the study from July to September 1987. The analysis included thorough briefings by VITA and AID staff. An on-site Washington review of VITA records and procedures, along with telephone interviews with a random group of VITA volunteer experts, were also undertaken. Interviews with selected recipients and users of VITA's services were carried out as well. Sherrod and I divided the on-site visits. He went to Thailand, while I traveled to Djibouti and Lusaka, Zambia. We also conducted discussions with officials of other non-governmental, international development organizations in Washington and in the field.

I traveled from mid-August to early September. Djibouti was the hottest place I had ever experienced on the planet. Leaving my air-conditioned room at the Hotel Plein Ciel, where the temperature never went below eighty degrees Fahrenheit, I felt as if I was stepping into a steam room. The highlight of my stay was a site visit to witness a development project in which a waste oil kiln had been developed with VITA information by a VITA volunteer. It represented the practical, operational outcome of a VITA-invented product that had been installed and placed in service and that was continuing to be managed by a volunteer. I spent several days in discussions and outdoor field trips. A stopover in Addis Ababa, en route to Lusaka, afforded me a welcome respite from the heat. I enjoyed the high-altitude breezes eight thousand feet above sea level. In Zambia, I was again impressed to see how information in a VITA publication had been transformed into a useful project for building low-cost housing by using inexpensive, indigenous materials. The professionalism of VITA resident staffs and volunteers in both countries, working under often vexing and demanding conditions, gave me a deep respect for their accomplishments. Sherrod and I found that VITA's services were far better known and appreciated in the developing world and international organization circles than they were in Washington. In our report we made a number of recommendations, and concluded that AID should reconsider its move to reduce support of VITA. It seemed unlikely that any other development program supported by AID at that time could generate as much widespread attention and develop so much good will for the United States. The program offered diverse forms of beneficial technical assistance to the developing regions of the world.

August 1987 marked the passing of someone who had toiled at my side during the exciting early years of the Maryland library education program. From the mid-1980's, Mary Lee Bundy suffered from acute emphysema. Before then, in spite of her outward appearance of frailty and physical weakness, Mary Lee had demonstrated her strength by laboring ceaselessly on innumerable causes. Her activism led to her recognition as librarianship's unquestioned leader in the cause of social and political justice. She never had the time or the patience to eat well, and she smoked incessantly. She continued almost to the end to write and speak out courageously. Her career in library education remains a testament to a devout belief that librarianship and libraries could not, and should not, be bereft of conscience. She was the colorful, articulate, energetic, and impassioned spirit behind the High John project, the Congress for Change, and library service to the disadvantaged and prisoners. She carried the banner in every battle, empowered by an urgent personal need to transform the field from the role of disinterested bystander to an activist and partisan role. Her disciples at Maryland and across the land were, and still are, countless. My personal association with Mary Lee grew tenuous in the early 1970's. Our personal goals diverged, and she felt that I had deserted the causes that propelled her until the very end of her life. We never lost respect for one another. In her waning months both of us sought and found again many of the common bonds that had first brought us together as colleagues and good friends. Many former students, practicing librarians, and others, whose work and whose lives had been influenced profoundly by her views, attended the memorial service on the Maryland campus.

Upon completing the VITA study, I accepted an appointment to become a member of the Advisory Committee for the Agency for International Development's Research and Reference Service in AID's Center for Development Information and Evaluation. These efforts were carried out as a contract program by the Academy for Educational Development. Over a five-year period, this Committee offered recommendations to the management of the AID library on its role in the provision of information products, services, technical assistance, and training to AID missions around the world. During this assignment, I enhanced my understanding of AID's priorities in meeting the information needs faced by AID specialists working in developing countries. I also strengthened my association with Maury Brown, Chief of Development Information at AID. He came regularly to the campus to meet with my seminar in international library and information science. He lectured on the changing issues that faced AID in its efforts to provide overseas research and information support.

Even though many of the reference projects I had carried out for Gale Research Company were no longer my responsibility, I continued to maintain my personal relationship with Fred Ruffner. Around 1985 Gale was sold to Thomson International, a Canadian based, international publishing conglomerate. Fred Ruffner's active involvement with Gale ended soon thereafter. Instead of turning to leisure after his long and productive life in publishing, Ruffner launched Omnigraphics, a new reference and media company headquartered in Detroit. Although his interests remained divided between the private Ruffner Foundation, Friends of the Library U.S.A., and Friends of the Library in the state of Florida, he applied himself vigorously to establishing the new firm. By the beginning of 1988, Ruffner engaged me in an editorial and research consulting capacity. I helped him in this role through 1991. Omnigraphics published a compendium titled *Privatization* in 1988. A number of source books were also published under the company's imprint. The first edition of *Moving and Relocation Sourcebook* appeared in 1992. My son Steven, in collaboration with Diane Barlow of the Maryland faculty, edited the book, while I served as an editorial advisor. In 1988, I also became a member of the editorial board of *Behavioral and Social Science Librarian*.

With the exception of the time I taught for brief periods at the University of Michigan and Western Reserve University in the 1960's, all my library school teaching experience in the United States had been at the University of Maryland. I often wondered what differences there might be in working with graduate students at other American library schools. During July and August of 1988, I had the opportunity to find out. I offered summer-term courses at the University of Hawaii, in Honolulu. I also accepted an invitation from Vespry at the Asian Institute of Technology and participated once more in his regional workshop in Bangkok.

In June of 1988, I spent five days at the Asian Institute of Technology. In 1986 I had offered a one-day management seminar to members of the Hong Kong Library Association. Dr. Kann, the director of the University Library, and of the program in library education at the University of Hong Kong, invited me to revisit Hong Kong in June 1988 to give a seminar for the students at her university. In Hong Kong, I gave a two-day course. The audience consisted of practicing librarians who were pursuing their studies while holding down full time posts in Hong Kong's public, academic, and special libraries. I occupied a room in the visiting faculty quarters for three nights. The university, itself, is located high at the top of a winding road. Its residential facility was perched at the edge of an imposing cliff, which towered over the university. From my room I could see the city far below, its harbor alive with colorful vessels. At night the city was a sea of twinkling lights beneath me. Myriad stars in the sky seemed near enough to touch. I felt as if I occupied some magical realm on the towering cliff.

By early July I was in Honolulu to start classes in library administration and business information services. My accommodation in Honolulu was a tastefully furnished, high-rise apartment with a balcony. I had sublet the apartment from a university faculty member. It overlooked a scenic canal and was equally distant between the university campus and the tourist area in Waikiki. My classes included students from the United States mainland, Hawaii, and the Asian and Pacific region. In many ways, this cross-cultural mix was similar to the groups I customarily found registered for my international seminar at Maryland. The students shared the same manner of dress and speech and ranged in age from their early twenties to middle age. The six-week term, with weekend outings around the island of Oahu and a visit to the scenic island of Kauai, gave me a more realistic sense of life in Hawaii. My prior visits had been for relaxation following protracted periods of work and long journeys from the Orient. Those short stays had an aura of romance. The scenic attractions made Hawaii seem the perfect place for a permanent home. Living there for six weeks, I came to appreciate how expensive it was to live on an island where so much of life's necessities had to be imported from distant places. I learned how the remote location of Honolulu made it far more difficult to remain current with the things I took for granted, such as daily access to *The New York Times* and the Washington media. I missed the cultural opportunities afforded by life in the nation's capital. Besides teaching, I gave a keynote address for the Hawaii State Library Commission. They were holding an all-day seminar for state library officials in Honolulu. I spoke to the group on management issues in library development.

In the fall of 1988, after four years of service, I resigned the chairmanship of the United States National Committee for FID. Tony Carbo Bearman of the University of Pittsburgh succeeded me. I continued on as a United States member of the

Education and Training Committee, which was still chaired by Marta Dosa at Syracuse University.

By 1989 the United States had withdrawn from UNESCO. The State Department decided to fill the vacuum in organizational involvement in international scientific activities by providing funds for American participation in the work of selected non-governmental, international scientific organizations. The U.S. National Committee for FID was one of the recipients. The arduous annual solicitation from the private sector was concluded. The sum owed for the four years from 1981 through 1984, when we had failed to meet our dues obligation, was never paid. With the start of 1989 I determined that I would disengage from the preparation of any further major reference book projects. Instead I acted only as advisor to my son, Steven, who, assisted by his sister, Jacqueline, was carrying forward *Statistics Sources*. The book by then had become an annual. Steven also continued with preparing the *Law and Legal Information Directory* for publication every second year.

Chapter Twenty

After my return from the Fulbright in Sri Lanka in 1987, I maintained ties in the country through correspondence with colleagues there. Strong links were continued with Cyril Ponnamperuma. He still directed the Institute for Fundamental Study in Kandy, while also teaching regularly and directing doctoral research in the Department of Chemistry and Biochemistry at Maryland. His vision to establish a model information center to serve the scientific staff of a Third World research organization had not yet been realized. He suggested that I work with a faculty team in the College of Library and Information Services to plan a workshop focused on the institute's goals. Members of the faculty oversaw the proposal and workshop planning with me. As a group, the faculty all shared an interest in scientific information, library technology, and information development in the world's less developed regions. The work was completed in the fall of 1989 and submitted to the National Science Foundation. The proposal sought travel support to Sri Lanka, where the group would conduct a seminar for several days in Kandy. The request for travel funding for the visiting group only covered the trip from Washington to Colombo. The Institute for Fundamental Study would cover the team's expenses on the ground in Sri Lanka. The conference won approval from the foundation. The group traveled to Sri Lanka in early January of 1990. Team members included Gary Marchionini, Jerry Kidd, Claude Walston, Peter Liebscher, and myself. For this trip, several of the wives came with us.

The institute's new facility for visiting scholars was ready by 1990. The accommodations were very modest compared to the deluxe Hotel Oberoi in Colombo, where we all stayed before going out to Kandy for the workshop. In his customary, generous fashion, Ponnamperuma had done everything conceivable to make our stay memorable. He made arrangements for us to be driven to several of the most celebrated tourist attractions in different regions of the country. The workshop drew strong attendance, not only from scientists in the country, but also from staff members of many of the other research organizations in Sri Lanka.

Once the professional portion of our trip was concluded, the Maryland team divided up. Some returned directly to Washington, while others made stopovers elsewhere in Asia. Krystyna and I went to Madras for several days. From there, we made a day trip to Kanchipuram and Mahabalipuram to explore historic temples that dated back many centuries. We then traveled on to Nepal and stayed at the Yak and Yeti Hotel in Katmandu. For two days we wandered about as typical tourists, gawking at the sights and admiring the crafts and indigenous architecture. We stopped in Bangkok on our journey home. There, Paul Steere, the United States Information Service regional librarian, arranged for me to give a lecture called "Library Survival in a Changing Environment" at Chulalongkorn University's Department of Library Science. The audience included students and faculty from four different Thai library schools, as well as members of the Bangkok professional library community.

Interesting developments took place during the spring of 1990, which would take me back to Asia again. The Maryland School of Public Affairs had entered into a three-year contract with AID to strengthen private- and public-sector activities. Glynn Cochrane, a widely experienced expert in building business infrastructure in developing regions, had accepted assignment as project director. He was already in residence in Sri Lanka. Cochrane's preliminary study, defining the scope and range of program initiatives, concluded that business and trade groups in Sri Lanka lacked the information framework needed to ensure the support of economic activity in the country. Cochrane's wife, Pauline Atherton Cochrane, a prominent American library educator and classification specialist, may have been a factor in his thinking. Cochrane reported to College Park that the improvement of business information systems in Sri Lankan chambers of commerce needed to be included in any project planning. Michael Nacht, Dean of the School of Public Affairs, invited me to participate in this effort as a consultant. In this capacity I traveled with Nacht to Colombo and participated in planning efforts held in July 1990. We met with AID officials, Sri Lankan government officers, and private sector representatives.

On another front, Arthur Vespry, at the Asian Institute of Technology (AIT), wanted to establish a first-rate, non-traditional graduate program in information science in the region. His ambitious plans were based on his previous experience offering annual institutes to individuals from surrounding countries. Located in Bangkok, the AIT was already a strong academic center for Southeast Asia. An international faculty there offered instruction in the English language for carefully selected students. Vespry felt that this technical university might also provide study for information scientists. Building upon the strength of AIT's computer and telecommunication technology, it would be natural to add a degree offering in information science. Vespry turned to the Thai Science and Technology Development Board for support for an analysis of this prospective new academic undertaking. Claude Walston and I were engaged to carry out this investigation.

I was able to carry out the two assignments — one in Colombo, the other in Bangkok — in sequence. For two weeks in late July and early August, I was in Colombo working with Nacht, Cochrane, and others associated with the Sri Lanka initiative. I undertook an analysis of private-sector business information needs, which would build the local capability for developing and offering current, accurate business information to the country's commercial organizations. I held conferences about the information needed for decision making with chamber of commerce officials and management personnel from several major companies. I also assessed the level of the information resources of the information centers that were available in the chambers and trade groups. I evaluated as well the preparation of the individuals who served as special librarians and business information officers. In the fall, I was to prepare a detailed timetable and plan for upgrading the information centers and for the training of key information workers in the chambers of commerce. In January 1991, I would return to Colombo to explain and discuss this plan.

From Colombo I traveled to Bangkok to form, with Claude Walston, our two-man, technical consulting team. For two weeks, we explored the feasibility of developing a graduate-level academic offering in information science and information management at the Asian Institute of Technology. The study received support from the United States National Research Council, a major sponsor of the Thai Science and Development Board. We reported to Thomas Cheatham, the resident advisor to the Science and Technology Board in Bangkok. We met first with the president of the Asian Institute of Technology and then with key faculty members who might teach courses in a new curricular offering in information science and information management. Walston and I conferred with Thai leaders in library education and with officials from the Technical Information Access Centers about the educational effort. Technical Information Access Centers had been established in Thailand by the Development Board to provide information processing and dissemination to the Thai scientific and research community. At the end of the site visits and interviews, we reported that a new master's degree program would be a useful academic offering. It would build upon existing elements in AIT's curriculum, so there would be no competition with existing Thai programs for the preparation of librarians. A regional offering was also more cost-efficient than dispatching graduate students to North America or to the United Kingdom for instruction. The investigators assured the AIT president and the Science and Technology Board of Thailand of their continued interest and of the potential for institutional relations between the University of Maryland and the Asian Institute of Technology, in whatever ways might be helpful to facilitate the prospective program. As a follow-up to this report, Jerry Kidd from Maryland was invited by AIT to spend a short period in Bangkok in early 1991. He went to consult with key faculty members and prepared a detailed curriculum, which would lead to the master's degree. Unfortunately, as with so many other attractive and innovative international educational aspirations, financial and political barriers proved too formidable. Ultimately, this promising new program at the Asian Institute of Technology was not implemented.

Summer 1990 marked the twenty-fourth and final offering of the annual Library Administrators Development Program at Maryland. When it began in 1967 it had been a unique, pioneer effort offering senior managers a two-week immersion in managerial concepts and practices. The curriculum had continued to focus on organization theory and processes, the human dimensions of organizations, and the managerial problems of innovation and change. Content elements were adapted to incorporate new issues, such as managing cultural diversity, and to augment the financial planning and budgeting component to make it a full day and a half presentation. Marketing and market research sessions were also increased to include a full day and evening. By 1990 John Rizzo had served faithfully as the director every year since 1968. By then he had grown weary of carrying the taxing responsibility of both resident director and substantive instructor for sessions on organizational behavior. Most importantly, the program could no longer attract the critical mass of participants needed to sustain it. From the outset, the Library Administrators Development Program was self-supporting. There was never any subsidy from the university; revenues from fees were used to cover all the costs incurred in conducting the program. To break even, the program needed about twenty-six enrollees. In 1990, participation fell below this number. With great reluctance we recognized that the time had come to end the long run. In twenty-four years 780 administrators attended the program. They came from all types of libraries — from the United States, Canada, and a number of foreign countries. Some of them still join fellow participants at national library conferences, where they continue to reminisce about their days spent at the Donaldson Brown Center on the scenic north bank of the Susquehanna River.

During fall 1990, I prepared a detailed prospectus for a program of training and development that was designed to upgrade the performance capabilities of the information personnel in the chambers of commerce in Colombo. The plan incorporated elements to be carried out during workshops in Colombo. The workshops would take place over a period of months. Maryland faculty in library and information science would offer classes in such topics as reference and information retrieval, data processing, and data base management. Several individuals from the Colombo program would be selected each year, over a three-year period, to come to Maryland for a three-week summer course in business information systems. A weeklong internship at the Information Center of the Chamber of Commerce of the United States in Washington would follow. And after that, participants would spend three weeks at INFOTEC in Mexico City working with its staff, which engaged in information work for the Mexican business community. Following review of my proposal by Michael Nacht and Glynn Cochrane, it was determined that I should return to Colombo for a two-week period in January 1991. I would present and explain my plan to the chambers of commerce there and to the AID liaison officers on the scene.

I had remained in communication with Arthur Vespry at the Asian Institute of Technology following the study for a new master's program. On learning of my prospective trip to Colombo, he asked me to participate in a conference in Hanoi, Vietnam, in January 1991. While I was amenable to traveling to Hanoi, there were serious difficulties in getting a visa. The State Department in Washington informed me that there was no U.S. government objection to my going to Hanoi to participate in a scientific meeting, even though the United States at that time had no representation there. The only place I could apply for a visa, however, was in Bangkok. I planned to stop there on my way to Colombo just long enough for a Vietnamese national employed by the Asian Institute of Technology to accompany me to the Vietnamese Consulate, where I could apply for a visa. The scheme worked. On January 3rd in Bangkok, the AIT driver and Ms. Lee, a Vietnamese national from Vespry's staff, were ready to take me downtown to the consulate. I received a visa after only half an hour's wait before returning to the airport.

The Best of Times

In Colombo I met with AID officials. I spelled out how, without proper investment in constructing sound business information centers and appropriately trained personnel, the Sri Lankan community would remain at a competitive disadvantage with other nations in the region. I explained that the training plan and timetable I had outlined in my analysis would enable Sri Lanka, in two years' time, to develop a cadre of qualified information personnel that could build a strong business and commercial information system. When I went to meet the chamber of commerce management officers, I already had the endorsement of both the AID officials and the Maryland project personnel. I left Colombo convinced that the plan I had advanced would be accepted and that the training sequence would get underway later in the year.

In Bangkok again, I spent the night at the campus hotel of the Asian Institute of Technology. I flew out the next day to Hanoi as part of a group that had been invited to participate in the Third All Country Congress on Scientific and Technological Information. Support for my participation came from the UNESCO General Information Program's regional office in Bangkok, directed by Delia Torrijos. I had last worked with her in 1976 when John Rizzo and I offered the UNESCO management seminar for the Southeast Asian region. My invitation to the conference came from Dr. Dinh, the director of the Vietnamese National Information and Documentation Center for Science and Technology in Hanoi. I gave the keynote address to the Congress and advised the center's management and the Deputy Minister of Sciences, Technology and Environment on information policy relations with United States institutions.

In early 1991, Hanoi had received few American visitors since the war. I was very curious about the reception I would be accorded by professional colleagues there. I was received cordially by everyone I encountered. Vietnamese sentiment seemed to be that they needed to learn from America in order to progress economically and technologically. The city was a peculiar blend of architectural reminders of the French colonial past along with the stern, controlling hand of government. At the same time, street vendors purveyed their products day and night with a newly tolerated capitalistic fervor. Cars were scarce, but the streets were alive with thousands of bicyclists. The January air was clear and fresh. Only the foreboding mausoleum of Ho Chih Minh remained as a symbol for American visitors of the horrors the nation had endured. I spoke to the three hundred delegates during the conference on information transfer and scientific communication. I sensed the zeal with which the country's information profession was striving to progress toward technical parity with more advanced nations. I left Hanoi with the feeling that this city, which I found so welcoming and tranquil, was hellbent to catch up with its envied neighbor, Bangkok. I was pleased to have seen Hanoi before development would turn its streets into jammed roadways reeking of exhaust fumes and its sky into a dense layer of smog.

Shortly following my return to the campus, I received frustrating news from Michael Nacht. In a communication from Glynn Cochrane, he had been informed that the Sri Lankan chamber of commerce officials had rejected my plan for training their information people. They had decided to give higher priority to the acquisition of equipment and the hiring of additional staff members. They saw manpower preparation as less attractive when measured against the less abstract alternative of augmenting staff and putting modern equipment immediately to work. As the recipients of AID support, local officials were entirely in charge of deciding how to allocate the resources. Experience with earlier unrealized international plans should have insulated me, yet I could not help but feel sorely disappointed. The considerable time and effort I had spent working on this project finally came to naught.

The spring of 1991 proved to be a trying time for the library education program at Maryland. The lean years of the late 1980's had been particularly troublesome for American academic institutions. Under continuing public scrutiny that demanded greater financial accountability, administrators and faculties on many campuses defensively re-evaluated academic priorities against what they conceived to be the institutional mission. The University of Maryland was not immune to such internal reassessment. For a number of months a university committee, Academic Programs and Curricula (APAC), had been assiduously reviewing the purposes, relevance, reputation, and consistency of overall objectives for every academic program. The intention was to make recommendations to the university policy-making body, the University Senate. The issues dealt with whether the university should consider the following: a reduction in scale, consolidation, or integration within other programs, or elimination of units, departments, colleges, or disciplines that were judged to be candidates for budget reduction. Months of solemn meetings, a review of countless documents, and reports from all campus units led APAC by the spring of 1991 to identify half a dozen prospective targets. The College of Library and Information Services was on this list. The danger was very grave. Small professional educational programs were especially vulnerable. Already, a number of comparable library schools across the country — most notably those at Columbia and Chicago — had been discontinued. Prior to submitting its recommendations to the University Senate, APAC saw fit to invite statements to the committee by scheduling public hearings where those interested could present their views.

The faculty and alumni of the library school were swift to react. Unlike other programs, which had less political experience and were on the defensive, the library education contingent rallied its forces and acted at once. They called upon a number of parties to attend the hearing: doctoral graduates; important Maryland and Washington, DC, institutional library leaders; publicly elected federal and state legislators; and other influential spokespersons. Those who could not attend wrote letters to APAC or to the university president. The president's office was deluged with letters affirming the significance and reputational esteem of the College of Library and Information Services. At the public meeting on May 1, 1991, the auditorium was filled to capacity with sympathetic supporters of our program.

When I was called upon to speak, I began by explaining that the program had not come into existence in the 1960's because of any powerful drive for its development by the College Park academic community. It was propelled into being by a broad cultural and political consensus that there was an important state and regional need to prepare individuals for service in libraries of every type. I described how the master's program had begun with a unique interdisciplinary faculty from North America and abroad. I talked about the carefully selected student body and about how, within three years from its inception, the school had received the endorsement of the University Senate to conduct a Ph.D. program to prepare members of the next generation of scholars for the discipline. I characterized the international dimension of the College's concerns by identifying the strong degree of faculty participation in significant efforts around the globe. To underscore an important element of political sensitivity, I explained that unlike other departments, the library program supported a student body at both the master's and doctoral levels that was roughly eighty percent female. I suggested that this represented an essential base for the professional development and research preparation of many outstanding women, affording them the opportunity to move toward senior responsibility in educational and administrative roles. I differentiated the professional school from other academic departments by calling attention to its close links with the world of practice and professional groups, while still requiring a strong research component to reinforce purely empirical current practice through insights derived from analytical study.

The Best of Times

The integrity of the program in my view militated for continued independent status. Subsuming the program within another academic unit would undercut dramatically its close associations with its alumni. It would demoralize the faculty and impede the attraction of new faculty members. I reasoned that any cost savings — which might come from reducing the scale of the program, reassigning it within another campus unit, eliminating the doctoral program, or even completely doing away with the college — would be negligible. I suggested that it was ironic that a proposal for reduction came precisely at a time when society clearly recognized that it was entering a new information age, and that library and information science was undergoing a fundamental transformation into a laboratory-based discipline. Finally, I argued that any reduction in scale would ensure only mediocrity and decline.

Many others — from public, professional, alumni, and faculty constituencies — made impassioned and eloquent statements supporting the college. Their participation had a strong bearing on the APAC decision. Unquestionably, another factor in our favor was the recent completion of Archives II of the United States National Archives, adjacent to the campus. Part of the rationale for this location had been to further the ties with the college faculty and student body. Another unforeseen check to the APAC plan was the extensive political clamor and press coverage defending the library education program. The College of Library and Information Services was the only academic program targeted for reduction or elimination that was spared in APAC's final recommendations to the Senate.

In 1991, Margaret Chisholm, director of the Graduate School of Library and Information Science at the University of Washington (and dean at Maryland from 1971 to 1975), invited me to teach a summer session in Seattle. I taught library administration and offered a seminar, which I had begun on an experimental basis at Maryland. The theme was Trends and Directions in the Information Field. In each session I treated what I perceived to be key elements of the main currents propelling library and information science forward conceptually, politically, technically, and operationally. By the end of this summer term, the topical outline and framework had reached the point that I was prepared to include this new seminar as a regular curricular offering at Maryland beginning in the academic year 1991-1992.

By that time I had begun to consider how best to take advantage of what would be my last sabbatical leave during the 1993-1994 school year. I decided to look into a second Fulbright grant. The brochure announcing research and lecturing awards for 1993-1994 revealed two opportunities — one in India, the other in Poland. India was seeking someone to teach graduate courses in any specialization. The preference was for an associate or full professor with substantial experience. The details failed to identify a specific academic institution where the courses would be offered, but in India, English was the customary language of instruction. The Polish listing at the University of Warsaw specified that they were looking for someone to teach courses and conduct seminars in any field. Possible fields of interest included acquisitions, information retrieval, library management, and library automation. Consulting on curriculum development and staff training was also part of the program. There would be opportunities for collaborative research on international information systems, international retrieval languages, and new trends in librarianship. Knowledge of the Polish language was preferred.

Fulbright applicants could only apply to one country. It appeared as if I might enjoy a competitive advantage for the Indian assignment. I had extensive experience in the region, and there was no foreign language requisite. I was put off, however, by the uncertainty of where the work would take place. The Polish award specified the University of Warsaw as the site. It also identified several substantive areas where I might contribute. Unfortunately, it was also made clear that a Polish speaker would have a competitive edge. I knew Warsaw, and I had followed with interest Poland's recent history — from the time of central control through the days of the Solidarity movement, and on to the reappearance of more democratic institutions and the resurgence of privatization. My FID experience had resulted in contacts with Polish colleagues in key information posts. Krystyna also had a wide circle of friends there, from when she had lived and worked in Warsaw. Pola Danecka, Krystyna's mother, was living in Lodz, some hundred kilometers from Warsaw. While Pola and I invariably had some difficulty comprehending each other in conversation, there were great mutual respect and very warm personal feeling between us. All these factors influenced my choice to apply for the Polish Fulbright. Tragically, by the time I was ready to submit my application in late spring 1992, Krystyna's mother had died.

Once again in 1992, I served as a member of another library school's summer school faculty. Jane Robbins, the very first alumna of the Maryland Ph.D. program, was the director of the library education program at the University of Wisconsin in Madison. When I mentioned during a professional meeting that I would enjoy a summer in Madison, Jane followed up soon thereafter with a formal invitation. I went to Madison for a relaxing six weeks. I lived in a university conference facility that was half an hour's scenic walk along the lake to my campus office. I taught library administration and conducted once again the seminar in Trends and Directions in Library and Information Science.

In winter of the 1992-1993 academic year, my name was forwarded to the Polish-U.S. Fulbright Commission in Warsaw on the recommendation of the U.S. Advisory Screening Committee in Library and Information Science. I was proposed as senior professor to the Institute of Library and Information Science at the University of Warsaw for the fall semester of 1993. From earlier experience with the award in Sri Lanka, I understood that a recommendation was not the same as an appointment. Judgements needed to be made by the Polish host organization about the selection of individuals and subject fields, based on a budget allocation that provided less than would be needed to choose all of the recommended candidates. An award for a professor in library and information science was in competition with grants to the individuals recommended in other subject areas. Final notification of awards was to be made on May 1, 1993. At that time I learned that I was designated the first alternate if any of the thirty or so other recipients failed to, or was unable to, accept an award.

I traveled to New York in late May to teach in the summer school program at the Palmer School of Library and Information Science at the C.W. Post College of Long Island University. I was still in limbo about the Fulbright. Selected candidates were not required to communicate their formal acceptance until the first of July. At C.W. Post, my courses were the same ones I had offered at the Universities of Washington and Wisconsin. It was not until I returned to Maryland in early July that I was informed about the disposition of the grant. Two recipients had decided not to accept, but they had failed to communicate their decisions until they were queried by telephone after the final date for acceptance had passed. I was therefore awarded the Fulbright professorship. Fortunately, my sabbatical leave for the fall term had been approved contingent on my receipt of the Fulbright. I still had most of July and part of August to prepare the materials I would need to ship to Poland and to prepare myself for the move to Warsaw.

The Polish assignment was far more structured than the Fulbright program in Sri Lanka. A precise job description was received from the Polish-U.S. Fulbright Commission in Warsaw. It indicated that I would be expected to teach two graduate-level courses at the University of Warsaw Institute of Library and Information Science. One of these was to be on business information services; the other would cover trends and issues facing libraries in the 1990's. I was also expected to serve as a consultant to the faculty on curriculum development. I would attend faculty meetings, advise on teaching methods, and hold office hours for students. Knowing in advance exactly which classes I would teach permitted me time to prepare outlines, reading lists, bibliographies, articles, book chapters, and the reproduction of three copies of everything I planned to use in the classes. All these materials were shipped to Warsaw for the classes, which would begin in October. I requested the United States Information Agency to acquire and send one copy of each book included in the course reading lists to the Institute. I also sent a number of personal volumes for student use. The University of Warsaw did not provide housing. Krystyna planned to travel with me to Poland to assist me in my search for a suitable apartment.

Early in August, USIA in Washington, DC, held a two-day conference for all the 1993-1994 Fulbright candidates going abroad. We received general briefings along with cultural and political orientation lectures. We were then grouped by country of destination for discussion sessions with State Department foreign desk officers, Polish academic specialists, and Fulbright professors freshly back from their in-country experiences. A high point of the conference was the address at the Library of Congress delivered by Joseph Duffy, who had recently been appointed director of the United States Information Agency from his former post in academia. In his speech, he stirringly characterized how vital the Fulbright exchanges were in advancing the cause of peace through international understanding.

Krystyna and I made our way to Warsaw via Scandinavia. We traveled first to Norway and then spent several days in Stockholm. Continuing south, we made a detour for a weekend stay in Sopot, a seaside vacation town where Krystyna revisited the place she had gone to as a young child with her mother for her summer holidays in the years immediately following World War II. After a brief visit to Gdansk, we flew on to Warsaw near the end of August. At the American Center, all the arriving Fulbrighters participated in a two-day orientation program offered by the local United States Information Service staff and the Polish Fulbright Office. Krystyna's Warsaw friends and former colleagues, who were knowledgeable about the tight local housing market, helped us locate a comfortable and centrally located, furnished apartment. Before moving in, I went to a two-week country introduction program in Krakow that was organized by the Polish Fulbright staff. Krystyna returned to the United States.

The country orientation program took place at Przegorzaly Castle, an imposing group of buildings situated on a hill in the outskirts of Krakow. The castle had been redesigned to serve as a conference center. All the elements made it a memorable experience — the lodgings, meals (the staff even obliged by setting up tables for vegetarians), the lecture program, the field trips, and the Polish language instruction. Great pains had been taken in selecting the most effective and well-informed Jagellonian University professors to provide briefings in excellent English. They gave a series of detailed introductions to the history, culture, economics, religion, politics, and educational characteristics of the society. Field trips in Krakow and around the general region were planned to integrate faculty presentations. Knowledgeable specialists accompanied us as guides to the infamous Auschwitz concentration camp, the Wawel Castle, and the Jagellonian University in Krakow. We visited the principal museums and galleries in the city. We also stopped in Nova Huta, the enormous, and enormously polluted, Soviet-style, steel-making suburb of Krakow. We stopped in the historic ghetto section in the Kazimierz district, as well. The weekend was spent in Zakopane, a picturesque mountain resort south of Krakow in the Carpathian Mountains.

Back in Warsaw, I settled into my apartment. I spent time at the institute preparing for the start of classes and getting to know my new colleagues. Jadwiga Wozniak, a lecturer in the Division of Information Systems who held an American Ph.D. and specialized in linguistic applications in information science, was assigned to offer assistance. She was exceedingly helpful to me in innumerable ways all during my stay. Most, but not all the faculty, were fluent in English. While the students were expected to be able to follow my lectures in English, I later learned that not all of them could.

My apartment was ideally situated. I could walk to my university office in half an hour and to the Fulbright office in another five minutes. There was frequent bus and streetcar transportation for use in inclement weather. I shopped in the neighborhood for breakfast and one other light meal a day. I learned a great deal during my two weeks of introductory Polish instruction in Krakow, but I did not have time to take further classes to improve my conversational skills. I made do with a simple vocabulary of essential words and a well-thumbed dictionary that bailed me out during shopping transactions. My apartment was also within easy

The Best of Times

walking distance of the Warsaw Opera House, the Symphony Hall, the city's reconstructed historic old town, and the shopping district. Many ethnic restaurants were available nearby, and I would take my main meal at lunch or dinner in one or another of them. Numerous hotel dining rooms also offered good meals close by. As had been the case in Sri Lanka, an important element of my apartment's furnishings was a short-wave radio, on which I listened to the BBC and Voice of America.

It was my good fortune to know quite a few people in Warsaw through Krystyna. Barbara Bolinska, who had been instrumental in helping me find an apartment, also arranged for a cleaning woman to come every Saturday. At Barbara's suggestion, the cleaning lady shopped for ingredients to prepare soup or vegetables for me that would last through the week. Zina Jancewicz, Krystyna's colleague from her working days in Warsaw, and Zina's husband, Kazik, adopted me as a member of their large, extended family. They welcomed me in their home for dinner and family celebrations. By a stroke of good fortune, Donald and Sydney Hausrath were posted in Warsaw during this time. Don was directing the library program of the American Center in Warsaw. He was responsible also for managing United States Information Service library programs that extended through Eastern Europe and through all the new countries of the former Soviet Union.

Lawrence Hussmann was one of my Fulbright colleagues in Warsaw. Like myself, he was there without wife or family. An English professor from the University of Dayton, Hussmannn specialized in late 19th and early 20th century American novelists. We shared common interests and got together frequently for dinner, concerts, and theater performances. Warsaw's Opera House and symphony hall were usually excellent and quite inexpensive. Tickets were usually available on the day of the performances. The hottest Opera House ticket of the fall season was for the musical, *Fiddler on the Roof*. The production on the grand stage was electrifying. The authentic *shtetl* set and lyrics sung in Polish somehow made the musical seem more realistic than it had when I saw it first in the United States.

I made numerous adaptations and changes to the courses I taught in Poland. Fifteen students were enrolled in each of my classes. Invariably, there were several visitors who sat in on particular sessions. These included two faculty colleagues, who tried to attend regularly. Others included graduate assistants and members of the professional library community. Wojciech Pirog, who in earlier years was the director of the Institute for Scientific and Technical Information, as well as chairman of the FID Education and Training Committee, honored me by attending two of my classes. About half of my students could follow the lectures in English. A graduate assistant or faculty colleague with fluency in English would have to sum up my remarks every five minutes during my talk. This slowed the pace considerably and reduced the amount of material we could cover, but it made everyone more comfortable. Questions and comments in Polish were translated for me. I took no attendance, but found the issues treated were of sufficient interest to ensure the regular appearance of the class members. Students interested in doing further study, reading, or research came to my office, where they could borrow material or ask questions. I invited them to speak in French or German if this would be easier for them; in this way we could enjoy a freer exchange of ideas.

The most interesting lesson of my teaching experience was how little the students in the business information class really understood about the workings of a capitalist economy. In order to explain the content and use of business information systems, I first had to describe private business ownership, financial markets, stocks and bonds, banking institutions, and credit transactions. It occurred to me that if these bright, young graduate students had little sense of the workings of the free enterprise market economy, then certainly their elders — who had lived their entire lives under a centrally administered economic system — would be even less informed. I gained an appreciation for just how difficult it is to bring about a radical, societal transformation that replaced centralized government ownership and control with a market-driven economy.

To assist me in my role as an advisor on curriculum development to the faculty, I had shipped a large body of material about American library and information science curriculum planning from Maryland. I attended a curriculum meeting of the faculty and student body. I distributed and explained the material and responded to questions. I also shared my personal perspectives on contemporary curricular problems in North America. My courses were not part of the normal curricular offering of the institute, yet they treated subject matter of concern to those engaged in instruction and practice in the field. The classes were seen as an important supplement to the institute's regular offerings. They also afforded the staff an opportunity to learn about new subject matter that might be worth adding to the curriculum. During my semester in Warsaw, I was also invited to give a public lecture at the American Center in Krakow. I spoke to an audience of faculty members and graduate students from the Jagellonian University. Library and information people from other Krakow institutions and interested members of the community also attended the talk on Information Transfer in Science.

Don Hausrath played an active role in library development in Eastern Europe and Russia. As part of his mission, he arranged for me to go to Moscow to offer several days of instruction to library groups. I had not been to Russia since 1972, when I spent most of my time in the airport detention center. I was both curious and apprehensive about going there again. I went there for the first week of December. I experienced two distinct Moscows. One was a capital city occupied by a newly moneyed class of financiers and entrepreneurs. The other Moscow included all the rest of the society. I stayed in one of the new luxury hotels. Everything there was exorbitantly priced and ostentatious. The streets were covered with piles of snow that had turned black with soot. Downtown, the streets were lined with men and women of all ages and classes. They seemed to be trying to sell every type of personal possession imaginable. People were displaying such things as plastic clothing hangers, empty wine bottles, and fine riding boots. There were no taxicabs. Instead, there were owners of private cars who would drive prospective passengers where they needed to go for a negotiated price. During my stay I caught a fierce cold. One of the local Moscow librarians accompanied me on visits to half a dozen pharmacies to try to find cough syrup or lozenges. Everywhere we went, we encountered long lines of people who were desperately trying, with no success, to find needed medication. The absence of over-the-counter drugs was only one symptom of the wider malaise afflicting Moscow's population. Moscow was in disarray. Nevertheless, my assignment went forward as planned.

For the first two days, I offered a seminar to librarians who came from the new American Studies Centers, which Hausrath had been opening in major Russian cities. The subjects I treated included Contemporary Concepts of Modern Information Service, Information Services to the Business Sector and to Public Policy Makers, and Issues in Structuring an Information Center as a Client Response Organization. I worked with a group of twenty participants. The course was given under the auspices of the United States Information Service in the conference rooms of the Russian Library of Foreign Literature. For the next two days, I lectured to a group of fifteen reference librarians from academic and research libraries in the Moscow region on Marketing Information Products and Services.

The Best of Times

By the time I was ready to leave, my cold had grown worse and I was anxious to return to Warsaw for medical attention.

Transportation in Moscow had been unreliable during my stay. I asked the staff of the United States Information Service to ensure dependable transportation for me from the hotel to the airport. I wanted to arrive at the airport well ahead of time. I was relieved when the driver appeared in the hotel lobby at the designated time. My bag was placed in the trunk of a nondescript, weathered vehicle. I congratulated myself on how well things were going as we started out on the forty-minute drive to the airport. It was late afternoon, and the sky was already growing dark. The streets were covered with melting snow. The car's windshield wipers were constantly in motion, clearing away slush that obscured our visibility. Halfway to the airport on the outskirts of the city, the engine made a loud noise, and the automobile came to an abrupt stop. The driver went out to see what had happened. He returned in a few minutes to let me know that the car could go no further. To relieve my distress, he announced that he would flag down another car to take me to the airport. After taking my suitcase from the trunk, we both positioned ourselves behind the car and tried to wave down passing vehicles.

By this time night had fallen. The only light came from rapidly passing vehicles. After ten minutes, we were splattered with mud and slush from the speeding traffic. I began to wonder whether I would ever leave Moscow that night. Finally, what looked like a station wagon came to a halt. On its side were the markings of a hospital ambulance. An animated discussion ensued. My driver then turned to me and announced that I would be driven the rest of the way to the airport if I would pay the ambulance driver ten American dollars. I accepted joyfully. Bidding my driver goodbye, and without any thought of what might become of him and his stranded car, I climbed up next to the ambulance driver, and off we went. The ambulance moved along satisfactorily, but there was a problem. The windshield wipers did not work. It was necessary to stop the ambulance by the side of the road every three or four hundred yards to clear away the mud and slush that impeded our visibility. It took us somewhat longer to reach our destination, but we arrived well ahead of my flight's departure. I gave the ambulance driver his money, thanked him profusely in words that were unintelligible to him, and alighted from the cab of the vehicle. It struck me that it must have been my preordained destiny to experience bizarre, unanticipated adventures every time I set foot in Russia.

The Best of Times

The sight of Warsaw's bright lights and the taxicab ride back to my apartment brought enormous relief. Unfortunately, my cold had become the flu. Antibiotics prescribed for me at a private clinic allowed me to recover fully in only a few days. The following week I gave a paper at a World Health Organization Conference in Warsaw. It was entitled "Databases and Computer Applications in Information Transfer in Science," and it made particular reference to the medical sciences. Virtually every aspect of my Warsaw experience was pleasurable — with one exception. Like most Americans from any region of the United States, I was depressed by the never-ending, gray days of cold, rain, mist, sleet, and damp. I made plans for Krystyna and me to fly to Tunisia for a sun-filled holiday. She was coming to Warsaw for the Christmas and New Year's holidays. The day after she arrived, we flew to North Africa for a week's stay there. We spent our time indolently basking in the sun, and savoring the native dishes and excellent wines. We also took in the tourist sights. While we were there, we had a chance to renew our acquaintance with Leila Ben Hamouda, a Maryland alumna who had been responsible for acquisitions at the Tunisian National Library in Tunis before her recent marriage.

Upon our return to Warsaw, we celebrated the New Year in the company of friends at my apartment. The night before Krystyna flew home we visited our friends Zina and Kazik for dinner. They lived in a typical, multi-floor apartment building with poorly lit hallways and staircases. As I was walking up the stairs, laden with bags that I planned to leave with them, I stepped down on a broken stair and twisted my foot. When Krystyna left for the airport early the next morning, my foot had swollen to twice its normal size. I could not put any weight on it. A doctor at the embassy arranged for me to have X-rays at a Polish government clinic. Zina and Kazik took me to the hospital and then, with X-rays in hand, to the embassy. My foot was fractured and required a heavy plaster cast for my foot and my leg. I could not step down or put any weight on my foot for some time. It was impossible for me to negotiate the staircases in my apartment building or at the university. The embassy doctor advised that I return to the United States. I had to cut short my stay in Poland by ten days, before classes were over. Don and Kazik carried me down from my apartment to a car waiting to take me to the airport. I spent the next twenty hours in a wheelchair, getting in and out of airplanes. Krystyna and Steven met me at the airport and managed to get me home in a rented wheelchair. The orthopedist who examined me a few days later was young enough to have never seen a plaster cast. He took further X-rays and

The Best of Times

recast my foot and leg in fiberglass. I was able to wear a special boot that made walking possible with the use of a cane.

During this convalescent period I was unable to drive. January of 1994 brought some of the worst Washington weather we had seen in many years. There were great amounts of snow, sleet, and ice, which made for impossible driving conditions. Many government agencies, schools, and universities remained closed during that month for several days. Spring term classes at Maryland started one week late. With driving help from Krystyna and Steven, I managed to meet my classes. I was also able to fulfill a commitment I had accepted while in Poland. This was a presentation for Latin American librarians called "Training and Education in Information Science in the Developing World" at the Inter-American Workshop for Agricultural Information Transfer and Networking. The presentation took place late in January in Washington, DC, during a conference sponsored by the Inter-American Development Bank and the National Agriculture Library. On February 7th, the doctor X-rayed my foot for the last time and declared it healed.

Chapter Twenty-one

Professors returning from a sabbatical must remain with the university for a year after the conclusion of their leave. But I had begun to give serious thought to retirement. I had turned seventy in January. Until the year before, the cessation of active teaching was mandatory upon reaching the age of seventy. This age limit was lifted in 1994. One could continue teaching indefinitely. I was not in any way weary of classroom interactions with students, but there were two compelling reasons for me to consider withdrawing from an active teaching role.

Since 1953, I had been instructing in academia, participating in faculty meetings, serving on university committees, advising students, and spending my workweeks in a campus office. Although I was not ready to relinquish intellectual and scholarly pursuits, the idea of letting go of workaday responsibilities held considerable appeal. There was another important consideration. Academia is in many ways similar to the military. In spite of expressions to the contrary, there is a table of organization that specifies the number of professors. Budget limits within different academic units dictate limits on levels of compensation. These arrangements are somewhat flexible, but a full professor fills a niche. Before he or she steps aside, it is not possible to add another professor at that rank or salary. By remaining in place, one person can block the capacity of the program to add another senior appointment to its roster. My sense was that it was time for me to move aside and make room for tomorrow. The college was going to celebrate its thirtieth anniversary in the fall of 1995. I timed my retirement for the close of that year. The Maryland Library Association Conference was held in Ocean City in the spring. The alumni association of the college arranged an anniversary celebration. Alumni going back as far as the first graduating class attended the event. Sharing observations with them about the program's history, and gazing at the sea of familiar faces and friends in the audience, I was reassured that the close of this year would be a fitting time to conclude my teaching career.

In the academic year 1994-1995, I was no longer participating actively in the work of the International Federation for Documentation or its Committee on Education and Training. My interest in the international field, however, still remained alive. I planned a paper for delivery to the August 1995 annual conference of the International Federation of Library Associations (IFLA) in Istanbul. The abstract of my proposed presentation was one of those selected in the spring of 1995 for inclusion in the program. Krystyna and I had not been to Turkey since 1977. Mary Berkmen helped us plan a week's holiday on the sea before the IFLA sessions in Istanbul. Her husband had died since we had last seen him in 1977, but Mary still lived in the same apartment overlooking the Golden Horn. She was still employed in the library of Robert College. A Turkish travel agent friend booked us into the Hotel Kismet in Kusadasi, a port and resort city on the southern coast.

Kusadasi is one hour from Izmir, and even nearer to the celebrated, ancient site of Ephesus. The Kismet (which means destiny) Hotel was idyllic. It was perched on a cliff at the edge of the city and was surrounded by the sea on three sides. The balcony of our room overlooked carefully groomed lawns that were ringed with colorful flower beds. Meals were included as part of the accommodation. They were served on an outdoor terrace, which looked out toward the harbor with its dazzling parade of sailboats and large vessels. The cuisine included traditional Turkish specialties as well as European fare. The wines served were among Turkey's best, including an old favorite from Ankara days, *Kavakladera*. It was with some reluctance that I left Kusadasi to spend half a day visiting the historical ruins at Ephesus. Everything about our stay at the Kismet, including the exceedingly modest price for our week-long stay, convinced us that our friend had led us to a rare and lovely resort.

The most striking feature of our Istanbul visit was the way the city had been transformed from the totally secular character we remembered so distinctly from the 1970's. Traditional Moslem attire was everywhere in evidence in the downtown area. Women of all ages were encased in cloth from head to foot. Istanbul itself remained the same bustling, colorful mélange of sights, sounds, and constant traffic. The smog, however, had grown more oppressive. The paper I gave during the IFLA Conference was called, "Developing New Information Products: A Revised Role for Librarianship in Advanced and Developing Countries." It was later published in the *IFLA Journal*, Vol. 21, No. 4, 1995. In the paper, I proposed two forms of prospective role transformation as particularly essential in less developed regions. The first included political behavior on behalf of clients, with librarians serving as vociferous spokespersons for adequate information resources. Using concerted expression to provoke action by governmental bodies, publishing companies, professional associations, and other generators of information tools, they could achieve their aims. The second proposition capitalized on the intellectual potential of individuals in the occupation — people who could take the initiative in creating new information products, services, or databases to fulfill client needs. The paper offered the philosophical and conceptual basis for such role adaptations and provided illustrations where proactive occupational behavior had taken place. The practical means for moving in this direction were also outlined.

In the fall semester of 1995, I announced my retirement from teaching. The final instructional responsibility I took on as a member of the Maryland faculty would take place in January. I was scheduled to travel to Beijing to teach in the Chinese government's Central Institute for Scientific and Technical Information. I intended to carry on with my research interests beyond my retirement from teaching. I worked with my colleagues Eileen Abels and Gary Marchionini during the fall to design an applied research project, which we planned to submit to the Kellogg Foundation for support. The effort had its genesis in the outline I had prepared as one chapter for my 1956 book, *Information for Administrators*. This detailed framework laid out the informational characteristics needed for developing a comprehensive set of economic, social, political, governmental, and cultural details about a community. We envisaged how, with updating and adaptations, this outline could serve as the basis for building a perpetual electronic inventory of a county's characteristics. Working in collaboration with a public library, we felt that the database could serve as a site for online searches to demonstrate an important value-added contribution to the library's constituency. We viewed the project as a means to demonstrate how library education could link with a public library, with operating practice serving as a laboratory for faculty and student participation. The final proposal, a joint undertaking between the University of Maryland College of Library and Information Services and the Montgomery County Public Library, was submitted in the fall of 1995 to the W. K. Kellogg Foundation. We requested support for a three-year period. A favorable response for support came from Kellogg late in the spring of 1996. A grant was awarded for a one-year pilot effort to begin in the fall of 1996.

The Best of Times

My trip to Beijing for three weeks in January 1996 was the first occasion that a Maryland faculty member had offered instruction in mainland China as part of a cooperative arrangement that had been established in the spring of 1995. Under its terms, American faculty were to travel to China to work with students in the master's degree program at the Institute of Scientific and Technical Information of China (ISTIC). The visiting faculty member was also expected to help select students to come to College Park for a semester as the final stage of their study. The two seminars I offered were Business Information Systems and Trends and Directions in Library and Information Science. Copies of instructional materials were shipped in advance of my arrival, so that all was in place when I arrived. I stayed at the very modern and comfortable Media Hotel. Many people from the Chinese Broadcasting Agency frequented the hotel. It was within easy walking distance of the institute. Students enrolled in the classes were required to be able to work in English. Zhang De, assistant director of the education and training program at ISTIC, was a helpful host and obliging mentor during my visit. A number of the students also participated in making my experience a pleasurable blend of instruction and tourism. They accompanied me on visits to all the renowned Beijing sites: from the Great Wall to Tiananmen Square. They shepherded me through the marketplaces as well. The institute was housed in a large building, where a staff of hundreds was employed. My stay was enriched during several official dinners that had been arranged in my honor. I sampled many exotic dishes. An associate savoring a special delicacy recommended it to me highly. I tried and thoroughly enjoyed the crunchy morsel and had two more before learning that I had consumed three fried scorpions.

If it was difficult for my students in Warsaw to understand many of the topics I discussed during the business information seminar, those subjects were even more incomprehensible to the Chinese students. There was a new, entrepreneurial class arising in the country, but central government control remained deeply rooted in the minds of the people and in fact. The very notion of business information systems implies a market-driven economy resting on a foundation of private banking and financial institutions, as well as securities transactions. It was essential for the students to understand the basic structure of capitalism. It was therefore necessary to inform their understanding by first describing fundamental forms of business ownership and private enterprise. From this I went on to explain the workings of capital markets, securities exchanges, the nature of stocks and bonds, and how they reflect private ownership or indebtedness of public corporations. I characterized for them the role of credit and banking as elements that drive business activity. A great deal of time was spent covering elements of an introductory course in economics and business finance. I could not get to my basic purpose — lecturing on business information systems — until we had covered this other information. After the lengthy explanations, many of the students remained quite confused by the concept of an economic order that was propelled by competitive market forces and in which the consumer is in control. We finally did move on to the substantive components of the seminar. The very same evening that I lectured on the importance of access to up-to-date, authenticated data for informed, business decision making, CNN television news reported on the Chinese government's decision to restrict the flow of economic and business information from foreign sources into China.

In my course on Trends and Directions, students showed the greatest interest by far in my discussion about inventing and designing new information products and services. Twenty-five to thirty students normally attended the seminar. On the morning that I dealt with new information product development, there were a dozen senior staff members present, from a number of different ISTIC departments. Questions raised during the class made it clear that even senior managers at ISTIC were perplexed by the notion of consumers as the determining factor in the economic equation. It was difficult for them to shake off the habits of mind that had held sway since the Great Revolution in 1949, when production and distribution judgements were made solely by the state. The very idea of fashioning information products and services that were derived from market research into consumer needs, preferences, and purchase patterns seemed alien. I learned later, during a dinner banquet with ISTIC management officials, that the agency had been put on notice. It was to transform itself within several years into a financially self-sufficient agency by generating revenue through the marketplace sale of its information products and services. It was only then that I understood the motivation of those who had come to audit the session on the invention and design of information products.

The weather in Beijing at that time of year was cold and crisp, without precipitation. The surprise was how dry the air was in January. I was obliged to run the shower all through the night during my stay in order to humidify the room enough so that I could sleep. Many young men and women, dressed in the high style of entertainment figures, could be seen in the Media Hotel at all hours. They seemed to be China's pop celebrities. When they were not being swept into and out of sleek Mercedes, Jaguars, and BMWs at the hotel's entrance, a youthful entourage constantly surrounded them. On the city streets were thousands upon thousands of people in nondescript outerwear, all of them pedaling in synchrony on modest bicycles in a sea of vehicular motion. The contrast between the hotel crowd and the city's ordinary citizens was striking.

On my last day in Beijing, Zhang De planned to accompany me to the celebrated Peking Opera. I was weary at the end of a long day at the institute and faced a very early departure the next morning. I proposed to him that we cancel the planned entertainment. Zhang De persisted, suggesting that I should not miss this unusual performance. I finally yielded. The event took place in a new theater building. We had box seats in the orchestra, where we were served peanuts and beer. The colorful performers danced, sang, juggled, and dueled with swords and knives. Large posters above the stage explained the plots. Program notes, all in English, provided descriptions of the three different main acts of the show. Never before had I seen more imaginative staging, costumes, and props. The skilled and energetic antics of the performers were a delight to watch as the skits unfolded. The precision of their animated body movements and their flawless dancing and singing were the hallmarks of these gifted artists. I remain indebted to Zhang De for his insistence that I not miss the justly celebrated Peking Opera.

When I returned from China, I learned that our research project with the Kellogg Foundation would begin in the fall, but for a one-year pilot or demonstration phase of the larger scale study. I was designated project director. Eileen Abels and Gary Marchionini were the associate project directors. The work was expected to test only method and process. We would not bring the full-scale, online database into being. Our efforts concentrated on demonstrating the usefulness of the information by focusing on three topical areas that were drawn from the fuller set of the approximately thirty subjects needed for a full-scale inventory. These topics were environment, quality of life, and business and economic concerns. The work would offer facts and figures on Montgomery County, consisting of hypertext links, data mounted on the system, and pointers to print or electronic sources on these subjects. Our strategy focused on several main components — system development, information gathering, forging relationships with agencies of the county, collaborative efforts with the public library staff, and laboratory use of Maryland Library School classes to afford student and faculty applied experiences in working on information needed for the project. An article appeared describing the research in *Journal of Education for Library and Information Science*, Summer 1997, Vol. 38, No. 3, "A Prospective Alternative Direction for Educational Practice: A Conceptual and Operational Model." Eileen Abels, Gary Marchionini, and Paul Wasserman authored the article.

As the research proceeded through the first year, responsibilities in carrying out the work shifted. Gary Marchionini's major contributions came at the early stages, when the basic decisions were made on the data structure and the implementation of systems configurations. Following this phase, he gradually withdrew from active involvement. Eileen Abels took over as project director, since she had taken on the heaviest burden of managing the research and supervising the work of the student research assistants. In the spring of 1997, negotiations began with the Kellogg Foundation for funding the second phase of the research. Kellogg approved the grant. The continuing research would lead to the completion of the construction and full implementation of an operational database by the end of 1998. In this later phase, my role had been reduced to that of consultant to the project. Eileen Abels served from there on as project director.

I maintained a limited degree of involvement with the project through 1998. I attended collaborative planning meetings with public library and other county officials. Before the contractual period had concluded by the end of the year, my contributions had grown less important. With the Kellogg grant nearing an end, the complete database included a full range of the subjects incorporated. The system included features to ensure that the file could be perpetually updated. The difficulty, however, was that once the Kellogg funding was no longer available, the funds needed to carry the work forward — mainly support for student assistant researchers, who would maintain and update the database content under faculty supervision — were absent. At the time the project had originally been designed, assurances had been sought from the public library to provide support beyond the term of foundation sponsorship. In the interim, however, the library's directorship changed hands. By 1999, the Montgomery County Department of Economic Development took over support for the county database. A small contribution also came from the Montgomery County Department of Public Libraries. Eileen Abels continues to direct the project, while I remain an advisor to the program.

Early in December 1995, I was privileged to enjoy a retirement party in the company of more than one hundred colleagues, friends, former students, and family members. Many touching communications were received from others who were not present. It was a very moving celebration. When I had the honor of offering the commencement address to the fall graduating class later in December 1995, I returned to a theme I had espoused from the inception of the Maryland program many years earlier. The talk was called "Change and the Maryland MLS Graduate." These remarks have never been published before, but they encapsulate many of the views and values I have long held and still hold about librarianship. Perhaps it is only fitting, therefore, that I conclude my story with these observations.

> The theme of my remarks is change. I plead guilty to having shrilly echoed this societal battle cry for many more years than I would like to confess. Still, let me revisit and bring into contemporary focus some comments I first began to make in print more than thirty years ago and suggest some guideposts for fresh entrants to the professional ranks of the occupation.
>
> I said then, "We live in a society whose only constant may be change. In this mass, complex technological society, the average citizen is engaged in changing jobs many times, perhaps even shifting careers in adapting to new cultural, educational, and economic circumstances. In such a context, the fair-minded observer of library instruction and library practice perceives how libraries, like many other institutional forms, are failing." I said that "libraries fail because they are morally and psychologically bound to physical plant and to physical objects rather than to clienteles and to problem solving. They fail because they identify with the status quo."
>
> Let me explain to you what led me to these conclusions and what I saw as impediments to far-reaching change for libraries. Before there can be broad and sweeping change, there must first be revised ideology. But earlier values are deeply ingrained in the hearts and minds of every practitioner community. The conceptual ideology, or if you will, the paradigm of the social organization, of which libraries constitute one illustration, is its tradition. Tradition exerts an enormous influence upon the minds of those committed to an institutional form and its practices, upon the sentiments of the occupation engaged in the activities carried out in the organization, as well as upon those who are sympathetic to, and supportive of, the institution and the people who work in it.
>
> The age-old, conventional norms or traditions, which have supported libraries, are two. The first has been the notion that a library stands

The Best of Times

alone and apart, enjoys an integrity unique to itself, and is intended solely for its own singular group of users. The second has been that the library, both in the mind's eye of librarians and of its users, is synonymous with its collection or its holdings. For libraries and for librarianship to forge new directions, these classic prescriptive definitions have stood, and still stand, in need of inversion. Grudgingly, yet inexorably, these traditional values are under assault. The stand-alone, independent, self-sufficient library yields to the system and the network. The zeal for holdings and inventory as a measure of distinction gives way to accepting effective response to the client as prime indicator of success. It all seems so obvious and simple. But the barriers to such a fundamental revision of classic beliefs and values and their translation into library practice are formidable indeed. These range across a very wide continuum — from reluctance by those holding authority to the notion of yielding administrative prerogatives in some libraries, all the way to recalcitrant faculty who believe they must have everything physically at hand. Fortunately, technology has come to serve as a new intervening variable, driving a far swifter pace of adaptation than might even have been imagined only a few years ago. Less sanguine has been the relentless economic assault upon libraries, making library managers and practitioners far more strictly accountable for their stewardship of an ever more remorselessly diminishing financial base. So we have been and are, willy-nilly, in the throes of dramatic change, sometimes through strategic calculation by our administrative class, but perhaps more often, driven by the sharp cost-effective scrutiny of those to whom libraries are responsible and from whom support is drawn.

Perhaps the cruelest irony is that these changes, these scale backs and reductions have been occurring precisely during the time when the world is experiencing what is tirelessly or tiresomely labeled the information age. Somehow, perhaps in consequence of our having failed to signal the incongruity of the denigration of library programs while simultaneously celebrating the dawn of a new information era, libraries continue to be reduced in scale and stature. Perhaps it has been because to the lay mind, the rise of the Internet bespeaks a time when users see the personal information garnering process as circumventing the intermediary through individual direct access to information in problem resolution. Perhaps it is because the pace of change in libraries and library practice has not swiftly or universally enough effected a thoroughgoing metamorphosis to the new paradigm of networks and user focus. Or it may be that we have not clearly enough enumerated our revised purposes, emphases, and targets, so that the practical effect is a user class that fails to comprehend that libraries and librarianship have changed and been enlisted in a revised agenda of arrangements, activities, and services to clients. Still, faulting users and obstreperous overseers and higher level officials for the ills of libraries, librarianship, and, yes, library education, is foolhardy, self-defeating, and purposeless.

In order to influence fortuitously, change for the better, we must accelerate the rate of change in new and imaginative ways. Ultimately, the relevance, value, and value-added measures of worth are in the eye of the beholder and not under the control of libraries or librarians. It seems to me that what is at issue here is the image of the library, the image of the librarian. The library, the librarian can be seen as indispensable, or they can be seen as marginal. How they are perceived by those in our society who decide upon resource allocation, as well as those who are the actual and potential users of libraries, profoundly affects our condition. High status for an agency and for an occupational class would confer not only an improved revenue base for libraries, but also greater parity for librarians with others in the professional class.

How then do we exploit the processes of change in order to enhance our status and reinforce our significance in a period of duress? My sense is that the likeliest avenue of opportunity is through role adaptation in ways that move the occupation from a reactive to a more proactive posture. Let me proffer a modest prescriptive list of seven recommendations to consider if you are to help ensure the future of a safer world for the field during your occupational lifetimes.

- *Add to the intellectual base of the discipline.*

    I have said elsewhere that many in librarianship like to think of themselves as intellectuals. Invariably their self-perception is based not upon substantive commitment to their own discipline, but rather to other fields. It is possible to distinguish between the intellectual librarian and the library intellectual. The intellectual librarian uses his or her intellectual capacity as part of the equipment in the vocational role. It is relevant to the problem-solving processes and to the nature of the personal contribution. While he or she see themselves basically as librarians, their intellectual side is exploited to advance librarianship. The library intellectual dismisses librarianship as a potential avenue of scholarly investigation and looks for such stimuli elsewhere. There are many library intellectuals, but relatively few intellectual librarians. I urge you to take seriously the intellectual side of librarianship — to ponder and analyze our problems, for they are innumerable, ranging from economics, to markets, to technical questions and beyond. I urge you to abjure the negativism, which implies that the problems of librarianship are unsuited to intellectualization — as if there were a fundamental dichotomy between thought and action, between theory and practice. Do not emphasize only action and responsibility for action, and downgrade contemplation and analytic pursuits. Contribute your thinking in professional forums and the literature of the field. For as our scholarly discourse grows, so does our esteem in the wider culture.

■ *Harness the emergent technology in purposeful ways.*

The case here is evident. No thinking librarian disputes this need any longer. Herein may reside the ultimate claim to professionalism. For even as we are in a time when the user may hold mastery in using electronic resources in a limited substantive field, the complexities of staying au courant in the protocols and arrangements across the gamut of knowledge has been rendered formidable indeed. In a simpler time we helped our users become their own librarians — wasn't this the consequence of teaching every one how to use the Dewey decimal classification and the *Reader's Guide*? It is unlikely that our expertise will often be relied upon when specialists like lawyers or professors seek information in their own narrow sphere — they'll doubtless continue to rely upon their own knowledge of the special systems of their disciplines or have their assistants do it for them. In a time when the range of information access stretches across literally hundreds of options, and when subject areas are constantly intersecting and overlapping, no one can hope to keep abreast of how to get at information across the full range of possibilities — or even to understand what the possibilities may be — except for those who specialize in keeping up with all of it. This of course is the stock in trade of the information professional.

Interestingly, while it may have been more unreasonable to lay claim to professional know-how when information recourse was simpler, in a period when it has become far more complex — with an innumerable and bewildering array of alternatives open — herein may well reside our unique means of enhanced status. So, staying on top of and controlling the perplexing variety of electronic options for clients holds clear promise for raising the visibility and perceived importance and status of the occupation among all those whose reliance and dependence upon librarian intermediation with data stores continues to grow.

- ■ *Build a personal substantive base in a subject matter area.*

In 1924 William Learned in a celebrated Carnegie study, *The American Public Library and the Diffusion of Knowledge,* first spoke of the need for "an intelligence personnel." Among the requisites Learned saw were "personal tact, quick intellectual sympathies and appreciation, a thorough knowledge of a certain field, precision and discrimination of thought and the power promptly to organize results." He said, "The reference expert must command all of the college teacher's familiarity with the literature of a field. It is important that the service go further than placing a pile of strange books or other printed material on the table before an applicant." To paraphrase, Learned saw that the librarian who serves clients must know the subject field and be more discriminating. This is the model for the fields of professional practice with which we would like to be compared. We defer to the doctor or lawyer because he knows and tells us how we may expect to solve the problem put to him. We must move beyond the level of performing as well-meaning generalists with a smattering of knowledge of many things, but no claim to the authority of expertise. We do have such types of librarians in our present ranks. They include the law librarians with legal preparation, the academic subject bibliographers, and the special librarians in many settings schooled in both librarianship and the subject matter of the fields they serve, from business to chemistry. Without a base of subject understanding, it is hard to imagine how the librarian may ever fully command the respect and attention of clients when answers to important substantive questions are sought rather than the simple identification of materials from which the user chooses. Subject expertise is built upon formal academic preparation or a serious program of self-study. Until librarians are far more widely seen as able to couple subject matter mastery with their information skills, the image of the occupation is less likely to improve markedly.

- *Consider the pursuit of entrepreneurial means in your work.*

If we were to characterize our time with any degree of accuracy we might identify it as the epoch of the entrepreneur. How can librarians climb aboard this engine of contemporary movement? Unlike most periods in our history, when the exclusive fate of all who entered the ranks was a destiny to play out their occupational histories in library bureaucracies, there are now a number of new avenues open to those educated for the profession. Those who gravitate toward these new paths may be a relatively small proportion of those in the field, but the number has been growing rapidly in recent years and continues to grow. For the skills and abilities honed through library education equip you to put your talents to work in a growing number of unconventional contexts. One is by hanging out a shingle and setting up as an information broker. Probably, this becomes a more viable option after some period of experience in practice. In a world in which information is understood as a crucial ingredient by many professionals and businesses, who may not be able to afford a full-fledged library, the consulting services of information specialists become an interesting alternative. Then there are roles in organizations that serve or sell to libraries. A fair number of library-trained individuals work as what might be termed information engineers — helping to install and train library staffs in the use of systems and technology. Some have moved into positions in the publishing world where their library training translates into working on reference works or databases, which are marketed to libraries. The corporate world has also beckoned to some who channel their abilities toward information and systems management assignments. In a time of growing privatization, a number of companies — some founded and run by librarians — carry out library contracts for government agencies or companies. They often employ library graduates, but the potential for librarians themselves to start such enterprises is clear. The number of these entrepreneurial outlets of expression continues to expand and holds promise for those of you with an independent cast of mind who might relish vocational expression in a non-traditional setting along with its potentially greater risks and rewards than the more orthodox library milieu.

■ *Use your ingenuity and expertise in the invention and design of information products.*

Certainly, inventiveness and innovation have been displayed by individual librarians many times during the history of the occupation. Indeed, classification schemes, cataloging systems, indexes to periodical literature, microformats, and advanced information systems have all been brought into being as the consequence of the imagination and creativity of forward-looking and pioneering librarians. Yet in more recent times, during the transition of the occupation into a bureaucratically bound class, the ritualization of performance rites has tended to create a more rigid self-definition among practitioners, which devolves more exclusively upon searching rather than inventing. There have been and continue to be instances of creative contributions among librarians, but the general perspective of the occupation is that inventive performance is a kind of aberration or unique class of phenomena outside the accepted definitions of the librarian's occupational role.

Built into the know-how of many who perform in librarianship are unique types of substantive and structural knowledge, which are perhaps unique in the society. Librarians often specialize in subject areas, research and operating fields, and the information requirements of disciplines and technologies, and so are especially sensitive to the range and types of information inquiries that arise and are being continuously modified through the changing conditions of the general culture and of specific subject fields. Reference work, moreover, affords an individual a special form of sensitivity to the way in which knowledge is organized and controlled and endows those who practice it with valuable insights into the ways in which useful constructions and syntheses might be made in order to build necessary new and workable information tools and systems.

What seems to be lacking is a fundamental revision of the conceptual basis for the occupational responsibility — that is, acceptance of a revised role definition for librarianship, or at least for some of those who practice it. Librarianship might well be redefined to include responsibility for more than simply providing information to clients based upon what can be found through searches; it might also embrace the responsibility for actively devising and planning needed new information products and services if they would valuably contribute to client requirements. Anything less, in my view, sells the profession short and conditions it to a lesser image among those from whom status and reputational esteem are perennially sought — the client group. The image of an occupation is the reflection of how it is perceived by those for whom it exists. To the extent that librarians serve but seldom create, limits are set on the stature and esteem to which the occupation aspires.

- *Engage in political activity on behalf of the occupation.*

Libraries are fundamentally influenced by the political world in which they are enmeshed. Yet many librarians are repulsed by the very idea of engaging in political processes, for they reason that every right-minded person knows how important libraries are. Isn't the library rhetorically referred to among other similar descriptors, as the "heart of the university?" Perhaps in every season except the budget time, when it is simply another competitor for a piece of an ever-shrinking pie. Many of the gains won by librarians in America, from the national to the local level, have been achieved only because of sophisticated strategic political engagement. From the early enactment of the Library Services and Construction Act to the latest referendum for a library purpose that finds its way to a county ballot, there has been forceful and imaginative political engineering by librarians and by those whom they have enlisted in their cause. In our negotiating, deal-making, polarized society, few gains for institutions or those who are employed in them are granted because of generosity, good will, or kindness. Gains are accomplished by building a constituent following, and then dexterously exploiting it through well-calculated political means. Have you ever considered why in some universities librarians enjoy faculty status while in most they do not? If you were to review the modern history of these institutions, you would learn that seldom was such a valued status achieved without there having been waged a bitter and protracted political war. Whether your work role takes you into a corporation, a public library, or an academic or research agency, political naivete will be a handicap. I would urge you to recognize that while its culture may differ, every organization represents a political playing ground where crucial decisions are as often based upon political as substantive considerations. While I do not admonish you to commit to memory every Machiavellian precept, I do strongly recommend that you study well and participate actively and purposefully in your organization's political machinations.

- *Understand always that change is possible in your organization.*

We often hear people talk about some omnipotent "they." One writer has suggested that we all, even the most competent people, carry over from childhood an emotional dependence upon adults, feeling ourselves to be helpless victims of circumstances beyond our control. We may mutter about the university administration or the county board or the corporate president, but feel it would be quixotic to assume that we can do anything to change the situation. So it is up to "them"—some vague authorities. We certainly cannot do anything to change anything for the better. "They" ought to do this or that. Thus, in a large library, the single individual is likely to believe that the only contribution one can make is to do his or her own limited job properly. Big changes that one may feel are needed seem hopelessly beyond reach.

Enmeshed in the system, many fail to use what leeway for expression or for improvement they have. So, librarians often assume — without testing the limits — that they would not be allowed to innovate or to make changes as they might wish to. If we feel helpless and behave as if we are helpless, then we become helpless. Libraries, because of their history and traditions of stability may not be swift paced, rapidly adapting environments. Yet perhaps precisely because this is so, there may be far wider latitude, particularly in threatening times, for there to be a heightened disposition for their leadership to be open to proposed alternatives. I urge you to speak up and speak out, not necessarily stridently, but calmly and resolutely, when you see a need for organizational change for the better. If we believe we can make a difference, we can make a difference. Even the prisoner being led to his execution can kick his jailer in the shins.

I have outlined for you a demanding set of marching orders. Doubtless they incorporate demands far beyond what was required of you as you underwent the tribal rites of entry into the field during your course of master's degree study. But then you are the future of the profession. In the time-honored tradition of occupational ambitions, it is your duty to stand on the shoulders of those who went before you and to see farther and more clearly the path ahead and to stride boldly forth. You have concluded a demanding course of study, during which you have developed habits of mind and the discipline to help you succeed toward your goal. Congratulations upon your commencement — your beginning! Aim high and continue as you have begun.

Publications and Professional Chronology

Publications

Editor, *Service to Business*, Brooklyn Public Library, 1949-1951.

"Are We Neglecting the Small Businessman?" *Wilson Library Bulletin*, 25 (8): 625, 1951.

Information for Administrators: A Guide to Publications and Services for Management in Business and Government, Cornell University Press, 1956.

"On Developing an Administration Library for a Foreign University," with Stephen A. McCarthy, *College and Research Libraries*, 17 (5): 375, 1956.

Book Review Editor, *Administrative Science Quarterly*, Cornell University, Graduate School of Business and Public Administration, 1956-1961.

Basic Library in Public Administration, Cornell University, Graduate School of Business and Public Administration, 1957.

"A Proposed Method for Finding a Position: Information Sources for Occupational Guidance by Geographic Area," *Personnel and Guidance Journal*, with Mason, 1958.

"Measuring Performance in a Special Library: Problems and Prospects," *Special Libraries*, 49 (8): 377, 1958.

Decision Making: An Annotated Bibliography, Cornell University, Graduate School of Business and Public Administration, with Fred S. Silander, 1958.

Decision Making: An Annotated Bibliography Supplement, 1958-1963, Cornell University, Graduate School of Business and Public Administration, with Fred S. Silander, 1964.

"Development of Administration in Library Service: Current Status and Future Prospects," *College and Research Libraries*, 19 (4): 283, 1958.

"Administration and the Special Library," *Bulletin of the Western New York Chapter, Special Libraries Association*, Winter 1959.

Publications — 1959 to 1962

Measurement and Evaluation of Organizational Performance: An Annotated Bibliography, Cornell University, Graduate School of Business and Public Administration, 1959.

Toward a Methodology for the Formulation of Objectives in Public Libraries: An Empirical Analysis, University of Michigan, 1960. (Ph.D. dissertation)

Managing Editor, *Sources of Commodity Prices*, with the Committee on Sources of Commodity Prices, Business and Finance Division, Special Libraries Association, 1960.

"Contrasts Between Information Consumers and Middlemen," *Bulletin of the Business and Finance Division*, Special Libraries Association, Spring 1960.

Editor, *Directory of University Research Bureaus and Institutes*, Gale Research Company, 1960.

Sources for Hospital Administrators: Publications and Facilities Serving the Health Administration Field, Cornell University, Graduate School of Business and Public Administration, 1961.

"Research Frontiers of Public Libraries," *Library Journal*, 86 (13): 2409, July 1961.

"Policy Formulation in Libraries," *Illinois Libraries*, December 1961.

Editor, *Health Organizations of the United States and Canada and Internationally*, Cornell University, Graduate School of Business and Public Administration, 1961; Second edition, 1965; Third edition, 1974, McGrath Publishing Company, Associate Editor, Joan Giesecke; Fourth edition, 1977, Anthony T. Kruzas Associates with Jane Bossart; Fifth edition, 1981, Gale Research Company.

Editor, *Statistics Sources: A Subject Guide to Data on Industrial, Business, Social, Educational, Financial, and Other Topics for the United States and Selected Foreign Countries*, Gale Research Company, with Charlotte Georgi and Anthony T. Kruzas, 1962; Second edition, with Eleanor B. Allen and Charlotte Georgi, 1965; Third edition, with Eleanor B. Allen and Charlotte Georgi, 1971; Fourth edition, Joanne Paskar, Associate editor, 1974; Fifth edition, Jacqueline Bernero, Associate editor, 1977; Sixth edition, Jacqueline O'Brien, Associate editor, Kenneth Clansky, Assistant editor, 1980; Seventh edition, Jacqueline O'Brien, Associate editor, Daphne A. Grace, Assistant editor, Kenneth Clansky, Assistant editor, 1982; Eighth edition, Jacqueline O'Brien, Associate editor, Daphne A. Grace, Assistant editor, Kenneth Clansky, Assistant editor, 1983; Ninth edition, Daphne A. Grace, Assistant editor, Kenneth Clansky, Assistant editor, 1984.

Publications — 1963 to 1967

Managing Editor, Management Information Guide Series, Gale Research Company, 1963-1982.

"One of a Species: The Special Library — Past, Present and Future," *Library Journal*, 89 (4): 797, February 15, 1964.

"A Management Resource," *Library Journal*, 89 (19): 4280, November 1, 1964.

The Librarian and the Machine: Observations on the Applications of Machines in the Administration of College and University Libraries, Gale Research Company, 1965.

"Management of Access to Information: Observations on the Problems of the Middleman," *West Virginia Libraries*, March 1965.

Managing Editor, *Executive's Guide to Information Sources*, Three volumes, Business Guides Company, with B. A. Olive (Distributed by Gale Research Company), 1965.

Manpower for the Library and Information Professions in the 1970's: An Inquiry into Fundamental Problems, University of Maryland School of Library and Information Services, with Mary Lee Bundy, 1966.

"The New School of Library and Information Services at the University of Maryland," *DC Libraries*, 20, Spring 1966.

"The Role of the Information Specialist in Industry," in *Management Information Systems and the Information Specialist*, Purdue University, Krannert Graduate School of Industrial Administration, and the University Libraries, 1966 (Proceedings of a Symposium held July 12-13, 1965).

"The Direction of Reference and Bibliographic Activities," in *Proceedings of the Second Biennial Department Workshop*, U.S. Department of the Interior, November 14-18, 1966.

Managing Editor, *Consultants and Consulting Organizations*, Cornell University, Graduate School of Business and Public Administration, with Willis R. Greer, Jr., 1966; Second edition, Gale Research Company, 1973; Third edition, Janice W. McLean, Associate editor, 1976; Fourth edition with Janice W. McLean, 1979; Fifth edition with Janice W. McLean, 1982.

"The Library and Information Professions in a Time of Change," *PNLA Quarterly*, January 1967.

"A Departure in Library Education: A Report of an Experimental Project at Maryland," with Mary Lee Bundy, *Journal of Education for Librarianship*, 124, 1967.

Publications — 1967 to 1969

A Program of Research into the Identification of Manpower Requirements, the Educational Preparation and the Utilization of Manpower in the Library and Information Professions: Proposal for Research and/or Related Activities Submitted to the U.S. Commissioner of Education for Support Through Authorization of the Bureau of Research, University of Maryland, College of Library and Information Services, 1967.

"Manpower Blueprint," with Mary Lee Bundy, *Library Journal*, 92 (2): 197, January 15, 1967.

"Professionalism Reconsidered," with Mary Lee Bundy, *College and Research Libraries*, 29 (1): 5, January 1968.

"The Character and Responsibility of a Graduate School," with R. Brian Land, Guy A. Marco, Andrew H. Horn, Perry D. Morrison, Kenneth R. Shaffer, Harold Goldstein, and Lawrence Allen, *Library Journal*, 93 (9): 1869, May 1, 1968.

Managing Editor, *Who's Who in Consulting: A Reference Guide to Professional Personnel Engaged in Consultation for Business, Industry and Government*, Cornell University, Graduate School of Business and Public Administration, 1968, Margaret Clark, Associate editor; Second edition, Gale Research Company, Janice W. McLean, Associate editor, 1973.

"The Gale Research Management Information Guide Series: A Publishing Effort by and for Librarians," *RQ*, 7 (4): 155, Summer 1968.

Managing Editor, *Reader Series in Librarianship and Information Science*, Microcard Editions, 1968-1979.

Co-editor, *Reader in Library Administration*, with Mary Lee Bundy, Microcard Editions, 1968.

Trends and Directions in Library Education and Library Practice, University of Denver, Graduate School of Librarianship, Isabel Nichol Lecture Series, February 21, 1968.

"Maryland's Manpower Project: A Progress Report," with Mary Lee Bundy, *Library Journal*, 93 (7): 1409, April 1, 1968.

"Elements in a Manpower Blueprint — Library Personnel for the 1970's," *American Library Association Bulletin*, 63 (5), 581, May 1969.

A Report on the Need for Additional Programs in Library Education at the Graduate Level in the Publicly Supported Higher Education System in the State of Ohio, Board of Regents of the State of Ohio in Columbus, 1969.

Publications — 1969 to 1970

A Program of Research into the Identification of Manpower Requirements: The Educational Preparation and the Utilization of Manpower in the Library and Information Professions (Final Report: Phase I), with Mary Lee Bundy, University of Maryland, School of Library and Information Services, 1969, printed by the United States Office of Education, Educational Resources Information Center, 1969.

Managing Editor, *Awards, Honors, and Prizes*, Janice W. McLean, Assistant editor, Gale Research Company, 1969; Second edition, Jeffrey Reed, Associate editor, Janice W. McLean, Assistant editor, 1972; Third edition, Janice W. McLean, Associate editor (Vol. 1), Krystyna Wasserman, Associate editor (Vol. 2), 1975; Fourth edition, Janice McLean, Associate editor (Vol. 1), 1978; Fifth edition, Gita Siegman, Associate editor (Vol. 1), Krystyna Wasserman, Associate editor (Vol. 2), 1982.

"Library and Information Center Management," with Evelyn Daniel in *Annual Review of Information Science, 1969,* 405, 1969.

Co-editor, *Reader in Research Methods for Librarianship*, with Mary Lee Bundy and Gayle Araghi, 1969.

Series Editor, *Contributions in Librarianship and Information Science*, Greenwood Publishing Corporation, 1969-1999.

"Professional Adaptation: Library Education Mandate," *Library Journal*, 95 (7): 1281, April 1, 1970.

A Study of the Executive in Library and Information Activity consisting of the following reports: *The Academic Library Administrator and His Situation*, with Mary Lee Bundy and Paul Wasserman, May 1970; *The Public Library Administrator and His Situation*, with Mary Lee Bundy and Jeanne O'Connell, June 1970; *The Administrator of a Special Library or Information Center and His Situation*, with Mary Lee Bundy and Jeanne O'Connell, August 1970; *The School Library Administrator and Her Situation*, with Mary Lee Bundy and Jeanne O'Connell, September 1970.

"The Birth of LIST: Report of a Seminar that Linked Library Education with Product Development," with Evelyn Daniel, *Library Journal*, 95 (20): 3879, November 15, 1970.

Managing Editor, *Library and Information Science Today (LIST)*, Science Associates International, 1970-1972, Gale Research Company, 1973-1974.

Publications — 1971 to 1975

Managing Editor, *Encyclopedia of Business Information Sources*, Gale Research Company, 1971-1983.

Coordinating Managing Editor, Information Guide Library Series, Gale Research Company, 1971-1983.

"Engineering Change in Librarianship: From Revised Paradigm to Prototypes of the Future," in *Library Lectures, 30*, Louisiana State University, March 24, 1972.

The New Librarianship: A Challenge for Change, R. R. Bowker Company, 1972.

"The Special Library Manager: A Profile," with Jeanne O'Connell, *Special Libraries, 63* (12): 568, December 1972.

"Project to Inventory Specialized Indexes in Libraries and Information Centers," in *Proceedings of the 36th Annual Meeting of the American Society for Information Science*, October 21-25, 1973, American Society for Information Science, 1973.

Managing Editor, *Museum Media: A Biennial Directory and Index of Publications and Audiovisuals Available from United States and Canadian Institutions*, Esther Herman, Associate editor, Gale Research Company, 1973; Second edition, 1980.

Commodity Prices: A Source Book and Index, with Diane Kemmerling, Gale Research Company, 1974.

"Educational Issues in International Information Systems Development," in *Proceedings of the International Seminar on Education in Information Science*, 1974 (presented at the Conference on Educational Problems in Information Science, FID/ET Committee, Veszprem, Hungary, September 14-16, 1972).

Managing Editor, *Consumer Sourcebook*, with Jean Morgan, Gale Research Company, 1974; Second edition, Jean Morgan, Associate editor, 1978; Third edition, Gita Siegman, Associate editor, 1980; Fourth edition, Gita Siegman, Associate editor, 1983.

"Recruitment and Utilization of Personnel: An Aspirational View," *Documentaliste, 11* (1), March 1974 (presented at the Seminar on Levels and Specializations in the Educational Preparation of Information Professionals, Paris, France, 1973).

Library Bibliographies and Indexes, Esther Herman, Associate editor, Gale Research Company, 1975.

"International Educational Patterns in Information Science: Characteristics and Issues," in *Information Resolution: Proceedings of the 38th ASIS Annual Meeting*, Boston, Massachusetts, October 26-30, 1975, American Society for Information Science, 1975.

"Entwicklungstendenzen der Erziehung und Ausbildung in der Informations und Documentations Wissenschaft: Spezifika, Probleme, und Vorschlage," in *Conference Proceedings* (Presented in the Colloquium on Information and Documentation by the Technische Hochschule in Ilmenau, German Democratic Republic) November 1975 (in German).

Co-author, *Outline for a Course in Administration for Managers of Information Services*, with John R. Rizzo, United Nations Educational, Scientific and Cultural Organization (UNESCO), 1976 (published also in French and Spanish).

Managing Editor, *Ethnic Information Sources of the United States*, Jean Morgan, Associate editor, Gale Research Company, 1976; Second edition, Alice E. Kennington, Associate editor, 1983.

"Use of Video-tape in Education for Information Science," and "Management Course for Administrators of Information Programs in Developing Countries — Experiences in Latin America and South East Asia" (Presented at the Seminar on Education and Training held in Mexico City, September 20-24, 1976, during FID Conference).

Managing Editor, *Festivals Sourcebook*, Esther Herman, Associate editor, Elizabeth A. Root, Assistant director, Gale Research Company, 1977; Second edition, Edmond L. Applebaum, Associate editor, 1984.

Self-Instruction Training Materials for Librarians and Information Scientists: The Use of Text and Video Learning Modules, FID/ET Committee, Warsaw, Poland, May 1977, author of modular units consisting of text and video lectures as follows:
1. An Introduction to Basic Elements in the Organization and Administration of Libraries,
2. The Administrative Process at Work in Library Administration,
3. An Introduction to Basic Information Sources in American Business and Economics.
All issued by Library Training Consultants, 1977.

Managing Editor, *Encyclopedia of Geographic Information Sources*, Third edition, James Sanders and Elizabeth Talbot Sanders, Associate editors, Gale Research Company, 1978.

Managing Editor, *Training and Development Organizations*, with Marlene A. Palmer, Gale Research Company, 1978; Second edition, Janice W. McLean, Associate editor, 1980; Third edition, Janice W. McLean, Associate editor, 1983.

Publications — 1979 to 1984

Member, Editorial Board, *Journal of Library Administration*, 1979-1989.

Managing Editor, *Speakers and Lecturers: How To Find Them*, Jacqueline Bernero, Associate editor, Gale Research Company, 1979; Second edition, Vol. 1, Jacqueline O'Brien and Daphne A. Rhudy, Associate editors; Vol. 2, Louise Hardy Hayman, Associate editor, 1981.

"Problems in Education and Training in Marketing and Marketing Research in Information Science," in *Education and Training: Theory and Provision*, with Gary Ford, International Federation for Documentation, 1979.

Managing Editor, *Newsletter on Education and Training Programmes for Specialized Information Personnel*, International Federation for Documentation, Quarterly, 1979-1982.

Managing Editor, *Learning Independently*, James Sanders and Elizabeth T. Sanders, Associate editors, 1979; Second edition, Edmond L. Applebaum, Associate editor, 1982.

Recreation and Outdoor Life Directory, with Steven Wasserman, Gale Research Company, 1979; Second edition, 1983.

Law and Legal Information Directory, with Marek Kaszubski, Gale Research Company, 1980; Second edition, with Marek Kaszubski, 1983; Third edition, Steven Wasserman, Associate editor, 1984.

Editor, "A Formal Course in Business Information Services," in *Education and Training for Information Services in Business and Industry in Developing and Developed Countries: The Needs, the Experience, the Newer Trends*, papers presented at the Education and Training Committee Workshop, Minneapolis, Minnesota, October 11-12, 1979, International Federation for Documentation, 1980.

"Marketing and Marketing Research: What the Library Manager Should Learn," with Gary T. Ford, *Journal of Library Administration*, 1 (1): 19, Spring 1980.

"Training and Development of a Library and Technical Information Staff," with Eileen Goldstein, *Special Libraries*, 72 (3): 290, July 1981.

Member, Editorial Board, *National Information System for Science and Technology (NISSAT), Newsletter*, New Delhi, 1982-1996.

Member, Editorial Board, *Education for Information: The International Review of Education and Training in Library and Information Science*, 1983-1987.

"Technological Innovation in Information Transfer: Strategies of Information Management," *Revista, AIBDA*, 5 (1): 1, January/June 1984.

"Review of International and Regional Programmes in Training Managers for the Information Profession," *Education for Information*, 2 (1): 3, March 1984.

The Teaching of Management as a Subject for the Preparation of Librarians, Documentalists, Archivists and Other Information Specialists. United Nations Educational, Scientific and Cultural Organization (UNESCO) International Symposium on Harmonization of Education and Training Programmes in Information Science, Librarianship, and Archival Studies, October 1984.

"Invention and Design of Information Products and Services," *Infomediary*, 1 (11): 1985.

Managing Editor, *Business and Management Sourcebook Series*, Oryx Press, 1985-1989.

Encyclopedia of Health Information Sources, Suzanne Grefsheim, Associate editor, Gale Research Company, 1987.

Encyclopedia of Senior Citizens Information Sources, Barbara Koehler and Yvonne Lev, Associate editors, Gale Research Company, 1987.

Encyclopedia of Legal Information Sources, Gary McCann and Patricia Tobin, Associate editors, Gale Research Company, 1988.

Encyclopedia of Public Affairs Information Sources, James R. Kelly and Desider Vikor, Associate editors, Gale Research Company, 1988.

Editorial Consultant, Omnigraphics, Inc., 1988-1991.

Member, Editorial Board, *Behavioral and Social Science Librarian*, 1988-1992.

Managing Editor, Where-To-Find-It Business and Management Series, Omnigraphics, Inc., 1989-1992.

Member, Editorial Board, *Privatization*, Omnigraphics, Inc., 1991.

"Information Transfer in Science and Technology: An Overview," *Asian Libraries*, 1 (2): 27, September 1991.

"Obieg Informacji w Nauce i Technice. The Information Communication and Transfer Process in Sciences," *Zagadnienia Informacji Naukowej*, 1-2: 5, 1994 (in Polish).

"Developing New Information Products: A Revised Role for Librarianship in Advanced and Developing Countries," *IFLA Journal*, 21(4): 287, November 1995.

"A Prospective Alternative Direction for Educational Practice: A Conceptual and Operational Model," with Eileen G. Abels and Gary Marchionini, *Journal of Education for Library and Information Science, 38*, 211, Summer 1997.

Professional Activities and Awards

1950's

Treasurer, Library Public Relations Council, 1951.

American Library Association Representative to the National Health Council, 1952-1953.

Chairman, Business Division, Special Libraries Association, 1952-1953.

Chairman, Business and Technology Committee, Reference Division, American Library Association, 1952-1953.

Chairman, Committee on Special Libraries/State Library Relations, Western New York Chapter, Special Libraries Association, 1955-1958.

Lecturer, American Management Association Seminars, New York, 1956-1958.

Chairman, *Sources of Commodity Prices* Project, Special Libraries Association, 1956-1960.

Member, Committee on Promotion and Development of Special Libraries, Special Libraries Association, 1957-1959.

Research and Editorial Consultant, Gale Research Company, Detroit, 1959-1960, 1963-1964.

1960's

Director, Section on Library Organization and Management, Library Administration Division, American Library Association, 1960-1961.

Member, Committee on Standards, Special Libraries Association, 1960-1962.

Member and later Chairman, Finance Committee, Special Libraries Association, 1960-1963.

Research Planning Consultant, Indiana University School of Business, 1961-1963.

Vice-Chairman and later Chairman, Section on Library Organization and Management, Library Administration Division, American Library Association, 1961-1964.

Professional Consultant, Special Libraries Association, 1961-1969.

Directed the development of a library in administration for Middle East Technical University in Ankara, Turkey, under terms of a Cornell-U.S. Agency for International Development contract, September 1963.

Recipient, travel financial award from the American Philosophical Society, 1963-1964.

Professional Activities and Awards — 1960's to 1970's

Tangley Oaks Fellow, United Educators, Inc., 1963-1964.

Chairman, Committee on Research Program Planning, Special Libraries Association, 1963-1965.

Member, New Reference Tools Committee, Reference Services Division, American Library Association, 1964-1969.

Member, Research Committee, Library Education Division, American Library Association, 1965-1970.

Member, Statistics Committee for Library Education, Library Administration Division, American Library Association, 1965-1970.

Board Member, Information Science and Automation Division, American Library Association, 1967-1970.

Representative to the Council of National Library Associations for the American Library Association, 1967-1970.

Research Director, Library Manpower Research Study, supported by the Office of Education, National Library of Medicine, and National Science Foundation, 1967-1970.

Planner and Lecturer, Library Administrators Development Program, University of Maryland, College of Library and Information Services, 1967-1990.

Isabel Nichol Lecturer, University of Denver, Graduate School of Librarianship, 1968.

Consultant, State of Ohio Board of Regents for a study of library education program needs, 1969.

Member, Education Committee, American Society for Information Science, 1969-1971.

1970's

Board Member, Documentation Abstracts, Incorporated (Publisher of *Information Science Abstracts*), 1970-1973; Vice-President, 1971-1973.

U.S. Member, Education and Training Committee of the International Federation for Documentation, 1970-1993; Chairman, 1979-1982.

Tutor on Inventing and Designing Information Products and Services, American Society for Information Science Conference, Denver, Colorado, November 1971.

Lecturer, Louisiana State University Library Lecture Series, 1972.

Professional Activities and Awards — 1970's

Director, Institute on Comparative and International Librarianship and Information Science, University of Maryland, Summer 1972.

Planning Committee Member, Institute on Educational Problems in Information Science, International Federation and Documentation Seminar in Hungary, September 1972.

Member, Committee on International Library Education, Library Education Division, American Library Association, 1972-1974, Chairman, 1974-1976.

Chairman, Federation for International Documentation, Education and Training Committee Working Group on Establishment of International Summer School in Librarianship and Information Science, 1972-1975.

Consultant, Redgrave Information Resources, Inc., 1972-1975.

Advisory Editorial Board Member, Social Sciences Citation Index, Institute for Scientific Information, 1972-1998.

Consultant to UNISIST Program of UNESCO on development of program for managers of national information systems in developing countries, 1973.

International Lecturer, European Summer School, sponsored by Liverpool Polytechnic, 1973.

Perrie Jones Lecturer, St. Paul Public Library, May 1973.

Member, Advisory Council of UNESCO Study on Convertibility and Standards in Graduate Education in Information Science, 1973-1975.

Seminar Director, Program for Officials, Economists, and Librarians for the Brazilian Institute for Space Research in San Jose dos Campos, January 6-17, 1975.

Co-director, International Seminar for Library Administrator Development, Mexico, August 1975, under UNESCO and CONACYT sponsorship; in the Phillippines, June 1976, under UNESCO and National Science Development Board auspices; and in Ankara, Turkey, June 1977 under UNESCO and TUR-DOK sponsorship.

Consultant to UNESCO, Bureau of Libraries, Documentation and Archives, on assignment to Santiago, Chile, assisting the University of Chile, Department of Library Science of the Faculty of Philosophy and Letters, on curriculum, teaching methods, and program content, December 1976 and July-August 1977.

Consultant to Organization of American States, Unit for Technological Change, on planning and offering of workshops for personnel of information for industry centers in Central America, 1976-1978.

Member, U.S. National Committee, International Federation for Documentation, 1978-1988, Chairman, 1985-1988.

Professional Activities and Awards — 1970's to 1980's

Workshop Director and Lecturer during U.S. Agency for International Development sponsored seminars on organizing and managing information centers and services for officials and library and information personnel of the government of Panama, held in Panama City, October 17-21, 1977, and October 23-27, 1978.

Director and Lecturer, Workshop on Organizational and Administrative Issues in Librarianship, for the College and Reference Libraries Division, Kentucky Library Association, April 6-7, 1978.

Consultant to UNESCO, General Information Programme, at the Seminar on Information for Planning and Economic Development for the African Region, held in Accra under the auspices of the University of Ghana, July 18-29, 1978.

Consultant to UNESCO on National Information Systems Development in Latin America, participated in REUNIBER-78 (Conference Iberoamericana sobre informacion y documentacion cientifica y tecnologica) in Madrid, Spain, September 13-15, 1978.

Member, Planning Committee for International Federation for Documentation Committee on Education and Training, Seminar on Education and Training, Edinburgh, September 1978.

Member, Advisory Screening Committee in Librarianship of the Council for International Exchange of Scholars (Fulbright Awards), September 1979-1981; Chairman, 1981-1982.

Professor in Charge of International Education Programs, University of Maryland, College of Library and Information Services, 1979-1982.

Consultant and Workshop Series Planner for Library and Technical Information Division, Institute for Electrical Research, Cuernavaca, Mexico, December 1979-1982 and Lecturer during seminar January 26-29, 1980, on Organization and Administration of Technical Libraries and Information Centers, and on Information Systems and Sources in Business, Science and Technology, March 16-18, 1981.

1980's

Director, Clearinghouse on Education and Training Materials in Librarianship, Documentation and Information Science, and Archives, carried out at the University of Maryland for the International Federation for Documentation, under contract with UNESCO General Information Programme, January 1980-1982.

Professional Activities and Awards — 1980's

Workshop Planner and Chairman for Seminar on Education and Training held in Copenhagen, August 13-15, 1980, sponsored by the Federation for Documentation Education and Training Committee as pre-conference to the International Federation for Documentation Biennial Congress.

Chaired and organized joint meeting of the International Federation for Documentation Committee on Education and Training, IFLA Education and Research Board, International Council for Archives Committee on Education and Training, UNESCO and invited observers, in Frankfurt, December 12-13, 1980.

Chairman, Conference on Training Materials in Library and Information Science, with Particular Reference to Needs of Developing Countries, sponsored by German Foundation for International Development in Berlin, December 15-19, 1980. Contributed paper, "Transferability of Curricular Models" on December 18, 1980.

Consultant to UNESCO, General Information Programme, and Lecturer during international workshop in management for library and information center administrators in the Asian region, New Delhi, December 29, 1980-January 10, 1981.

Lecturer, Department of Librarianship, University of Guanajuato, Mexico, on Trends in Library Management and Information Systems, March 20, 1981.

Instructor in Seminar on Business and Economic Information Sources for Practicing Librarians, April 22, 1981, Washington, DC; and June 26, 1981, San Francisco, sponsored by AJ Seminars.

Chairman of Technical and Business Meeting of FID Education and Training Committee at the University of Ibadan, Nigeria, May 6-9, 1981, on the theme, Identifying Training Needs for Library and Information Services in a Predominantly Non-Literate Society.

Lecturer, Federal Institute of Industrial Research in Lagos, Nigeria, on May 11, 1981, on Business and Economic Information during United Nations Industrial Development Organization Workshop.

Consultant to INFOTEC, Mexican Government Information Service to Industry, on its Industrial Inquiry Service in Mexico City, July 27-August 5, 1981. Lectured to professional staff on Client Relationships; Marketing of Information Products; Search Strategy; Information Systems in Science and Technology; and Business and Economics. Advised professional staffs of industrial consulting, information resources, and marketing departments.

Professional Activities and Awards — 1980's

Workshop planner and Chairman of seminar held in Hong Kong, September 1982, sponsored by the International Federation for Documentation Committee on Education and Training, during the International Federation for Documentation 1982 Conference and Congress.

Member, Technical Program Review Committee for the December 1982 joint meeting of the American Society for Information Science and the Egyptian Society for Information Science, Cairo, Egypt.

Member, Advisory Board, UNESCO, for the planning of the 1984 International Conference on Harmonization of Education Programs in Librarianship, Documentation, and Archives, Paris, France, May 1983.

Attended Workshop on Management Education for the Information Professions sponsored by the International Federation of Library Associations (IFLA), International Federation for Documentation (FID), and International Council on Archives (ICA), Vienna, Austria, August 17-18, 1983.

Chairman, Editorial Advisory Board, *Education for Information: The International Review of Education and Training in Library and Information Science*, meeting held during the International Federation of Library Associations Conference, Munich, West Germany, August 20-21, 1983.

Director, Workshop for the Organization of American States Unit for Technological Change and National Technical Information Service for participants from Latin America, Miami, Florida, December 12-16, 1983. The theme was Microcomputers in Technical Information Centers. Offered lectures in business and technical information services and management, and coordinated technical sessions and panel discussions.

Project Director, Institute for International Information Programs, University of Maryland, College of Library and Information Services, January 1985-Summer 1986.

Attended seminar of Joint Education and Training Committees of FID/IFLA/ICA in Varna, Bulgaria, June 3-8, 1985. Delivered paper on the Harmonization of Management Instruction for Librarianship, Documentation, and Archives.

Consultant to the International Atomic Energy Agency, Summer 1986, to plan regional workshop on information center management and development in Mexico in December 1986.

Member, Advisory Committee, U.S. Agency for International Development, Center for Development Information and Evaluation, 1986-1990.

Professional Activities and Awards — 1980's to 1990's

Fulbright Professor, University of Kelaniya, Colombo, Sri Lanka, and consultant to the Institute for Fundamental Research in Kandy, Sri Lanka, Spring 1987.

U.S. Information Agency regional lecturer in India at Madras, Bangalore, Calcutta, Delhi, Chandigarh, Bombay, and Poona, April 1987.

Lecturer at Asian Institute of Technology seminar for regional information personnel in Bangkok, May 22, 1987, and June 22-28, 1988.

Consultant to Volunteers in Technical Assistance (VITA) for evaluation of U.S. Agency for International Development three-year contract for conducting the VITA Inquiry Service to Developing Countries, June-October 1987. Conducted site visits in Djibouti and Zambia.

Director, Seminar in Library Management held at University of Hong Kong for students in the library education program, June 29-30, 1988.

Recipient, Alumni Recognition Award, University of Michigan, School of Information and Library Studies and Alumni Society, 1988.

Keynote speaker, State Library Advisory Commission of Hawaii Seminar, July 23, 1988, in Honolulu, on management issues in library development.

1990's

Principal investigator, U.S. National Science Foundation project to develop a model information center for a Third World research institute in Kandy, Sri Lanka. Led a seminar with collaboration from four colleagues in Kandy at the Institute for Fundamental Studies, January 2-5, 1990.

Lecturer on Library Survival in a Changing Environment in Bangkok at Chulalongkorn University on January 19, 1990, under sponsorship of U.S. Information Service and the University Department of Library Science to students and faculty from four Thai library schools and invited professionals.

Consultant, University of Maryland, School of Public Affairs, Sri Lanka Policy Support Unit, in Colombo, Sri Lanka, July 26-August 3, 1990. Analyzed private-sector business information system needs and participated in policy planning meetings under terms of U.S. Agency for International Development contract for strengthening private- and public-sector activities. Revisited Colombo, January 4-16, 1991, to review and discuss planned development of training programs for information staffs of the Sri Lankan chambers of commerce.

Technical consultant, U.S. National Research Council to analyze the need for graduate programs in information science and information management at the Asian Institute of Technology in Bangkok, Thailand, August 3-17, 1990.

Professional Activities and Awards — 1990's

Keynote speaker at Third All Country Congress on Scientific and Technological Information in Hanoi, Vietnam, January 17-19, 1991, speaking on science information transfer issues. Advised the director of the National Information and Documentation Center for Science and Technology on various aspects of information policy relations with U.S. institutions.

Fulbright Professor, Warsaw University, Institute of Library and Information Science, Warsaw, Poland, September 1993-January 1994.

Lectured on November 15, 1993, at the American Center in Krakow to faculty members and graduate students of Jagellonian University, library and information people from other Krakow institutions, and interested members of the public on Information Transfer in Science — Development, Characteristics, and Current Trends.

Offered a seminar in Moscow under the aegis of the United States Information Service — Moscow and the Russian Library of Foreign Literature, December 3 and 4, 1993 on Contemporary Concepts of Modern Library Service, Services to the Business Sector and Public Policy Makers, and Issues in the Structuring of an American Information Center as a Client Response Organization. The workshop was attended by librarians drawn from the new American Study Centers. On December 6, offered a one-day course on Marketing Information Products and Services to reference librarians drawn from academic and research libraries in the Moscow region.

Gave a paper on Communication and Information Transfer in Science, with particular reference to medical sciences, in Warsaw during the World Health Organization Conference on Databases and Computer Applications on December 9, 1993.

Recipient, International Federation for Documentation Centennial Medallion, 1995.

Visiting Professor, Chinese Institute for Scientific and Technical Information, Beijing, China, January 1996.

Member, Board of the American Library in Paris, USA Foundation, 1996-present.

Recipient, Distinguished Member Award, Business and Finance Division of the Special Libraries Association, 1996.

Co-director of research project to build database of economic and community characteristics of Montgomery County, in collaboration with Montgomery County Public Library, under terms of a Kellogg Foundation Grant, 1996-December 1998.

Professional Activities and Awards — 1990's

Recipient, Gale Research Award for Excellence in Business Librarianship, 1997. Received during ALA conference in San Francisco, California, June 1997.

Recipient, 1998 International Landmark Award, University of Maryland, presented at Annual International Affairs Banquet, October 23, 1998.

Index

A

A. J. Seminars, workshops for librarians, 304
Abels, Eileen
  associate project director of Kellogg Foundation project, 366-367
  designing an applied research project, 363
Aberystwyth, University, Wales, 266
Aboyade, Bimpe, head of University of Ibadan library education program, 304
Academia, similar to the military, 361
"The Academic Library Administrator and His Situation," one of the final reports in the Manpower Research Project, 226
Academic programs, need fresh perspectives, 203
Academic standard, needed at University of Md, 215
Academy for Educational Development, AID contract, 336-337
Accounting Systems as Performance Measures and Control, course in Maryland Library Administrators Development Program, 212
Accreditation from ALA, January 1967, 207
Active librarianship, librarians anticipate client needs, 145
Adams, Scott, led sessions of Institute on Comparative and International Library and Information Science, 247
Adams Morgan, party, 67
Adaptation, means for occupational survival in librarianship, 217-218
Addis Ababa, stopover, 335
Adelaide, Victorian architectural style, 319
Adkinson, Burton
  director of American Geographic Society, 247
  director of Office of Science Information, National Science Foundation, 306
Administration, James Thompson and William McEwen, informal tutors, 153
Administrative activities, 159
Administrative process, common elements, 140
Administrative Science Quarterly
  Paul Wasserman, book review editor, 149
  planning stages, 153
  Robert Presthus, editor, 157
"The Administrator of the Special Library and Information Center and His Situation," one of the final reports in the Manpower Research Project, 226
Advertising copywriter, landing a job, 94
Advertising job, 95
Advisory Screening Committee in Library and Information Science of Council for International Exchange of Scholars
  appointed member in 1979, 298-299
  chairman, 298-299

Aeroflot

Aeroflot, cancelled Saturday flight to Helsinki, 257
Agency for International Development (AID)
  advisory committee in AID's Center for Development Information and Evaluation, 336
  Cornell University contract for Indonesian work, 183
  officials, met with Paul Wasserman about Sri Lanka, 346
  three-year contract with Maryland School of Public Affairs to strengthen private- and public-sector activities, 342
Agra, Taj Mahal visit, 303
AID—*See* Agency for International Development
Air conditioning, needed in McKeldin Library, 199
ALA convention
  daily paper, 128
  Eleanor Roosevelt, speaker, 128-129
ALA Daily Reporter, 129
Alabama, Craig Field, 76-79
Aldrich, Henry, played by Ezra Stone, 38
Allen, Eleanor
  contributor to *Sources of Commodity Prices,* 173
  wrote portion of *Encyclopedia of Business Information Sources,* 242
Allen, Larry, assistant editor on ALA convention daily, 128-129
Amateur radio transmitter, used to communicate with Brazil, 271
American Documentation Institute
  contributions and limitations in regard to library automation, 191
  later known as American Society for Information Science, 191
  member, 218-219
American Express travelers checks, payment in Brazil, 274
American librarianship, characterized by indifference, 245
American Library Association (ALA)
  accreditation process for University of Maryland, 207
  annual meetings, 152
  Committee on International Library Education of the Library Education Division, chairman, 270
  contributions and limitations in regard to library automation, 191
  invited to become member of committee, 130
  Library Education Division, chairman from 1974 to 1976, 245
  Library Organization and Management Section of the Library Administration Division, 177
  member since 1949, 120, 127
  Organization and Management Section of the Library Administration Division, 186
American Management Association
  Ernest Dale, writer, 148
  lecture series on information for management decision making, 158
American overseas librarianship, 184-185
American Participants Program in India, Speakers and Artists Program, 330
American Philosophical Society in Philadelphia, travel funds, 187
American Political Science Association, Edward Litchfield, executive secretary, 133, 148-149
American Society for Information Science (ASIS)
  member, 218-219
  presented paper at Boston meeting, 277
Analytic pursuits for librarianship, 371
Anand, Mrs. A. K., director of University of Chandigarh library, 332

Anderson, John
  director of San Francisco Public Library, 223-224
  refusal to allow publication of San Francisco Public Library material, 224
Anglophone African nations, conference sponsored by University of Ghana, 294
Ankara, Turkey, travel as consultant in September 1962, 183-185
Ann Arbor
  move to graduate student housing, 165
  taught summer school in 1961, 181-182
Annual Review of Information Science, work with Evelyn Daniel on chapter, 219
Applebaum, Edmond, associate editor of *Learning Independently,* 296
Applying measurement tools to performance, 159
Araghi, Gayle, acknowledgments in *The New Librarianship,* 236
Archeological artifacts, data retrieval system, 189
Archives, U.S. National, Archives II building completed near University of Maryland, 349
Arlington Branch Library in Brooklyn, 50
Army
  discharge scoring system, 88
  final physical at discharge, 10% disabled, 92, 93
  food, lost weight, 71
Army Air Corps
  base in Miami Beach, 74
  cancellation of training, 76
  flight training, 73-74
  qualification for navigator or bombardier, 74
  recruitment campaign, 73-74
  shortage of gunners, 75
Army Signal Corps
  laboratory exercises, 70
  rotating schedule, 70
  trained as radio repairman, 69-70
  training and instruction, 69-70
Army Specialized Training Program, 72-73
Arntz, Helmut, president of FID, 261
Artifacts, data retrieval system, 189
Asheim, Lester, ALA Committee on Accreditation, chairman of visiting committee, 207
Ashkenazi heritage, 46
Asia, sabbatical, 318
Asian Institute of Technology (AIT)
  five days in 1988, 337
  in Bangkok, 342, 343
  institutional relations with University of Maryland, 344
  program not implemented, 344
Asian Libraries, published "Information Transfer in Science and Technology: An Overview," 330
ASIS Education Committee, 219
ASLIB, 204
Aspnes, Grieg
  chairman of SLA's nominating committee, 173
  librarian of Cargill Corporation, 173
Assessment of performance, impossible until values, objectives, and goals are articulated, 161
Atanasov, Lyuben, professor in the faculty of library and information science at University of Sofia, 316
Athens, Greece, 316
Atlantic crossing
  10-day voyage to England, 80
  perennial seasickness, 80
Auschwitz concentration camp, visited in Poland, 353
Austin, Pat, acknowledgment, viii

Australia

Australia, two-day seminar at School of Library and Information Studies of Kuring-gai College of Advanced Education, 319-320
Australian library education, 319
Austria, 88-91
  army of occupation, 88-89
  weekly newspaper, *The Thunderbolt* jeep available, 89
  photographer who called himself Weegie, 89
  true Army home, 89-90
Austrian participant at Turkish UNESCO training seminar
  disruptive influence, 292
  supporter of the program, 292
Automated retrieval systems, research investigations at Stanford Research Institute in California, 189
Automation, class at Case Institute of Technology, 188
Autonomous University of Mexico, faculty of philosophy and letters, sponsor of Mexico City lecture series, 283
Aviation Cadet program, written examination, 74
Awards, Honors, and Prizes: A Source Book and Directory
  issued by Gale Research Company, 220
  second edition, 237
Awards, Honors, and Prizes: International and Foreign
  details of prizes given by international bodies, organizations, and institutions around the world, 270
  published in 1975, 270
Ayesteran, Antonio, work with Eileen Goldstein on Mexican information problems, 293

B

Babb, Janice, editor of *Real Estate Information Sources*, 181
Bagon, Harry, high school and college classmate, 99
Bali, vacation with Marilyn and Ed Foodim, 320-322
Bangalore, India, National Aeronautical Laboratory, 332
Bangkok
  arrival, 303
  Asian Institute of Technology, 343
  Erewan Hotel, 321
  lectured for five days to librarians in residence for a several-week-long regional workshop for information personnel, 334
  stayed on campus of Asian Institute of Technology, 334
Bar mitzvah, 19
Barber, Nathan Miller, 29-30, 98
Barber, Red, favorite announcer, 17, 41
Barlow, Diane, editor of *Moving and Relocation Sourcebook*, 337
Barnard, Chester, modern behaviorist, 153
Baseball
  in the Catskills, 33
  major league game, 16
  passion for sports-addicted boys, 17
Basic training, at Camp Edison in New Jersey, 71
Basie, Count, in Washington, DC, 66
Battle of the Bulge
  high American casualties, 87
  turning point for Germany, 81
Batty, David
  OAS workshop, 284
  taught workshop at Technical Information Department at Institute of Electrical Research in Cuernavaca, 299
  used taboo military example in Brazil, 273

work on Brazilian workshop on information science, 271-274
Baum, Winifred, contributor to *Sources of Commodity Prices,* 173
Beach, sun's effects, 44
Bearman, Tony Carbo, new chairman of U.S. National Committee for FID, 338
Beijing
  first time Maryland faculty member offered instruction in mainland China as part of a cooperative arrangement established in 1995, 364
  teaching in Chinese government's Central Institute for Scientific and Technical Information, 363
  weather in January, 365
Belarus, birthplace of Joe Wasserman, 2
Bellagio, Italy, meeting, 300-301
Belon, Herbie
  Adams Morgan party, 65
  jazz, 65
Ben Hamouda, Leila, responsible for acquisitions at Tunisian National Library in Tunis, 358
Bengal Library Association, Calcutta, 332
Bennett, William
  lesson in the ways of Turkey, 184
  University library director in Ankara, Turkey, 184
  USIS regional librarian for West Africa, based in Accra, 295
Bergen, Daniel, assistant professor at University of Maryland, 203
Bergmann, Barbara, opponent of Ph.D. for SLIS at University of Maryland, 216
Berkmen, Mary, helped plan week's holiday in Turkey, 362
Berkmen, Salim and Mary, Istanbul's art, literary, and academic communities, 293

Bernstein, Sidney "Sonny"
  childhood friend, 23-24
  joined Army Air Corps, 69
  married and moved out of neighborhood, 125
Bhattacharya, Professor, director of Documentation Research and Training Center, 332
Bi-National Committee in Information Science between the United States and Mexico, established by National Science Foundation, 268
Biblical history class, 20
Bibliographic titles, competing in library market where acquisition budgets had not kept up with inflation, 311
Bicycle, for commuting, 49-50
Biennial FID Congress in Budapest, 246
Bierman, Harold, taught finance and managerial accounting at Cornell University, 154
Big Band sounds, 52
Big Little Books, 16
Biology class at City College Business School, 97
"The Birth of LIST: Report of a Seminar that Linked Library Education with Product Development," with Evelyn Daniel, 225
Bishop, Charles, chancellor at University of Maryland, 241
Black market, travelers checks in Brazil, 274
Bleeding ulcer, 185-186
Bloomington, Indiana, 178
Board of Trustees, endorsement of Ph.D. program at University of Maryland, 215-216
Boarding house in Washington, DC, 63-68
  air of a coed dormitory, 66
  rent hike, 66

Bolino, August

Bolino, August
 from Catholic University, 208
 wrote technical report in Manpower Research Project, 236
Bolinska, Barbara, helped with arrangements in Warsaw, 354
Bombay, spoke at U.S. Center, 332
Bonk, Wallace
 reference instructor at University of Michigan, 167
 reference specialist on dissertation committee at University of Michigan, 171
Book project, testing ideas put forward in book on four successive student groups at Cornell University, 149
Book selections, boyhood, serendipitous, 50
Book to encompass the sum of views on leadership, 232
Books for College Libraries, prepared by Charles Shaw, 166
Borko, Harold
 library educator at UCLA, at International Seminar on Education in Information Science, 250
 president of ASIS, 218-219
Borys, Cynthia, arranged lecture at American Center to students and faculty from several universities in Bangkok, 321-322
Boston trade show, 100
Bourne, Charles, Stanford Research Institute, 189
Bowker Company, R. R., publisher of *The New Librarianship,* 235-236
Brasilia, International Association of Agricultural Librarians and Documentalists, invitation arrived late, 313-314
Brazil
 body search, 274
 compensation in U.S. dollars, 274
 costly telephone charges, 271
 ingenious alternative communication mode, 271
 political discourse taboo, 273
 ruling military junta, 273
 Brazilian National Institute for Space Research, 271
 Brazilian workshop on information science, 271-274
 compatible instructional trio, 273
 police clearances, 272
Brewster, Beverly, prepared index for *The Librarian and the Machine,* 191-192
Brighton Beach, 43-44
British Airways, flight to London from Lagos, Nigeria, 306
Brittany, France
 greatest danger from artillery shells and frostbite, 87
 surrounded Germans, 86
Broderson, Irving "Ike", boyhood friend, 30
Brooklyn, Ringelescus move, 2
Brooklyn Academy, school library project, 122-124
The Brooklyn Daily Eagle, stringer, 42
Brooklyn Dodgers, 41
Brooklyn Public Library
 Central Library, Grand Army Plaza, 125, 126
 in-service training, 113
 Montague Branch Business Library, 113
 orientation series, 117
 public relations department, 113
 Saratoga Branch Library, 105
 want ad in *The New York Times,* 104
Brooklyn Technical High School, 26
Brooks, Earl, taught personnel management and human relations at Cornell University, 154
Brown, Maury, Chief of Development Information at AID, 336-337

Bryfonski, Dedria, editor on Gale Management Information Guide Series, 181
Bucharest
  Center for Scientific and Technical Information, 252
  lecture at Social Science and Political Science Information Center, 255-256
  visit in fall 1972, 247
  visited National Museum, Opera House, and National Theater, 253
Budapest
  arts and media community, New Year's Eve party, 240
  attractive conference venue, 250
  Hotel Royale, 248
  lavish banquet, 251
  New Year's Eve, 239-240
Buddha, supposedly authentic tooth in Kandy, Sri Lanka, 328
Bulgaria
  conference to bring together representatives of education and training committees of FID, IFLA, and ICA, 315
  shortages of consumer products, 316
Bundy, Mary Lee
  acknowledgments in *The New Librarianship*, 236
  associate director of manpower project, 208
  associate professor at University of Maryland, 203
  co-director of High John Library, 210
  collaborations sparked discussions, debates, and heated arguments, 213
  disappointed and annoyed by Wasserman's resignation as dean of SLIS, 232
  emphysema and death, 336
  faculty advisor for minority program at University of Maryland, SLIS, 218
  faculty in Maryland Library Administrators Development Program, 212
  librarianship's unquestioned leader in cause of social and political justice, 336
  Library Research Center at University of Illinois Library School, 181
  necessity for transformation of librarianship, 209-210
  provocateur, 205
  review of Ph.D. proposal at University of Md, 215
  societal concerns examined at scholarly level, 220
  taught class on library services for previously ignored constituencies, 209-210
  team teaching library administration course with Wasserman, 205-206
  wrote technical report in Manpower Research Project, 236
Bureau of Research, grant funding, 208
Burma
  authoritarian military junta, 334
  eight-day tour, 334
  ubiquitous black market, 334
Burton, Barry, planned full-day workshop under auspices of Hong Kong Library Association, 322
Bus, hitching rides, 9
Business and Management Source Book Series, 19 titles, 317
Business correspondent, Zuckerberg Company, 100
Business courses at City College, pragmatic, 96
Business in Washington, DC, small-town flavor, 64-65
Business information sources, proposed undergraduate course, 124

Business library

Business library at Brooklyn Public Library
  experiment in alternative methods of answering questions, 119-120
  network of subject specialists, 119-120
  patrons, 118
  promotion to assistant business librarian, 118
  reference assistant, 115
  richness of resources, 116
Business management subjects, 180
Business reference library at Brooklyn Public Library, 120
Business reference tools, analysis, 120-121
Bustamante, Jorge
  effective teacher, 277
  Mexican management consultant, 275
  taught workshop at Technical Information Department at Institute of Electrical Research in Cuernavaca, 299
Byam, Milton
  assistant director of the Brooklyn Public Library, 110
  director of the District of Columbia Public Library, 110
  librarian of the Queensborough Public Library, 110

C

C.W. Post College of Long Island University, taught in summer school program, 351
Calcutta, Department of Library Science of Jadavpur University and Bengal Library Association, 332
Calisthenics, whipped into shape, 78
Camp Edison, in New Jersey, 71
Canberra, 319

Candy store
  public telephone booths, 15-16
  pulp magazines, 17
Capitalism, incomprehensible
  to Chinese students, 364
  to Polish students, 355
Cappadocia, 292
Card playing, 2, 6
Career advice
  from Cecile Lynch, 107
  from David Thomas, 157
  from Francis St. John
    about Cornell University, 134-135
    about role in public library administration, 124-125
Career in journalism, 43
Carmichael, William
  dean at Cornell University's business school, 190
  Wasserman expressed desire to change appointment at Cornell University, 193
Carpathian Mountains, 353
Carrion, Guadalupe
  met Wasserman in Mexico City, 275
  resident director at Mexican seminar, 274, 276
  work with Eileen Goldstein on Mexican information problems, 293
Carroll, Stephen, faculty in Maryland Library Administrators Development Program, 212
Carter, Mary Duncan, on dissertation committee at University of Michigan, 171
Casablanca, tourism, 296
Case Institute of Technology
  audited two classes, 188
  taking computer classes, 187
Cassavant, Mrs., library's circulation assistant at Cornell University, 137
Cassouto, Mrs., articulate woman, 53

Cassouto, Stella, friend of Clara Sadacca, 53
Castro, Beatriz, director of National Center for Information and Documentation in Santiago, 289-290
Catskill Mountains
 family visit, 32-33
 part-time job, 34
Cayuga Heights
 Hutchinses' spacious home, 142
 Litchfield home, 140
Cellar clubs, illegal rental arrangement, 51, 52
Center for Adult Education, University of Maryland
 home away from home, 197
 setting for University of Maryland CLIS summer institute, 245
Center for Documentation Research, at Western Reserve University, helpful colleagues, 189
Center for Scientific and Technical Information, in Bucharest, 252
Central America, information for industry centers program, 310
Central Intelligence Agency in Chile, 290
Central Library, branch of Brooklyn Public Library, chief of science and industry division, 125-136
Central Park, 31
Chamber of Commerce of the United States in Washington, DC, internship for Colombo, Sri Lanka, participants, 345
Chandigarh, two-day workshop at University of Chandigarh, 332
Change and the Maryland MLS Graduate, commencement address, 367-377
Change Institute on Frontiers in Librarianship, planned and directed by Gilda Nimer, 220

Channel crossing, 81-84
 panic, rescue, and survival, 84
 torpedo strike, 82
Characteristics of Large Organizations, course in Maryland Library Administrators Development Program, 212
Cheatham, Thomas, resident advisor to Science and Technology Board in Bangkok, 343
Cherbourg, France,
 hospital, 84-86
 New Year's Eve, 86
Chiang Mai, 322
Chichicastenango, Guatemala, 281
Chile
 book burnings and bodies found floating, 289
 Central Intelligence Agency, 290
 curfew, 289
 discussion of political topics taboo, 288
 no entry to casino, 290
 resort weekend in Vina del Mar, 290
 reviewed procedures and management practices, 289
 University, Department of Library Science, advisory role, 288
China
 government
  Central Institute for Scientific and Technical Information, teaching in Beijing, 363
  decision to restrict flow of economic and business information from foreign sources, 365
 greatest interest in discussion about inventing and designing information products and services, 365
 mainland, first time Maryland faculty member offered instruction as part of a cooperative arrangement established in 1995, 364

China
  pop celebrities, seen in the Media Hotel at all hours, 365
Chinese Broadcasting Agency, 364
Chinese Institute of Scientific and Technical Information, American faculty working in master's degree program, 364
Chinese National Museum, 322
Chinese opera, 322
Chisholm, Margaret
  dean at University of Maryland, CLIS, 243
  director of Graduate School of Library and Information Science at University of Washington, 349
  endorsed proposal for sabbatical, 247
Christmas in a Cherbourg hospital, 84-85
Chulalongkorn University's Department of Library Science, lecture on library survival in changing environment, 342
City College
  business school, 60-61, 95
  disappointment, 58
  first library job, 56
  Gothic architecture, 55
  immaturity, 56-57
  Latin requirement, 56
  long commute, 55-56
  men only, 55
  proposed undergraduate course, 124
  ROTC program, 56
Civil service position, Government Printing Office, 61, 62
Clay, General Lucius, work with Edward Litchfield as director of civil affairs in Germany, 132
Clearinghouse on Education and Training Materials in Library and Information Science
  corollary effort of FID Education and Training Committee, 297-298
  cited as key resource, 301

Cleveland
  colloquium lectures offered by visiting scholars, 189
  post-doctoral study at Western Reserve University, 187-190
CLIS — *See* College of Library and Information Services at University of Maryland
Club Raleigh
  disbanded, 70
  entertaining girls, 52
  gambling, 51-52
  party headquarters, 53
CNN television news, reported on Chinese government's decision to restrict flow of economic and business information from foreign sources into China, 365
Coblenz region, 88
Cochrane, Glynn
  informed Michael Nacht of bad news about Sri Lankan project, 347
  preliminary study concluded that business and trade groups in Sri Lanka lacked information framework needed to ensure support of economic activity in the country, 342
  project director of three-year contract with Maryland School of Public Affairs to strengthen private- and public-sector activities, 342
  review of Wasserman proposal for Colombo program, 345
Cochrane, Pauline Atherton, prominent American library educator and classification specialist, 342
Cohen, Esther, distant family member, 99
Cohen, Herbert, executive of Greenwood Press, 238
Cohen, Leo, neighborhood, high school, and college friend, 99
Colegio de Mexico in Mexico City, 268

Collaborative efforts among non-governmental organizations in information field, UNESCO's General Information Program, 309
Collection and Analysis of Cost Data, course in Maryland Library Administrators Development Program, 212
Collection development policy at Cornell University, 144
College
  choices, Brooklyn College or City College, 55
  little enthusiasm for enrolling just before war, 69
  readmission, 95-96
College and Research Libraries, printed "Development of Administration in Library Service, 158
College life
  difficulties, 57
  Latin and math courses, 57
  political factions, 57
College of Library and Information Services at University of Maryland (CLIS)
  association with Institute for Fundamental Study in Kandy, Sri Lanka, 333
  evaluated by University Senate, 347-349
  name change with reorganization of University of Maryland administration, 241
  only academic program targeted for reduction or elimination that was spared in final recommendations to University Senate, 349
  support for program in danger, 347-349
  Wasserman's speech, 348-349
College Park Woods, community near University of Maryland campus, 199

Colombo, Sri Lanka
  almost exactly half way around the world from Washington, DC, 325
  analysis of private-sector business information needs, 343
  apartment, transportation, and arrangements, 326, 327, 329
  bombing of central market, 332
  individuals from program selected each year, over a three-year period, to travel to Maryland for three-week summer course in business information systems, 345
  martial law, 332
  plans to evacuate all U.S. citizens, 333
  three weeks at INFOTEC in Mexico City, 345
  visited major libraries and information centers with Jaya Lankage, 328
Colson, John, assistant professor at University of Maryland, 203
Columbia University
  business courses, 117
  business school teachers, 117-118
  Dwight Eisenhower president, 117
  exploring possibilities, 107-108
  first Master of Library Science class, 108
  gender ratio, 108-109
  library school teachers, 109-110
  notification of admission, 108
  second master's degree, 116, 122
  visit looking for Ph.D. program, 162
Commencement address, offered to graduating class in December 1995, 367-377
Committee for International Library Education, member for the 1972-1974 term, 245
Commodity Prices: A Source Book and Index, published in 1974 by Gale Research Company, 270

Communication and Libraries

Communication and Libraries, required course at University of Maryland library school in original curriculum, 201-202

Communication methods, evolution of scientific, paper presented in Colombo, Sri Lanka, 330

Communication Processes in Organizations, course in Maryland Library Administrators Development Program, 212

Community, *Information for Administrators*, informational characteristics needed for developing comprehensive set of economic, social, political, governmental, and cultural details, 363

Commuting with father, 59

Comparison of performance results with standards, 159

Comprehensive examinations at University of Michigan, 170

Computer industry, influence on future directions for libraries, 191

Computer technology, gaps in understanding, 186

CONACYT (Consejo Nacional de Ciencia y Tecnologia)
  invitation as part of North American team to plan graduate degree program in library education in Mexico, 267
  UNESCO contract for local arrangements for seminar, 274

Concentration camp survivors, 91

Coney Island, 43-44

Conference of the Southwestern Library Association, lecture, 209

Congress for Change, Mary Lee Bundy's work, 336

Congress of FID, decision making body of FID, 249

Consejo Nacional de Ciencia y Tecnologia — *See* CONACYT

Consolidated Laundries, interview process, 102-105

Consultants and Consulting Organizations complementary volume to *Who's Who in Consulting*, 214
  published by Cornell University Press, 206

Consulting in Ohio, 221

Consumer Sourcebook, published in 1974 by Gale Research Company, 270

Contribution Series in Librarianship and Information Science, monographs, research material, advanced texts, essays, and symposia on topics of concern, 238

Convalescent period coincided with bad weather in Washington, DC, area, 359

Cook, Michael, British archivist, 316

Copyright, Wasserman retained in some publications, 312

Cornell Social Science Research Center, 161

Cornell Studies in Policy and Administration, Cornell University Press series, 151

Cornell University, 131-164
  association perceived as an asset, 193
  association with Middle East Technical University in Ankara, Turkey, 183
  campus, 132
  centralized library system, 137
  commute to College Park, 197
  criteria for tenure, 139
  culture, 152
  development of effective reference service, 139
  faculty members, 139-140
  full professorship, 190
  hospital administration monograph, 179-180

408

lecture on information for decision making, 211
library
　measured against University of Pennsylvania's Wharton Business School and Stanford University, 147
　Paul Wasserman's allegiance was to specialty, 147
　research and writing, 139
　second semester's teaching smoother than the first, 144
　settling in, 138
　special colloquia, 149
　Wasserman's office, 137
Cornell University Press, published *Information for Administrators,* 150
Cost analysis, research investigations at Stanford Research Institute in California, 189
County's characteristics, perpetual electronic inventory, 363
Courrier, Yves, chief of section for Training of Specialists and Users in UNESCO's General Information Program, 316
A Course in Administration for Managers of Information Services: Design, Implementation and Topical Outline, published by UNESCO in English, French, and Spanish, 290-291
Covered bazaar in Istanbul, 185
Craig Field in Alabama, 76-79
Crain, Leon
　fellow student at Columbia University library program, 109
　work on ALA convention daily, 129
Creating new information products, services, and databases to fulfill client needs, 363
Cross, Jesse
　New York Public Library Economic Department, 113

respected as scholar and collection builder, 118
supervisor in business library, 115
Cuadra, Carlos, editor of *Annual Review of Information Science,* 219
Cuernavaca, Mexico
　return in March 1981, 304
　seminar for Institute of Electrical Research staff on Information Systems and Sources in business, Science, and Technology, 304
　Technical Information Department at Institute of Electrical Research, 299
Culler, Lois, assistant editor of *Encyclopedia of Health Information Sources,* 318
Curfew in Chile, 289
Curricular adaptations, reflective of emerging technological directions in practice of librarianship, 191

D

Dakar, Senegal, addressed students of principal library education program in francophone Africa at University of Dakar, 296
Dale, Ernest
　adjunct professor at Cornell University, 148
　industrial relations instructor at Columbia University, 117
　writer for American Management Association, 148
Dance jamboree in Santo Domingo, 284
Dancing in the Club Raleigh, 52
Danecka, Pola (Krystyna Wasserman's mother) died in Lodz, Poland, 350
Daniel, Evelyn, worked on *Annual Review of Information Science,* 219
Daniell, Lorna, contributor to *Sources of Commodity Prices,* 173

Data Processing for Libraries

Data Processing for Libraries, required course at University of Maryland library school in original curriculum, 201

Davis, Ann
  guided Wasserman's understanding of higher education scene in Turkey, 185
  U.S. Information Services librarian, 184-185

Davis, Norman, acknowledgment, viii

Day, Melvin, led sessions of Institute on Comparative and International Library and Information Science, 247

Day, Thomas, campaign to reorganize campus administrative structure at University of Maryland, 241

De, Zhang
  assistant director of education and training program at ISTIC, 364
  insistence that Wasserman not miss Peking Opera, 366

de Chazeau, Mel
  acting dean at Cornell University, 154
  economist at Cornell University, 139

De Mendonza, Dr.
  asked Wasserman to organize team to offer two-week workshop on information science in San Jose dos Campos, 271
  ingenious alternative communication mode, 271
  met to discuss extra work hours, 273

Dean, John, Cornell Social Science Research Center, 161

Decision making, survey in behavioral and scientific fields, 158

Decision Making: An Annotated Bibliography
  collaboration with Fred Silander, 188
  follow-up effort, 159
  published by Cornell University Press, 158

Decision Making: An Annotated Bibliography (Supplement 1958-1963), 188-189

Deep South, protests against racial discrimination, 220

Delhi
  Department of Library and Information Science of University of Delhi, 332
  Indian National Scientific Documentation Center, 332

Delinquent dues from United States to FID, 308

Denmark, two-day stopover in April 1970, 233

"A Departure in Library Education: A Report of an Experimental Project at Maryland," published in *Journal of Education for Librarianship*, 210

Depression, Great
  childhood treats, 15
  money concerns in evidence, 14
  movies were inexpensive, 20

Deutsche Gesellschaft fur Dokumentation, 233

"Developing New Information Products: A Revised Role for Librarianship in Advanced and Developing Countries," paper at IFLA Conference in Istanbul, 362

"Development of Administration in Library Service," article in *College and Research Libraries*, 176

Devereux, Edward, Cornell Social Science Research Center, 161

Diaz, Albert
  director of Washington office of Microcard Editions, 214
  OAS workshop, 284
  ran series of workshops for librarians, 304

Dictating equipment, used for reference books, 174
Dinh, Dr., director of Vietnamese National Information and Documentation Center for Science and Technology in Hanoi, 346
Directory of University Research Bureaus and Institutes, editorial work, 169, 171
Disability, Veterans Administration classification, 92
Discharge from Army, 93
Discharge scoring system from the Army, 88
Dissertation
  committee at University of Michigan, 171-172
  oral defense, 175
  problem retrieving material from doctoral committee, 172
Distance education in library science, offered in Australia in 1986, 320
Divorce from Clara, 267, 268
Djibouti, work on VITA project, 335-336
Doctoral dissertation, measurement concerns in public librarianship, 160
Donaldson Brown Center, Maryland Library Administrators Development Program, 212, 345
Dordick, Beverly, editor of *Real Estate Information Sources,* 181
Dorsey Brothers, Big Band sounds, 52
Dosa, Marta
  advisor to Sam Kotei, 294
  chairman of FID Education and Training Committee, 309, 338-339
  professor at Syracuse University, 309
Draft, thinned ranks of young men at corner hangout, 69
Dubester, Henry, adjunct lecturer at University of Maryland library school, 204
Dudley, Edward, head of library education program at Northwestern Polytechnic in London, 265
Duffy, Joseph, director of U.S. Information Agency, 352
Dynamics and ills of the library profession and its professional groups, 221
Dysentery, 299-300

E

East Berlin, visit to Central Institute for Information and Documentation, 247, 262
East Germany
  Colloquium on Information and Documentation, 277
  conference
    chilly political climate, 279
    translated paper delivered, 279
Eastern Europe
  Don Hausrath played active role in library development, 356
  first trip, 238-240
  travel problems, 256
Ebbets Field, 17
Economic assault on libraries, relentless, requires accountability, 369
Edinburgh
  offered paper with Gary Ford, 296
  planning seminar, 294
Education and Training: Theory and Provision, conference proceedings issued by FID, 296
Education and Training Committee of FID
  efforts to expand membership and participation, 298
  monthly newsletter, 297
  moved to University of Maryland for four years, 297
  pre-conference seminar in Mexico City, 288

Education and Training Committee of FID
proceedings published by FID workshop in Minneapolis, 298
Education for Information
editorial board's first meeting, 310
membership on editorial advisory board, 310
Egg cream, soda fountain drink, 15
Eisenhower, Dwight D.
appointed Quincy Mumford as Librarian of Congress, 135
president of Columbia University, 117
Electronic inventory, perpetual, of a county's characteristics, 363
Elementary school, survival strategy, 23
"Elements in a Manpower Blueprint—Library Personnel for the 1970's," published in *ALA Bulletin*, 209
Elephant, rode in Thailand, 322
Elkins, Wilson
became president of all higher education institutions in Maryland, 241
president of University of Maryland, 194
ratified faculty selections, 198
Ellington, Duke, in Washington, DC, 66
Emotional dependence on adults, handicap in adults, 376
Encyclopedia of Business Information Sources
published on an experimental basis, 182-183
quick acceptance and widespread use, 242
England, seemed paradise after first Atlantic crossing, 80
English Channel crossing, 81-84
English language
spoken in Sri Lanka, 326
ubiquity, 254
use by faculty and students in Warsaw, 353, 355
Enhanced status for librarians, may lie in controlling perplexing variety of electronic options for clients, 372

Enoch Pratt Library, Emerson Greenaway, director, 155
Entrepreneurial work in library work, 373-374
Entrepreneurship, avenues open to those educated for librarianship, 373-374
Ephesus, Turkey, 362
Epner, Dinah, later Lindauer, fellow student at Columbia University library program, 109
Essex Street, apartment, 4
Ethnic Information Sources in the United States, 279
Ethnic neighborhoods of New York, acceptance of lot in life, 41
Ethnic Source Book, second edition, 317
Eugenics, studied in biology class, 97
Europe, two-day stopover in Paris in 1962, 183
European education and research centers, sabbatical tour, 246-266
Evaluation of performance, impossible until values, objectives, and goals are articulated, 161
Evolution of scientific communication methods, paper presented in Colombo, Sri Lanka, 330
Ewha Womens University Library School, 323
Executive's Guide to Information Sources, published on an experimental basis, 182-183
Explosion during English Channel crossing, 82

F
Faculty colleagues at Cornell University, close links, 139
Faculty library committee at Cornell University, 144

Familiarity with literature of a field, required of librarians, 372
Family life with Clara
  disintegrating in the early 1970's, 232
  move to Ithaca, 141
Family matters, turn for the worse, 130-131
Family restaurant, 3-4
Family ties occupied much time, 125
Fang, Josephine, adjunct lecturer at University of Maryland library school, 204
Far Rockaway, seashore rental, 102
Farina, Ms. B., from National Research Council in Rome, at International Seminar on Education in Information Science, 250-251
Father — *See* Wasserman, Joe
Federal civil service exam, 61
Federal government support for international information efforts, reduced dramatically in early 1980's, 306
Federal Institute of Industrial Research on Business and Economic Information in Lagos, lecture for workshop, 304
Feirstein, Bernard "Bookie," boyhood friend, 30
Feliu, Ximena
  head of library education program at University of Santiago before Pinochet, 289
  library staff with international social science organization regional office in Santiago, 289
Ferguson, Milton J.
  director of Brooklyn Public Library system, 104
  retiring from Brooklyn Public Library, 111
Fernandez de la Garza, Guillermo
  hired Eileen Goldstein, 293
  hired Guadalupe Carrion, 274
  of Consejo Nacional de Ciencia y Tecnologia in Mexico, at International Seminar on Education in Information Science, 250
  senior officer of CONACYT, 267
Festivals Sourcebook
  first edition, 279
  second edition, 317
Fetzer, Erwin, started program to build network of technology and industrial development centers in Latin America, 281
FID — *See* International Federation for Documentation
FID Education and Training Committee
  active role, 269
  encouragement of U.S. National Committee, 294
  first business and technical session in Africa in 1981, 304
  meeting in April 1970 in Frankfurt, 233
  met with IFLA Education and Research Board and ICA Committee on Education and Training to discuss implementing practical cooperative measures, 301
  secretariat in Warsaw, 222
Fiddler on the Roof at Warsaw Opera House, 354
Field experience, 199-200
Final Army training before crossing to France, 80-81
Financial Planning and Budgeting, course in Maryland Library Administrators Development Program, 212
Finkel, Murray
  boyhood friend, 30
  married and moved out of neighborhood, 125
  wounded in Italy, 91
First car for Paul Wasserman, 125

First-generation immigrants

First-generation immigrants, 5
First grandchild, Paul Wasserman, 12
First teaching experience, 143-144
Fish and chips, discovered, 81
Flagler Hotel in Catskills, 33
Flamm, Martin "Mooky," boyhood friend, 30-31
Floating gardens of Xochimilco, Mexico, 277
Florence, Italy, meeting of International Informatics Association, 264
Food in England, bland, 81
Foodim, Ed
  married Marilyn Wasserman, 125
  returned to United States from Bangkok, 322
Foodim, Marilyn and Ed
  starting family in Huntington, Long Island, 152
  vacation in Bali, 320-322
Foodim, Marilyn
  ill, 130
  returned to United States from Hong Kong, 322
Forceful performance style, Wasserman's, 195
Ford, Gary
  co-authored paper, 296
  OAS workshop, 284
  paper about OAS and Cuernavaca programs, 300
  taught marketing and market research as full-day component of Maryland Library Administrators Development Program, 284
  taught workshop at Technical Information Department at Institute of Electrical Research in Cuernavaca, 299
Formative years, first part of book, vii
Forsman, Caroline, acknowledgments in *The New Librarianship*, 236

Fort Dix, New Jersey
  discharge center, 92
  transfer from Alabama, 79-80
Fort Monmouth, training in radio repair, 71-72
Fort Rucker
  near Dothan, Alabama, 76-77
  rumors, 79
Foskett, Douglas
  book royalties used to throw lavish banquet in Budapest, 251
  from University of London, at International Seminar on Education in Information Science, 250
Foskett, Tony
  drove to Wasserman's train station for London, 266
  head of South Australian Institute of Technology Department of Library Studies in Adelaide, 319-320
Fractured foot in Warsaw, 358-359
Frank, Nathalie, advertising agency librarian, 120
Frankfurt, closing days of 1980, 301
Freeman, Mrs., high school English teacher, 39-40
Frontiers in Librarianship: Proceedings of the Change Institute 1969, 221
Fulbright Commission in Warsaw, Wasserman designated first alternate, 351
Fulbright grant, second, India or Poland, 350
Fulbright professorship
  applied, 318
  in Sri Lanka, 325
Fulbright teaching and research awards, work on screening committee, 298-299
Fund-raising to raise FID dues for United States, 314-315
Furlough, New York, 76

G

Gale Directory of University Research Bureaus and Institutes, 180
Gale Information Guide Library Series
  a little over 200 books, 311
  coordinating editor, 237-238
Gale Management Information Guide Series, 38 volumes, 181
Gale Research Company
  annual contribution to FID dues, 315
  bought by Thomson International, 337
Gardin, Jean Claude, archeologist, 189
Garment district, job, 47
Gdansk, brief visit, 352
Georgi, Charlotte
  collaborator on *Statistics Sources,* 175
  contributor to *Sources of Commodity Prices,* 173
  effort to complete first edition of *Statistics Sources,* 182
  librarian of Graduate School of Business at University of California, Los Angeles, 175
  wrote portion of *Encyclopedia of Business Information Sources,* 242
German Foundation for International Development, five-day conference in West Berlin, 301
German instructor, innuendoes about Nazi spies, 60
German P38 pistol, only souvenir from World War II, 90
German submarine installations on French coast, 86-87
Ghana, modest meals with small portions, 295
GI Bill
  effect on makeup of university faculties, 147-148
  end of stipend, 122
  stipend, drawing to a close, 116
Giegengack, August, U.S. public printer, 65
Gietz, Ricardo, from Centro de Documentacion Cientifica in Buenos Aires, at International Seminar on Education in Information Science, 250
Ginsberg, Eli, course in history of economic thought at Columbia University, 117
Gjelness, Rudolph
  chairman of dissertation committee at University of Michigan, 171
  chairman of library science department at University of Michigan, 162
  invitation to teach summer school at University of Michigan, 190
  requirements for Ph.D. at University of Michigan, 167
Glaser, Mr., academic advice and summer job, 58-59
Goal definition, 159
Goff, Marie, contributor to *Sources of Commodity Prices,* 173
Goldberg, Adolf (uncle), 3
Goldberg, Charlie (cousin)
  attended college full-time, 55
  studious boy, studied law at Fordham University, 4
Goldberg, Gussie (cousin), 4
Goldberg, Willy (Velvel) (cousin), 4
Golden Sands, resort area on the Black Sea, 315
Goldstein, Eileen, later Abels
  directed workshop for International Atomic Energy Agency, 319
  head of one of Mexico's most important special libraries at Institute for Electrical Research in Cuernavaca, 293
  paper in *Special Libraries* with Wasserman, 299

Goldstein, Eileen

went to Mexico as CONACYT summer intern, 293
workshop series for Technical Information Department at Institute of Electrical Research in Cuernavaca, 299
Goldwyn, Alan, managed Center for Documentation Research at Western Reserve University, 188
Golub, Ben, boyhood friend, 30
Gomulka government in Poland, about to fall, 238
Goodman, Bernard "Buggy"
  boyhood friend, 30
  joined Coast Guard, 69
Goodman, Charles, faculty in Maryland Library Administrators Development Program, 212
Goodman, Dorothy
  assistant at Central Library at Brooklyn Public Library, 126-127
  recommended for promotion, 135
Goodrich, Robert, contributor to *Sources of Commodity Prices*, 173
Goodrum, Charles, Columbia University student body president, 110
Gore, William
  political scientist at Cornell University, 148
  work in behavioral sciences, 149
Gorski, Adam, FID Education and Training Committee, Polish chairman, 233
Government pace, 64
Government Printing Office, civil service job, 62
Graduate Record Examination, required for admission to University of Maryland library school, 201
Graduate School of Business and Public Administration, Cornell University, lecture on information for decision making, 211

Graf, Karl, translator, 279
Great Revolution in 1949, habits of mind in China, 365
Great Wall, tourism, 364
Greenaway, Emerson
  director of Enoch Pratt Library in Baltimore, 155
  librarian at Philadelphia Free Library, 155
Greenwood Press, Contributions Series in Library and Information Science, 238
Grefsheim, Suzanne, associate editor of *Encyclopedia of Health Information Sources*, 318
Guanajuato, addressed audience of library staff and library school students at University of Guanajuato, 304
Guatemala seminar
  covered organizational and administrative problems inherent in setting up and organizing a center, 282
  first in a series of workshops meant to prepare information personnel, 282
  first workshop in OAS initiative, 281
  second week did not go well, 282
Guayabera shirt, bought in the Philippines, unfit for Chilean casino, 290

H

Haar, George (cousin), 1
Haar, Gladys (cousin), 1
Haar, Ida (aunt), 1-2
Haar, Jesse (cousin), 1
Haar, Uncle
  made room for Sadie and Joe Wasserman, 1-2
  business failed, 11
Haas, Jim, president of Council on Library Resources in Washington, DC, 301

Habib, Irving "Itskil," boyhood friend, 30
Habib, Mr., 46
Hagelstein, Robert, president of Greenwood Press, 238
Hague, the, FID Conference in fall 1984, 314
Hamouda, Leila Ben, responsible for acquisitions at Tunisian National Library in Tunis, 358
Hanley, Tullah
  heiress and benefactress of the arts, 240
  New Year's Eve party, 240
Hanoi, Vietnam
  blend of architectural reminders of French colonial past with stern, controlling hand of government, 346
  conference in January 1991, 345
  Third All Country Congress on Scientific and Technological Information, 346
  trying to catch up with its envied neighbor, Bangkok, 347
Harasic, Oscar
  representative of Organization of American States, 282
  started program to build network of technology and industrial development centers in Latin America, 281
Harlem, Jewish neighborhood in Manhattan, 2
Haro, Robert, second librarian at University of Maryland CLIS, 246
Harris, Lt., company commander, 86
Hausrath, Donald
  coordinator of overseas library program of USIA, 284-285
  director of library program of American Center in Warsaw, 354
  director of USIS library program in India, 330
  played active role in library development in Eastern Europe and Russia, 356
  posted in Warsaw with Sydney, 354

Hawaii State Library Commission, keynote address, 338
Hawaii, University, Honolulu
  invited to teach by Ralph Shaw, 192
  taught summer-term courses, 337
Hawaii, visit, 323
Health management field, literature and bibliography, 180
Health Organizations of the US, Canada and Internationally, directory of organizations in the health field, 180
Hebrew school, 19-20, 22, 25-26
Heckelman, Louis "Chink"
  bachelor uncle, 44-46
  boyhood friend, 30
  passion for homing pigeons, 45
  uncle's scam, 45-46
Hegeman Avenue, apartment, 39
Heho, sorrowful conditions of life in Burma, 334
Heiliger, Ed, data processing installation at University of Illlinois, 189
Helfand, Esther, work on ALA convention daily, 129
Helplessness breeds helplessness, 376
Helsinki, visit, 247, 259-260
Herman, Esther
  associate editor
    for *Festivals Source Book,* 279
    for *Museum Media,* 267
  co-editor of *Library Bibliographies and Indexes,* 270
  responsible for Student Contribution Series at University of Maryland, 220
Herman, Gilbert, principal of Library Training Consultants, 285
Hermanson, Roger, faculty in Maryland Library Administrators Development Program, 212
Heumann, Karl
  president of American Documentation Institute, 306

Heumann, Karl

worked to transfer responsibilities for FID from American Documentation Institute to newly created Office of Documentation in National Research Council of National Academy of Sciences, 306

Heyerdahl, Thor, Kon-Tiki museum, 260

High John Library, directed jointly by Mary Lee Bundy and Richard Moses, 210

High John project, Mary Lee Bundy's work, 336

High school
 basketball leagues, 40
 English teacher, Mrs. Freeman, 39-40
 friends, 99
 habitual user of school library, 39-40
 high school newspaper, 37
 journalism teacher, Mr. Pearl, 37-39
 last year, 54
 options, 26-27
 orphanages, basketball, 40
 venturing beyond boundaries, 40

High school newspaper
 cub reporter, 42
 Ezra Stone interview, 37-39
 feature column, 42
 immersion in work, 50
 sports reporter, then editor, 42

Higher education, transformation in ranks, 147

Hill, Frank, reference librarian at Saratoga Branch, 115

Hillhouse, Miller
 national authority on municipal administration and public finance at Cornell University, 139
 seminar in municipal administration, 159

History, class with Professor Brandt, 96-97

History of books, printing, and publishing, fascinating course at University of Michigan, 168, 170

History of Libraries and Their Materials, required course at University of Maryland library school in original curriculum, 201-202

Hitchhiking, 43

Hitler, Adolph
 became chancellor of Germany, 15
 in newsreels, 21
 made plight of Jews seem hopeless, 41

Ho Chih Minh, mausoleum in Hanoi, 346

Hockey at Cornell University, 152

Hoftorah, sacred text, 26

Hogg, Frank
 British Council consultant to National Public Library Board in Colombo, Sri Lanka, 333
 principal of Wales College of Librarianship in Aberystwyth, 266

Holmes, Robert "Ducky," associate professor at Cornell University, 139

Hong Kong
 FID Congress and Conference, 307
 taught two-day course, 338
 University, 337-338

Hong Kong Library Association, one-day management seminar, 322, 337

Hopping, Ann, regional U.S. Information Service librarian, 289

Hornbake, R. Lee
 advocate on behalf of SLIS at University of Maryland, 206
 became vice-president at state level, 241
 beginning of political journey toward Ph.D. approval at University of Maryland, 215
 informed of Wasserman's resignation as dean of SLIS, 231
 interview in College Park, 194
 ratified Wasserman's faculty selections, 198
 traveled to Ithaca, 193
 vice-president for academic affairs at University of Maryland, 192-194

418

Hospital administration
  need for review and analysis of information facilities, 179-180
  program at Cornell University, 148
Hospital in Cherbourg, France, foot and ankle, 84-86
Hotel Kismet in Kusadasi, Turkey, 362
Hotel Royale in Budapest, New Year's Eve party, 240
House, first, built in Ithaca, 160
House, two-family, in New York, 12
Hsio, Yu, acknowledgment, viii
Hu, James, chairman of library science education program at National Taiwan University, 322
Human Relations Laboratory, course in Maryland Library Administrators Development Program, 212
Hurricane, struck the Philippines during workshop, 287
Hussmann, Lawrence, Fulbright colleague in Warsaw, 354
Hutchins, John G.B., 139
  affluent, 147
  stormy differences with Paul Wasserman, 142
  taught transportation economics and interstate trade at Cornell University, 139
Hutchins, John and wife, social call, 141-142

I

Illich, Ivan, director of school in Cuernavaca, Mexico, 275
Illinois, University, visit looking for Ph.D. program, 162
Illinois Libraries, issue about management topics, 181
Image of the library and librarian, indispensable or marginal, 370

Impact of Technology on Information Organizations, course in Maryland Library Administrators Development Program, 212
Imperialist United States, Irani's objections to workshop director, 303
Implementation of Change in Organizations, course in Maryland Library Administrators Development Program, 212
Incunabula, taught by Hellmut Lehmann-Haupt at Columbia University, 110
Indexers in education, training, 208
India
  abject poverty, 303
  first visit, UNESCO program, 301-303
  insulated from sight of poverty, 331
  Krystyna befriended homeless blind woman and her child in the park, 303
  obtaining a visa from Indian consulate in Colombo, Sri Lanka, 331
  possible Fulbright grant, 350
  second visit, USIS program, 330-332
Indian National Information System for Science and Technology Newsletter, 313
Indian National Science Development Board, host organization for New Delhi seminar, 302
The Individual in the Organizational System, course in Maryland Library Administrators Development Program, 212
Indonesia, University, Cornell University built public administration library, 183
Indonesian National Museum in Jakarta, 321
Induction notices, 69
Infantile paralysis, 33-34
Infomediary, new library periodical in 1985, 316
Information age, coincides with financial reductions for libraries, 369

Information and systems

Information and systems management, work for people trained in information professions, 373

Information broker, work for people trained in information professions, 373

Information engineer, installing and training library staffs in use of systems and technology, work for people trained in information professions, 373

Information for Administrators: A Guide to Publications and Services for Business and Government
  dedication to parents, 151
  genesis of research project in mid-1990's, 363
  guide through the maze of information resources in business and governmental management, 150
  informational characteristics needed for developing comprehensive set of economic, social, political, governmental, and cultural details about a community, 363
  received comments on limits of the book, 182
  redesigning a reference book, 182
  work leading to personal philosophy of librarianship, 145

Information for industry centers programs in Central and South America, 310

Information Handling Services, publisher of Reader Series in Library and Information Science, 312

Information products and services
  annual seminar in inventing and designing, 313
  development and catalysis, major interest, 269

Information products, services, and databases, librarians can create to fulfill client needs, 237, 363

Information transfer and dissemination, 221

INFOTEC in Mexico City
  Mexican quasi-governmental industrial consulting organization, 306
  participation by Colombo, Sri Lanka, participants, 345

Innovation, means for occupational survival in librarianship, 217-218

Institute for Fundamental Study in Kandy, Sri Lanka
  association with College of Library and Information Services at University of Maryland, 333
  Cyril Ponnamperuma suggested faculty team in CLIS to plan workshop focused on the institute's goals, 341
  description of campus, 328

Institute for Information Science, Inventions and Law in East Germany, 277

Institute for Scientific Information's Social Science Citation Index, member of editorial advisory board, 247

Institute of Scientific and Technical Information of China (ISTIC), American faculty working in master's degree program, 364

Institute on Comparative and International Library and Information Science, Krystyna Ostrowska, student, 247

Intellectual discourse, appropriate level needed at new library school at University of Maryland, 202-203

Intellectual librarian vs. library intellectual, 370-371

"Intelligence personnel," William Learned saw a need, 372

Inter-American Development Bank,
sponsor of Inter-American Workshop for Agricultural Information Transfer and Networking, 359
Inter-American Workshop for Agricultural Information Transfer and Networking, presentation for Latin American librarians on Training and Education in Information Science in the Developing world, 359
Inter-Organizational Relationships, course in Maryland Library Administrators Development Program, 212
Interdisciplinary instructional cadre at University of Maryland
  adjunct lecturers, 203
  joint appointments with other campus facilities, 203
  regular faculty, 203
Interdisciplinary links at University of Maryland, with computer science, social science, and history faculties, 215
Interdisciplinary orientation, important at University of Maryland library school, 203
International and comparative librarianship and information science
  melange of students, 242
  seminar, 242
International Association of Agricultural Librarians and Documentalists in Brasilia, invitation arrived late, 313-314
International Atomic Energy Agency, planning workshop for the agency's regional information centers in the hemisphere, Mexico City, 319
International Council for Archives (ICA)
  Committee on Education and Training, met with IFLA Education and Research Board and FID Education and Training Committee to discuss implementing cooperative measures, 301
  met with FID and IFLA, education and training committees met in Varna, Bulgaria, 315
  encouraged to eliminate redundancy with IFLA and FID, 300
  work with FID and IFLA as forerunner to UNESCO symposium, 309
International Federation for Documentation (FID)
  biennial Congress, planning for Budapest, 239
  Burton Adkinson, colleague of Krystyna's from Warsaw, 247-248
  chairman of the National Committee, 313
  Congress in Budapest, 248
  encouraged to eliminate redundancy with IFLA and ICA, 300
  established in Holland and headquartered in the Hague, 314
  friendships, continued for years, 234
  German secretariat, meeting in Frankfurt, 233
  international counterpart of elements of ASIS and SLA, 219
  met with IFLA and ICA, education and training committees in Varna, Bulgaria, 315
  mostly European organization, 306
  recommended major commitment to work of the Education and Training Committee, 234
  structure based on designation in each member country of national member, 307
  work with IFLA and ICA as forerunner to UNESCO symposium, 309

421

International Federation of Library Associations

International Federation of Library Associations (IFLA)
- conference in Istanbul, 362
- Education and Research Board, met with FID Education and Training Committee and ICA Committee on Education and Training to discuss implementing cooperative measures, 301
- encouraged to eliminate redundancy with FID and ICA, 300
- met with FID and ICA, education and training committees in Varna, Bulgaria, 315
- serves international community, 307
- work with FID and ICA as forerunner to UNESCO symposium, 309

International field, interest remains alive, 362

International Journalists Center
- haven among shortages in Bulgaria, 316
- near Varna, Bulgaria, 315

International Seminar on Education in Information Science in Veszprem, Hungary, 246, 250

International study in librarianship, Maryland, University, CLIS, potential to be an important center, 245

International Symposium on Classification Research, Jean Perreault, 208

International Symposium on Harmonization of Education and Training Programmes in Information Science, Librarianship and Archival Studies in Paris, 310

Internet, users see personal information garnering process as circumventing the intermediary through direct access to information, 369

Intourist, Moscow airport, 257

Intravenous fluids for dysentery, 299

Inventory, perpetual electronic, of a county's characteristics, 363

Isabel Nichol Lecture Series, University of Denver, 217

Istanbul
- covered bazaar, 185
- IFLA conference, 362
- smog, 362
- traditional Moslem character in 1995, 362
- University, visit, 185

Ithaca
- Cornell University, main business, 151
- ideal setting for raising a family, 134
- impressive, 133-134
- settling in, 138
- small-town living, 151
- South Hill, 146
- stayed at YMCA, 137
- Wassermans purchased building lot at auction and built a house, 160
- winters and summers, 152

J

Jackson, Eugene
- chairman of U.S. National Committee for FID, 219
- librarian of General Motors Corporation Library, 174
- opponent in SLA election, 174
- taught at University of Texas in Austin, at International Seminar on Education in Information Science, 250

Jackson, Miles, dean of University of Hawaii library school, 323

Jadavpur University, Calcutta, 332

Jagellonian University in Poland, professors provided briefings in excellent English, 353

Jakarta
  Indonesian National Museum, 321
  met Marilyn and Ed Foodim, 320
  public lecture to members of library community on the American library scene, 320
  teeming crowds and traffic congestion, 321
  University, speaking engagement at U.S. Center, 320
Jancewicz, Kazik and Zina, welcomed Wasserman as member of extended family, 354
January, Mr., headmaster at Brooklyn Academy, 122
Japan, invasion, 88
Japanese war, over, 88
Jassi, Romania
  birthplace of Joe Wasserman, 2
  visit to maternal grandparents' town, 253-255
Jazz
  Herbie Belon, 67-68
  Washington, rich center, 65-66
Jerome Street, 12
Jewish communities in New York City, 40-41
Jewish community, religious fervor for Franklin D. Roosevelt, 41
Job-seeking campaign
  after World War II, 94
  during final term of college, 101-105
Johnson, Herbert, executive of Greenwood Press, 238
Joint efforts encouraged among IFLA, FID, and ICA, meeting in Bellagio, Italy, 300-301
Joint workshop with OAS and U.S. National Technical Information Service, workshop director, 310
Journal of Library Administration, editorial board, 313

K

Kalaydzhieva, Kostadinka
  director of National and University Library in Sofia, 251
  eager to establish association between Maryland library school program and training courses offered at National Library, 251
Kaltenbach, Margaret, assistant dean at Western Reserve University, 188
Kanchipuram, 342
Kandy, Sri Lanka, model information system for Institute for Fundamental Studies, 326-328
Kangaroos, 320
Kann, Dr., director of University of Hong Kong library, 337
Kaszubski, Elizabeth (sister-in-law), acknowledgment, ix
Katmandu, Yak and Yeti Hotel, 342
Kauai, visit, 338
Kavakladera, old favorite Turkish wine, 362
Kazimierz district, historic ghetto section, 353
Kelaniya University in Sri Lanka
  framework for graduate education offering in library and information science, 333
  library operated while classes were suspended, 328
  looking for professor of library administration, 318
  students boycotting, 326
Kellogg Foundation
  approved grant funding for second phase of research, 367
  Eileen Abels served as project director, 367
  research project funded for one-year pilot project, 366

Kellogg Foundation
    support sought for designing an applied research project, 363

Kelly, James, associate editor of *Encyclopedia of Public Affairs Information Sources,* 318

Kemmerling, Diane, co-compiler of *Sources of Commodity Prices,* 270

Kenner, Frances, adjunct lecturer at University of Maryland library school, 204

Kerr, Clark, former chancellor of University of California higher education system, addressed audience in New Delhi, 302

Kerwin, Brit, vice-chancellor for academic affairs at University of Maryland, 241

Kessler, Rose Ringelescu (aunt)
    acknowledgment, viii
    caregiver for Sadie Wasserman, 131
    Christmas visit, 143
    family ran dry goods store, 143
    loaned Paul a suitcase, 63
    managed retail store, 49
    parents and children, 2-4
    shared apartment with Mollie and Hyman Ringelescu, 10, 21, 22, 24

Kidd, Jerry
    prepared curriculum for master's degree at Asian Institute of Technology, 344
    work in Sri Lanka at Institute for Fundamental Study, 341-342
    work on State Department Leaders Program, 288

Kilgour, Raymond, taught history of books and libraries at University of Michigan, 168, 170

Kilim rug in Turkey, 293

Kimchi, 323

Knight, Bob, Effie's husband, 311

Knight, Effie
    acknowledgments in *The New Librarianship,* 236
    died of heart attack, 317
    involved in all phases of book development and production, 237-238
    kidney dialysis, 310
    Paul Wasserman spoke at memorial service at University of Maryland Chapel, 318
    poor health, 310-311
    productive achievements in many series, 269
    promotion to secretary to the dean at University of Maryland, SLIS, 206
    reference book projects, 311
    resigned as dean's secretary and head of administrative office at University of Maryland, SLIS, 235
    scrupulous monitoring of publication efforts, 267
    work on *Encyclopedia of Business Information Sources,* 242
    work on Maryland Library Administrators Development Program, 235

Koala bears, 320

Koehler, Barbara, associate editor of *Encyclopedia of Senior Citizens Information Sources,* 318

Kon-Tiki museum in Oslo, 260

Korean Women's University, 323

Kosciala, Sinikka, contact person in Helsinki, 260

Kotei, General
    arrested on charge of financial corruption and executed, 295
    brother of Sam, 295

Kotei, Sam
    head of library education program at University of Ghana, 294
    left Ghana with family for Botswana, 295

Kowloon, 322
Krakow
  travel at Christmas time, 238
  two-week country introduction program organized by the Polish Fulbright staff, 353
Kramer, General Herman, 77-78
Kruse, Paul, contributor to *Sources of Commodity Prices,* 173
Kruzas, Anthony
  collaborator on *Statistics Sources,* 174-175
  effort to complete first edition of *Statistics Sources,* 182
  instructor in the library school faculty at University of Michigan, 169-170
Kuala Lumpur, National Mosque, 321
Kuhn, Thomas, seminal study, *The Structure of Scientific Revolutions,* basis for lecture, 247
Kuring-gai College of Advanced Education, two-day seminar at School of Library and Information Studies, 319-320
Kusadasi, Turkey, 362
Kyonju, Korea, 323

L

Ladino, primary language for Sephardim, 46
Lagos, Federal Institute of Industrial Research on Business and Economic Information, lecture for workshop, 304
Lake Cayuga
  in Ithaca, 132
  view from office at Cornell University, 137
Lancour, Harold, dean of University of Illinois library school, 162
Langostinas in Panama, 294
Langridge, Derek
  from North London Polytechnic, at International Seminar on Education in Information Science, 250
  in London, 265
Lankage, Jaya, head of library education program and director of Kelaniya University library, 326
Latin American librarians, workshop in Washington, DC, 359
Latin American opportunities, 275
Laundry companies, 100
Law and Legal Information Directory, published every other year, 339
Lazar, Peter
  consultant to United Nations Development Organization, 304
  Hungarian information scientist active on Council of FID, 304
Le Havre, port of embarkation, 91
Leadership in librarianship, 226
Leadership Theory and Styles, course in Maryland Library Administrators Development Program, 212
Learned, William, spoke of need for "an intelligence personnel," 372
Learning Hebrew, 19-20, 25-26
Learning Independently
  preparing second edition, 317
  published by Gale Research Company, 296
Lee, Ms., Vietnamese national from Arthur Vespry's staff, 345
Lee, Pongsoon, Korean member of FID Education and Training Committee, 323
Left Bank hotel in Paris, 265
Lehmann-Haupt, Hellmut, rare books, manuscripts, and incunabula, 110
Leigh, Robert, dean of Columbia University's library school, 162

Lend-lease program

Lend-lease program to the British, 60, 65
Leningrad, visit, 247
Leopoldville
   African crew commandeered lifeboats and deserted vessel, 85
   freezing water, 83
   greatest number of men lost in any troop transport incident of World War II, 85
   jump overboard, 83
   man crushed, 82
   torpedo strike, 82
Leski, Mr., snoring, 248-249
Letter about hiring at Philadelphia Free Library, 157
Lev, Yvonne, associate editor of *Encyclopedia of Senior Citizens Information Sources,* 318
Lewis, Chester
   library director at *The New York Times,* 163
   Wasserman's substitute teacher at Cornell University, 163
Liberty Bell — See High school newspaper
Librarian(s)
   creating new information products, services, and databases to fulfill client needs, 363
   need familiarity with literature of a field, 372-373
   political behavior on behalf of clients, 363
   proactive occupational behavior, 363
   responsibility for timeliness of resources, 121
   sensitive to range and types of information inquiries that arise, 374
The Librarian and the Machine: Observations on the Applications of Machines in the Administration of College and University Libraries, plan to write, 190

Librarian as an Administrator in Complex Organizations, course in Maryland Library Administrators Development Program, 212
Librarianship
   adding to intellectual base of the discipline, 370-371
   applied pursuit, 199-200
   building personal substantive base in a subject matter area, 372-373
   considering pursuit of entrepreneurial means in library work, 373-374
   engaging in political activity on behalf of the occupation, 375-376
   enhanced image, 180
   future of the profession, 377
   harnessing emergent technology in purposeful ways, 371-372
   need for change, 158
   understanding that change is always possible in organizations, 376
   using ingenuity and expertise in invention and design of information products, 374-375
   Western Reserve University reinforced Wasserman's identification, 189-190
Libraries
   "heart of the University," 375
   scarcely influenced by insights from other disciplines, 176
   stand-alone, independent, and self-sufficient yields to the system and the network, 369
Library administration
   practice in libraries ahead of theory, empirical analysis, and research, 158
   study and teaching, 158
Library administration course
   adaptation of course for business and public administration students, 176
   first offering of Paul Wasserman's course, 176

required course at University of Maryland library school in original curriculum, 201
revision and reduction in demands on students, 181-182
team teaching with Mary Lee Bundy, 205-206
Library administrators
directors of fundamental reorientation in librarianship, 226
unlikely to be change agents, 226-227
Library Administrators Development Program at Maryland — *See* Maryland Library Administrators Development Program
"The Library and Information Professions in a Time of Change," published in *PNLA Quarterly,* 209
Library and information science management, chapter in *Annual Review of Information Science,* 219
Library and Information Science Today: An International Register of Research and Innovation
Gale Research Company took over publishing, 225
published in 1970 by Science Associates, 225
Library automation and computer technology, required course at University of Maryland library school, 202
Library Bibliographies and Indexes, co-edited with Esther Herman, 270
Library contracts for government agencies or companies, work for people trained in information professions, 373
Library education
link with public library, 363
prevailing wisdom was that library school was something to endure, 200-201

skills and abilities to work in growing number of unconventional contexts, 373-374
Library intellectual vs. intellectual librarian, 370-371
Library manpower requirements, U.S. Department of Labor's Office of Manpower, Automation and Training, 208
Library of Congress, association developed with University of Maryland's SLIS, 198
Library profession, dynamics and ills, 221
Library school library, 200
Library schools, many understaffed, 207
Library service to disadvantaged and prisoners, Mary Lee Bundy's work, 336
Library Services and Construction Act funds, U.S. Office of Education, 217
result of political engineering by librarians, 375
Library Training Consultants, company formed to prepare and deliver USIA products, 285
Library use study in New York City
27 in-depth interviews, 178-179
assaulted basic tenet of library faith, 179
Licea de Arenas, Judith, director of library school at Autonomous University of Mexico, 283
Lieberman, Elias, principal at Thomas Jefferson High School, 27, 37
Lieberman, Irving
doctoral student at Columbia University, 127
on Brooklyn Public Library's senior management team, 127
Liebowitz, Samuel, criminal lawyer, 29-30
Liebscher, Peter, work in Sri Lanka at Institute for Fundamental Study, 341-342

Liese, Fred

Liese, Fred
  office assistant at University of Maryland, SLIS, 228
  work with Manpower Research Project, 228
Liesener, James, second acting dean at University of Maryland, SLIS, 241
Life in Ithaca, small-town living, 151
Lifelong zeal for travel, 35
Lincoln Theater, in Washington, DC, mecca for jazz, 66
Lindauer, Dina Epner
  fellow student at Columbia University library program, 109
  from Baltimore's Enoch Pratt Library, 110
  returned to Brooklyn Public Library, 110
Linderman, Winifred, reference work, 110
Linz, Austria
  Army printed currency, 90
  citizens looked to Americans for supplies, 89-90
  exchange rates, 90
  paid rent with doughnuts, 88-91
  rented room in a civilian family apartment, 88-91
Lipschitz, Maxie
  boyhood friend, 30
  Club Raleigh's finest dancer, gave dance lessons, 52
  gunner in the Air Corps, 52
Litchfield, Ann, diagnosed with cancer, 149
Litchfield, Edward
  appointment to discuss prospective volume with director of Cornell University Press, 145
  articulate and spell-binding speaker, 133
  assured needed financial resources to build a great library at Cornell University, 133
  belief in universality of the administrative process, 133
  cocktail parties for faculty at Cornell University, 140
  dean of Graduate School of Business and Public Administration at Cornell University, 132
  dynamism of office, 132
  executive secretary of American Political Science Association, 133, 148-149
  home in Cayuga Heights, 140
  influenced Wasserman's career, 153
  managerial assignment with Panama Canal Authority, 139
  moved to University of Pittsburgh as chancellor, 154
  perception as self-promoter, 153-154
  saw commonalities between business and public administration, 140
  senior role in post-war civil governance of Germany, 139
  strategy, 148
  support of library needs at Cornell University, 138
  work on public administration, 139
  work with General Lucius Clay, as director of civil affairs in Germany, 132
  wrote preface for *Information for Administrators*, 151
Liverpool Polytechnic, two weeks as visiting international lecturer at European Summer School offered by library school, 269
London
  lecture at Northwestern Polytechnic, 247, 265
  pubs, discovered, 81
  wartime shortages, 81
Long Island University
  C.W. Post College, taught in summer school program, 351
  lectured on program planning, 221
  proposed undergraduate course, 124

Lorient, Channel port, 86
"Lost Horizons," 35
Louisiana State University Library Lecture Series, spoke publicly for first time about many ideas elaborated in *The New Librarianship,* 247
Low, Edmon
  active in American Library Association, 166
  taught seminar in library technical services at University of Michigan, 166-167
Lubbock, Mrs. G., from Istituto Nazionale de Informazione in Rome, at International Seminar on Education in Information Science, 251
Luhn, Hans Peter, new approaches to handling and retrieving information, 177
Lusaka, Zambia, work on VITA project, 335-336
Lynah Rink, Cornell University's hockey games, 152
Lynch, Cecile
  branch librarian at Saratoga Branch Library of Brooklyn Public Library, 105
  career advice, 107
  quiz on classes, 111

M

Macklin, David, wrote technical report in Manpower Research Project, 236
Madison, University of Wisconsin, Wasserman on summer school faculty, 350-351
Madras, India
  Department of Library and Information Science of University of Madras, 332
  tightly scheduled program, 331-332
  tourist visit, 342
Madrid, REUNIBER-78, Conference on National Systems Development in Scientific and Technological Documentation in Latin America, 296
Mahabalipuram, 342
Mainland China, first time Maryland faculty member offered instruction as part of a cooperative arrangement established in 1995, 364
Malacca, remains from Portuguese imperial period, 321
Male culture, 28-29
Malott, Deane, president of Cornell University, 190
Mamaliga, cornmeal, 254-255
Management consulting, 159
Management Information Guide Series, 38 volumes, 311
Management roles in librarianship, 211
Managerial and Subordinate Development, course in Maryland Library Administrators Development Program, 212
Managerial characteristics, common to all kinds of organizations, 202
Mandalay, sorrowful conditions of life in Burma, 334
"Manpower Blueprint," with Mary Lee Bundy, published in *Library Journal,* 209
"Manpower for the Library and Information Professions in the 1970's: An Inquiry into Fundamental Problems," report prepared with Mary Lee Bundy, 208
Manpower Research Project
  concluding efforts, 232
  funding, 225
  volatile meetings, 222
  work with Mary Lee Bundy, 226

Manual labor

Manual labor, 59
Manuscripts, taught by Hellmut Lehmann-Haupt at Columbia University, 110
Marban, Rocio, handled local arrangements for Guatemalan workshop, 281
Marchionini, Gary
  associate project director of Kellogg Foundation project, 366-367
  designing an applied research project, 363
  work in Sri Lanka at Institute for Fundamental Study, 341-342
Marcos bureaucracy, functionaries were teachers in Manila workshop, 286
Maria Cristina, favorite hotel in Mexico City, 287
Market-driven economy, incomprehensible to Chinese students, 364
Marketing and market research, co-authored paper with Gary Ford, presented in Edinburgh, 296
Marketing issues essential for library and information managers, work with Gary Ford, 284
Marriage
  to Clara Sadacca
    civil ceremony in Selma, Alabama, 79
    religious ceremony, 80
  to Krystyna Ostrowska in Upper Marlboro, Maryland, 268
Martin, Elaine, assistant editor of *Encyclopedia of Health Information Sources*, 318
Martin, Lowell, associate dean at Columbia University library program, 109
Martin, Lynne, U.S. cultural affairs officer in American consulate in Taipei, 322
Maryland, University, College Park
  Center for Adult Education, home away from home, 197
  College of Library and Information Services
    institutional relations with Asian Institute of Technology, 344
    international efforts in library and information science, 297
    international summer institute, 245
    joint undertaking with Montgomery County Public Library, 363
    potential to be an important center for international study in librarianship, 245
    ultimate responsibility for success of Manpower Research Project, 223
  decision to launch a new library school, 193
  high aspirations for its master's degree, 201
  High John Project, protests against racial discrimination, 220
  invitation to apply as dean of new library school, 192
  new library school program, 82 students, 201
  original curriculum, 201
  requirements for admission to library school, 201
  School of Public Affairs, three-year contract with AID to strengthen private- and public-sector activities, 342
  School of Library and Information Services
    deanship, five-year term, opportunity to build academic program from scratch, 195, 199
    doctoral program, 204
    elements put on hold at first, 204
    executive development program for managers, 204
    faculty research projects, 204
    first admissions, 198
    first class, 80% female, virtually all white and middle class, 202

highest priority was accreditation from American Library Association for the master's degree, 204
hiring first faculty, 198
in the vanguard of movement for change in librarianship, 210
one small program in a large University, 206
Maryland Department of Education's Division of Library Extension and Research
support for research, 198, 210
support for research on public library issues, 203
Maryland Library Administrators Development Program
applications from overseas library people, 268
budget, 211
decision making, 211
Donaldson Brown Center, 212
final offering in summer 1990, 344
financial controls, 211
in 1974 included people from Turkey, Mexico, and Colombia, 270-271
leadership, 211
marketing and market research as full-day component, 284
organizational behavior, 211
relationship with United Board for College Development in Atlanta, 280
self-supporting, 344
studied comments with John Rizzo, 271
suitability of program for non-U.S. nationals without any American organizational experience, 271
UNESCO program, 265
work with Effie Knight, 235
Maryland Library Association
Bill Wilson, president, 246
conference in Ocean City in 1995, 361

Maryland state legislature, authorization of establishment of School of Library and Information Services at University of Maryland, 198
Master of Library Science curriculum at University of Maryland, 198
Matthews, Ann, abstracting and editorial activities for *Decision Making,* 188
McCann, Gary, associate editor of *Encyclopedia of Legal Information Sources,* 318
McCarthy, Eugene, strained relations with investigators on Manpower Research Project, 222-223
McCarthy, Stephen
advice about SLA first vice-presidency, 173-174
approved academic year as post-doctoral scholar at Western Reserve University, 187
cordial relationship, 186
differences with Paul Wasserman, 146-147
director of Cornell University library, 132
displeasure with rapid rate of Cornell University business library's expansion, 146
on a Fulbright professorship in Egypt, 137
return from Fulbright year, 146
McCullough, David, *The Path Between the Seas,* 294
McDonough, George, first director of admissions at University of Maryland, SLIS, 227-228
McEwen, William
anthropologist at Cornell University, 148
support of work on library administration, 158
work in behavioral sciences, 149

McGraw Hall at Cornell University, 132
McKeldin Library
  limited quarters for new library school, 194
  overcrowding, 216-217
  SLIS working and classroom areas on two top floors, 199
McKinsey Company, leading management consulting firm, 159
McKinsey Foundation for Management Research, submission of proposal to support research about information for managerial study and practice, 158
McLean, Janice
  associate editor
    of *Awards, Honors, and Prizes*, 220
    of *Training and Development Organizations*, 291
  editor of *Consultants and Consulting Organizations* and *Training and Development Organizations*, 313
  Measurement and Evaluation of Organizational Performance, published by Cornell Graduate School of Business and Public Administration, 163
Measurement in public libraries
  qualitative standards absent, 159
  system of faith in numerical counts, 159
Measurement tools, applying to performance, 159
Measuring performance in public libraries, 159
Mechanic, Sylvia, head of department of social sciences at Central Library, 126-127
Mechanization of library processes, book, 191
Media Hotel
  China's pop celebrities seen at all hours, 365
  in Beijing, 364

Mein Kampf, 15
Melbourne, Royal Melbourne Institute of Technology Library School, 319
Menou, Michel
  independent library consultant for international organizations in Africa, at International Seminar on Education in Information Science, 250
  met flight in Paris, 265
Mexican education plan, 268
Mexico
  Autonomous University, faculty of philosophy and letters, sponsor of Mexico City lecture series, 283
  first effort at international library administrators development program, 271
Mexico City
  advisor to professional staff at INFOTEC, 306
  Colegio de Mexico, 268
  consultant for International Atomic Energy Agency, planning workshop for the agency's regional information centers in the hemisphere, 319
  devaluation of the peso, 287
  INFOTEC, participation by Colombo, Sri Lanka, participants, 345
  weekend during Mexican seminar, 277
  work with group in charge of local arrangements for FID Conference, 283
Meyriat, Jean
  FID friendship, 234
  from the Sorbonne, at International Seminar on Education in Information Science, 250
Miami, joint workshop with OAS and U.S. National Technical Information Service, 310

Miami Beach
  exams, 75
  for Jacqueline Wasserman's health, 130-131
  New Year's Eve, 75
  quarantine, 75
Michigan, University
  first library building for undergraduate students, 217
  language exams, 165-166
  requirement of competence in two foreign languages, 163
  taught summer school, 176
  teaching course on business information sources, 167
  visit looking for Ph.D. program, 162
Micou, Madame
  arranged for trip to Jassi, Romania, 253
  at Social Science and Political Science Information Center in Bucharest, 252
  director of research institute on social science and political science information in Bucharest, 250
  her story, 254
Microcard Editions
  Albert Diaz, director of Washington office, 214
  publisher of Reader Series in Library and Information Science, 312
Middle East Technical University in Ankara, Turkey
  association with Cornell University, 183-185
  new curriculum in administration, 183-185
Mikhailov, Professor
  director of VINITI, 248
  promised to arrange Wasserman visa in Moscow, 249
Military occupational specialty, 77
Miller, Glenn, Big Band sounds, 52

Miller, Gormley, librarian of the School of Industrial and Labor Relations at Cornell University, 152
Miller, Nathan, barber, 29-30, 98
Millinery industry, 3, 10, 13
Mills, Jack
  first contractual grant at University of Maryland, SLIS, 208
  in London, 265
  Northwestern London Polytechnic, 189
  one-year appointment as visiting lecturer at University of Maryland, 203-204
Milton Berle's Texaco Hour, 100
Minority program at University of Maryland, SLIS, 218
MLS program at Columbia University, drawing to a close, 116
Mohawk Airlines, 141
Montague Branch Library, branch of Brooklyn Public Library, 113
Montgomery County, Maryland
  Department of Economic Development, took over support for county database, 367
  Department of Public Libraries, contribution for county database, 367
  Public Library, joint undertaking with University of Maryland, College of Library and Information Services, 363
  research project to offer facts and figures, 366
Morgan, Jean, associate editor for *Ethnic Information Sources in the United States,* 279
Morocco, tourism, 296
Morris, Thelma, contributor to *Sources of Commodity Prices,* 173
Moscow
  airport, 256
  caught fierce cold, 356
  city in disarray, 356

Moscow
  seminar for librarians who came from new American Studies Centers, 356
  two distinct Moscows, 356
  unreliable transportation, 357
  visit, 247
Moses, Richard
  co-director of High John Library, 210
  protests against racial discrimination, 220
  staff member of the Enoch Pratt Free Library's Community Action Program in Baltimore's inner city, 210
Moses, Robert, public lecture at Cornell University, 149
Mother — *See* Wasserman, Sadie Ringelescu
Movie house, 50
Movies
  compared with books, 50-51
  "Kings Row," 65
  "Lost Horizons," 35
  serials, 21
  source of childhood pleasure, 20-21
Moving and Relocation Sourcebook, 337
Mumford, Quincy
  ALA presidency, 135
  appointment as Librarian of Congress, 135
  candidate for ALA presidency, 130
Munich, first meeting of editorial board for *Education for Information,* 310
Munn, Ralph, director of Carnegie Public Library in Pittsburgh, 194
Munn, Russell
  called Wasserman a risk-taker, 194-195
  dean of libraries at University of West Virginia, 194
Museum Media, published by Gale Research Company, 267
Museum of Natural History, 31
Mussolini, Benito, in newsreels, 21
Mykonos, Greece, 316

N

Nacht, Michael
  dean of School of Public Affairs at University of Maryland, 342
  gave bad news about Sri Lankan project to Wasserman, 347
  review of Wasserman proposal for Colombo program, 345
Nash, Allan, faculty in Maryland Library Administrators Development Program, 212
National Agriculture Library
  association developed with University of Maryland's SLIS, 198
  sponsor of Inter-American Workshop for Agricultural Information Transfer and Networking, 359
National Cash Register Company, publisher of Reader Series in Library and Information Science, 312
National Library of Medicine
  association developed with University of Maryland's SLIS, 198
  Extramural Program, grant funding, 208
  funding cited in support of Ph.D. program at University of Maryland, SLIS, 216
National Science Development Board, conference planning, 286
National Science Foundation
  Burton Adkinson, director of Office of Science Information, 306
  funding cited in support of Ph.D. program at University of Maryland, SLIS, 216
  Office of Science Information Service, grant funding, 208
  reduced contribution to FID, 307
  travel support to Sri Lanka, 341
National Taiwan University, 322
Nazi party, 15

Needham, Chris, in London, 265
Neighborhood, boyhood
  friends, 99
  public library branch, 50
Nepal, 342
Nestle Center, location of Mexican seminar, 276
Neustadt, Richard
  joined Columbia University's political science department, 148
  taught administration at Cornell University, 140
New academic enterprise at College Park, prospect of bringing into being, 192
New Deal, 6
New Delhi
  director and lecturer in two-week UNESCO workshop for library and information center administrators in Asia, 301-303
  first-class arrival, 301
  International Center
    Indian conference site, 302
    oasis in desert of human misfortune, 303
    provided library and weekly public lectures, 302
  seminar, participants from India, Iran, Mongolia, and Afghanistan, 302
The New Librarianship: A Challenge for Change
  outgrowth of comprehensive research on manpower issues, 235-236
  product of thinking, theorizing, speaking, and manpower studies since moving into library education, 235-236
New Mexico State University in Las Cruces, 243
New Year's Eve
  in Budapest, 240
  in Cherbourg, France, 86
  in Miami Beach, 75

New York, housing shortage, 93
The New York Times
  no daily access in Hawaii, 338
  preferred newspaper in college, 56
  stringer, 42
Newark, New Jersey, 1-2
Newspaper
  habit of reading, 56
  selling in Catskills, 34
Nice, weekend stay in 1970, 233
Nigeria
  departure postponed indefinitely, 305
  national strike against government, 304-306
  thriving economy, 304
Nilsson, Arthur, professor at Cornell University, 139
Nimer, Gilda, planned and directed Change Institute on Frontiers in Librarianship, 220
Nitollo, Peter, assistant librarian at Cornell University library, 144
Norman, Henry, president of VITA, 335
Normandy, bivouac in countryside, 86
North Africa, week's stay, 358
Northwestern Polytechnic in London, lecture, 265
Norway, 352
Nova Huta, steel-making suburb of Krakow, 353
Nuremberg, Nazi war crimes trials, 90

O

O'Connell, Jeanne
  acknowledgments in *The New Librarianship*, 236
  assistant on the Manpower Research Project, 223
  associate editor of *Library and Information Science Today*, 226

O'Connell, Jeanne

worked with Mary Lee Bundy and Wasserman on reports in the Manpower Research Project, 226
wrote article with Wasserman for *Special Libraries*, 267

Oahu, weekend outings, 338

OAS — *See* Organization of American States

Oberhof, in East Germany, 278

Objectives and Objective Formulation, course in Maryland Library Administrators Development Program, 212

Occupational history, second part of book, vii

Occupational survival in librarianship, 217-218

Office of Education
  funding cited in support of Ph.D. program at University of Maryland, SLIS, 216
  grant funding, 208

Office of Science Information Service, National Science Foundation, grant funding, 208

Ohio
  invitation to consult by preparing study and report on library education needs in the state, 221
  shortage of librarians, 221

Ohm's law, 70

Olive, Betsy Ann
  asset as assistant business librarian at Cornell University, 154
  business and public administration librarian at Cornell University, 190
  daily management of library at Cornell University, 154
  directed business library at Cornell University, 163
  highly regarded in library community, 186

index of *Sources for Hospital Administrators*, 180
prepared index for *Information for Administrators*, 151
wrote portion of *Encyclopedia of Business Information Sources*, 242

Olson, Edwin, wrote technical report in Manpower Research Project, 236

Olympic Hotel in Catskills
  entertainment, 33
  selling newspapers, 34

Omnigraphics, reference and media company headquartered in Detroit, 337

On-the-job training, 199-200

Operations research, class at Case Institute of Technology, 188

Opportunities to practice German
  insight into consequences of war for ordinary civilians, 91
  interviewing civilians and war refugees, 91

Opportunity to build academic program from scratch, deanship at University of Maryland, 195

Organization of American States
  engaged Wasserman as consultant, 281
  initiative to foster technology transfer system in developing nations of South and Central America, 281
  joint workshop with U.S. National Technical Information Service, theme of three-day meeting, micro-computers in technical and information centers, 310
  series of workshops, 283-284
  supported attendance at Madrid meeting, 296
  Unit for Technical Change of the Science Secretariat, 281

Organizational assessment, heightened interest, 159

Oryx Press in Phoenix, books aimed at library market, 317
Oslo, visit to Oslo University library, 247, 260
Ostrowska, Krystyna
  arrival in United States, 242
  decision to marry, 267
  married in Upper Marlboro, Maryland, 268
  met in Frankfurt, 233
  planning for Budapest FID biennial Congress, 239
  promised to visit in Warsaw in fall 1970, 233
  studied at Pratt Institute's Library School, 242
  vilified to National Academy of Sciences for incompetence, 233
  visit to United States, 240
  work status in United States subject to question by Immigration and Naturalization Service, 247
Overcrowding, McKeldin Library, 216-217

P

Pacific Northwest Library Association Conference in Portland, Oregon, speech, 209
Pagan, sorrowful conditions of life in Burma, 334
Palmer School of Library and Information Science at C.W. Post College of Long Island University, taught in summer school program, 351
Palmour, Gene
  OAS workshop, 284
  taught workshop at Technical Information Department at Institute of Electrical Research in Cuernavaca, 299

Pan-American Seminar on Information Systems and Services: Present Status and Future Directions, given in Washington, DC, 288
Panajachel, Guatemala, 281
Panama Canal
  feelings running high about control, 294
  watched in operation, 294
Panama Canal Authority, Edward Litchfield as manager, 139
Panama City, five-day workshop under auspices of U.S. AID, 294
Paris
  first visit, 87
  Gardin seminar, 189
  meeting with UNESCO officials about Accra seminar, 296
  Symposium on Harmonization of Education Programs in Librarianship, Documentation and Archives, 309
  UNESCO International Conference on Harmonization of Education Programs in Librarianship, Documentation, and Archives, 314
  visit to UNESCO, 247, 265
Park, Myung Soon, faculty member at Ewha Womens University Library School, 323
Parker, Ralph, director of library at Washington University in St. Louis, 189
Patterson, James, marketing professor at Indiana University, 177-178
Pealy, Robert, public administration representative on dissertation committee at University of Michigan, 171
Pearl, Mr.
  faculty advisor for high school newspaper, 42
  high school journalism teacher, 37-39
Pearl Harbor, 61-62

Peking Opera

Peking Opera, 366
Pellowski, Anne, adjunct lecturer at University of Maryland library school, 204
Penang, Malay Peninsula, Eastern and Oriental hotel, 321
Pennsylvania Avenue, apartment, 13-14
Perella, Sue, reference assistant at Cornell University library, 163
Performance, measuring and evaluating, 159
Performance Appraisal, course in Maryland Library Administrators Development Program, 212
Performance evaluation, research investigations at Stanford Research Institute in California, 189
Performance measurement systems, selecting, 159
Performance standards, 159
Perihera, procession in Kandy, Sri Lanka, 328
Perpetual electronic inventory of a county's characteristics, 363
Perreault, Jean
  International Symposium on Classification Research, 208
  lecturer at University of Maryland, teaching cataloging and retrieval courses, 204
Perrie Jones Lecture at St. Paul Public Library, spoke about future directions for public libraries in an era of change, 269
Personal history, first part of book, vii
Perth, spoke to library community about general directions in American library and information science, 320
Pest, New Year's Eve, 239-240
Ph.D. degree, offering at University of Md, 215
Philadelphia Free Library, opening for director of personnel, 155-156

Philippines
  developing local workshop, 286
  hurricane during workshop, 287
Phillips, Deborah, acknowledgment, viii
Pietsch, Erich, FID friendship, 234
Pinochet administration, removed from office all those who had held senior positions during Allende period, 288-289
Pinochet, General, and military junta in control in Chile, 288
Pinochle, 6
Pirog, Wojciech
  attended Wasserman's classes in Warsaw, 355
  chairman of FID Education and Training Committee, at International Seminar on Education in Information Science, 250
  director of Central Institute for Scientific and Technical Information, 355
  introduced Wasserman to Professor Mikhailov, 249
Plaxe, Davey
  boyhood friend, 24
  joined the Navy, 69
  married and moved out of neighborhood, 125
  work for Mr. Russo, 46-49
Plaxe, Yetta, 24
Poland
  colleagues in key information posts, 350
  difficulty of explaining capitalist economy, 355
  Fulbright grant, 350
  Gomulka government about to fall, 238
  government transition carried out without incident, 238-239
Polio epidemic, 33-34
Polish Central Institute for Scientific and Technical Information, secretariat of FID Education and Training Committee in Warsaw, 222

Polish Fulbright assignment, more structured than Fulbright program in Sri Lanka, 351-352
Polish Fulbright Office, two-day orientation program in Poland, 352
Polish instruction in Krakow, 353
Polish-U.S. Fulbright Commission in Warsaw, Wasserman designated first alternate, 351
Political activity
  on behalf of clients, 363
  on behalf of librarianship, 375-376
Political engineering by librarians, needed in our society, 375-376
Political machinations of organizations, participation by librarians, 376
Political naivete, handicap for librarians, 375
Political topics, discussion taboo in Chile, 288
Ponnamperuma, Cyril
  director of Institute for Fundamental Study in Kandy, Sri Lanka, 326-327
  made stay in Sri Lanka memorable, 341-342
  maintained strong links, 341
  science advisor to president of Sri Lanka, 327
  suggested faculty team in CLIS to plan workshop focused on information program goals of Institute for Fundamental Study in Sri Lanka, 341
Pontigo, Jaime, translator at Mexico City lecture series, 283
Poona, two-day seminar for local librarians at University of Poona, 332
Pope's weekly audience, 264
Posner, Eugene, boyhood friend, 30
Post, C.W., College of Long Island University, taught in summer school program, 351
Post-doctoral study, proposal for year, 187

Powers, Jimmy, idol at *The Daily News*, 42
Prague, visit with George Toman as guide, 247, 262-263
Prat, Ana Maria, faculty member at University of Santiago before Pinochet, 289
Pratt Institute's Library School, Krystyna Ostrowska's studies, 242
Pre-flight instruction, 76
Pre-teen years, 16
Prefabricated house in Ithaca, 160
Pregnancy
  Clara's first, 112
  Clara's second, 131
Premaratne, Bogoda, Fulbright director, 326
Prendiville, Christina, acknowledgment, viii
Prentice, Ann, dean of the University of Maryland College of Library and Information Services, acknowledgment, ix
Preoccupation with girls, 51
Presthus, Robert
  editor of *Administrative Science Quarterly*, 157
  from University of Oregon, 209
  taught public administration at Cornell University, 154
  wrote technical report in Manpower Research Project, 236
Price Sources
  book of current market prices, 121
  committee of business librarians, 144
  outline, 144
  updated edition, 144, 173
Prince George's County Public Library, support for research, 210
Proactive information producer, librarian, 316-317
Proactive occupational behavior by librarians, 363

Proactive posture

Proactive posture for librarians, seven recommendations, 370-377
Proactive stance in librarianship, shift in emphasis, 237
Problem Solving, course in Maryland Library Administrators Development Program, 212
"Professional Adaptation: Library Education Mandate," published in *Library Journal*, 221
Professional library groups, dynamics and ills, 221
"Professionalism Reconsidered" response to writings, 213
  with Mary Lee Bundy, published in *College and Research Libraries*, 213
A Program of Research into the Identification of Manpower Requirements: The Educational Preparation and the Utilization of Manpower in the Library and Information Professions, substantial grant, 208
Promotion and tenure committee at Cornell University, need to publish, 141
Promotion to associate professor at Cornell University, 151
Provence, summer, 88
Przegorzaly Castle, on the outskirts of Krakow, country orientation program, 353
Public health clinic, 31-32
Public libraries
  evaluation measures, 159
  service, legislative standard undefined, 161
  Wasserman doctoral dissertation on measurement concerns, 160
"The Public Library Administrator and His Situation," one of the final reports in the Manpower Research Project, 226

Public school, 13
Public speaking, lifelong lesson in high school class, 27-28
Publication activities, accelerated pace, 237-238
Publishing by committee, frustrating, 173
Publishing industry and its impact on the library, 221
Publishing reference works and databases, work for people trained in information professions, 373
Punctuality, cultural difference in Guatemala, 282-283
Purple Heart for *Leopoldville* disaster, 84-85
Putnam, Lee, administrative staff member of University of Hawaii library, 323
Pyramids in Mexico, 277

Q

Quarantine, Miami Beach, 75
Queens Hotel, Kandy, Sri Lanka, 328
Quevedo, Jose, director of INFOTEC in Mexico City, 306

R

R. R. Bowker Company, publisher of *The New Librarianship*, 235-236
Radio broadcasts, 6, 16, 41
Radio repair training
  at Fort Monmouth, 71-72
  frustration, 73
Radio shows, 41
Raffles Hotel in Singapore
  in crumbling disrepair, 321
  Somerset Maugham Suite, 321
Rangoon
  Shwedegon Pagoda, 334
  sorrowful conditions of life in Burma, 334

Rare books, taught by Hellmut Lehmann-Haupt at Columbia University, 110
Rate of change, libraries need to accelerate, 370
Rathmell, John "Mac," assistant professor of marketing at Cornell University, 139
Rathskeller, dining club for faculty at Cornell University, 140
Ravages of war, 91
Reader for course work, 213-214
Reader in Library Administration
  commercially viable, 221-222
  first volume in a series of readers, 205
  published in 1968, 214
Reader in Research Methods in Librarianship, work with Mary Lee Bundy, 222
Reader Series in Library and Information Science
  24 volumes, 214, 312
  copyright, 214
  Greenwood Press officials knew the series, 238
  series editor, 214
Reading tastes, eclectic, 51
Reagan administration, retrenchment initiatives, 307
Real Estate Information Sources, 181
Reconstructing the past, 1
Recreation and Outdoor Life, published by Gale Research Company, 296
"Recruitment and Utilization of Personnel: An Aspirational View," published in *Documentaliste,* 269
Rees, Alan, junior faculty at Center for Documentation Research at Western Reserve University, 188
Reference books
  designing and mounting projects for new editions of earlier efforts, 269
  planning process, 174
  projects, 311
  topics about which statistics might be sought, 175
Reference work, sensitivity to how knowledge is organized and controlled, 374
Refugees in Austria, 91
Reichmann, Felix, director of technical services department at Cornell University, 137
Relevance of libraries, 221
Religious rituals, 26
Reorganized infantry division, 77-79
Research and development in progress, building a database, 225
Research investigations of automated retrieval systems, performance evaluation, and cost analysis at Stanford Research Institute in California, 189
Research proposal for dissertation, measurement of performance in public libraries, 160
Resignation as dean at University of Maryland, SLIS, freedom to concentrate exclusively on personally important matters, 231, 234
Restaurant — *See* Family restaurant
Retirement from teaching, announced in fall 1995, 363
Retirement thoughts, 361
REUNIBER-78, Conference on National Systems Development in Scientific and Technological Documentation in Latin America, held in Madrid, 296
Review of military history, 77
Revised role definition for librarians, devising and planning information products and services for client needs, 374-375
Revision of classic beliefs, formidable barriers, 369
Reynolds, Michael, acting dean at University of Maryland, SLIS, 235

Rhineland

Rhineland, occupying forces, 87
Ringelescu, Goldie (aunt)
  born in 1912 in Harlem, 3
  chronically ill, 24
  shared apartment with Mollie and Hyman Ringelescu, 21, 22, 24
Ringelescu, Hyman (grandfather), 7
Ringelescu, Mollie (grandmother), 7-8, 10
Ringelescu, Morris (uncle)
  accident, 7-8
  bookkeeper for a large distributor of linens, 58
  introduced Paul Wasserman to the theater, 25
  introverted, 24
  part-time evening student at City College, 55
  serious reader, 25
  shared apartment with Mollie and Hyman Ringelescu, 21, 22, 24, 25
  supported Sadie's side in argument about Paul's Hebrew lessons, 19
  younger brother of Sadie, 3
Ringelescu, Rebecca (aunt), 2, 3, 7
Ringelescu, Rose—*See* Kessler, Rose Ringelescu (aunt)
Rio de Janeiro, loud music at hotel, 272
Riverdale Avenue, apartment, 12
Rizzo, John
  director of Maryland Library Administrators Development Program for 22 years, 344
  editor of *The Journal of Library Administration*, 300
  joined Paul and Krystyna in Mexico City, 276
  residential director at Maryland Library Administrators Development Program, 212
  studied comments about Maryland Library Administrators Development Program, 271
  travel to Istanbul, 293
  work in Philippines, 286-287
  work in Turkey, 290-293
Robbins, Jane, director of library education program at University of Wisconsin in Madison, 350-351
Robert College in Istanbul, visit, 185
Rock Creek Park, 66
Rockaway Beach, 43
Rocq, Margaret, contributor to *Sources of Commodity Prices*, 173
Rodriguez, Amalia
  director of library education program at University of Chile, 288-289
  husband was high-ranking officer in Chilean Air Force, 288-289
Romania, birthplace of Joe Wasserman, 2, 3
Romanian language, lecture remarks, 255-256
Romantic encounters at the Club Raleigh, 52
Rome, visited Vatican, 247, 264
Roosevelt, Eleanor, speaker at ALA convention, 128-129
Roosevelt, Franklin D.
  death, 87
  declares war, 62
  hero and defender of the working class, 41
  improving conditions during the Depression, 14
  Jewish support, 41
Root, Elizabeth, associate editor for *Festivals Source Book*, 279
ROTC at City College, 56
Rovelstad, Howard
  director of University of Maryland library, 198
  McKeldin Library director, 217
Rubin, Herman "Cousin Chaim"
  boyhood friend, 30
  had friend in Washington, DC, 62
Rubin, Leo, boyhood friend, 30

Ruffier, Marino
  deputy director of central library programs, 126-127
  reviewed drafts of chapters, 150
  visit in Ithaca, 135
Ruffner, Frederick G., Jr.
  annual contribution to FID dues, 315
  asked Wasserman to name managing editors for titles, 312
  decided to publish bibliographic guides in subject fields, 237-238
  encouraging about proposed series for Gale Research Company, 180
  Gale Research Company, 169
  guest lecturer, in Wasserman's class at University of Michigan, 168-169
  launched Omnigraphics, 337
  loathe to encumber Wasserman's study with too much responsibility, 189
  publishing *Executive's Guide* on an experimental basis, 182-183
Ruffner Foundation, 337
Rugaas, Ben, director of Oslo University library, 260
Rumburg, Lt. Colonel Chris, hero of the *Leopoldville* disaster, 85
Rummy, 6
Russ Togs, 49
Russia
  Don Hausrath played active role in library development, 356
  locked and guarded detention center, 256
  ride in ambulance, 357
  unanticipated adventures, 357
Russian Library of Foreign Literature, conference rooms used for Moscow seminar, 356
Russo, Eli, 46-49
Russo, Irving "Shorty," 46-49
Russo, Mr., summer job, 46-47

Rybon, Beulah
  office manager at University of Maryland, SLIS, 206
  secretary at new library school at University of Maryland, 197

S

Sabbatical
  decision to pursue a doctorate, 160
  fall semester 1972, 246-266
  itinerary of lectures and professional visits in Asia, 318
Sadacca, Clara
  goodbye, 63
  letters, 79
  marriage, 79
  sister of Ralph, at the Club Raleigh, 53
  visit to Fort Rucker, 79
Sadacca, Fred, living in Miami Beach, 130-131
Sadacca, Hy (brother-in-law)
  and Paul Wasserman, bought two television sets, 100
  call about Steven's birth, 141
  married Ray Sarfaty, 98-99
Sadacca, Hy and Ray, occasional evening visits, 111
Sadacca, Ralph, boyhood friend, 23
Sailing to America, Joe and Sam Wasserman, 3
St. John, Francis
  ALA convention chairman, 127
  candidate for ALA presidency, 130
  career advice
    about Cornell University, 134-135
    about role in public library administration, 124-125
  daily newsletter during ALA convention, 128
  director of Brooklyn Public Library, 111

St. John, Francis
- hired Irving Lieberman, 127
- innovative leadership, 112
- New York City library systems, commissioned study of readership patterns of library use, 178
- promising to lead the Brooklyn Public Library, 112
- rapport ended with disagreement, 179
- stewardship of ALA convention, 129-130

St. Nazaire, Channel port, 86

St. Paul Public Library, Perrie Jones Lecture, spoke about future directions for public libraries in an era of change, 269

Salesmen, attitudes, 60

Samuelson, Kjell
- did research and lectured on information science at Stockholm University and Royal Institute of Technology, at International Seminar on Education in Information Science, 250
- dinner in Stockholm, 260

San Francisco
- Bay area, first visit to study two libraries, 223-224
- de Young Memorial Museum, Tullah Hanley, benefactress, 240
- public library, visited every three months, 224

San Jose dos Campos, 273

Santiago, 288

Santo Domingo
- black market transactions on bus, 284
- dance jamboree, 284
- local organizing institution for marketing workshop was Banco Centrale, 284

Saracevic, Tefko, junior faculty at Center for Documentation Research at Western Reserve University, 188

Saratoga Branch Library
- evening meals, 111
- learning about branch operations, 106-107
- pleasingly arranged, 106

Sarfaty, Ray, married Hy Sadacca, 98-99

Saunders, Wilfred, University of Sheffield, 189

Scarecrow Press, founded by Ralph Shaw, 192

Schiller, Arthur
- fellow soldier, 80, 81
- letter from brother, 85
- similar backgrounds, 81

Scholarly discourse for librarianship, 371

Scholarship support available at University of Michigan for Ph.D. program, 163

School athletics, corruption, 42-43

"The School Library Supervisor and Her Situation," one of the final reports in the Manpower Research Project, 226

Schultheiss, Louis, data processing installation at University of Illlinois, 189

Schur, Herbert, FID friendship, 234

Science and Technology Board in Bangkok, 343

Scientific communication methods, evolution, paper presented in Colombo, Sri Lanka, 330

Scientific community, time for United States to take strong role in building professional ties to the world, 306

Scorpions, fried, 364

Seashore, place for meeting girls, 44

Seasickness during Atlantic crossing, 80

Second Fulbright grant, India or Poland, 350

Segal, Stanley
- from State University of New York at Buffalo, 209
- wrote technical report in Manpower Research Project, 236

Selecting performance measurement systems, 159
Selective Service System, 60
"Self-Instruction Training Materials for Librarians and Information Scientists: The Use of Text and Video Learning Modules," paper at FID Committee meeting, 291
Seminar in the Invention and Design of Information Products and Services, attempt to inspire students to create information tools, 237
Senate Committee on New Courses and Programs, review of Ph.D. program at University of Maryland, SLIS, 215-216
Senegal, addressed students of principal library education program in francophone Africa at University of Dakar, 296
Seoul, Korea, 323
Sephardic Jews, 46
Serials, movies, 21
Shannon, Bill, taught accounting at Cornell University, 139
Shaw, Artie, Big Band sounds, 52
Shaw, Charles
  librarian of Swarthmore College, 166
  taught academic library administration at University of Michigan, 166-167
Shaw, Ralph
  applied machine processes at Department of Agriculture Library, 192
  differences of opinion, 192
  founder of Scarecrow Press, 192
Sheffield Avenue, apartment, 22
Shepherd, G. F., Jr.
  acting librarian at Cornell University, 137
  return to role as assistant librarian at Cornell University, 146
  unforgettable evening with family, 138

Shepherd, Margaret, unforgettable evening with family, 138
Sheppard, C. Stewart
  advice about SLA first vice-presidency, 173-174
  approved academic year as post-doctoral scholar at Western Reserve University, 187
  dean at Cornell University, 157, 195
  inconsistency, 186
Sheppard, Corrine, director of central library programs, 126
Shera, Jesse, dean of Western Research University library school, 186-188
Sheremytov Airport
  landing, 256
  passengers cheered when aircraft took off, 259
Sherrod, John, collaboration on project with Volunteers in Technical Assistance, 334-336
Shilling, Charles, representative for United States on FID Education and Training Committee, 219
Short-wave radio
  in Sri Lanka, 327
  in Warsaw, 354
Shortages
  in London, 81
  in United States, 91
Shoup, Carl, seminar on tax policy at Columbia University, 117
Shrewsbury, Miss, assistant librarian at Saratoga Branch Library of Brooklyn Public Library, 106
Shwedegon Pagoda in Rangoon, 334
The Sid Caesar Show, 100
Siegman, Gita, editor of *Consumer Sourcebook* and *Awards, Honors, and Prizes,* 313

Silander, Fred

Silander, Fred
  associate professor at DePauw University, 188
  doctoral student in administration and economics, 158
Simon, Herbert, modern behaviorist, 153
Singapore, disabling fever and cold, 321
Singhalese, native language in Sri Lanka, 326
Singhalese Buddhist community, majority in Sri Lanka, 327
Sinus condition
  cleared by country air, 33
  doctors and treatments, 31-33
Skin cancers, 44
Skipper, James, University of California at Berkeley, 223
Skipping a grade, 23
Sloan Foundation, supported establishment of Sloan Institute of Hospital Administration at Cornell University, 148
Sloan Institute of Hospital Administration
  empirical study of decision making, 158
  need for review and analysis of information facilities serving hospital administration, 179-180
  support from Sloan Foundation for establishment, 148
Smidt, Seymour (Sy)
  helpful with dissertation, 161
  taught managerial economics at Cornell University, 154
  two-year visiting professorship in Ankara, Turkey, 184
  visits to Turkish colleges, 185
Smith, Karen G. and Thomas E., assistant editors of *Encyclopedia of Health Information Sources*, 318
Smoking, 54
Smookler, Idair, contributor to *Sources of Commodity Prices*, 173
Snoring in Budapest, 248-249
Social independence, 54
Social justice, Mary Lee Bundy's involvement in movement, 232
Social life
  during school, 97-98
  marking time before war, 69
  minimal during library school, 111
Social Science and Political Science Information Center in Bucharest, 252
Sofia, Bulgaria
  crowded with tourists, 315
  romantic aura, 247, 252
Sopot, Poland, weekend stay, 352
Sources for Hospital Administrators: Publications and Facilities Serving the Health Administration Field, 180
Sources of Commodity Prices: A Project of the Special Libraries Association Business and Finance Division
  first edition published by committee, 173
  revision published by SLA, 269-270
South America, information for industry centers program, 310
South Hill, Ithaca, 146
Southeast Asia, developing local workshop, 286
Soviet Union, application for visa denied, 248
Spanish, resolved to learn to speak language, 268
Spanish National Research Council, meeting in Madrid, 296
Speakers and Artists Program in the American Participants Program in India, 330
Special Libraries Association (SLA)
  annual meetings, 152
  business division, 173

business division project, 144
chairman
  of business division, 152-153
  of finance committee, 186
conference, potential contributors to Gale Management Information Guide Series, 181
contributions and limitations in regard to library automation, 191
member, 120
nominated for first vice presidency, 173
Spencer, Miss, children's librarian at Saratoga Branch Library of Brooklyn Public Library, 106
Sports world, cynicism, 42-43
Sri Lanka
  active schedule of special programs, conferences, and seminars, 329
  apartment, 326
  chambers of commerce
    needed improved business information systems, 342
    officials rejected plan, 347
  conflict between majority Singhalese Buddhist community and Tamil Hindu minority, 327
  consultant to directors of libraries, 329
  correspondence with colleagues, 341
  food, 329
  lull in conflict between administration and students, 329
  met with AID officials, 346
  need for proper investment in constructing sound business information centers and appropriately trained personnel, 346
  one time in a university class during entire semester in Sri Lanka, 329
  professor in library education program of University of Kelaniya, 325
  project came to naught, 347
  south Asian version of Latin America, 326
  travel support from National Science Foundation, 341
Sri Lankan Library Association, two-day conference in Colombo for public and academic librarians, with Frank Hogg, 333
Sri Lankan National Academy of Sciences, public lecture in Colombo, 328
SS Leopoldville, 81
Standards for performance, 159
Stanford Research Institute in California, field trip, 189
Starting high school, 27
State Department Leaders Program for Policy Officials from Latin America, 288
Statistical Abstract of the United States, 174
Statistics Sources
  became an annual, 339
  effort to complete first edition, 182
  first edition published in 1962, 175
  went from biennial to annual publication, 312
Statler Hotel School building, 140
Statue of Liberty, object of loving regard, 92
Status quo, libraries fail when they cling, 368
Steckler, Phyllis, president of Oryx Press, 317
Steere, Paul, U.S. Information Service regional librarian in Bangkok, 342
Stemmy, Linda, worked with Janice McLean, 313
Stockholm
  public library, 260
  several days, 352
  University, public talk, 247, 260

Stone, Ezra

Stone, Ezra, actor who played Henry Aldrich, 38
Student Contribution Series, at University of Maryland, 220
Subject expertise, built on formal academic preparation or self-study, 372-373
Subject matter, librarians need familiarity, 372
Sullivan, Dr., senior academic official at Brooklyn Academy, bribery scheme, 123-124
Summer job in garment district, 47
Summers, William, work on Mexican education plan, 268
Summerskill, John, resident psychologist at Cornell University, 152
Sunbathing, 44
Survey of Midwest library directors, implications for education in librarianship, 191
Susquehanna River, Maryland Library Administrators Development Program, 345
Swanson, Rowena
  OAS workshop, 284
  taught information retrieval and information handling systems in Guatemalan workshop, 281
Sydney
  opera house, 319
  two-day seminar at School of Library and Information Studies of Kuring-gai College of Advanced Education, 319-320
SYNTOL, data retrieval system for artifacts, 189
Szentmihalyi, Janos
  FID friendship, 234
  planning for Budapest FID biennial Congress, 239
  took Krystyna and Paul to lunch in Budapest, 239

T

Taft, Philip, instructor at Columbia University, 117-118
Tagaytay, two hours from Manila, 287
Taipei
  Ambassador Hotel, 322
  earthquake, 322-323
  Taiwan Library Association, 322
Taiwan Library Association in Taipei, 322
Taj Mahal, visit, 303
Talmud Torah
  bar mitzvah tutor from the school, 25
  privately run school, 14
Tamil, native language in Sri Lanka, 326
Tamil Hindu community, minority in Sri Lanka, 327
Tamkang University, spent a day, 322
Tangley Oaks Foundation of United Educators, Inc., fellowship support, 187
Taraboi, Victor
  head of research center in Bucharest, 250
  member of FID Education and Training Committee, 252
Taube, Mortimer
  died before starting appointment as adjunct lecturer at University of Md, 204
  president of Documentation, Inc., 204
Tauber, Maurice, editor of *College and Research Libraries,* 109
Taunggyi, sorrowful conditions of life in Burma, 334
Taylor, Frederick Winslow, work in scientific management, 153
Taylor, Nettie, director of Maryland Department of Education's Division of Library Extension, 198
Teaching load, maximum of 15 hours at University of Maryland library school, 203

"The Teaching of Management as a Subject for the Preparation of Librarians, Documentalists, Archivists and Other Training Specialists," presented formally at International Symposium on Harmonization of Education and Training Programmes in Information Science, Librarianship and Archival Studies in Paris, 310

Technical Information Access Centers, established in Thailand by Development Board to provide information processing and dissemination to the Thai scientific and research community, 343-344

Technical Information Department at Institute of Electrical Research in Cuernavaca, 299

Technical University of Chemical Engineering, in Veszprem, Hungary, 251

Technology
  drives swift pace of adaptation, 369
  potential for library associations to get involved, 191

Tees, Miriam, professor of management at McGill University library school, 316

Tejada, Miguel, started program to build network of technology and industrial development centers in Latin America, 281

Tejak, Bojo
  died soon after returning to Zagreb, 270
  director of University of Zagreb's library education program, 263
  experiences in furthering information science in Yugoslavia, 270
  lecture tour in United States, 270

Telephone linesman, 71-72

Television set, bought first, 100

Thackston, Frances, librarian and lecturer at University of Maryland, 200

Thai Science and Technology Development Board, 343

Thailand
  Sherrod visited for VITA project, 335
  Wassermans visited as tourists, 342

Thanksgiving on the high seas, 80

Theories of Motivation and Behavior, course in Maryland Library Administrators Development Program, 212

Thesis, research evidence might further effective practice of administration of public libraries, 181

Thiagarajan, Major, hired lecturers for New Delhi seminar, 302

Thomas, David
  career advice, 157
  dissertation for University of Michigan Business School, 145
  taught accounting at Cornell University, 140

Thomas Jefferson High School
  almost covered city block, 14
  possibility of attending, 27
  principal, Elias Lieberman, 37

Thompson, James
  left Cornell University for University of Pittsburgh with Edward Litchfield, 154
  sociologist at Cornell University, 148
  teaching required course in administration, 148
  work in behavioral sciences, 149

Thompson, Victor, faculty in Maryland Library Administrators Development Program, 212

Thomson International, bought Gale Research Company, 337

The Thunderbolt
  travel to Vienna, Munich, and Nuremberg, 90
  weekly Army newspaper in Linz, Austria, 89

Tiananmen Square

Tiananmen Square, tourism, 364
Time, 1
Tobin, Patricia, associate editor of *Encyclopedia of Legal Information Sources*, 318
Tobin, Sporn and Glaser, summer job, 58-60
Tocatlian, Jacques
  arranged contractual details with UNESCO for Maryland Library Administrators Development Program, 265
  arranged for Wasserman to serve as consultant on development of program for managers of library and information systems in developing countries, 268
  Maryland program should provide model for international programs, 271
Toman, George, guide in Prague, 262
Tompkins, Miriam, ethos of readers' services, 110
Tompkins County Hospital, diagnosis of bleeding ulcer, 185
Toplova, Todora
  director of State Library Institute in Sofia, Bulgaria, 315
  political connections, 316
Torah, 19
Torrijos, Delia
  director of UNESCO General Information Program's regional office in Bangkok, 346
  liaison from National Science Development Board in Manila, 286
Tosi, Henry
  faculty in Maryland Library Administrators Development Program, 212
  professor of management in the business school at University of Maryland, 212

"Toward a Methodology for the Formulation of Objectives in Public Libraries," dissertation, 175
Townsend Harris High School, 27
Tradition, influence on minds of those committed to an institutional form and its practices, 368-369
Training Materials in Library and Information Science with Particular Reference to the Needs of Developing Countries, five-day conference in West Berlin, 301
Translation of important American books into Turkish, 185
Trautman, Ray, superintendent of wartime book and library programs, 109
Travel
  lifelong zeal, 35
  to Asia, 318
  to Bangkok, 303, 342
  to Bellagio, Italy, 300
  to Brazil, 272
  to Casablanca, 296
  to Cuernavaca, 299, 304
  to Frankfurt, 301
  to Greece, 316
  to Istanbul, 293
  to Kanchipuram, 342
  to Katmandu, 342
  to Madras, 342
  to Mahabalipuram, 342
  to Mexico City, 283
  to Nepal, 342
  to New Delhi, 301
  to Panama, 294
  to Poland, 352
  to Santiago, 288
  to Thailand, 342
  to the Bronx, 11
  to Vienna, 309-310
Trenchfoot, second short hospital stay, 87

Trends and Directions in Library Education and Library Practice, developed from University of Denver lecture series, 217
Trolley in Washington, DC, 63, 64
Troubles
 brewing around the world, 54
 in Europe
  anti-Semitism, 15
  threatening international order, 43
Tunisia, week's stay, 358
TURDOK, the Turkish National Documentation Center in Ankara, host agency for UNESCO training seminar, 291
Turkey
 help with identifying indigenous faculty from former students, 291
 regional management workshop, 290-293
 travel as consultant in September 1962, 183-185
Turkish, translation of important American books, 185
Turkish wine, 362
Types of libraries, series of reports about managers, 226
Typing
 hunt and peck method, 93
 trying to learn touch method, 94

U

U.S. Agency for International Development (AID)
 sponsored five-day workshop in Panama City, 294
 sponsored VITA project, 334-336
U.S. delinquency in paying FID dues, 314
U.S. Department of Labor's Office of Manpower, Automation and Training, library manpower requirements, 208

U.S. Information Agency (USIA)
 contractual relationship with University of Maryland for series of learning modules on subjects normally taught in library school, 284-286
 training program for indigenous staff in libraries around the world, 285
U.S. Information Service (USIS)
 reception and buffet dinner for delegates in Ghana, 295
 sponsored seminar for librarians who came from new American Studies Centers, 356
 two-day orientation program in Poland, 352
USIA training program for indigenous staff in libraries around the world, 285
U.S.-Mexico Bi-National Committee, 275
U.S. National Committee for FID
 elected chairman in 1985, 314
 encouraged joint efforts among IFLA, FID, and ICA, meeting in Bellagio, Italy, 300-301
 invited to become member, 294
 recipient of State Department funds, 339
 resigned chairmanship, 338
U.S. National Research Council, major sponsor of Thai Science and Development Board, 343
U.S. National Technical Information Service, joint workshop with OAS, theme of three-day meeting, microcomputers in technical and information centers, 310
U.S. Office of Education
 Educational Research Information Centers Training Program, first contractual grant at University of Maryland, SLIS, 208
 Library Services and Construction Act funds, 217
 support for research, 210

Ufizzi

Ufizzi, visited in Florence, 264
Ulcer, bleeding, 185-186
Undergraduate libraries, trend in the 1960's, 217
UNESCO
  consultant in arranging and contributing to seminar on information planning and economic development in Africa, to be held in Accra, Ghana, 294-295
  destination in Paris, 265
  General Information Program advisory board member, 309
  consultant, 296
  regional office in Bangkok, Wasserman support, 346
  Maryland program should provide model for international programs, 271
  regional training seminar held in Ankara, Turkey, participants came from countries in Africa, the Middle East, and Europe, 291
  sponsoring overseas participants in Maryland Library Administrators Development Program, 265
  support for FID Education and Training Committee efforts, 297-298
  work in Turkey, 290-293
  workshop in New Delhi, 301-303
  workshops, presentation in Mexico City, 288
Uniquely male culture, 28-29
United Board for College Development in Atlanta, relationship with Maryland Library Administrators Development Program, 280
United Nations Development Organization, Peter Lazar, consultant, 304
United States
  delegation to FID Congress and Conference in Hong Kong, delinquent in paying dues, 307
  lecture tour, American Library Association's Committee on International Library Education of the Library Education Division, chairman, 270
Universality of the administrative process, divided opinions, 140
University, democracy of the intellect, 148
University librarians, some have faculty status while most do not, 375
University of Aberystwyth, Wales, 266
University of Chile's Department of Library Science, advisory role, 288
University of Dakar, addressed students of principal library education program in francophone Africa, 296
University of Denver, invitation to serve as advisor to the Graduate School of Librarianship, 217
University of Guanajuato, addressed audience of library staff and library school students, 304
University of Hawaii in Honolulu
  cross-cultural mix of students, 338
  invited to teach by Ralph Shaw, 192
  taught summer-term courses, 337
  weekend outings around Oahu and visit to Kauai, 338
University of Hong Kong, 337-338
University of Ibadan in Nigeria, 304
University of Illinois, visit looking for Ph.D. program, 162
University of Illinois at Chicago, field trip, 189
University of Indiana Graduate Business School, consulting visits, 186
University of Indonesia, Cornell University built public administration library, 183
University of Jakarta, speaking engagement at U.S. Center, 320

University of Kelaniya in Sri Lanka
  assignment for Fulbright professorship, 325
  looking for professor of library administration, 318
University of Maryland — *See* Maryland, University
University of Michigan — *See* Michigan, University
University of Poona, two-day seminar, 332
University of Stockholm, public talk, 260
University of Washington (state), offered Wasserman seminar on trends and directions in information field, 349
University of Wisconsin in Madison, Wasserman on summer school faculty, 350-351
University of Zagreb, visit to library education program, 263
University Senate at University of Maryland
  endorsement of Ph.D. program at University of Maryland, 215-216
  evaluated CLIS, 347-349
Urban libraries, special problems, 221
USIA project, presentation in Mexico City, 288

V

Van Riper, Paul, taught federal civil service and governmental history at Cornell University, 139
Varna, Bulgaria, conference to bring together representatives of education and training committees of FID, IFLA, and ICA, 315
Vassallo, Paul
  administrative aide, 225
  OAS workshop, 284

Vatican, saw the Pope, 264
Vespry, Arthur
  goal to establish first-rate, non-traditional graduate program in information science in Bangkok, 342-343
  invited Wasserman to Hanoi conference, 345
  librarian of Asian Institute of Technology, 334
  regional workshop in Bangkok, 337
Veszprem, Hungary
  International Seminar on Education in Information Science, 250
  proceedings of seminar published in Budapest by Hungarian Technical Library and Documentation Center in 1974, 251
  seminar, 247
Veteran, compensation, 93-94
Veterans Administration classification, 92
Video lecture series for USIA
  actual use, 286
  difficulties, 285
Vienna
  four-power military administration, 90
  Museum of Natural History, lodging, 309
Vienna meeting
  Wasserman's two reports, 310
  working group of FID, IFLA, and ICA, 310
Vietnam, visa, 345
Vikor, Desider, associate editor of *Encyclopedia of Public Affairs Information Sources*, 318
Vina del Mar, Chile, resort weekend, 290
VINITI, centralized Soviet documentation and information system, 248
VITA
  collaboration on project with John Sherrod, 334-336
  evaluation of effectiveness, 335

VITA

services better known in developing world and international organizations than they were in Washington, DC, 335-336

Vogel, Helen, reference librarian at Business library, 115

Voluntary enlistment, thinned ranks of young men at corner hangout, 69

Volunteers in Technical Assistance — *See* VITA

Voyage home from World War II, 10 days, 91

W

Wales, 265-266

Wales College of Librarianship in Aberystwyth, largest library school in United Kingdom, 266

Walker, Julia, acknowledgment, viii

Walking to and from the office, 146

Walston, Betty, travel to Brazil 272

Walston, Claude
 caught hepatitis in Brazil, 274
 taught classes in library automation and data processing, 204
 work in Sri Lanka at Institute for Fundamental Study, 341-342
 work on Brazilian workshop on information science, 271-274
 work with Paul Wasserman on investigation of Thai Science and Technology Development Board, 343

Walters, J. Hart
 background in psychology and marketing research, 178
 from George Washington University, 209

Wang, Shih Hsion, director of University libraries at Tamkang University, 322

War in Europe, going badly, 60

Ward, Geoffrey, 320

Ward, Patricia Layzell, director of Western Australian Institute of Technology library education program, 320

Warsaw
 airport, teeming with military, 238
 celebrated New Year in company of friends, 358
 Christmas and New Year's holidays, 358
 FID Education and Training Committee, 291
 gave paper at World Health Organization Conference, 358
 gave public lecture at American Center in Krakow, 356
 opera house, *Fiddler on the Roof,* 354
 Polish-U.S. Fulbright Commission, Wasserman designated first alternate, 351
 secretariat of FID Education and Training Committee, 222
 ubiquitous shortages, 238

Wartime disruptions, 62

Washington, DC
 area, potential to be an important center for international study in librarianship, 245
 boarding house, 63-68
 city made for walking, 66
 cultural opportunities, 338
 finding housing, 62-63
 job at Government Printing Office, 62-68
 left in shame, 68
 public library branch, 65
 rich center of jazz, 66

Washington University in St. Louis, field trip, 189

Wasserman, Clara
 amicable divorce settlement, 268
 birth of second child, 141
 clerical position in department store chain, 93, 101
 father's death, 98

454

flew to Ithaca, 141
followed Jacqueline to California, 233
mother
  helped with new baby in Ithaca, 141
  moved in, 98
  spoke Ladino, 98
parents' apartment, first home for newlywed Paul and Clara, 93
pregnant with second child, 131
reluctance to leave her family, 134
visit in California to discuss divorce, 267

Wasserman, Jacqueline
  began kindergarten, 146
  birth, 118
  editorial work on *Statistics Sources* and *Law and Legal Information Directory*, 317
  graduation from high school, 232
  healthy, 131
  recurrent respiratory infections, 130
  relocated in 1971 to Los Angeles area, 232-233
  stopover in Los Angeles, 267
  time in Miami for health, 130
  work on *Statistics Sources*, 339
  working on several publications, 312

Wasserman, Joe (father)
  angry episode, 9
  anguish at Sadie's illness, 136
  background and early history, 1-7
  baseball game, 6
  card player, 6
  close to his brother Sam, 7
  death, 143
  deferential and respectful relationship with Paul, 9-10
  encouraged Paul to go to Cornell University, 134
  enthusiasm for cigars and hot peppers, 5
  evicted, 98
  good-natured disposition, 9
  heart attack, 143
  naive, accepting outlook, 9
  spoke English and Yiddish, 7
  Thanksgiving visit to Ithaca, 142-143

Wasserman, Joe and Sadie, relocated to an apartment, 125

Wasserman, Krystyna and Paul
  enrolled in beginning evening Spanish class at University of Maryland, 275
  four-week immersion course in Cuernavaca, Mexico, 275

Wasserman, Krystyna
  acknowledgment, viii
  arrived in Turkey from Italy, 293
  director of Library and Research Center of National Museum of Women in the Arts, 325
  flew to Warsaw, then Tunisia, 358
  took Paul home from airport in rented wheelchair, 358
  travel
    to Asia, 318
    to Bangkok, 303, 342
    to Bellagio, Italy, 300
    to Brazil, 272
    to Casablanca, 296
    to Cuernavaca, 299, 304
    to Frankfurt, 301
    to Greece, 316
    to Istanbul, 293
    to Kanchipuram, 342
    to Katmandu, 342
    to Madras, 342
    to Mahabalipuram, 342
    to Mexico City, 283
    to Nepal, 342
    to New Delhi, 301
    to Panama, 294
    to Poland, 352
    to Santiago, 288
    to Thailand, 342
    to Vienna, 309-310
  two-week train tour of Mexico, 276

Wasserman, Marilyn

Wasserman, Marilyn (sister)
  birth, 12-13
  evicted, 98
  married Ed Foodim, 125
  See also Foodim, Marilyn
Wasserman, Paul
  advisor to Sam Kotei, 294
  editor on ALA convention daily,
  faculty in Maryland Library Administrators Development Program, 212
  first teaching experience, 143-144
  OAS workshop, 284
  principal of Library Training Consultants, 285
  project director of the Kellogg Foundation project, 366
  representative for United States on FID Education and Training Committee, 219
  taught workshop at Technical Information Department at Institute of Electrical Research in Cuernavaca, 299
  work in Sri Lanka at Institute for Fundamental Study, 341-342
  work with Claude Walston on investigation for Thai Science and Technology Development Board, 343
  wrote "Professionalism Reconsidered" with Mary Lee Bundy, 213
  wrote technical report in Manpower Research Project, 236
Wasserman, Pearl (cousin), 11
Wasserman, Sadie Ringelescu (mother)
  appreciation for scholarly pursuits, 4
  background and early history, 1-5, 7-10, 14
  cancer, 131
  cooking, 8
  death, 136
  decided Paul should start Hebrew school, 19
  evicted, 98
  "fixing yourself," 13
  homemaking frugality, 6
  hospital stay for Marilyn's birth, 13
  moved to a nursing home, 136
  opinion that delicatessen foods were unhealthy, 8
  outdoor food markets, 8-9
  personification of dedicated motherhood, 7
  serious operation, 130
  turn for the worse, 135-136
Wasserman, Sam (uncle)
  background and early history, 2, 3
  close to his brother Joe, 7
  economic success, 10-11
  entrepreneurial schemes, 11
  ties to union leadership, 10
Wasserman, Sidney (cousin)
  exploring the neighborhood, 11
  Loew's Paradise, 11
  penny collection, 11
Wasserman, Steven
  associate editor of *Recreation and Outdoor Life,* 296
  birth, 141
  chose New Mexico State University in Las Cruces, 243
  editor
    of *Encyclopedia of Physical Sciences and Engineering Information Sources,* 318
    of *Moving and Relocation Sourcebook,* 337
  editorial direction of *Statistics Sources* and *Law and Legal Information Directory,* 317
  entered first grade in Ann Arbor, 165
  graduated from high school in June 1971, 242
  graduated from University of Maryland in mid-1970's, 312

took Paul home from Warsaw in rented wheelchair, 358
work on *Law and Legal Information Directory,* 339
work on *Statistics Sources,* 339
working on several publications, 312
Wasserman, Sylvia (aunt), 10-11
Waste oil kiln, VITA-invented product in Djibouti, 335
Wawel Castle, visited in Poland, 353
Weber, Felix
  director of Institute for Information Science, Inventions and Law, 277
  from Technische Hochschule in Ilmenau, at International Seminar on Education in Information Science, 250
Weber, Max, on bureaucracy, 153
Weegie, photographer on *The Thunderbolt,* 89
Weekly colloquium at University of Maryland, political, philosophical, or conceptual issues bearing on library work, 200
Weequahic, neighborhood in Newark, New Jersey, 1-2, 4-5
Weimer, Arthur
  dean at Indiana University, 178
  engaged Wasserman as consultant to help design program for Indiana Graduate School of Business, 178
Welbourne, James, activist movement demanding social responsibility from ALA, 220
Welsh Student Mafia Society, placard denoting honorary membership, 266
Werdel, Judith
  left National Academy of Sciences, 307
  secretary of U.S. National Committee for FID, 222
Wersig, Gernot
  chairman of FID Education and Training Committee, 291
  from Freie Universitat in Berlin, at International Seminar on Education in Information Science, 250
  visited East Germany, 278
  West German member of FID Education and Training Committee, 261
Wesner, Jean, contributor to *Sources of Commodity Prices,* 173
West Berlin
  five-day conference, 301
  opulence, 247, 261
Western Australian Institute of Technology, distance education program, 320
Western Reserve University
  Center for Documentation Research at the library school
    new approaches to handling and retrieving information, 177
    post-doctoral scholar, 187, 188
    freedom to pursue independent course of study, 189
    manuscript about study year, 190
    taught library administration, 189
White, Rodney
  from Trent University, 209
  wrote technical report in Manpower Research Project, 236
Who's Who in Consulting
  biographical directory, 214
  complementary volume to *Consultants and Consulting Organizations,* 214
Whyte, William Foote, Cornell Social Science Research Center, 161
Wiley, Paul, contributor to *Sources of Commodity Prices,* 173
Willard Straight Hall, Cornell University's student union, 140
Wilson, Bill
  president of Maryland Library Association, 246

Wilson, Bill

profound influence on development of CLIS at University of Maryland, 246
Wilson, Louis Round, joint authorship with Maurice Tauber of treatise on academic librarianship, 109
Winde, Dr. B., director of Central Institute for Information and Documentation in East Berlin, 262
Wisconsin, University, in Madison, Wasserman on summer school faculty, 350-351
Woods, Bill, executive secretary of SLA in New York, 153
Woolworth's Five and Dime, 14
Work Analysis, course in Maryland Library Administrators Development Program, 212
Working conditions, important at University of Maryland library school, 203
Works Progress Administration (WPA), free performances in Central Park, 25
World Health Organization Conference, gave paper in Warsaw, 358
World War II
in Europe, 53
prospects for American involvement, 56
United States involvement seemed inevitable, 60
Woy, James
managing editor of *Encyclopedia of Business Information Sources*, 313
wrote portion of *Encyclopedia of Business Information Sources*, 242
Wozniak, Jadwiga, lecturer at University of Warsaw, 353
Wright, Kieth, dean at University of Maryland, 297
Writing a book
procrastinating, 145
work in earnest, 145-146

Wysocki, Adam
appointed Wasserman as member of UNESCO's Advisory Council to study convertibility and standards in graduate education in information science, 269
director of UNESCO's Division of Libraries, Documentation and Archives, 250
UNESCO sponsoring participation in Maryland Library Administrators Development Program, 265

X

Xochimilco, floating gardens in Mexico, 277

Y

Yak and Yeti Hotel, Katmandu, 342
Yankee fan, 17
Yankee Stadium, 17
Yiddish
everyday language of European Jews, 20
primary language for Ashkenazim, 46
Yugoslavia, visit to University of Zagreb's library education program, 263

Z

Zagreb, University, visit to library education program, 247, 263
Zakopane, mountain resort in Carpathian Mountains, 353
Zambia, work on VITA project, 335-336
Zihuatenejo, Mexican resort city, 299-300
Zuckerberg, Sam, 99-101
Zuckerberg Company, flexible part-time job, 99-101